Negotiating India in the Nineteenth-Century Media

Negotiating India in the Nineteenth-Century Media

Edited by

David Finkelstein

and

Douglas M. Peers

First published in Great Britain 2000 by
MACMILLAN PRESS LTD
Houndmills, Basingstoke, Hampshire RG21 6XS and London
Companies and representatives throughout the world

A catalogue record for this book is available from the British Library.

ISBN 0–333–71146–7

 First published in the United States of America 2000 by
ST. MARTIN'S PRESS, LLC,
Scholarly and Reference Division,
175 Fifth Avenue, New York, N.Y. 10010

ISBN 0–312–23465–1

Library of Congress Cataloging-in-Publication Data
Negotiating India in the nineteenth century media / edited by David Finkelstein
and Douglas M. Peers.
     p.   cm.
     Includes bibliographical references and index.
     ISBN 0–312–23465–1
     1. Press—India—History—19th century. 2. Press—Great Britain—History–
–19th century. 3. India—In mass media—History—19th century. I.
Finkelstein, David, 1964– II. Peers, Douglas M.

PN5373 .N44 2000
079'.54—dc21
                                                                  00–027823

This book is printed on paper suitable for recycling and made from fully managed and sustained
forest sources.

10   9   8   7   6   5   4   3   2   1
09 08 07 06 05 04 03 02 01 00

Printed and bound in Great Britain by
Antony Rowe Ltd, Chippenham, Wiltshire

Contents

List of Illustrations

Notes on the Contributors

Kelly Boyd lectures in British and gender history at Middlesex University, London. She is the editor of the *Encyclopedia of Historians and Historical Writing* (London and Chicago, 1999), has published several articles on the construction of masculinity in the boys' story paper, and is author of the forthcoming *Wait Till I'm a Man: Manliness and the Boys' Story Paper in England, 1855–1940*.

Antoinette Burton is Associate Professor of History at the University of Illinois. She is the author of *Burdens of History: British Feminists, Indian Women and Imperial Culture, 1865–1915* (Chapel Hill, North Carolina, 1994) and *At the Heart of the Empire: Indians and the Colonial Encounter in Late-Victorian Britain* (Berkeley, 1998). She has also published numerous articles on race, nation, empire, feminism and colonialism. She is currently at work on an edited collection of essays about colonialism and modernity, and a book-length project on Indian women writers and architectural idioms of memory and home.

Nupur Chaudhuri teaches at Texas Southern University in Houston. She has written on gender and imperialism, and is the co-editor of *Western Women and Imperialism: Complicity and Resistance* (Bloomington, Indiana, 1992) and *Nation, Empire, Colony: Historicizing Gender and Race* (Bloomington, Indiana, 1998).

David Finkelstein is Head of the Media and Communication Department at Queen Margaret University College, Edinburgh. He has published articles on print culture studies, book history and the nineteenth-century media in such journals as *Victorian Periodicals Review, Text: an Interdisciplinary Annual of Textual Studies* and *Publishing History*. He is author of *An Index to Blackwood's Magazine, 1901–1980* (Aldershot, 1995), *Philip Meadows Taylor* (Queensland, 1990), and co-editor of *Nineteenth-Century Media and the Construction of Identities* (Basingstoke, 2000).

Mark Harrison is Senior Lecturer in History at Sheffield Hallam University, where he teaches both the history of medicine and the history of British imperialism in South Asia. He is author of two monographs on Indian medical and environmental history: *Public Health in British*

India: Anglo-Indian Preventive Medicine 1859–1914 (Cambridge, 1994) and *Climates and Constitutions: Health, Race, Environment and British Imperialism in India, 1600–1860* (Oxford, 1999). He is currently co-editing a collection of essays on health and medicine in India, and co-ordinating a history of smallpox in India, funded by the Wellcome Trust.

Javed Majeed was Lecturer in the Department of South Asia, SOAS, University of London from 1992 to 1999. He currently holds a lectureship in the Department of English and Drama, Queen Mary and Westfield College, University of London. His publications include *Ungoverned Imaginings: James Mill's 'The History of British India' and Orientalism* (Oxford, 1992) and, with Christopher Shackle, *Hali's Musaddas: the Flow and Ebb of Islam* (Delhi, 1997). He is currently working on the thought of Iqbal, Nehru and Gandhi.

John McBratney teaches English at John Carroll University in Cleveland, Ohio. He has published articles on Kipling, Tennyson and Paul Scott, and is currently working on a study of Kipling, race, nation and empire.

T.R. Moreman is a Lecturer in War Studies at King's College, London. He has published articles on the military in British India in various periodicals such as the *Journal of Imperial and Commonwealth History* and *Journal of Strategic Studies* and is the author of *The Army in India and the Development of Frontier Warfare, 1849–1947* (Basingstoke, 1998). He is currently completing a study of the British, Indian and Australian armies in the Far East during the Second World War and is working on a book on the 1897–98 Tirah Campaign.

Hyungji Park is Assistant Professor of English at Union College, Schenectady, New York, where she teaches courses on the Victorian novel, detective fiction and Asian American Literature. She has published on Shakespeare and on Victorian literature and is completing a book on empire, Englishness, and masculinity in the Victorian novel.

Douglas M. Peers is Associate Professor of History at the University of Calgary. He is the author of *Between Mars and Mammon: Colonial Armies and the Garrison State in Early Nineteenth Century India* (London, 1995) and co-editor of *J.S. Mill's Encounter with India* (Toronto, 1999). He has published articles on discipline, sexuality and sexually transmitted diseases in the Indian Army, and the Indian Army in the Victorian press in such journals as the *Journal of Imperial and Commonwealth History*, *International History Review*, *Medical History* and *Modern Asian Studies*.

Laura Peters is a Lecturer in English at Staffordshire University, where she lectures on Victorian literature and contemporary Canadian literature. She has published essays in these areas in such journals as *The Dickensian*, and has two forthcoming books: *Orphaned Texts: Victorian Orphans, Culture and Empire* (Manchester), and a reader on Race.

A. Martin Wainwright is Associate Professor of History and Director of World Civilizations at the University of Akron. He is author of *Inheritance of Empire: Britain, India, and the Balance of Power in Asia, 1938–55* (Westport, Conn., 1994) and is currently working on a second book about the Indian diaspora in Britain and the formation of identities within the imperial context.

Glenn R. Wilkinson received his PhD from the University of Lancaster and now lectures on European and Intellectual History at Mount Royal College in Calgary, Alberta. He is currently working on a book regarding the cultural depictions and images of warfare in late-Victorian and Edwardian newspapers concerning the origins of the First World War.

Acknowledgements

We would like to thank the University of California Press for permission to use material which originally appeared in Antoinette Burton, *At the Heart of Empire: Indians and the Colonial Encounter in Late-Victorian Britain* (1998). The illustration from the *Civil and Military Gazette* (1885) is reproduced by permission of the British Library (reference 98E0367B). Permission to reproduce illustration from *The Black and White Christmas Issue* (1897) was kindly granted by the University of Toronto Library. Thanks also to the University of Calgary Library for reproducing the full-page illustration of the *Illustrated London News* (5 August 1854).

We would also like to thank Napier University and the University of Calgary for travel funding which allowed us to plan and complete this collection, and the Calgary Institute for the Humanities for assisting in its final production. We would especially like to thank our editor at Macmillan, Charmian Hearne, for her support, patience and faith in this project.

1
'A Great System of Circulation': Introducing India into the Nineteenth-Century Media

David Finkelstein and Douglas M. Peers

'Our Empire in India is an empire of opinion', stated the *Friend of India* in 1836, acknowledging the role that information and social communication processes played in upholding and defining the British presence in India (*Friend of India*, 27 October as quoted in Bayly 1996, 218). By the time the Indian Rebellion broke out in 1857–58, the role of the press had become more complex and its potential influence had grown. The consolidation of colonial rule in India resulted in an increased flow of information between India and Britain. While the periodical press in India was initially launched by Europeans with their expatriate communities in mind, it did not take long before Indians adapted such instruments of communication to their own purposes, ensuring that the mass media was simultaneously a site where knowledge of India could be acquired and put to imperial use as well as a place from whence challenges to the empire could be raised. Not surprisingly, the outbreak of the Indian Rebellion of 1857–58 raised fears amongst British officials that they no longer had any effective control over the flow of information. Few at the time doubted the potential power of the press, and while there were those officials who urged an immediate crackdown, they were outweighed by those who argued that it was impossible to turn back the clock. One such voice came from Mountstuart Elphinstone, one-time governor of Bombay, who lamented that:

> I am afraid it is too late to put any effectual restraint on the press in India. The Press is a great system of circulation, of which the types and printing machines form only a part. When the art is once understood, a very small quantity of printing even in a language not more

generally understood than English in India, is enough to furnish materials for a great quantity of manuscript, as well as of declamation, conversation, dissemination of rumours and alarms. (Wilson 1861, 105n)

It is this 'great system of circulation', the exchange and interchange of news, ideas and technologies of communication between India and Britain, between Indians and Britons, and between different groups within each of those communities, that is the focus of this collection of essays.

How India was represented to audiences in Britain as well as in India has spawned much critical work over the past decades. A great deal now exists on the language, images and ideologies created and sustained in the travel accounts, diaries, official records, and the literary imaginations of participants in the development and maintenance of colonial rule in India. Cultural critics such as Edward Said, Gayatri Spivak, Anne McClintock, Mary Louise Pratt, Homi Bhabha, Sara Suleri, Sara Mills, Robert Young and Patrick Brantlinger have all contributed important and provocative analyses of colonial discourse as presented in a variety of printed formats (see, for example, Brantlinger 1990; McClintock 1994; Mills 1992; Pratt 1992; Said 1978, 1992; Spivak 1999; Suleri 1992; Young 1991). While often disagreeing profoundly in their interpretations, Edward Said and John MacKenzie both stress the extent to which Victorian Britain was thoroughly saturated with imperial imagery (MacKenzie 1984, 1986, 1995; Said 1978, 1992). As noted by Nicholas Dirks (1992, 3) in his introduction to a collection of essays entitled *Colonialism and Culture*, 'Colonial knowledge both enabled colonial conquest and was produced by it; in certain ways, culture was what colonialism was all about'. Obviously print media had a role to play in this; in the words of the first editor of the *Calcutta Review*, readers were attracted to his journal because of its 'decidedly Oriental character' (as cited in Chanda 1987, 252). Yet orientalism is a powerful but annoyingly imprecise term; overuse, emotional overloading, and academic politics have transformed what might have been an instrument for careful dissection into a blunted axe, encouraging statements such as Deirdre David's 'Victorian attitudes toward empire are almost always unambiguously racist' (David 1995, 8). Racist, perhaps, but definitely not unambiguous, for as the essays in this collection demonstrate, empire and its ideologies were inescapably ambiguous.

Studies of imperial discourse have for the most part been confined to a limited range of genres, such as novels, travel accounts, autobiographies and works of history. Often absent from such discussions is an awareness of and accounting for the limited audience reached by these works. For example, novels published in Britain from the time of Walter Scott in the 1820s through to the 1890s were generally issued initially in small print runs of 750–1000 copies, often in expensive formats accessible only to those wealthy enough to purchase them or subscribe to a circulating library.

Similarly, nineteenth-century travel accounts, memoirs and histories were invariably aimed at a limited readership, priced to remain beyond the reach of an increasingly literate working-class public. Ironically, many of these texts had first appeared in the pages of Victorian periodicals where they had been serialized and also reviewed, meaning that their initial readership was very different to that which consumed them when they were subsequently published in book form. An example of this is afforded by John Lang's short novel of Anglo-Indian life, *The Wetherbys – Father and Son*. (We are using Anglo-Indian as it was used in the nineteenth century, namely to denote the British expatriate community in India, and not necessarily peoples of mixed ancestry. The term itself symbolized this community's sense of difference from Indian society as well as its distance from Britain.) First published in installments in the *Mofussilite* (an English-language paper published in Meerut, near Delhi), it was later serialized in *Fraser's Magazine* before appearing as a book (Peers 1997).

Thus a valid question that must be asked is, why has there been no major work done on the cultural values found in the more ephemeral, more available and perhaps more influential pages of the periodical press – the dailies, weeklies, monthlies and quarterlies whose massive circulation made them *the* mass media of Victorian Britain and its empire? For, as the editors of a recent stocktaking exercise in the history of the Victorian periodical press have noted, 'the circulation of periodicals and newspapers was wider and more influential than that of books in Victorian society' (Vann and VanArsdel 1996, 3). Contemporaries were equally convinced of the importance of such publications; in the words of one reviewer in *Bentley's Magazine*, 'periodical publications are a surer index of the state of progress of the mind, than works of a higher character' (Chaudhuri 1996, 175).

Fifteen years ago, Ann Parry (1985, 254) complained that 'It is a commonplace of literary criticism to acknowledge the importance of the periodical press in Victorian England and then consign it to the realm of "background"'. Unfortunately, little has been done on this subject since then, especially as far as the empire and India are concerned. As

Lyn Pykett (1990) has similarly noted, the situation has not improved much since Shattock and Wolff (1982) identified that there had been no systematic study of the Victorian periodical press. Others too have remarked on this lacuna (Maidment 1990). An example of this continuing lack of engagement with the Victorian press can be found in *Writing India*, a recent and important collection on the subject of India's representation in British literature (Moore-Gilbert 1996). Nowhere in its pages does it address the periodical press.

This is not to say that nothing has been written in this area. David Spurr has studied the relationship between journalism and imperialism in a broad-ranging study that is particularly useful in identifying several of the repeating motifs and rhetorical forms in journalistic accounts of the wider world. His work is informed by the assumption that 'The question that matters...is, finally, not how one literary form differs from another, but how writing works, in whatever form, to produce knowledge about other cultures' (Spurr 1993, 11). In his emphasis on culture, and how journalism contributed to the production of ethnological meanings, Spurr offers an alternative way into colonial discourse. However, like so many studies that are purportedly about colonial discourse, his story begins around 1870, and therefore implies that the popular consumption of imperialism came at a later date than the evidence suggests.

There have been a number of studies over the years that have located the history of the press in India within a traditional political narrative where the focus is on press freedom. While many of these situate this history unproblematically within a liberal paradigm (Natarajan 1962), some have adopted a more critical approach (Kaul 1993, 1997). Kaul's study (1993) of the domestic press at the time of the Ilbert Bill crisis (1884), for example, demonstrates just how powerful the press could be in determining the tone and direction of political debates. So too does Wong's recent study (1998) of the origins of the Arrow War illustrate the power of the press in prodding a reluctant Parliament to adopt a more aggressive imperial stance.

Much less has been written on how India came to be conveyed in the pages of British literary and professional magazines. Some moves in this direction are afforded by Amal Chatterjee (1998) who builds his analysis in part on articles culled from literary magazines. Somewhat surprisingly, India makes no appearance in Altick's definitive study (1997) of the early years of *Punch*, despite the fact that India was often the subject of its cartoons. Nor, it should be added, is there much of an imperial presence in this book.

Media historians are also prone to skipping over the Victorian empire, seemingly concluding that the mass media began with the first issue of the *Daily Mail* in 1896, and then subsequently exploded with the advent of cinema, radio and television (see, for example, Williams 1998). In essence this fascination with the twentieth century has left a large hole in critical work in media studies. Nor can we look to colonial studies for insight into this topic. Media and colonial studies alike either ignore the Victorian press or simply strip-mine it for pithy quotes. For example, authors often uncritically cite a statement from the *Times* to confirm someone's motive or state of mind, or isolate texts from their contexts. Examples of the latter are the frequent analyses of Joseph Conrad's *Heart of Darkness* which fail to account for its first appearance in 1899 as a serial in the very pro-empire monthly *Blackwood's Edinburgh Magazine* (Finkelstein 1995). Two of the essays in this book offer examples of how important it is to contextualize literary production and media utilization. In their studies of Charles Dickens's and Wilkie Collins's linking of different media genres, Laura Peters and Hyungji Park document the significance of the press in fostering cultural intertextuality. They illustrate how Dickens and Wilkie Collins transfer and transform news from one textual form, in this case news reportage and illustrations in the *Illustrated London News*, into another, serialized fiction and short stories in *Household Words* and *All the Year Round*.

India in the British media

Print media, namely newspapers, literary periodicals and professional trade journals issued daily, weekly, monthly and quarterly, was the mass media of Victorian Britain, particularly after the reduction of advertising and newspaper taxes in the 1830s, and most significantly after the abolition of all taxes on print material in the 1850s. These initiatives encouraged the production and circulation of a wide range of periodicals and printed media, from the illustrated weekly *Penny Magazine* (founded in 1832 to provide 'improving literature' for the masses), whose circulation briefly exceeded 200 000, to Charles Dickens's *Household Words* (founded in 1850) which during its brief career averaged 40 000 copies a week, and *All the Year Round* (1859) which claimed an average weekly circulation of 300 000 (Sullivan 1984, 173).

As far as newspapers were concerned, similar growth in circulation occurred. In 1834, it was estimated that weekly sales of unstamped papers exceeded 130 000 copies (Altick 1957, 340). Newspaper circulations rose substantially in the second half of the nineteenth century: The *Times*, for example, averaged a stable 50–60 000 copies a day during the 1860s, rising to 100 000 by 1882; the *Daily News* boasted a circulation of 150 000 by the time of the Franco-Prussian war in 1871; and the *Daily Telegraph* sold 200 000 copies daily around the same period (Altick 1957, 355). By 1899, the *Daily Mail* claimed a staggering circulation of 540 000 copies a day. Such figures reflect only a small percentage of the sheer volume of mass printed media cascading into the daily lives of an increasingly literate public. It is worth noting that sales of this magnitude were not limited to newspapers. The *Boy's Own Paper*, for example, had a print run of 153 000 per week in 1888 (Reed 1997, 86).

Newspapers and magazines seeking stories for their ever-increasing readership did not overlook India. Yet their attention to India did not grow uniformly across the nineteenth century. As Kelly Boyd's contribution to this collection makes clear, while India did figure in contemporary literary production, it was not the all-pervasive constant that we have sometimes assumed it to be. Instead, it grew fitfully, rising, as Glenn Wilkinson shows us in his essay, during times of war, and falling back during peacetime. Other examples of this fascination with battles in far-off places, and from an earlier period, are the accounts of British struggles with Tipu Sultan to be found in the pages of the British domestic press in the 1790s (Marshall 1992). Not surprisingly, crises like the Indian Rebellion of 1857–58 were well covered, though it is a mistake to assume, as some do, that there was little or no coverage before those dates, for interest in India had been there all along, though not necessarily with the same fervour or volume. Publications like the *Oriental Herald* and the *Journal of the Royal Asiatic Society* emerged at the beginning of the nineteenth century, catering to a market largely comprised of returned officials from India and armchair travellers. Other British newspapers and magazines slowly and somewhat spasmodically began to take an interest in India. Coverage picked up in the late 1820s when newspapers like the *Times* addressed subjects like thuggee and suttee. Nevertheless, war continued to fascinate readers in Britain, and whether it was a literary magazine like *Blackwood's Edinburgh Magazine* or a specialist journal like the *United Service Journal*, there were many more mentions of India during bouts of war than there were in peacetime.

Much of this growth in the mass media correlates with a parallel growth in production technologies. As Reed (1997, 44) has argued, the 'second half of the nineteenth century saw a complete transformation of the printing trade'. With the development of the rotary press, introduction of cheap paper in place of expensive linen rag material, and the implementation of faster modes of transport (such as trains and steam-boats), the potential for the production, marketing and distribution of print media increased dramatically. Likewise, the laying of telegraph cables from the 1850s onwards enabled quicker transmission of news from hitherto isolated areas and imperial arenas (Headrick 1981, 1988; Kaul 1997).

Before the era of telegraphs, information from India was secured through a number of sources. These included official, semi-official and unofficial letters from India sent via the sea or overland (including many anonymous correspondents), contributions from individuals kept on retainer (for example, the *Times* regularly printed letters from India filed by Philip Meadows Taylor), gossip from returned civil and military officials, the occasional 'leaked' report from government sources, and copies of Indian newspapers and magazines that found their way to Britain (Marshall 1992). Seaborne and overland communications did cause some delay in the transmission of news: the quickest route, the one that went via the Red Sea, cut the voyage to 30 days. Moreover, with the cost of telegraphs precluding all but the most vital political and commercial intelligence, these pre-telegraph modes of communication still had a role to play (Kaul 1997).

It is important to note the reciprocal relationship that existed between British publishers and editors and their audience. Just as they depended on Indian 'experts' for their information, they also looked to them as its consumers. Some journals were dedicated almost exclusively to such groups; here one can point to the *Oriental Herald*, the *Overland Mail* and *The Indian Magazine*, which is the subject of Antoinette Burton's essay. Then there were those groups with increasingly strong ties to India, for example, missionaries, engineers, physicians and surgeons, and military officers. As suggested in the articles by Harrison, Wainwright and Moreman, India was an important site for the promulgation of these professional identities.

Other publications targeted individuals with longstanding personal or family connections to India as well as members of the political and cultural elite. Eugenie Palmegiano found in her 1991 study of the Victorian press and the Indian Revolt of 1857 that British journals like *Bentley's Miscellany*, *Blackwood's Edinburgh Magazine*, and *Fraser's* increasingly focused their attention on India with an eye to this market. *Blackwood's* was especially persistent in appealing to those with an interest in the British empire in general and India in particular. During the course of the Afghan War and after, it published many articles on this campaign and the so-called 'Great Game' which was then taking place between Britain and Russia (see, for example, the articles by Alison 1833, 1836, 1838 and 1840). Its regular inclusion of articles on India and other parts of the empire, as well as on the Army, ensured that it was widely available in the libraries and messes of the British empire. In 1843, *Blackwood's* even launched a colonial edition, though it must be added that its market was smaller than it had anticipated. Its initial print run of 1000 copies per month was soon reduced to 350 (Milne 1985). Nevertheless, *Blackwood's'* commitment to the empire would last until well into the twentieth century (Finkelstein 1995).

Plenty of other evidence exists to show how India was being taken up by a range of magazines aimed at domestic audiences, including miscellanies, women's journals and children's periodicals. Essays in this collection by Chaudhuri and Boyd provide examples of how India filtered into the Victorian household through such print media. Such domestic spaces encouraged gendered refigurations of imperial themes, for the empire enabled British women to establish new public roles for themselves. However, as noted before, Boyd adds the important caveat that India was not the ubiquitous canvas upon which writers inscribed such identities. Other arenas, such as Africa and the settler colonies of Australia, New Zealand and Canada, proved equally important in formulating imperial agendas.

Nevertheless, miscellanies like *Household Words* and *All the Year Round* placed great stock on India as the subject or setting for fiction and prose. Over 90 articles on India have been identified in the 1850s in *Household Words*. With average sales of 40000 copies per week (compared to around 6000 for *Blackwood's* and 15000 for the *Edinburgh Review* at its peak), this profitable weekly disseminated news and views of India to a wider audience than that reached by monthlies and quarterlies (Fetter 1965; Lohrli 1973; Milne 1985). To that extent, Lohrli's claim that 'the Crimean War and the Indian Mutiny were strongly reflected in *Household Words* pages but not dealt with in any reasoned or analytical manner' (1973, 7) is only partially true: as Peters and Park demonstrate in their essays in this collection, Dickens and Wilkie Collins, among others, used *Household Words* and *All the Year Round* to comment on Britain's place in and obligations to India.

This growing engagement with Indian and imperial themes, however, while challenging specific aspects of Britain's imperial mission, rarely produced sustained critiques of the whole. This is not surprising because writers, editors and publishers were generally loath to tackle directly the status quo. As one reviewer in the *Westminster Review* said of the *Edinburgh Review*, 'periodical literature depends upon immediate success. It must therefore patronize the opinions which are now in vogue, the opinions of those who are now in power' (Pykett 1990, 13; Shattock and Wolff 1982). Writers and editors tailored their writings with such factors in mind.

Introducing print media into India

Mass print media in India has a number of important characteristics that distinguish it from domestic productions. While the technology and culture of mass media was at least initially largely borrowed from Europe, its audience was much more fragmented by language, region and race. Interestingly enough, the British were among the last of the European powers active in India to introduce the printing press into their enclaves. It was not until 1761 that the British in India acquired a press, and even then it was a press that had been taken from the French (Dharwadker 1997). Its role was primarily the production of official documents and texts. Printing for popular consumption came much more slowly. The first newspaper in Calcutta came out in 1780, followed by one in Madras in 1785 and Bombay in 1789 (Natarajan 1962, 9). By the mid-nineteenth century, newspapers and magazines were common elements in Anglo-Indian life. As one commentator noted in 1851, 'The newspaper is as necessary an adjunct to the breakfast table in Calcutta as it is in London' (Hobbes 1851, 362).

Anglo-Indian newspapers rarely challenged the status quo. This was partly the result of the government's occasional efforts at curtailing the freedom of the press. The first attempt at controlling the press came in 1799 when regulations were passed which obliged editors to submit copy to the government prior to publication. However, as threats to British authority receded and the legislation proved unwieldy, these laws fell into disuse. Further attempts to control press activity were mounted in 1823, 1856, 1867 and 1878 (Natarajan 1962).

Submission to the status quo was also predicated on the sense of beleaguerment that pervaded the Anglo-Indian community. As a result of this anxiety, ideological divisions within the Anglo-Indian community were subordinated to the need to demonstrate political and cultural unity. While some publications like the *Mofussilite* occasionally annoyed the government by taking up minor grievances, they rarely attacked the government on partisan grounds. As one writer informed his readers, 'Let a man have been ever so violent a Tory or zealous a Whig, six months in India will generally find him, so far as his discourse can testify, neuter' (Hobbes 1851, 365).

Another example of the kinds of subtle differences that separated British periodicals from their Anglo-Indian counterparts can be glimpsed in their political cartoons. The self-mocking and self-critiquing quality of cartoons in domestic British magazines like *Punch* was largely absent from cartoons in Anglo-Indian magazines (Mitter 1997). No doubt this was largely due to the fact that British rule was deemed to be inseparable from British character, and hence any mockery of the latter could very well threaten the former. Instead, the most common caricatures in the Anglo-Indian magazines were of Indians, and relied upon a fairly standard and often very crude set of racial stereotypes. Interestingly, caricatures in the vernacular press were truer to the British ideal for they did engage in self-criticism, mocking in particular those Indians who eagerly and unquestioningly mimicked their colonial rulers.

A second source of print media in India was the missionary societies. The East India Company's antipathy to their activities in the subcontinent forced many of them to locate their operations in territories outside Company control. For example, presses in the Danish enclave at Serhampore were used to print missionary tracts and other devotional literature in English as well as in indigenous languages. This in turn stimulated the establishment and development of a vernacular press.

From these small beginnings came a spectacular growth in the production of newspapers and magazines in English and in vernacular languages in India. It has been estimated that 14 000 newspapers and periodicals were launched in India during the course of the nineteenth century, though the caveat should be added that many of these publications were short-lived (Dharwadker 1997, 126). Anglo-Indian publishers often made grandiloquent claims for their periodicals: for example, one heralded its imminent arrival in the following manner:

In the press, and will be published on the 1st of July, and continued monthly, a new periodical, entitled 'The British India Magazine, and Daily and Monthly Treasury', a most useful Writing and Reading Table Manual of Reference, Memoranda, Expenditure, and Literature, to which is added a Precis of the news of the past month, Political, Fashionable, Social, Commercial, Humorous, and Scientific. It is equally adapted for ladies in general, as for Gentlemen of the Civil, Military, and Uncovenanted Services, Members of the Legal and Medical Professions, Merchants, Indigo and Sugar Planters, and Planter's Assistants, Captains and Officers of Ships, Clerks in Mercantile Houses, etc, or in fact, for all Persons by whom due order and regularity in the expenditure of their Time and Income is considered an Object

Worthy of Notice. It is compiled upon a method perfectly novel in the annals of the Press, be it American, Asiatic, or European, and may be had (per dak) in all parts of British India. (Hobbes 1851, 363)

Despite such lofty pretensions, this journal apparently never materialized, thus demonstrating the volatility of the marketplace. Even the *Calcutta Review*, which had over the course of its first decade reached 1500 subscribers, teetered on the edge of financial ruin in its early years (Chanda 1987, 253).

The English-language press suffered competition from imported British periodicals. Customs figures indicate that by 1843 India was the single largest colonial export market for British publishers (Fraser 1997). One medical officer in the Bengal Presidency informed readers in Britain that 'in a knowledge of the periodical literature of the day, the society of India is particularly conversant', concluding that it was common to find 'the *Quarterly*, the *Edinburgh*, *Blackwoods*, *Fraser*, *New Monthly*, and many others, on the table of an Anglo-Indian in Upper Hindostan within four months and a half after their appearance in England' (Spry 1837, 86). However, it would be a mistake to assume that there was a seamless connection between British publishers and Anglo-Indian readers. As Priya Joshi has found in her 1998 study of the reception of the novel in colonial India, readers did not necessarily purchase the books which British publishers tried to direct them towards.

The Anglo-Indian press was also hampered by poor internal transportation links, and the fact that many of the British in India lacked either the income to purchase or the ability to read these publications. In 1832, a Parliamentary Committee looking into the administration of the East India Company was told that the combined circulation of the English press in 1832 was about 3000 (Chaudhuri 1996). The total British population in India at that time was around 30 000 (though of that, a little over 20 000 consisted of the European rank and file of the East India Company's army and king's regiments stationed in India, a good number of whom would have been illiterate). Similar problems were encountered by the vernacular press, who also had to contend with regional and linguistic differences, and an even smaller potential audience. In 1875, India had 382 vernacular newspapers and what were then termed 'Anglo-Vernacular Papers', that is papers published by Indians for Indians but produced in English, and 166 English papers (Digby 1877, 362). Yet each paper had only limited numbers of readers: it was estimated that each of the vernacular papers could count on no more than 400 subscribers (Digby 1877). In practice, this meant that few vernacular papers operated at a profit, contributors were paid little if anything, and publishers and editors tended to bring out these papers more for political or cultural reasons than as a strictly business undertaking (Das 1991, 259). As one observer claimed, 'the Indian vernacular journal had a greater effect upon the mind of the reader than an English paper can have upon an Englishman, because, practically, it is all the reading the *ryat* [agriculturalist], and even a member of some higher classes has access to' (Digby 1877, 381). Brief histories of many of these journals have been provided by Mrinal Kanti Chanda (1987).

It is also worth noting that the vernacular press had to compete with already established communication networks. A precolonial tradition of handwritten newsletters persisted even in the face of the emerging vernacular print culture. Such newsletters initially reached a wider readership and frequently were written in a much more inflammatory style. As late as 1850, the Nawab of Awadh still had 65 newswriters on staff (Natarajan 1962, 87; for more on the newswriter tradition, see Fisher (1993) and Bayly (1986)). However, by the 1890s print and print media had become a defining and ubiquitous presence in Indian village life, as a noted scholar of Indian languages remarked: 'there is now scarcely a town of importance which does not possess its printing-press or two. Every scribbler can now see his writings in type or lithographed for a few rupees, and too often he avails himself of the power and the opportunity' (Grierson, *Vernacular Literature*, as quoted in Bayly 1996, 343).

A good number of those journals that survived and in some cases even flourished did so because they either targeted a niche market or enjoyed official patronage. One particularly important sector was the Army. A number of publishers deliberately and directly appealed to them. While this is most obvious in journals which dealt with the professional demands of the profession, such as the *East India United Service Journal* and the *British Indian Military Repository*, even newspaper editors wrote with an eye on the Army. We can see this in John Lang's *Mofussilite*, published in Meerut. His account of the founding of this journal, published in *Household Words*, places great stress on the importance of the military market to his success, for officers not only subscribed to but wrote for the paper (Lang 1853; Stanley 1998, 230). British publishers were also quick to capitalize on such markets, as John Sutherland (1986) explains in his comments on Henry Colburn's role in publishing the *United Service Journal*. Yet even this market was not as lucrative as it might have appeared. Unlike military periodicals in the United Kingdom which could enjoy a long life (Tucker 1994), journals like the *East India United Service Journal* and the *British Indian Military Repository* lived a hand-to-mouth existence, and often lasted only a short while. The former had on average 300 subscribers per month while the latter's circulation peaked at 400 (Chanda 1987, 73–4, 164).

Other examples of niche journals include those associated with engineering and medicine as explored here in the essays by Wainwright and Harrison. The importance of patronage is brought out by Moreman and Majeed who illustrate that purchases by government agencies of military and Urdu periodicals ensured their survival. In the case of the military press, such support had its price – a loss of autonomy. This was also discovered by publishers of vernacular papers; as one commentator remarked,'Rich natives now make handsome presents to the editors of Native papers, as well as subscribe for their publications, and the sense of their editorial power is increasing' (as quoted in Bayly 1996, 343).

Recently scholars have credited this print capitalism with introducing into India the ideologies and practices of Enlightenment Europe, thereby subordinating India to western material and discursive forces (Anderson 1991; Chatterjee 1993). Yet it is important to note that the print culture which emerged did not merely mimic British forms: instead, it was hybrid and hence it cannot be accounted for in such simple terms (Dharwadker 1997). Its intrinsic qualities ensured that it was not a pale shadow of what had happened in Europe, and hence it needs to be studied on its own terms, as Majeed demonstrates in this collection. The periodical press in Urdu provides an interesting example of this. Although published mainly in Urdu, such newspapers contained occasional items in English, with translations alongside. The resulting mistranslations, the untidy process of turning official English-language proclamations into the vernacular, whereby original meaning could be lost and subverted, yields important insights into cultural transformations, cultural values and cultural subversion. Subversion was also present in the press's frequent juxtaposition of news items with each other, irrespective of whether they referred to events in India or Europe, as well as the intermingling of scientific and practical items with poetry, legends, fables and philosophy.

Linking India and Britain

The process of creating, disseminating and incorporating representations of India required the coupling together of Indian, Anglo-Indian and British interests. The Indian, Anglo-Indian and British media borrowed freely from each other, drawing on common sources, and calling on each other to validate positions taken up in their writing. The regular exchange of information between these three arenas was crucial to the integration of metropole and periphery. One sees this, for example, in the bylines in the *Times*; many of its articles on India were reprinted from Anglo-Indian newspapers. And, as captured here in the essays by Moreman, Harrison and Wainwright, professional and trade publications also gained from this two-way flow of information. This exchange in turn informed and shaped the evolution of these professions as the century progressed.

This tradition of including copies of articles from India was in turn replicated by newspapers in India who repeatedly ran copies of articles from the *Times* as well as other British papers and periodicals. The *Madras Male Asylum Herald*, for example, often reprinted articles from *Blackwood's Edinburgh Magazine* and the *Edinburgh Review*.

All this begs the question: who was responsible for these representations of India? As Bart Moore-Gilbert (1996) has noted, insufficient attention has been paid to the matter of who was writing on India and how familiar were they with it. Many contemporaries with Indian experience frequently found representations of India in the British press wanting. Such complaints were widespread amongst Anglo-Indians who, while they were acutely and perhaps even pathologically conscious of their British identity, were nevertheless separated from Britain by subtle cultural differences, many of which were exaggerated by the press. J.W. Kaye (1846) wrote critically of the crude stereotypes and inaccuracies which commonly crept into many British discussions of India. He and others were especially upset at the caricature of the amoral and avaricious British Nabob that often found itself in print. In other cases, India was little more than a convenient and exotic backdrop upon which narratives could be draped. Boyd's essay considers this in more detail as it relates to Victorian boys' papers. She shows us how India was often tangential to the actual story, and through this calls into question common assumptions about the degree to which India was instrumental in shaping young men's visions of empire.

For those with perhaps first-hand knowledge of India, the subcontinent was a more complex and ambiguous site of reference. McBratney's essay explores the ambiguities embedded in Kipling's early and often overlooked journalistic writings, thus providing a more nuanced reading of the place of India and Empire in Kipling's work. The concept of hybridity, popularized by Bhabha (1990), Young (1995) and Malchow (1996) among others, is a helpful way of approaching cultural mediators like Kipling. By emphasizing the porous rather than the fixed nature of colonial boundaries, hybridity allows us to concentrate on the slippages of meaning that one finds when reading imperial texts. For such critics, hybridity is synonymous with ambiguity. Yet there is another way of looking at hybridity that has been suggested by Dharwadker (1997), namely that hybridity is a form of cultural ambidexterity.

Hybridity as ambidexterity could be applied to many of the authors, editors and publishers active in the nineteenth-century media. Their role as cultural brokers, participating in the formation and distribution of images of India, was informed by their migration between metropole and periphery. One example of this is J.H. Stocqueler who, following his career in India where he edited *The Englishman* (which had begun life as the *John Bull*) and founded and edited the *East India United Service Journal* and the *Bengal Sporting Magazine* (Chanda 1987, 170, 399), returned to England where he edited the *Naval and Military Gazette* and gave public lectures on Indian topics.

J.W. Kaye is another example of a writer moving between India and Britain. He went to India as a cadet in the Company's artillery but was soon swept up into the publishing world of Calcutta. Not only did he serve briefly as the editor of one of Calcutta's most popular English newspapers, the *Bengal Hurkaru*, but he was also instrumental in founding the *Calcutta Review*, a journal modelled on the lines of the *Edinburgh Review* and the *Quarterly Review*, and to which he contributed many articles until his departure for Britain (Singh 1986). In Britain he wrote many articles on Indian affairs, especially for the *North British Review*. He was instrumental in establishing newspapers specifically aimed at Anglo-Indians moving between Britain and India.

Other efforts were made to bridge the gap between domestic and Anglo-Indian spheres by both India-based and British-based publications. This often took the form of offering spaces where competing voices could be heard. This coupling together of Imperial Indian and domestic agendas is, for example, the subject of Antoinette Burton's analysis of *The Indian Magazine*. This was the official monthly journal of the National Indian Association (NIA), which was founded in 1870–71 by Mary Carpenter, an energetic philanthropist chiefly remembered for her promotion of the Ragged Schools system. It was published continuously between 1870 and 1914. What makes this journal exceptional is that, though edited and run by Britons from Britain, it served as a site where Indian men and women could address and contest interpretations of Indian culture and society offered by well-meaning British observers and reformers. Writing from Britain and India, their views recorded in letters to the editor, editorials, features or in transcribed speeches at NIA annual meetings, Indian reformers used the periodical space to shape, contest and articulate views of India as part of a printed dialogue, a dialogue that evolved as events were recorded and ideologies were challenged.

Media culture and media history

In the field of cultural studies and media history, the analysis of media and cultural artefacts as cultural commodities has more often than not been bound up in post-Marxist and postmodernist concerns with political hegemony and the role of culture within a capitalist system of production and commodification. The political agendas of such analyses often mask the more fundamental importance of considering such issues, namely that analysing the process of social transaction can enrich our understanding of social meanings, activities and identities as they are constructed through the social communication process, through texts and mass media. Print and mass media studies provide valuable sites for analysing representations of society as cultural objects and as integrated parts of 'the subcultures, class fractions, social movements that produce and consume them', to quote one advocate of mass media analysis (M. Denning, as quoted in Schneirov 1994, 17).

As the essays in this collection seek to demonstrate, the 'Empire of opinion' that is claimed for India by *The Friend of India* is not a monolithic construct, but a complex, evolving and disparate creature, particularly when viewed through the lens of the nineteenth-century press and print media. One finds that the pages of the century's general and specific periodical publications become sites of contestation, forums for debates on and evolving definitions of nationhood, gender and class, as well as on and of emerging professional and social identities. As Stuart Hall notes in a now classic study of media voices and the popular press, the printed page of such ephemeral commodities become the 'products of a social transaction between producers and readers', whereby 'successful communication in this field depends to some degree on a process of mutual confirmation between those who produce and those who consume' (Stuart Hall, introduction to Smith 1975, 22).

Subsequent to such a pronouncement, some critics have followed through on these implications for print media and cultural analysis, among them Matthew Schneirov and Richard Ohmann, whose studies of nineteenth-century US magazines have examined the manner in which such cultural commodities can be read as 'a product of human action or agency within certain structural contexts and as a cultural form or "object"' (Schneirov 1994, 19). Their work reflects an interesting side of current trends in media culture studies, many of whose practitioners have generally tended to ignore print media history in favour of reflective work on recent visual and mass media trends. Yet, as Douglas Kellner suggests, one point shared in common by all is the healthy transdisciplinarity of such work, where such approaches to culture and society cross over and transgress the borders of various academic disciplines. Indeed, as he rightly suggests, reiterating themes flowing through contemporary work in literary and historical studies, 'One should not stop at the border of a text, but should see how it fits into systems of textual production, and how various texts are thus part of systems of genres or types of production and have an intertextual construction' (Kellner 1995, 27–8).

Studying the process of social transaction as it is played out in the printed pages of Victorian and Indian mass print media is one way to refresh debate on colonial and post-colonial issues and theories. The matter is how to untangle the complex and interweaving connections between producer and consumer, to join disparate and competing views on defining these social groupings within society, whether through the sociologist Pierre Bourdieu's articulation of literary 'fields' as common social, intellectual and ideological arenas linking producers (publishers, editors and authors) of texts, or as Stanley Fish's 'interpretive communities' of textual production, or through utilization of variations of Jurgen Habermas's articulation of the 'public sphere' as the major arena for the construction of public opinion. Such methodologies have much in common with the manner in which colonial and postcolonial theory has attempted to deal with issues of transculturation and hybridity: all could be said to be testing the manner in which culture mediates communication, at the same time that communication mediates culture.

Conclusion

This brings us back to the main point of this collection. What we seek to do is offer considerations of the nineteenth-century mass media as sites of contestation, of reflections of wider cultural agendas than those found in travel, historical and fictional treatments of colonial matters, published in expensive formats for the few. The mass media, that is, the print media of the nineteenth century, with dailies, weeklies, monthlies and quarterlies reaching audiences ranging from a few thousand to 500 000 an issue, present sites of reference potentially more influential and valuable in discussions of otherness, colonial, national, ethnic, gender and professional identities, than those often sought and sometimes found between book covers.

More importantly, the analysis of the production, dissemination and reception of such texts can provide powerful indices of cultural responses shaping and being shaped by various interpretive communities, the 'imagined communities' of Benedict Anderson (1991). Past theoretical strategies have not often addressed the fissures and slippages to be found in reconciling texts with contexts, in illustrating how cultural values are shaped within textual spaces. As Tim Youngs notes in reference to recent work on explorers' narratives, a point that could be applied equally well to the analysis of India in the mass media, too often published accounts 'have been taken as straightforward evidence of their authors' claims without any critical attention being paid to the conditions of their production, their literary and ideological constructions, or their reception' (Youngs 1995, 5). All of the essays in this collection, in one form or another, reply to Youngs' concern, though they approach this problem in different ways and from different directions.

While colonial discourse is now seen to be far more fractured and contested than was once the case, owing to the varieties of agendas and agents at work, the various genres through which discourse is produced, and the shifting material and ideological contexts in which they are played out, it would be a mistake to assume that there are no patterns or commonalities. There are some particular themes and plots which resonate throughout writings on the empire in general, and India in particular. Among these we find the constant drive to produce ethnological mappings of the empire, those all-important classificatory schemes that enable racial, class and gender hierarchies to be plotted and preserved. This is not to say that such efforts went unchallenged, or that they remained frozen in aspic (see, for example, Loomba 1998; Sarkar 1994).

Finally, a word of caution is in order. In our excavations into the Victorian worldview, we must take care that we do not commit the same sin that we commonly accuse them of, namely essentializing them into our 'others' (Lorimer 1996). The Victorians were never as culturally monolithic as some studies imply; nor were they as necessarily and systematically intolerant as we are often encouraged to assume. They were in many ways as diverse a society as we are today, and there is therefore a very real risk that we could end up offloading our own anxieties and prejudices onto them, a process which could obscure the extent to which many of their assumptions about race, class and gender can still be found amongst us today.

The point is, understanding the processes of production and dissemination, composition and reception can present significant sites of reference for current and future critical interpretations of the nineteenth-century media. Similarly, considerations of the processes of mediation of intended meanings through unseen filters, such as editorial policies, mostly undiscussed and often untraceable due to the anonymity of such textual production, should be central to discussions of nineteenth-century media responses to India. They play their part in the ephemeral pages of newspapers and journals, often in form of differing editorial policies, conflicting voices, even in considerations of the placement of advertising material and the spaces and places allocated to individual topics. The result is an engagement of discourses reflecting not a consensual view of India, but a fractured one: a multiplicity of voices within and outside Indian borders, real and imagined borders, many interpretive communities from which individuals shift and slide to, from and in between, contesting cultural, religious, ethnic and gendered identities, shaping and being shaped through rhetoric and debate.

Works cited

Alison, Archibald. 'The East India Question', *Blackwood's Edinburgh Magazine* 33 (1833), 776–803.
Alison, Archibald. 'What is our External Policy and Condition?', *Blackwood's Edinburgh Magazine* 39 (1836), 780–92.
Alison, Archibald. 'Affairs in the East', *Blackwood's Edinburgh Magazine* 44 (1836), 769–78.
Alison, Archibald. 'The Afghanistan Question', *Blackwood's Edinburgh Magazine* 47 (1840), 241–52.
Altick, Richard. *The English Common Reader*. Chicago, 1957.
Altick, Richard. *Punch: the Lively Youth of a British Institution, 1841–1851*. Columbus, Ohio, 1997.
Anderson, Benedict. *Imagined Communities: Reflections on the Origin and Spread of Nationalism*. London, 1991.
Bayly, C.A. *Empire and Information: Intelligence Gathering and Social Communication in India, 1780–1870*. Cambridge, 1996.
Bhabha, Homi (ed.). *Nation and Narration*. London, 1990.
Brantlinger, Patrick. *Rule of Darkness: British Literature and Imperialism, 1830–1914*. Ithaca, 1990.
Chanda, Mrinal Kanti. *History of the English Press in Bengal, 1780–1857*. Calcutta, 1987.
Chatterjee, Amal. *Representations of India, 1740–1840: the Creation of India in the Colonial Imagination*. London, 1998.
Chatterjee, Partha. *The Nation and its Fragments: Colonial and Postcolonial Histories*. Princeton, 1993.

Chaudhuri, Brahma. 'India', in J. Don Vann and Rosemary VanArsdel (eds), *Periodicals of Queen Victoria's Empire: an Exploration*. Toronto, 1996, 175–200.

Das, Sisir Kumar. *A History of Indian Literature: Western Impact, Indian Responses, 1800–1900*. New Delhi, 1991.

David, Deirdre. *Rule Britannia: Women, Empire and Victorian Writing*. Ithaca, 1995.

Dharwadker, Vinay. 'Print Culture and Literary Markets in Colonial India', in Jeffrey Masten, Peter Stallybrass and Nancy Vickers (eds), *Language Machines: Technologies of Literary and Cultural Production*. New York, 1997, 108–36.

Digby, William.'Native Newspapers of India and Ceylon', *Calcutta Review* 65 (1877), 356–94.

Dirks, Nicholas B. (ed.). *Colonialism and Culture*. Ann Arbor, 1992.

Fetter, Frank W. 'Economic Controversy in the British Reviews, 1802–1850', *Economica* 32 (1965), 424–37.

Finkelstein, David. *An Index to Blackwood's Magazine, 1901–1980*. Aldershot, 1995.

Fisher, Michael H. 'The Office of Akhbar Nawis: the Transition from Mughal to British Forms', *Modern Asian Studies* 27 (1993), 45–82.

Fraser, Angus. 'John Murray's Colonial and Home Library', *Papers of the Bibliographic Society of America* 91 (1997), 339–408.

Headrick, Daniel R. *The Tools of Empire: Technology and European Imperialism in the Nineteenth Century*. Oxford, 1981.

Headrick, Daniel R. *The Tentacles of Progress: Technology Transfer in the Age of Imperialism, 1850–1940*. Oxford, 1988.

Hobbes, Robert George. 'Calcutta', *Bentley's Miscellany* 30 (1851), 361–8.

Joshi, Priya. 'Culture and Consumption: Fiction, the Reading Public, and the British Novel in Colonial India', *Book History* 1 (1998), 196–220.

Kaul, Chandrika. 'England and India: the Ilbert Bill, 1883: a Case Study of the Metropolitan Press', *Indian Economic and Social History Review* 30 (1993), 412–36.

Kaul, Chandrika. 'Imperial Communications, Fleet Street and the Indian Empire, c.1850s–1920s', in Michael Bromley and Tom O'Malley (eds), *A Journalism Reader*. London, 1997, 58–86.

Kaye, J.W. 'English Literature in India', *Calcutta Review* 5 (1846), 202–20.

Kellner, Douglas. *Media Culture: Cultural Studies, Identity and Politics between the Modern and the Postmodern*. London, 1995.

Lang, John. 'Starting a Paper in India', *Household Words* 7 (March 1853), 94–6.

Lohrli, Anne (ed.). *Household Words: a Weekly Journal, 1850–1859, Conducted by Charles Dickens*. Toronto, 1973.

Loomba, Ania. *Colonialism/Postcolonialism*. London, 1998.

Lorimer, Douglas A. 'Race, Science and Culture: Historical Continuities and Discontinuities, 1850–1914' in West, Shearer, ed. *The Victorians and Race*. Aldershot, 1996, 12–33.

MacKenzie, John M. *Propaganda and Empire: the Manipulation of British Public Opinion, 1880–1960*. Manchester, 1984.

MacKenzie, John M. (ed.). *Imperialism and Popular Culture*. Manchester, 1986.

MacKenzie, John M. *Orientalism: History, Theory and the Arts*. Manchester, 1995.

Maidment, B.E. 'Victorian Periodicals and Academic Discourse', in Laurel Brake, Aled Jones and Lionel Madden (eds), *Investigating Victorian Journalism*. London, 1990, 143–54.

Malchow, H.L. *Gothic Images of Race in Nineteenth-Century Britain*. Stanford, 1996.

Marshall, P.J. '"Cornwallis Triumphant": War in India and the British Public in the Late Eighteenth Century', in Lawrence Freedman, Paul Hayes and Robert O'Neill (eds), *War, Strategy and International Politics: Essays in Honour of Sir Michael Howard*. Oxford, 1992, 57–74.

McClintock, Anne. *Imperial Leather: Race, Gender, and Sexuality in the Colonial Context*. London, 1994.

Mills, Sara. *Discourses of Difference: an Analysis of Women's Travel Writing and Colonialism*. London, 1992.

Milne, Morris. 'The Management of a Nineteenth Century Magazine: William Blackwood and Sons, 1827–1847', *Journal of Newspaper and Periodical History* 1 (1985), 24–33.

Mitter, Partha. 'Cartoons of the Raj', *History Today* (September 1997), 16–21.

Moore-Gilbert, Bart (ed.). *Writing India, 1757–1990: the Literature of British India*. Manchester, 1996.

Natarajan, S. *A History of the Press in India*. New Delhi, 1962.

Palmegiano, Eugenie. 'The Indian Mutiny in the Mid-Victorian Press', *Journal of Newspaper and Periodical History* 7 (1991), 3–11.

Parry, Ann. 'Reading Formations in the Victorian Press: the Reception of Kipling, 1888–1891', *Literature and History* 11 (1985), 254–63.

Peers, Douglas M. '"Those Noble Exemplars of the True Military Tradition": Constructions of the Indian Army in the Mid-Victorian Press', *Modern Asian Studies* 31 (1997), 109–42.

Pratt, Mary Louise. *Imperial Eyes: Travel Writing and Transculturation*. London, 1992.

Pykett, Lyn. 'Reading the Periodical Press: Text and Context', in Laurel Brake, Aled Jones and Lionel Madden (eds), *Investigating Victorian Journalism*. London, 1990, 3–18.

Reed, David. *The Rise of the Popular Magazine in Britain and the United States, 1880–1960*. Toronto, 1997.

Said, Edward. *Orientalism*. London, 1978.

Said, Edward. *Culture and Imperialism*. London, 1992.

Sarkar, Sumit. 'Orientalism Revisited: Saidian Frameworks in the Writing of Modern Indian History', *Oxford Literary Review* 16 (1994), 205–24.

Schneirov, Matthew. *The Dream of a New Social Order: Popular Magazines in America, 1893–1914*. New York, 1994.

Shattock, Joanne and Michael Wolff (eds). *The Victorian Periodical Press: Samplings and Soundings*. Leicester, 1982.

Singh, Nihar Nandan. *British Historiography on British Rule in India: the Life and Writings of Sir John William Kaye, 1814–1876*. Patna, 1986.

Smith, A.C.H. *Paper Voices: the Popular Press and Social Change, 1935–1965*. London, 1975.

Spivak, Gayatri Chakravorty. *A Critique of Post-Colonial Reason: Toward a History of the Vanishing Present*. Cambridge, 1999.

Spry, Henry. *Modern India*. London, 1837.

Spurr, David. *The Rhetoric of Empire: Colonial Discourse in Journalism, Travel Writing, and Imperial Administration*. Durham, 1993.

Stanley, Peter. *White Mutiny: British Military Culture in India*. London, 1998.

Suleri, Sara. *The Rhetoric of English India*. Chicago, 1992.

Sullivan, Alvin. *British Literary Magazines, vol. 3: The Victorian and Edwardian Age, 1837–1913*. Westport, Conn., 1984.

Sutherland, John.'Henry Colburn: Publisher', *Publishing History* 19 (1986), 59–84.
Tucker, Albert. 'Military', in J. Don Vann and Rosemary T. VanArsdel (eds), *Victorian Periodicals and Victorian Society*. Toronto, 1994, 62–80.
Vann, J. Don and Rosemary T. VanArsdel (eds), *Periodicals of Queen Victoria's Empire: an Exploration*. Toronto, 1996.
Williams, Kevin. *Get me a Murder a Day!: a History of Mass Communication in Britain*. London, 1998.
Wilson, John. 'Short Memorial of the Honourable Mountstuart Elphinstone, and of his Contributions to Oriental Geography and History', *Journal of the Bombay Branch of the Royal Asiatic Society* 6 (1861), 97–111.
Wong, J.Y. *Deadly Dreams: Opium and the 'Arrow' War (1856–1860) in China*. Cambridge, 1998.
Young, Robert. *White Mythologies: Writing, History and the West*. London, 1991.
Young, Robert. *Colonial Desire: Hybridity in Theory, Culture and Race*. London, 1995.
Youngs, Tim. *Travellers in Africa – British Travelogues, 1850–1900*. Manchester, 1995.

2
Institutionalizing Imperial Reform: *The Indian Magazine* and Late-Victorian Colonial Politics

Antoinette Burton

In January 1886 the National Indian Association (NIA) announced a new name, a new look, and a renewed sense of purpose for its monthly magazine. The *Journal of the National Indian Association* (hereafter, *JNIA*) henceforth became *The Indian Magazine* (hereafter, *IM*), a name that would be modified again in 1891 to *The Indian Magazine and Review* (hereafter, *IMR*). Despite these periodic changes of title, the NIA's journal enjoyed an uninterrupted run from 1870 to 1914, during which time it provided its subscribers in Britain and in India with 'the best tendencies and aspirations of Indian thought' as well as 'a true chronicle of educational reforming activity'. The name changes were not simply cosmetic. They reflected both the success of the journal in publicizing Indian affairs during the first 15 years of its existence and the need – born of that very success – to carve out a niche for itself in a domestic British market that was inundated in the 1880s and after with Indian news and images. Attention to progressive Indian opinion and to educational reform projects for India had been among the founding concerns of the NIA, and it was these which the editor of the newly reinvented *IM* chose to highlight as its distinctive contributions to the late-Victorian press scene. Writing in the first issue in 1886, Elizabeth Adelaide Manning remarked,

> We would remind our readers ... that while other periodicals relating to India treat of political, religious, or commercial subjects, this *Magazine* is, perhaps, the only one which is mainly occupied with educational, literary and social matters: yet these are of immense importance at the present time, and on their advance depends the solution if many serious problems.

The social if not the political purpose of the NIA's periodical was thus made explicitly clear: 'we therefore commend the *Indian Magazine* to its supporters in India and in England, with the hope that, by the help of their exertions, it may become more and more a source of encouragement to workers in good movements, and of stimulus to others to go and do likewise' (Manning 1886, 2).

Manning's insistence on the link between journal reading and social reform work could easily be read as a cynical attempt to bolster slumping subscriptions. Indeed, whenever the NIA changed the title or the look of its monthly magazine, the editor took the opportunity to lament the failure of the journal to come to the notice of a wider circle of readers and issued a call for promoting 'the highest good of others' by enlarging the list of subscribers (Manning 1886, 2).[1] The history of the NIA and its connections with female reform communities in Victorian Britain suggests, however, that Manning's equation of periodical reading and social improvement was not unique to the NIA, even if it was a philosophy untypical of other mainstream Victorian monthlies (including those which paid attention to India). Like the *Englishwomen's Review*, a feminist monthly which was contemporary with it, and like a host of short- and long-lived female reform and suffrage periodicals between 1860 and 1915, the *IM* was a conspicuous organizational site for a diverse set of people interested in and committed to social reform in India and, more specifically, to the 'uplift' of Indian women through education (Burton 1994). As suffrage journals did for the British women's movement, the *IM* represented its organizers' schemes to the public and helped to institutionalize their reform concerns in a centralized yet geographically far-reaching public space. The NIA (which was based in London after 1877) had no permanent public offices (Manning 1879, 389). It was run out of Manning's home in Maida Vale, which was where many of the NIA soirées also occurred. Its annual meetings and occasional lectures took place in a variety of meeting places available in London and it was affiliated with the Northbrook Club (a reading room for English and Indian 'gentlemen'), but it had no fixed institutional site. In the absence of a physical, bricks-and-mortar home, the *IM* came to embody not just the NIA, but the 'imagined community' of colonial reformers and others sympathetic to its projects. In both a symbolic and a material sense, the magazine had by 1886 become one of the chief public faces of secular reform for India in Victorian Britain.

As the institutional expression of much Victorian social reform opinion about India, the *IM* furnished its readers with fairly stereotypical, orientalist images of Indian social and cultural life and especially of

Indian women. A September 1880 article entitled 'Self-Love of Orna-
ments among Bengali Ladies', together with dozens of pieces on the
long-suffering qualities of Hindu women over a quarter of a century,
attempted to fix 'the Indian woman' as helpess and degraded – images
that were disrupted from time to time either by accounts of contemporary
Indian women's social reform activities or by the speaking voices of
Indian women themselves (Singha 1880, 507–13). Child-marriage and
widow remarriage were common topics especially after 1884, when
Behramji Malabari's 'Notes on Enforced Widowhood' was published
and the trial of Rukhmabai, a child-bride who contested her husband's
claim to conjugal rights in court, was publicized first in Bombay and
then throughout Britain via the London *Times* (Malabari 1890; Gidumal
1888). Contributors wrote about Indian female education, but they also
reviewed books published in English, Hindi, Gujarati and Urdu on
Indian subjects and commented on all manner of events having to do
with India – from the celebrations of the Queen's Jubilees to the difficulties of 'crossing the black waters' for Hindus to the opening of new
hospitals, schools and widows' homes all over the subcontinent. Addi-
tionally, the proceedings of the NIA's annual meetings were covered
extensively. There was a regular column called 'Indian Intelligence' which
detailed the activities of individuals and groups in India, especially
those connected with NIA branches, and one called 'Personal Intelligence' which documented the comings and goings of Indians to Britain,
as well as their educational achievements (those called to the Bar, those
passing medical examinations, and so on). Excerpts from Indian newspapers on a number of topics were commonly reprinted both with and
without editorial commentary. Information about and analysis of India
was thus extraordinarily varied, with all of it justified under the rubric
of 'aiding social progress and education in India', which became the
NIA's official motto in the 1880s.

The fact that the *IM* in its various incarnations was exclusively devoted
to reportage of Indian events and concerns makes it unique enough
among nineteenth-century secular periodicals. That the *IMR* succeeded
in institutionalizing the otherwise rather disparate calls for imperial
reform and that it had organizational connections to an Indian
and Anglo-Indian readership in India through NIA branches there also
differentiates it from most if not all of its contemporaries in the late-
Victorian press. What makes the *IM* truly exceptional is that although it
was run by Britons from Britain, it served as a public space where Indian
men and occasionally Indian women could speak to, engage with, and
in many cases contest the interpretations of Indian society and culture

that apparently well-meaning English reformers offered as unalterably true. Whether they were writing from India (where many contributors were already well-known reformers or local leaders), whether they wrote from Britain (where many came to study law and medicine), or whether their voices were recorded as they spoke up at NIA annual meetings (which many attended if they were semi-permanent residents or just passing through London), Indians worked to influence the terms upon which India and its 'problems' were defined and discussed in the metropole. No matter what their speaking position, in other words, Indians participated in and actively shaped the direction of social reform on behalf of India not just in the *IM* but, as we shall see, in the domain of practical reform as well. They did so during an extended historical moment when, with the advent of Indian Civil Service reform and the emergence of the Indian National Congress, Britons at home were increasingly uneasy about the claims to self-representation and participation being made by Indian nationalists – a number of whom, including the Ghose brothers and Dadabhai Naoroji, were NIA regulars. Indian women, for their part, articulated their concerns about 'the problem of Indian womanhood' in the pages of the *IM* at a time when even their most ardent supporters – British feminists – emphasized the Indian woman's silence and passivity in order to enlist such images in the cause of imperial feminism (Burton 1994).

If the *IM* was potentially an instrument of cultural and social imperialism, its success in that regard was limited, thwarted even, by the persistent, interruptive speech of Indians who made their presence known to metropolitan readers. It functioned, therefore, not just as a site for the production of British images of India, but as a space where those images, together with the very principles of imperial rule, might be challenged and reformulated. As evidence of the ways in which India captured the Victorian imagination, the *IM* is virtually unparalleled. As historical evidence of how Indians both in the metropole and outside of it helped to shape discourses about empire, it is an important archive from which the agency of colonial peoples in constructing the parameters and presumptions of imperial rule can be discerned.

When historicizing its own origins, the NIA tended to attribute its beginnings to the inspiration of Mary Carpenter. Upon her death in 1877 the special issue of the journal devoted to her memory was trimmed with a black border and Carpenter was eulogized as the person 'to whom the National Indian Association owes its origin' (*JNIA* 1877, 89). Although she has been chiefly remembered for promoting the Ragged Schools system, which laid the foundation for primary and industrial education in the 1840s and 1850s, Carpenter was also involved in phil-anthropic activity in India from the late 1860s til her death in 1877. Her trips to India (she made four in all) convinced her that 'the problem' of Indian women (that is, child-marriage and early widowhood) could be solved by teacher training schemes for young Indian girls and women. Such schemes would delay their age of marriage and hence rescue colonial India from the decay and degeneration into which it was destined to fall, she believed, unless benevolent English women like herself could be encouraged either to staff training programs or support them with charitable donations. Carpenter was impressed by the desire expressed by high-caste Hindu men whom she met in India to have educated wives and mothers for their children, but she worried that without the supervision of England-trained women teachers to help them Indian women could not realize their full potential. Her two-volume travelogue, *Six Months in India* (1868), which detailed her experiences, identified Hinduism as a social pathology afflicting the colonial body politic and therefore as the biggest obstacle to be overcome by progressive Indian reformers seeking companionate marriages and female emancipation, along with all the other cultural attributes of 'civilization'. *Six Months in India* was enormously popular with the British female – and especially the British feminist – reading public. Carpenter founded the NIA and its monthly journal two years after its publication in order to keep the need for teacher training before the British public eye but also to spread knowledge about India more generally among the British population – and so to promote the cause which was to become central to Victorian female and feminist imperial reform commitments: the education and uplift of 'the Indian woman' (Manton 1976; Ramusack 1992; Burton 1995).

In fact, it was not just Carpenter's trip to India in 1866–67 but also Keshub Chunder Sen's trip to Britain in 1870 which provided the inspiration for the NIA. Sen was a theist who had been instrumental in the formation of the Brahmo Samaj, a reformist organization in Bengal (Borthwick 1977). He met Carpenter on her first trip to India and while in Britain he lectured extensively on a number of topics, including female education. It was on one of these occasions that the idea for establishing a society to promote Indian female education in Britain was first publicly articulated. Carpenter was speaking to the Society of the Arts on Indian women's education; after her speech, Sen was invited to speak on the subject. In the discussion session that followed, Sen suggested 'the formation of a society in England for the promotion of female education in India. This idea was warmly supported by Miss Carpenter'.

Significantly, a member of the Religious Tract Society objected, arguing that societies (like his) already existed for that object, but Sen rejoined that 'they were of a sectarian character, and that what was wanted was secular instruction, apart from...the doctrines of...[any] creed' (Sen 1871; *JNIA* 1877, 206). In a situation that was to anticipate the discursive framework of the *IM*, the very conception of the NIA itself was the product of dialogue between English and Indian reformers, with Sen in this case insisting that its philosophical basis be de-linked from the Christian proselytizing mission. His insistence, combined with Carpenter's commitment to keeping the Association's work separate and distinct from proselytizing in the mission field, secured the NIA and its journal as decidedly secular institutions.

If Sen's influence was crucial to the founding of the NIA, Carpenter's hard work, reform commitments, and Indian connections undoubtedly brought it to life and gave it visibility in Bristol and across the United Kingdom during its early years. Carpenter travelled all over Britain, speaking frequently to Social Science Association congresses about the need for Indian female education (Manton 1976; Ramusack 1992). When her talks were reprinted in the monthly magazine, they suggested how intertwined she believed the work of the NIA and that of its journal to be. The first purpose of the Association, she told an audience in Leeds, was 'to impart information about the condition and requirements of India'. The principal method of doing this, she went on, was 'by means of circulation of the *Journal*' – a conviction she echoed at the second annual meeting in October 1873. There she explained to the membership that her first task after founding the NIA had been to establish a journal. Its publication, she believed, had already been 'the means of awakening up in the people of this country a desire for further knowledge of India, and of securing for Hindu gentlemen and others a friendly reception in England' (*JNIA* 1873, 482–3). For Carpenter, 'intercourse with natives of India' was equally essential to the dissemination of knowledge about India, and the journal consequently featured accounts of lectures given by Indians in India and also in Britain (*JNIA* 1873, 486). 'Intercourse' in this sense could be had – and was in fact orchestrated – by the act of journal reading itself. To this end, the visit of Sasipada Banerjee and his wife received a lot of coverage, as did his public speaking. As had Sen, Banerjee echoed much of what Carpenter said about the need for Indian women's education, and he was especially keen to underscore her emphasis on the lack of trained female teachers. But significantly, in the reprint of his address in Birmingham in the NIA journal for September 1871, it was not the errors of Hinduism but the repugnance with which

Britons, and especially British women, regarded it, that he saw as the chief obstacle to Indian women's education. Such people 'did not mix enough with the native population, but were rather against them, and hated everything Hindu' (Banerjee 1871, 176). The burden was on the English to 'let the people of India know they wish them to rise in the scale of nations, and the word of sympathy carried through seas and oceans would do more to unite the two nations than hoards of money sent from England' (*JNIA* 1871, 64–72; 1871, 79–83; 1871, 123–35). Banerjee's comments may have been intended as an oblique criticism of Carpenter, whose distaste for Hindu ritual and for Hinduism in general is evident throughout much of *Six Months in India* (Burton 1995, 563–4). In any event, he gave the project of Indian female education a different urgency than had Carpenter. And his was by no means the only 'native' voice to do so. Readers of the NIA journal up to Carpenter's death and beyond would have been persuaded to embrace the necessity of Indian social reform as much because they understood that England was failing in its duty to Indians as because, as Carpenter had it, Hinduism had corrupted Indian culture and society from within.

After Carpenter's death, the NIA moved to London and fell into the capable hands of Elizabeth Manning, who had been the treasurer of the London branch since the early 1870s. Under her guidance, the NIA and its journal provided a continuous public forum over the next 20 years for debates about the nature and direction of colonial social reform – debates in which Indians and Britons in India and at home vigorously participated. Because my space here is limited, I want to focus on three of the issues which dominated the *IM* from the beginning of Manning's editorship until the end of the century (and beyond). These are: (1) women's medical education for India; (2) the debates on child-marriage and enforced widowhood; and (3) the superintendence of Indian students in Britain. Although there were some in the NIA membership who lamented that the organization was straying from Carpenter's founding principles, each of these issues in fact grew out of the Association's original concerns about education as the right and proper route toward Indian progress. Each one stimulated pages and pages of analysis, response and engagement between men and women, between Britons and Indians, between Britons and Britons, and between Indians and Indians. So vigorous were these debates that the *IM* came to serve as both a kind of public committee room and an important policy organ for Indian social reform from which readers gleaned not just knowledge about India but also an understanding of what was at stake – for Britain as well as for India – in the 'civilizing' mission of empire.

Just before her death Carpenter had, together with Lady Anna Gore-Langton, developed a scheme for female teacher training in India which was broadcast initially through the journal ('Lady Anna Gore Langton on Hindu Women' 1877, 105–7). Elizabeth Manning carried on that tradition, linking the NIA with the Froebel Society and other metropolitan training schools and trying to interest Indian women in considering education as a career. As debates about English women entering the medical profession gained publicity in the mainstream press the 1870s and early 1880s, the *IM* became a place for the free exchange of ideas on that subject (Blake 1990). It was at an NIA meeting in December 1882 that Elizabeth Beilby, a former missionary in India, first brought before the British public her conviction that women needed credentialed medical training before they could go to India in an healing capacity. In this sense, NIA anticipated the creation of the Countess of Dufferin's Fund for Supplying Female Aid to the Women of India (1885) (*JNIA* 1882, 681–4; Burton 1996). The *IM* ended up becoming a kind of clearing house of information about employment opportunities for English women in India until the First World War. Through it the NIA – which was patronized by ex-viceroys and subscribed to by ex-civil servants and prominent feminist reformers – helped advertise women's educational successes in the medical field, and brought the activities of women in India before the British public. It sponsored speakers, gallery talks and other public forums having to do with women and medicine all over the United Kingdom (Brander 1889, 285–8). In the wake of Carpenter's death, it also raised money for scholarships in her name and regularly reported on events sponsored by its regional branches in the United Kingdom and throughout India (*JNIA* May and June 1879). In the words of the *IM*, the NIA was, together with the Victorian feminist community, 'the needed link' between those in India and those at home who were invested in securing a place for women in colonial medicine (Manning 1892, 2).

The movement for medical women for India, however, was contested from the start. The premise upon which the first generation of English women physicians based their case for female medical aid to India was that the Indian women in the *zenana* [women's quarters] were unwilling to be examined by European male practitioners and therefore required the care of newly professionalized 'lady doctors'. Frances Hoggan, who trained at Zurich and got on the British medical register in 1876, was one of the most outspoken advocates of the need for medical women in India. She published frequently in the NIA journal, attended a number of annual meetings in the 1880s, and as early as 1881 was calling for the establishment of a government medical service for women equivalent to the one already in place for men (Hoggan 1882, 23–32). In keeping with the rhetoric of Victorian female social reform, and in order to bolster her particular claim that English women doctors could better represent Indian women's needs than European men, Hoggan claimed in the January 1882 issue of the magazine that in the person of British-trained female physicians like herself, 'the inarticulate cry of Indian women has at length found a voice' (Hoggan 1882, 23). Hoggan's arguments were hotly contested by male medical officials in and outside India who scoffed at the notion that *zenana* women either wanted or needed treatment by doctors of their own sex. But she was also called to account in the *IM* by Indians who did not so much dispute her arguments as they did her claims to authoritative knowledge about the condition of Indian women. Directly following Hoggan's article came a one-page letter from Narendra Nath Mitra, a correspondent from Bengal. In it he acknowledged that it was 'a recognised fact that we are in great need of qualified women doctors in Bengal', but he disputed her assertion that Indian men never called on European male doctors to treat their wives or female relatives. He also conceded that there were 'certain diseases of women' for which women's special knowledge was appropriate – and in that case, he argued, patients had *dhais* (midwives), 'whose business is to attend to all classes of women at the time of the birth of children'. Mitra was not refusing the work of European women doctors in India but he made it clear that they were a supplement to, and not the sine qua non of, medical practice in India ('we shall be too glad to have ... [their] *assistance*' (*JNIA* 1882, 33). His letter to the *IM* was, rather, an intervention in Hoggan's attempt to claim exclusive and authoritative knowledge of Indian women. It represented a subtle but unmistakable rejection of her claim to speak on behalf of the 'inarticulate' mass of Indian women – as well as an implicit assertion that that task belonged to Indian men and Indian men alone.

The method by which the *IM* chose to present Mitra's contestation suggests that as the editor, Manning was interested in fostering a dialogue about such matters rather than in foreclosing one. Mitra's letter appeared on the page directly opposite Hoggan's piece, and was introduced in this way: 'the following opinion of a Bengali gentleman on the subject of Mrs. Hoggan's paper, forms an appropriate P.S.'. If the designation 'Post Script' implies that Mitra's objections were given the status of an afterthought, the publication of a full-length article entitled 'A Native View of Lady Doctors for India' under the pen-name 'Losain' in the April 1882 issue of the magazine points to the dialogic nature of the debate.

Losain, whose gender is not self-evident, did not object to the fact that
'Mrs. Hoggan has used her voice on behalf of the voiceless millions confined in the *zenana*' (Losain 1882, 235). She/he did take issue, however,
with Hoggan's plan for a full-scale medical service, arguing that it
would make medical care prohibitively expensive and echoing Mitra's
call for 'assistance' rather than an organizational takeover. Losain pushed
Hoggan and the readers of the *IM* to consider that training native
women would be far less expensive, and far more effective for the
purposes of *zenana* practice, in the long run. 'Having been brought up
similarly with their patients', s/he went on, 'they will be better able to
sympathize with them than is possible with English lady doctors'. Of
equal concern to Losain were the differences between high- and low-caste
women, and between what kind of 'foreign' medical care *zenana* patients
in Indian cities were willing to submit to as opposed to the reluctance of
those in more rural areas to seek treatment by European practitioners.
The cultural challenges faced by Hoggan and others who wished to
practice in the *zenana* were, she/he concluded, not simply attributable
to gender seclusion but to the kinds of indigenous cultural systems under
colonialism which, Losain implied, even well-intentioned lady doctors
could not necessarily fully appreciate (Losain 1882, 235).

Manning prided herself on the fact that the NIA journal 'presents the
views . . . and elicits opinions from thinkers of various races and creeds'
(Manning 1882, 1). The triangular conversation to which I have referred
above is evidence of this commitment in action. But Manning was
clearly not the only one controlling the exchanges. Indians could and
routinely did use the *IM* as a means of intervening in a metropolitan
conversation that was putatively 'about' them and their deficiencies, in
order to reassert their right to author their own interpretations of the
matter at hand. In this particular case, Mitra and Losain succeeding in
turning the discussion into a conversation about *British* reformers that
underscored both the latter's deficiencies *and* the inadequacies of an
exclusively metropolitan perspective on Indian social reform. They also
made manifest to careful readers of the *IM* that English women and
Indian men had different investments in the body of the Indian woman
and that those differential investments reflected the ways in which
power was asymmetrically distributed according to gender and race
under colonial rule. The fact that the journal was produced at and distributed from the heart of the empire to its peripheries (whether those
peripheral locations were Bengal or Leeds) may have signalled to some
that the centre still held. At the same time, the proliferation of resistant
and recalcitrant voices may also have destabilized metropolitan (and

also Anglo-Indian) presumptions about who could – and who should – govern discussions about 'the progress of India'.

The long-term impact of these kinds of discursive manoeuvres is hard to measure. Emphasis on training English women as doctors first, with native women to follow, was characteristic of the British medical women's movement as it was embodied by the Dufferin Fund. This did not prevent Indian women from coming to London or Edinburgh and qualifying as medical doctors as early as the late 1880s, as the careers of K. Ganguli and Rukhmabai illustrate (Forbes 1994; Lal 1994; Karlekar 1993). But Losain's protest that Indian women ought to be trained was not sufficient in and of itself to reorient metropolitan policy, despite the fact that the NIA and Manning in particular were instrumental in overseeing much of the medical scholarship funding. Manning, for her part, was perceived by Cornelia Sorabji, a Parsi Christian who came to Britain initially to train as a doctor, as someone who preferred to promote English women to posts for which Indian women like herself were equally qualified (Sorabji 1892). In the more immediate confines of the *IM*, however, contests over who was authorized to speak for or about Indian women did much to shape the ideological debate on the civilizedness of Indian culture, especially insofar as 'the Hindu marriage system' was concerned. The controversy over Behramji Malabari's 'Notes' as well as the publicity given to the Bombay trial of Rukhmabai in the mid-1880s generated a series of responses in the *IM* which in turn helped to solidify the links between Indian women's sexuality, Indian female education and the British civilizing mission in the late-Victorian empire. The equation in the public's mind between the condition of Indian women and India's progress more generally was not produced in any kind of unilateral way by British social reformers but was the result of spirited exchanges among a variety of actors, including Indian women themselves – some writing anonymously, some emerging into the public as self-naming, self-determining subjects.

Although by the end of the 1880s it would have been difficult for readers to imagine discussions of child-marriage and enforced widowhood apart from the names of Malabari and Rukhmabai, in fact both aspects of the so-called Hindu marriage system had been matters for consideration in the NIA's journal practically from its beginnings. This was because Carpenter had made the question of Hindu conjugality the centerpiece of her reform projects in *Six Months in India*, but also because Indian male social reformers did the same (Sarkar 1992, 231). Interest in the twin subjects of child-marriage and widowhood was manifest in the NIA's journal in a variety of ways. Reprints of articles from 'native papers', full-length essays, accounts of lectures given in India and Britain, short stories and other fictional pieces – all these were the means by which readers of the *IM* might be witness to what was often referred to as the primary 'evil' of Hindu social custom with regard to girls and women. Even pieces not ostensibly about Hindu marriage, as in the case of an essay reprinted from *The Argus* in May 1873, took it as their invariable starting point for any general discussion of 'female education' in India (*JNIA* 1873, 325–8). If there was a basic consensus about the corrosive effects of the marriage system on Indian women's lives and hence on Indian society as a whole, contributors to the journal differed widely in their attitudes towards and their recommendations for redressing the problem of conjugal arrangements. Some, like William Knighton, saw the situation as a tragedy and the Indian woman as its pathetic protagonist. Hindu women were 'unspeakably sad', not just because they were married young but because they accepted their lots with 'sublime self-renunciation' – a quality he found appealing in its nobility. His three-part series on 'Hindu Women' had, incidentally, been prompted by Florence Nightingale's request for some examples of such Indian female nobility, suggesting that English men might gain credibility in the eyes of English female reformers when they cast the Other woman as the helplessly self-sacrificing victims of Hindu tradition (Knighton 1878, 226). For Knighton, the solution was education through the offices of the NIA, a remedy echoed by Nightingale herself in the pages of the NIA journal: 'we want education to prevent the family and custom from making the lot of the poor widow intolerable' (Nightingale 1879, 537). Others were less sanguine about the salutary effects of the westernisation of Indian women through education. 'A.R.', an Indian correspondent writing from Bombay in 1880, expressed concern that such a path gave rise to the fear that higher education would 'make our women clerks'. In the end, 'A.R.' reassured his readers that education would not make women mere public functionaries but would instead 'draw out their resources and energies, and when deprived of their natural supporters . . . [would] prevent their being utterly helpless and dependent for their bare maintenance'. At the same time he emphasized that female education should not be viewed as a rejection of Hinduism, but as a component of it. It was not, he argued, 'incompatible with Manu's requirements in a wife'. What's more, 'the codes, the shastras and the legends fully testify to the existence in Ancient India of exemplary female characters – of women not only studying, but *teaching* the Vedas and being proficient in metaphysics and ethics, as well as the "liberal arts", such as music, vocal and instrumental' ('A.R.' 1880, 344).

Whereas English reformers, male and female, advocated women's education in order to break the hold they believed Hinduism had on Indian society, Indian reformers like 'A.R.' were determined to educate Hindu girls so that they profited just enough from western influence to revitalize an already 'progressive' religious tradition, but not so much that they corrupted it. The distinctions between these two positions can be read as a ratification in microcosm of the arguments Lata Mani, Partha Chatterjee and Gayatri Spivak have made about the ways in which Indian women were the discursive terrains upon which colonizing and colonized men fought battles and made bargains in the context of patriarchal colonial rule (Mani 1989; Chatterjee 1989; Spivak 1988). Such postures as we have seen articulated also provide evidence that one of the audiences for this negotiation was the middle-class, metro-politan reading public in the late-Victorian period. That same public was also made privy to Indian women's – and in the case of Pandita Ramabai, to an Indian *widow's* – agency in the social and political realm. Ramabai was a Hindu widow who made news in the early 1880s because she could read the Vedas, discuss Hindu sacred texts with the pandits, and speak publicly on the question of Indian female education and the need for women doctors (Kosambi 1988; Chakravarti 1989; Burton 1995). The NIA journal followed Ramabai's career closely, reporting on a testimonial address made by Hindu women to her in Calcutta in 1878. The testimonial, read by Miss Radha Rani Lahory, praised Ramabai as evidence of 'the glory of Indian womanhood' and of 'what excellence in learning our women can attain by observing the cus-toms and manners of ancient Hindus'. Ramabai responded by exhorting her audience to learn Sanskrit, read the Vedas, and discover in them examples of women's heroism from ancient times. She also took the opportunity to condemn early marriage, insisting that it was not an ancient practice and that education did not corrupt as some opponents of Indian women's education asserted. Thus were British readers treated to the spectacle of Indian women's 'progress' through the words of Indian women themselves. It was a spectacle, of course, which the NIA journal helped to produce and for which it took much of the credit. Manning prefaced the above account by observing that 'such a meeting would a few years ago have been an impossible event' and that 'the cul-tivated Indian ladies' to whom Ramabai spoke owed their education 'to English influences and to the spread of western thought' (*JNIA* 1878, 492). Manning may not have intended to displace Ramabai from the centre of attention, but one of the effects of her preface was to make educated Indian women appear to be little more than the successful realisation of a decade of the NIA's educational training schemes. In this sense the Association's journal displayed the contested, multivocal nature of reform on behalf of Indian women even as it attempted to contain some of the 'native' voices who were working to define the terms upon which Indian women's emancipation should be negotiated.

In spite of Manning's efforts to represent colonial reform as a project originated and determined by English philanthropists, by the mid-1880s readers of the *IM* could not have helped noticing that the metropole was incidental to the direction debates on social reform were taking in India. The controversy over child-marriage and the age of consent sparked by the publication of Behramji Malabari's 'Notes' and exacerbated by the trial of Rukhmabai made the NIA's marginality quite clear. Manning published excerpts from Malabari's 'Notes', which outlined what he believed to be the regressive aspects of Hindu conjugality for Indian women and their welfare. Malabari was a Parsi and editor of a Bombay newspaper which he used as platform for publicizing his campaign against child marriage and 'cold suttee' (enforced widowhood). His solution was government intervention, a suggestion that divided Hindu communities all over India and provoked particularly heated responses from orthodox pandits in India, who viewed legislation as a breach of the policy of non-intervention promulgated by the Queen's government since 1857 (Sinha 1995; Kosambi 1995). The NIA journal alluded to these objections but its focus was on Malabari's schemes, to which Manning was personally sympathetic – so much so that in January 1885, she printed a prospectus for 'an association for practical reform' in Bombay which Malabari had sent to her in London. Among the objectives of the Association was the regulation of age of marriage, the bête noire of many Hindus, both reformist and orthodox. Publication of the prospectus prompted an essay in the March 1885 journal by P. Bishan Narayan Das. Das, who had a degree from Cambridge, lived in London and was vice-president of the Indian Society, a local group founded by Naoroji and others for Indian 'gentlemen' (Das 1885, 481). Das' piece, which he called 'Social Reform in India: A Suggestion', was full of admiration for Malabari's plan but plainly vetoed even the possibility of embracing legislation regulating age of marriage. He told his NIA audience that Malabari's scheme had no hope of success in India, that it would only be embraced 'by Anglicised renegades', and that he would have a much better chance if he abandoned 'social' reform for a programme of 'educational' reform instead. He also intimated that Malabari's plan was not original, since a very similar one had been proposed by Pandit Pran Nath the year before in Lucknow (Das 1885, 481). Malabari's credibility was thereby challenged on two points: he was not the original thinker he seemed to be and worse, he might well be one of those 'Anglicised renegades' himself.

Das was not the only Indian to enter into this debate in the pages of the NIA journal. In April 1885 a contributor who identified herself simply as 'an Indian Lady', wrote a piece called 'Our Social Customs', in which she outlined some of the experiences of child-brides and child-widows. She acknowledged the current popularity of the topic and added her voice to those who argued that 'infant marriage lies at the root of all social evils' ('An Indian Lady' 1885, 221). Even if contemporary accounts of the misery experienced by its victims were exaggerated, she argued, the fate of child-wives and widows had to be ameliorated. 'An Indian Lady' ended her essay by siding with proponents of government legislation, though she never mentioned Malabari by name and in fact, sought to differentiate her position from his with the following stipulation: 'of course, positive coercion of any kind on the part of the Government will be productive of much evil' ('An Indian Lady' 1885, 221). Malabari's proposal got even more attention in the journal in late 1885, when Manning published two letters that Rukhmabai, who was then the defendant in a conjugal rights suit in a Bombay court, had written to the *Times of India*. Rukhmabai had been married at the age of 11 but had lived with her mother and stepfather until 1884, at which time her husband requested that she live with him. She refused and he sued her, causing a huge scandal in Bombay and propelling Rukhmabai to the public stage in India and in Britain (Kosambi 1995). Rukhmabai's letters to the *Times of India* defended Malabari's call for legislation, but like the essay by 'An Indian Lady', they were not merely imitative or repetitive of his aims. In addition to embracing government interference, Rukhmabai articulated an impassioned critique of both British imperialism and Hindu patriarchy and tried to shame opponents of reform into understanding how early marriage and female education were incompatible ('A Hindu Lady' 1885, 420). This was followed by a five-point outline of what such legislation might look like, including provisions to raise the age of marriage to 15 for girls and 20 for boys, and one to require young men who married below the stipulated age to give up their right to university. Although Rukhmabai's essay had begun as a letter to the editor (hence the 'Sir' in the above citation), by the end she was addressing the leaders of the Hindu community who claimed to have the best interests of Indian women at heart ('A Hindu Lady' 1885, 423). Like Malabari, she was persuaded that it was the duty of the British government in India to take action, but she framed her appeal in terms of Indian reformers' co-operation with government rather than their submission to it. In so doing, Rukhmabai may be said to have argued more forcibly and more persuasively than Malabari or perhaps anyone involved in the debate had done in the pages of the NIA magazine for an equation between Indian women's education and Indian civilization's progress (Burton, 1998b).

Opinion about the subjects of child-marriage, enforced widowhood and Indian women's education in the *IM* was diverse, and it was not limited to engagement with the pros and cons of Malabari's scheme. There were Indians both in India and outside it who chose to ignore the controversy swarming around Malabari and to carry on with concrete schemes for seeking government subsidies for female education, as in the proposal M. Bhownaggree laid out in the journal's account of an NIA meeting in spring 1885 (*JNIA* 1885, 242). Two Indians who were also present debated his scheme with no reference whatsoever to the Malabari plan (*JNIA* 1885, 242–3). What this suggests is that, beyond the publicity which the debates on Hindu conjugality received in the *IM*, there were a variety of Indians competing with English reformers and perhaps with each other for influence over how and under what conditions reform for India would proceed. It is quite possible that being on the spot (in London, at the various NIA soirées, lectures and public meetings) gave men like Bhownaggree an advantage in this regard – a possibility that Malabari may have come to realize, since he came to London in 1890 specifically to plead his case before the British public when an Age of Consent Bill was pending in India (Malabari 1893; Sinha 1995; Burton 1996). On the other hand, the NIA had an official policy of non-interference in political affairs to which it adhered quite insistently. The naivety of this particular position must have been obvious to readers of the journal, who witnessed the NIA's involvement in the politics of social reform at every turn; it was an irony that was not lost in any event on at least one member, who wrote to the magazine to object to the leadership's hypocrisy in imagining that its work was neither politics nor interference in Indian customs (Etherington 1875, 267–70). And yet, technically, the NIA was true to its word: it did not petition Parliament (as, for example, feminists interested in India did in this period); it did not raise money for lobbying; and it did not pick up on Malabari's 1885 call for an association for 'practical reform'. The point is not that proximity to London guaranteed Indian reformers more or less influence on metropolitan opinion, then, but rather that London was not necessarily the centre of imperial reform. As the *IM* illustrated month after month, the metropole was a convenient if necessary stage for the rehearsal of proto-nationalist arguments and ultimately, for the performance of nationalist claims to self-government – claims articulated via that quintessentially Victorian expression of civic participation and belonging, the commitment to 'social improvement'.

It was precisely this sense of civic responsibility and national belonging among Indians which the NIA wished, at least theoretically, to encourage. The Association's early interest in education had quickly translated into a commitment to fostering opportunities for Indian students coming to Britain to study. There were few Indian students who passed through London in the late nineteenth century who did not attend the 'At Homes', soirées or lectures sponsored by the NIA. Several Indian women, including Sorabji and Rukhmabai, lived temporarily with Manning or visited her home in Maida Vale. Manning was keen not just on bringing Britons together with Indians – which was among the purposes of the Association – but on linking expatriate colonials up with each other for the duration of their stay in the United Kingdom as well. Sorabji, who privately told her parents she did not enjoy Rukhmabai's company, was none the less thrown together with her at Miss Manning's during their term breaks and had to make the best of it (Sorabji, MSS EUR F 165/2, 2 February 1890). Even Gandhi could be found at Miss Manning's events during his student days in London. He recalled in his autobiography that whenever he went to NIA gatherings at her home he 'used to sit tongue-tied, never speaking except when spoken to'. She introduced him to Narayan Hemchandra, a Bengali writer, at an NIA function, and their friendship helped sustain Gandhi during the rest of his time in England, not least because Hemchandra was also a vegetarian, an identity Gandhi was struggling to maintain in the face of various metropolitan pressures to eat meat (Gandhi 1990, 61–4).

At the same time that the Association extended hospitality to Indian students in Britain, it monitored their numbers and kept an eye on their activities through the *IM*. Notice of who came and went and for what purposes was a regular feature of the 'Indian Intelligence' column from the 1870s onwards. In 1879 the journal published formal 'Rules' on how it would manage and guide Indian students (implicitly men), starting with an invitation to parents who wished to their children to be supervised to write six months in advance of arrival for application to be 'superintended' by the NIA. In exchange for 'an annual charge to defray minor expenses' (50 Rs to 100 Rs), the NIA would meet the student on arrival, secure lodgings for him (the Indian student population was overwhelmingly male), make arrangements for his education and even, if the parents wished, oversee the disbursement of his allowance to him (*JNIA* 1879, 388). A special committee was created to oversee these details. Perhaps most tellingly, the editor hoped that 'the new arrangements proposed for the extension of... [the NIA's] work will greatly add to the usefulness and permanence of the Association' (*JNIA* 1879, 389). In this way was the future of the NIA bound up not just with the lofty ideals of bringing Britons and Indians together through social intercourse but more pointedly with the surveillance of Indians in Britain.

As more and more Indian students came to Britain in the 1880s to pursue courses of study at London, Oxbridge and Edinburgh, the business of 'superintendence' began to emerge as a preoccupying function of the NIA. The *IM* began to publish tables that enumerated exactly which Indians were studying where, what they were studying, and also from what part of India they came (*JNIA* 1885, 1–9). Cornelia Sorabji's arrival at Oxford (where she studied law) prompted an article by the Somerville College principal and a collaborator specifically aimed at Indian women interested in coming west for higher education, but the majority of the information the NIA broadcast continued to apply chiefly to men (Hobhouse and Shaw-Lefevre 1891, 141–7). In September 1885 the Association announced that it was producing a circular advertising what the NIA was prepared to do to help Indian students who came to the United Kingdom. Among the services now more formally offered was help in securing lodgings, in gaining exposure to 'English home life', and in choosing the appropriate clothing to wear while exposed to the English climate.[2] Indian students were encouraged to consult the Association's *Handbook* before leaving India, follow its advice, make the kinds of housing arrangements it suggested and take the precautions it offered seriously – down to what kinds of clothes to buy and where to purchase them (*JNIA* 1885, 407). More broadly, the advice on clothing suggest how far some Britons were willing to go in order to anglicize their 'fellow Indian subjects'. It may help explain why Gandhi was so intent on procuring the outfit of an English gentleman while he was a student in London: whatever anxieties Indians might have experienced about the appearance of colonial difference were not just anticipated but intensified by the NIA. However, not everyone conformed. Sorabji was determined to wear saris during her time at Somerville, even though she had worn more westernized clothing growing up in Poona. And although she was quite Anglophilic in other respects, she routinely used her dress as part of a defiant performance of a certain version of Indian womanhood rather than submitting to the kind of westernization the NIA encouraged (Sorabji, MSS EUR 165/1, 12 December 1889 and 165/2, 26 January 1890; Burton 1998a).

Significantly, perhaps, Indians who contributed pieces to the *IM* on life in the metropole or at British universities were all but silent on the dress question, focusing instead on what courses students were advised to take, what sights they should be sure to see or, most revealingly, the kinds of money problems they were likely to have (Satthianadhan 1880, 603–16; *JNIA* 1880, 386–91). They detailed what life in a British university was like for readers in India who were either considering studying in the United Kingdom or who were the parents of potential students worried about sending their children into unknown cultural waters thousands of miles away (Satthianadhan 1880, 603–16). As one 'native' correspondent remarked, 'ten or twenty years ago the visit of a Hindu in London was a thing almost unknown'. Thanks in part to the influence of the NIA, he conceded, 'the advantages of a stay in this country are [now] more and more appreciated in India every day' ('Piyarilal' 1884, 281). The 'Superintendence Committee' of the NIA, on the other hand, saw itself as promoting 'friendly guidance' to Indian students whom it believed were disinclined to live 'under supervision' while in Britain (*IMR* 1891, 203). The Association's concern was unabashedly paternalistic: an editorial in the *IM* of 1891 worried that Indian students were 'frequently sent to England when they have scarcely passed boyhood' and that in these circumstances they were in danger of falling into bad company (Pinhey 1891, 228–9). And if the magazine's editor was prepared to be euphemistic, there were others ready and willing to declare the civilizing mission behind the whole notion of 'superintendence'. Mary Pinhey wrote a lengthy piece for the *IMR* in May of 1891 in which she was quite candid about her concerns. 'The astute Oriental mind rather delights in crooked ways', she wrote. She continued:

> There is a certain lumpiness about the Oriental character, a want of pluck and backbone, and a general ignorance of what is expressed by the word 'honour', which can only be got rid of, if at all, by a thorough immersion in the spirit of English life...nothing can be more dangerous than to send youths to England, at a most critical age, to live far away from their natural guardians; deprived of the sanctions of caste and of their religion; entirely free for the first time in their lives from all control; well supplied probably with money and exposed to all the temptations and seductions of great city like London. (Pinhey 1891, 230)

Pinhey wished to control not just Indian students but their encounters with their fellow-subjects in the metropole. Nothing less than the preservation of imperial rule – and with it, the social-cultural hierarchies of colonialism in everyday life at home – was at stake. For 'even where no serious evil comes of their sojourn to England, young men are tempted to forget here their real place in the social side of their own country'. The average Englishman who encountered 'orientals' on his own soil, she concluded, 'regards all . . . [of them] as of one class' – and this was clearly a mistake (Pinhey 1891, 230). The ramifications of such a misreading were implicit, if unspoken. Failure to notice that Indian students were neither equivalent to the masses of India nor on a par with Englishmen might lead to notions about the possibilities of political equality – possibilities which in the Victorian period, even among Britons sympathetic to the cause of Indian reform, were quite unthinkable. For Pinhey, as perhaps for other readers of the *IM*, the social aspirations of Indian students had to be curbed so that, in keeping with the colonial project writ large, they remained in a state of permanent tutelage and at one remove from their British 'fellow subjects' (Burton, 1998b).

Whether her opinions were the result of Pinhey's personal encounters with Indians – at NIA events, perhaps – is not known. Less than a decade earlier, the debate over the Ilbert Bill (which proposed to extend the power of Indian judges to try Europeans in criminal cases to Europeans residing outside presidency capitals, among whom numbered white women) had polarized opinion in India and England. British female reformers sympathetic to India women's education, like Annette Ackroyd Beveridge, had made it clear that certain boundaries had to be maintained at all costs, the boundary between white women and Indian men being chief among them (Sinha 1992). Pinhey may have been among those who agreed and who found the need to reiterate that position given the increase in Indians coming to Britain and making their way into London society in this period. In any event, her views did not go unchallenged. Angry and disheartened responses from Indian correspondents appeared in the June issue of the *IMR*, and while the NIA appeared in its editorial to side with Pinhey, the weight of 'colonial' opinion was against her. One contributor called her account 'fiction' while another insisted that for every Indian student who floundered, there were plenty who succeeded and returned to India having achieved their educational goals. Another claimed that she had exaggerated 'the dark picture of the life of an Indian student in London' while still another called her article 'nothing but very painful reflections cast on the natives of India'. 'All pleasure must go', wrote one correspondent who signed him/herself 'S.A.M.S.', 'if we are spoken of thus, or . . . [if] English people think of us in the way intimated in the article' (*IMR* 1891, 304–8).

This short-lived contretemps does not appear to have affected the operation or the direction of the NIA in any significant way. Indians continued to submit articles for the *IMR* detailing their views of 'the modes of living in England' and even occasionally waxing rhapsodic about the joys of imperial citizenship. Professions of loyalty sometimes bordered on the saccharine, but they should not necessarily be dismissed as such. They often had their own subtle political effects, if not their expressly political purposes. Syed A.M. Shah, who spent an afternoon at the Tower of London in the spring of 1893, for example, wrote enthusiastically about his afternoon out and expressed his pride at having been

> born in the glorious reign of our noble Queen-Empress Victoria. Through her government we are protected from all sort of dangers, and also our property and our sacred religions: this is the real blessing which we, the British subjects, enjoy under our good Queen-Empress, upon whose rule the sun never sets. (Shah 1893, 209)

Shah's attitude may have been prompted by hearing about all those who had been subjected to execution at the Tower through the ages, and, indeed, he expressed thanks that he had not been born under the reign of a medieval English monarch. But the historical function of the Tower and its message about the benefits of subjecthood – and the dangers of disloyalty – were not lost on him. As did other British visitors, no doubt, Shah came away from the Tower feeling grateful for being a 'British subject'. And along with his delight at the many 'wonders and curiosities' London had to offer, his essay for the *IM* announced his confidence that his claim to that status was as sound as that of any other Briton (Burton, 1998a).

It was this confidence that made would-be barristers and Indian Civil Service applicants a potential threat to the cultural norms of everyday life in the imperial metropole no less than to the future of the empire itself. For more than one Indian student who came to Britain in order to obtain credentials in the law or the colonial bureaucracy in the 1860s and 1870s rose to prominence in the Indian nationalist movement and returned to the metropole in the late 1880s and 1890s to demand a measure of political equality and representation for his fellow-subjects in India. As Rozina Visram notes, the list of those who studied in Britain reads like 'a roll call of the Indian [political] elite', with Gandhi, Nehru, Jinnah and, in the twentieth century, Indira Gandhi representing just four of the names best known outside India today (Visram 1986, 177–8). In the late nineteenth century, reform of the colonial Civil Service was one of the first avenues through which ambitious and nationally-minded Indians sought to equalize the structure of imperial power. Even the London *Times* recognized it as being among 'the first rank of national problems' (14 May 1884, 4). Among the Indian leaders of this reform effort was Manomohun Ghose. He and his brother Lalmohun were English-educated barristers who were regular attenders at NIA functions. The Ghose brothers, who travelled back and forth between Britain and India from the 1860s (when Manomohun was among Carpenter's favourite visitors at the Red Lodge), were among the most active Indians in Britain in the last quarter of the nineteenth century. They made deputations to Gladstone and Ripon, promoted conferences on Indian questions and in 1883, Lalmohun ran unsuccessfully as a Liberal candidate for Deptford (Visram 1986, 78; *Times* 1 February 1884, 10 and 29 January 1885, 7). It was in his capacity as a delegate for the Indian National Congress that Manomohun traveled to England in 1885 in order to try to influence the parliamentary elections. In response to this delegation and to the increasingly visible presence of Indian nationalists generally, the *Saturday Review* offered one of the most succinct and unguarded statements about the threat such Indian men posed to the fate of the British empire to be articulated in the Victorian period: 'when the question of admitting native Indians to civil employment was first raised, it can scarcely have occurred to the most zealous advocate of equality that they would claim seats in the House of Commons' (*SR* 16 July 1887, 67).

As an example of understatement such a view is quite remarkable, especially when juxtaposed with the rather more impassioned responses to which Indian nationalists in Britain and, in the process, the British reading public, were treated. The 1885 delegates were cast as 'a batch of young cuckoos' who 'talk as men might whose fathers had defended the Star Chamber or lost their heads on Tower Hill'. They were dubbed 'vapouring, gushing rhetoricians' and the Congress they represented, 'an irresponsible association' peopled with 'busy-bodies, notoriety-seekers and incendiaries'. Congress' claims to government were nothing more than 'pretensions' and their desire to 'superintend the reconstruction of the Government of India can be regarded as a dull joke' (*SR* 21 March 1885, 386; 5 January 1889, 12). While the vehemence of these reactions can hardly be surprising, it is important to note that it is the capabilities of the Indian men *qua men* in their midst of which these Britons are contemptuous. To be sure, the very concept of India as a nation was unimaginable, if not reprehensible, to those who ruled the Victorian empire. As one journalist put it, 'the Nation of India is a pure fiction' (*SR* 15 February 1890, 203). But it was at base the capacities of Indians – and their inadequacies as 'English' men as evidenced by their behaviour in Britain – that was at issue. Those who proposed self-government, wrote a contributor to the *Saturday Review*, 'must have an amazing trust in their own impudence and in the credulity of Englishmen ... our Empire was not built by the Baboo's oratory, but by Englishmen's force of character' (*SR* 5 October 1889, 382). Resisting the nationalist onslaught thus became a test of the mettle of English manhood in the face of Indians who were pretenders by any other name.

The *IM* remained aloof from these public battles, possibly because they were too patently political. But traces of the antagonisms that were publicly articulated elsewhere in the British press did make their way into the pages of the NIA's journal – in this case, in the minutes of a London NIA meeting. Moving to make a resolution in support of the work of carried out by the NIA, Sir Lepel Griffin urged all the members of the Association to be mindful that it was committed to 'social' reform and that it was sworn to leave aside 'the polemical ground of religion and politics, where conflict raged as fiercely as on the battle-fields of the Soudan'. He continued:

> This Association would do its work best if it induced native gentleman, such as those present, some of whom were among his personal friends, to apply themselves to the social regeneration of their country, [and] to leave aside those barren political studies, which were of no use to England and of little use to India. It was not to Indian students at the Universities or in London that we look for illumination on the vexed questions of English policy. In England when we required a wise and carefully considered opinion on a political or religious question, on the pacification of Ireland or the enlargement of the franchise, we did not ask English schoolboys for their opinion. If the Association directed the attention of those young men over whom it could exercise a legitimate influence to those points which were of far more importance than any political agitation, such as the enlightenment of their own countrymen, the instruction of their wives and daughters, and the removal of prejudices from the minds of Hindus, it would do far more good to them and to their country than by seeking to intrude their opinions into the vexed political questions that now disturbed India today. (*JNIA* 1884, 142–3)

If Lalmohun Ghose, who was recorded as being in the audience, replied, it was not noted in the account of the meeting as represented in the NIA journal. But as they had from the beginning of the journal's publication, Indians engaged with this authoritative claim to knowledge about what route was best for Indian progress and in the process, articulated a polite but firm response to Griffin's imperially minded diatribe. Hamid Ali Khan seconded Griffin's resolution, agreeing that the objects of the Association deserved support: 'the prosecution of them would be the best service England could render to India, and none of them would be more important than the promotion of female education'. He also reminded the crowd that was gathered, as well as the readers of the magazine, that

> there could not be a really stable Empire which did not rest upon the foundation of the popularity of the governing classes with the gov-erned. He hoped, therefore, the natives of India and the people of England would, in their joint interest, endeavor to promote the social condition of the people of India, and would heartily co-operate in a work which was honourable alike to England and to India. It was a great thing to conquer India, but it was still a greater thing to govern India with justice and impartiality. Much good had been done by this Association much good still remained to be done; and in doing it the Association deserved the cordial support of both countries. (*JNIA*, 1884, 144)

Khan may have been trying to smooth over the waters, but as his coun-trymen had done for years in the context of the NIA journal, he offered a different, more co-operative view than Griffin on how reform should come about – and he made it quite clear that nothing less than the stability of the empire was at issue. The resolution was passed and the meeting adjourned, but not before N.N. Mitra had his say. Mitra, who had been the one to contest Hoggan's proposal for women's medical education, pressed the meeting to endorse government support for edu-cation for women medical doctors, arguing that 'if Government were truly liberal it should display its liberal principles by liberal acts'. He added his agreement that Indian students resident in Britain 'should not interfere in politics'. But his final comment was not without its ambiguous reference to the possibility of political redress for Britain's colonial subjects. 'Indian society was full of social grievances, and it was their duty to try and remove them', he observed. 'If they were successful in that there would be no difficulty in getting rid of the political griev-ances' (*JNIA* 1884, 146).

Readers of this exchange in the NIA journal would hardly have feared for the future of the British empire as they knew it. Indeed, those Indian men involved in the creation of the early Indian National Congress – several of whom were friends of the NIA – sought not the end of empire but a more representative role in it (Low 1988). What the *IM* dramatized for its reading public was that Indians were not content to have the terms of their inclusion in the imperial nation-state dictated to them even by well-meaning and ostensibly apolitical sympathizers at home. Journal reading might also have signalled how little control the NIA finally had over what uses its 'social' reform projects were being put by Indians, both practically and symbolically. For, as the discussion in the Association's annual meeting makes clear, Indians were content to have women's education categorized as 'social' precisely because they understood what its 'political' implications might be in the short as well as the long term. The NIA continued to support female education, to debate the Hindu marriage system, to monitor Indian students in Britain, to foster dialogue between 'natives' and Britons, and to diminish the symbolic distance between the United Kingdom and its colonies from the 1880s until the turn of the century and beyond. The promotion of social intercourse between home and the empire – a founding concern of the NIA – was thereby realized, though not without disturbing some of the presumptions which Britons had about their fellow Indian subjects. Discerning readers of the journal over the years may have become aware that the battle for nationalism was being waged on the domestic front, in Britain, as fiercely as it was being fought in the more distant terrains of empire during the late-Victorian period. The *IM* was one of the technologies through which these contests were brought home. Among the effects of the way it institutionalized imperial reform was that its readers were required to confront the traffic of ideas circulated by the traffic of colonial subjects in their midst.

Notes

Some sections of this essay are drawn from my book, *At the Heart of the Empire: Indians and the Colonial Encounter in Late-Victorian Britain* (Berkeley, 1998), and are reprinted with permission.

1. There is little evidence to suggest what circulation might have been. The price was 5 shillings in 1886 (3 rupees) and 6 shillings (5 rupees) in 1897 (per annum). 1000 copies were printed monthly in the early 1870s. See *JNIA* (January 1873), 1. The annual report for 1884 reported approximately 300 subscribers. not counting the Indian branches. See *Fourteenth Annual Report*, 20–9.
2. For a fuller context for this kind of superintendence, see Burton, *At the Heart of the Empire*, ch. 1.

Works cited

'A Hindu Lady', 'Child Marriage in India', *JNIA* (September 1885), 416–23.

Anagol-McGinn, Padma. 'The Act of Consent Act (1891) Reconsidered: Women's Perspectives and Participation in the Child-Marriage Controversy in India', *South Asia Research* 12, 2 (November 1992), 100–18.

'An Indian Lady', 'Our Social Customs', *JNIA* (April 1885), 218–23.

'A.R.'. 'Hindu Domestic Reform', *JNIA* (June 1880), 342–50.

Banerjee, Sasipada. 'On the Social Condition of Women in India', *JNIA* (September 1871), 169–76.

Blake, Catriona. *The Charge of the Parasols: Women's Entry into the Medical Profession*. London, 1990.

Borthwick, Meredith. *Keshub Chunder Sen: A Search for Cultural Synthesis*. Calcutta, 1977.

Brander, Mrs. 'Report', *The Indian Magazine* (June 1889), 285–8.

Burton, Antoinette. *At the Heart of the Empire: Indians and the Colonial Encounter in Late-Victorian Britain*. Berkeley, 1998a.

Burton, Antoinette. *Burdens of History: British Feminists, Indian Women, and Imperial Culture, 1865–1915*. Chapel Hill, 1994.

Burton, Antoinette. 'Colonial Encounters in Late-Victorian England: Pandita Ramabai at Cheltenham and Wantage, 1883–1886', *Feminist Review* 49 (Spring 1995), 29–49.

Burton, Antoinette. 'Contesting the Zenana: the Mission to Make "Lady Doctors for India", 1874–1885', *Journal of British Studies* 35 (July 1996), 368–97.

Burton, Antoinette. 'Fearful Bodies into Disciplined Subjects: Pleasure, Romance, and the Family Drama of Colonial Reform in Mary Carpenter's *Six Months in India*', *Signs* 20 (Spring 1995), 545–74.

Burton, Antoinette. 'From "Child-Bride" to "Hindoo Lady": Rukhmabai and the Debate about Sexual Respectability in Imperial Britain', *American Historical Review* 104, 4 (October 1998b), 1119–46.

Burton, Antoinette. 'The Wanderings of a "Pilgrim Reformer": Behramji Malabari in Late-Victorian London', *Gender and History* 8 (August 1996), 175–96.

Chakravarti, Uma. 'Whatever Happened to the Vedic *Dasi*?', in Sangari and Vaid (eds), *Recasting Women*, 27–87.

Chandra, Sudhir. 'Whose Laws? Notes on a legitimising myth of the colonial Indian state', *Studies in History* ns 8 (1992), 187–211.

Chatterjee, Partha. 'The Nationalist Resolution of the Women's Question', in Sangari and Vaid (eds), *Recasting Women*, 233–53.

Chaudhuri, Nupur and Margaret Strobel (eds). *Western Women and Imperialism: Complicity and Resistance*. Bloomington, 1992.

Das, P. Bishan Narayan. 'Social Reform in India: A Suggestion', *JNIA* (March 1885), 139–44.

Engels, Dagmar and Shula Marks (ed.). *Contesting Colonial Hegemonies: State and Society in Africa and India*. New York, 1994.

Etherington, Ellen. 'Education in the North-West of India', *JNIA* (December 1875), 267–70.

Forbes, Geraldine. 'Managing Midwifery in India', in Engels and Marks (eds), *Contesting Colonial Hegemonies*, 159–61.

Fourteenth Annual Report of the National Indian Association in Aid of Social Progress and Education in India. Bristol, 1885.

Gandhi, M.K. *An Autobiography, or, the Story of My Experiments with Truth.* Ahmedabad, 1990.

Gidumal, Dayaram. *The Life and Life-Work of Behramji M. Malabari.* Bombay, 1888.

Hobhouse, Mary and Madeleine Shaw-Lefevre. 'Colleges for Women in England', *IMR* (March 1891), 141–7.

Hoggan, Frances. 'Women Doctors in India', *JNIA* (January 1882), 23–32.

Karlekar, Malavika. *Voices from Within: Early Personal Narratives of Bengali Women Writers.* Delhi, 1993.

Knighton, William. 'Hindu Women', *JNIA* (June 1878), 226–31.

Kosambi, Meera. *At the Intersection of Gender Reform and Religious Belief.* Bombay, 1993.

Kosambi, Meera. 'Women, Emancipation and Equality, Pandita Ramabai's Contribution to Women's Cause', *Economic and Political Weekly* 29 (October 1988), 15–63.

Kosambi, Meera. 'Gender Reform and Competing State Controls over Women: the Rakhmabai Case (1884–1888)', *Contributions to Indian Sociology* ns 29 (1995), 265–90.

'Lady Anna Gore Langton on Hindu Women', *JNIA* (April 1877), 105–7.

Lal, Maneesha. 'The Politics of Gender and Medicine in Colonial India: the Countess of Dufferin's Fund, 1885–1888', *Bulletin of the History of Medicine* 68 (March 1994), 29–66.

Losain. 'A Native View of Lady Doctors for India', *JNIA* (April 1882), 233–43.

Low, D.A. (ed.). *The Indian National Congress: Centenary Highlights.* Delhi,1988.

Malabari, Behramji. *An Appeal from the Daughters of India.* London, 1890.

Malabari, Behramji. *The Indian Eye on English Life; or, Rambles of a Pilgrim Reformer.* Westminster, 1893.

Mani, Lata. 'Contentious Traditions, The Debate on *Sati* in Colonial India', in Sangari Vaid (eds), *Recasting Women,* 88–126.

Manning, E.A. 'The "Indian Magazine"', *The Indian Magazine* (January 1886), 1–2.

Manning, E.A. 'Indian Students in England', *JNIA* (January 1885), 1–9.

Manning, E.A. 'Nota Bene', *The Indian Magazine and Review* (January 1897), 1.

Manning, E.A. 'Ourselves', *IMR* (January 1892), 1–5.

Manning, E.A. 'The Principles and Work of the National Indian Association', *JNIA* (January 1882), 1–4.

Manton, Jo. *Mary Carpenter and the Children of the Streets.* London, 1976.

Nelson, Cary and Lawrence Grossberg (eds). *Marxism and the Interpretation of Culture.* Urbana, 1988.

Nightingale, Florence. 'Can We Educate Education in India to Educate Men and Women? [Part III] ', *JNIA* (October 1879), 527–57.

Pinhey, Mary. 'England as a Training Ground for Young India', *IMR* (May 1891), 228–32.

'Piyarilal'. The Hindus in England', *JNIA* (June 1884), 281–93.

Ramusack, Barbara. 'Cultural Missionaries, Maternal Imperialists, Feminist Allies, British Women Activists in India, 1865–1945', in Chaudhuri and Strobel (eds), *Western Women and Imperialism,* 119–36.

Sangari, Kumkum and Sudesh Vaid (eds). *Recasting Women: Essays in Colonial History*. Delhi, 1989.

Satthianadhan, S. 'Indian Students and English Universities', *JNIA* (November 1880), 603–16.

Sarkar, Tanika. 'The Hindu Wife and the Hindu Nation, Domesticity and Nationalism in Nineteenth Century Bengal', *Studies in History* ns 8 (1992), 213–35.

Sen, Keshub Chunder. *Keshub Chunder Sen in England: Diaries, Sermons, Addresses, and Epistles*. Calcutta, 1980 (first edition, 1871).

Shah, Syed A.M. 'A Visit to the Tower of London', *IMR* (April 1893), 208–17.

Singha, Dwarkanath. 'Self-Love of Ornament among Bengali Ladies', *JNIA* (September 1880), 507–13.

Sinha, Mrinalini. '"Chathams, Pitts, and Gladstone in Petticoats": The Politics of Gender and Race in the Ilbert Bill Controversy, 1883–84', in Chaudhuri and Strobel (eds), *Western Women and Imperialism*, 98–118.

Sinha, Mrinalini. *Colonial Masculinity: the 'Manly Englishman' and the 'Effeminate Bengali' in the Late Nineteenth Century*. Manchester, 1995.

Sorabji Cornelia. Correspondence, 1892, OIOC (London) MSS EUR F 165.

Spivak, Gayatri. 'Can the Subaltern Speak?' in Nelson and Grossberg (eds), *Marxism and the Interpretation of Culture*, 271–313.

Visram, Rozina. *Ayahs, Lascars and Princes: Indians in Britain, 1700–1947*. London, 1986.

3
Issues of Race, Gender and Nation in *Englishwomen's Domestic Magazine* and *Queen*, 1850–1900

Nupur Chaudhuri

By the mid-nineteenth century imperialism had become a cornerstone of British national identity, and domination of non-western countries – especially India, the crown jewel of the British empire – further strengthened British notions of their unique and inherent superiority. The British were not only convinced of their own superiority, but felt they were under an obligation to improve the physical fabric and moral fibre of indigenous society (Parry 1972, 18). Many Victorian women's periodicals wanted their female readers to participate in Britain's imperial mission. One journal, for example, noted when Queen Victoria took the title of Empress of India in March 1876 that:

> There is a great destiny to be accomplished, and there is a great responsibility on us. It may not be that a future monarch of the country may add to the title 'Emperor of India' the words 'and Australasia,' for the colonies may be constitutionally independent; but they will be 'of us,' if not 'ours,' and the history of the world in the twentieth century will be really the history of the English-speaking people of the globe. (*Englishwomen's Domestic Magazine* March 1876, 121)

This essay examines nonfictional writings published in two women's magazines (*Englishwomen's Domestic Magazine* and *Queen*) during the second half of the nineteenth century. It analyses the interpretation of India in British upper- and middle-class periodicals and illustrates how Indian spaces helped to define and redefine the relationship between private and public spheres. It also suggests the avenues and the methods through which views of India filtered into domestic British discourse in the second half of the nineteenth century and helped to fashion a gendered legitimation of British rule in India. In representing India in this fashion, British women's periodicals gave the memsahibs a national identification within a contextualized Indian landscape. *Englishwomen's Domestic Magazine* and *Queen* wanted their female readers to be a part of this 'English-speaking people of the globe'.

In the second half of the nineteenth century, women were an essential component of the imperial mission. The number of women travelling to India increased considerably. A number of them wrote about India and Indians, and often called on their experiences to help promote an imperial ethos. Nationalism, which is historically a modern phenomenon, takes many forms with changing foci and directions in different times and places (Gellner 1983). We must remember that nationalism, according to Anne McClintock (1993, 67), is 'invented, performed and consumed in ways that do not follow a universal blue print'. Nationalism can be revolutionary ideologies concerned with resisting domination, or dominant ideologies legitimizing the interests of established elites (Jackson and Penrose 1993). Women play an important role in the discourse of nationalism, as Nira Yuval-Davis and Floya Anthias (1989) suggest when they describe the ways in which women become players in formulating and shaping some distinctive marks in national identities. In their recent article on Irish nationalism, Breda Gray and Louise Ryan (1998) have emphasized the interconnections that exist between feminism, national identities and colonialism.

Periodicals, especially women's periodicals, constitute an important source for the study of women's history and social history. Since the early 1980s scholars on both sides of the Atlantic have used these periodicals to shed light on the cultures that produced and consumed them. For example, Margaret Beetham (1996, ix) has used Victorian women's magazines to interrogate concepts of class, nation and religion in British domestic spaces. She also argues that these periodicals performed an important function as a medium of exchange between women (Beetham 1996, 2). Similarly, Marjorie Ferguson (1983, 1) has shown us how women's journals in Britain helped to construct both how women viewed themselves and how society viewed them. A parallel development can be found in Jennifer Scanlon's use of the *Ladies' Home Journal* to link American women's lives with the rise of modern consumer culture (Scanlon 1995, 2). And, most recently, Kathryn Castle (1996) has examined history textbooks and popular books and magazines for themes and tropes intended to impress certain imperial values and ideals on British children. Yet to date there has not been a sustained study of how the treatment of India in women's magazines, especially articles of an instructive or didactic nature, created and recreated gendered and racialized identities for their readers.

It was quite common for nineteenth-century women's periodicals to publish feature articles and question and answer columns about India and travel to India. Woman's periodicals, such as *Eliza Cook's Journal, Queen, Ladies' Treasury, Englishwomen's Domestic Magazine (EDM)*, and *Ladies' Cabinet of Fashion and Music and Romance*, published numerous editorials, articles, fiction, and letters to the editors that drew upon Indian settings. This was especially true after 1857 when, in the aftermath of the Indian Revolt which led to Crown Rule being put in the place of the East India Company, there was an influx of British emigrants to India. This migration was caused partly by an increase in the British military garrison in India, partly by growth in the bureaucracy, and partly by an expansion in the commercial and service sectors. Prior to 1857, many of the British residents in India would have had extensive family connections extending back over several generations. This was not necessarily the case with many of these new expatriates and consequently there was a demand for publications that would prepare them for life in India. Many women's periodicals responded to this need. For example, *Queen* frequently published articles and correspondence on such topics as appropriate clothing for travel to and use in India.[1] In this regard, these periodicals served as an active channel for women to gain and give information about India and its peoples, thereby conforming to what Jennifer Scanlon has found from her analysis of women's periodicals in the United States: namely that a tension existed in such magazines between the anxieties underlying reader's queries and the reassurances which such periodicals proferred (Scanlon 1995, 5). One can conclude from such examples of readership response that there was a loyal and regular readership for these journals.

I have selected *Englishwomen's Domestic Magazine (EDM)* and *Queen* because they more than most made frequent use of and reference to India in their features and columns. Although they shared the same publisher and many of the same writers, there were important differences between these two journals: *EDM* targetted women readers from the British middle classes while *Queen* looked higher up the social scale.

Samuel Orchard Beeton published *EDM* and *Queen*, and his wife Isabella Beeton was a major force in editing the *EDM*. First published in London in 1852, each copy of the *EDM* cost only two pence, instead of the usual one shilling for a monthly (White 1970, 44; Beetham 1996, 59). By 1857, *EDM* claimed to have around 50 000 subscribers (Preface, *EDM* vol. VI, 1857). The intention of *EDM* was to reach women of the middle class. Beetham notes that the title was likely intended to associate middle-class domesticity with Englishness (Beetham 1996, 63). English national pride was bound up with its imperial ambitions, and, in this context, India was an important site for such expressions. This was the case with *EDM* whose publisher and editor, not having visited India, hired writers who did have some Indian experience. For example, in 1878 a writer was specifically contracted to provide a series of articles on daily life in India under the pseudonym of 'E.J.'. The rationale provided for this series, as indicated in its issue of January 1878, was,

> We have received so many letters asking for information on the subject of outfits for India, and regarding the necessaries for housekeeping to be taken out to that country, that we have arranged with a lady, qualified by a residence in India to be an authority, to contribute a series of articles which we feel assured will be found useful. (*EDM* January 1878, 90)

Queen was equally attentive to individuals seeking information about India. *Queen* claimed to be 'for women', 'about women' and 'EDITED BY A LADY.' *The Queen* was variously titled *The Queen and The Ladies' Newspaper*. These statements of editorial identity have obvious class implications, as Watkins suggests when she claims that *Queen* had a 'wide' and 'wealthy' readership (Watkins 1982, 91). Likewise, in *Women's Magazines, 1693–1968*, Cynthia A. White suggests that *Queen* 'provided women with more topical and factual information than the orthodox magazines, and soon achieved the status of being the foremost periodical for ladies of rank and breeding' (White 1970, 50). As the editor of *Queen* acknowledged, 'The Problem which we have set ourselves is how to provide a weekly record and Journal which ladies can read and profit by; one in which their understanding and judgment will not be insulted by a collection of mere trivialities but which will be to them a help in their daily lives.'[2]

From its inception in 1861 until the turn of the century, it frequently featured articles and editorials on Indian topics. The subjects it addressed varied considerably from the dramatic to the mundane, from the religious oppression experienced by Hindu women to the story of a children's party thrown by an Indian prince.[3] Through regular columns like Leaders, Gazette des Dames, Balls, Bazaars, Boudoir, Charity, Cuisine, Drama, Dress, Illustrations and Library, *Queen* was able to inform and educate its readers about India. By featuring authors who were familiar with India, like Emily

Kinnaird or 'E.J.' who was also a contributor to *EDM* on India, *Queen* was able to reinvent and recreate India for its readers (Castle 1996, 7).

Both *EDM* and *Queen* published columns that touched on fashion. For example, an unsigned article was published in *EDM* in 1854–55 that described Indian women's clothing. It distinguished between Hindu, Muslim and Christian women on the basis of their clothing. It described Hindu women's clothing as: 'Long piece of silk or cotton tied around the waist, and hanging in a graceful manner to the feet; it is afterwards brought over the body in negligent folds; under this they cover the bosom with a short waistcoat of satin, but wear no linen ... their ears are bored in many places, and loaded with pearls.'[4]

In contrast, Muslim women were described in the article as having 'adorn[ed] themselves with a variety of jewels, worn over a close gown of muslin, with long sleeves and short waist; silk or satin drawers reach to the ankles, and a transparent veil covers the head'. It further claimed that when 'the Hindoos and Mohammedans are baptized into the Christian faith, the women lay aside their Eastern dress, and put on a jacket and petticoat'. Hindu and Muslim men, on the other hand, were described wearing similar apparel, such as turbans, sashes and long white gowns. There were some differences: Muslim men, for example, were sometimes described as having a short dagger in their girdle and wearing full-length trousers, usually of satin and with a gold and silver flower pattern embroidered on them. And when Hindus and Muslims became Christian, they were depicted as wearing 'as much of the European apparel as they can, with the exception of a coat and stockings, which are only worn on festivals and days of ceremony'.

Religious differentiations in fashion were accompanied by class-based distinctions as attention was drawn to differences between the Indian upper and lower classes. The *EDM* observed that the 'lower class of females often wear only a single garment, like a sheet, which wrapped round the body and tucked in under the arms, descended to the ankle'. On the other hand lower-class Indian males were often described in terms like the following, 'men of the working-classes ... wear a very limited quantity of clothing'. This description of their near-nakedness could well stem from the fact that British incomers first encountered Indian males as boatmen and servants (Cohn 1989, 331).

In describing the clothing of upper-class males, *EDM* used Hyder Ali as an example. Hyder Ali, a ruler of Mysore State in Southern India in the second half of the eighteenth century, was a particularly formidable opponent of the British, and as such would have been a familiar figure to many readers. It described Hyder Ali's clothing as 'consist[ing] of a robe of white muslin, with a turban the same. The vest, which is fashioned much like the gown of an European lady . . .' (*EDM* 1854–55, 21). There is an interesting subtext in the latter statement reflecting the tendency to feminize Indian males, even ones with such a martial reputation as Hyder Ali. This article further pointed out that in India men and women devoted much time to embroidery: 'it is not unusual to see several of the former seated cross-legged on a mat, employed in a manner that in Europe would be considered as effeminate, and quite below the dignity of the nobler sex' (*EDM* 1854–55, 23). Again, we see the same theme of Indian men being effeminate.

The above *EDM* article illustrates how something as specific as dress can embody many of the values and preconceptions of nineteenth-century British imperialism. Clothing within the colonial context was especially important in setting out the criteria through which Indian society functioned and was judged (Tarlo 1996, 23). Even differences in how clothing was produced and worn was exaggerated in this periodicals, and therefore contributed to the creation of false distinctions between Indian communities. For example, *EDM* described Hindu women as wearing saris which required no tailoring or stitching which while presented in a positive way, nonetheless was intended to distinguish them from Muslim women who were seen as favouring stitched gowns. What *EDM* failed to recognize was that Hindu women also wore stitched gowns such as the northern Indian *ghagra*, or stitched skirt.

Indian women's clothes remained an interesting topic even toward the end of the century. One woman, calling herself 'ayah', wrote in the *Queen* on 27 May 1899 to answer a query: 'They [Indian dresses] consisted mostly of plain skirts, with a loose jacket and light sleeves coming halfway to the elbow, bordered with embroidery, the Hindoos wear them longer.' She went on to describe the saree and claimed that silver bangles and a necklace of sequins and embroidered slippers completed the outfit. This seemingly benign description in fact emphasizes the 'otherness' of the Indian woman, because while the clothing itself might seen nondescript, the accompanying accessories draw attention to the difference between Indian and European women (Tarlo 1996, 26–35). Thus, Indian clothing became yet another indicator of the hierarchy to be found in the relationships between British rulers and Indian subjects in this period.

As we have seen in the case of clothing, religion was a recurring theme. Both *EDM* and *Queen* offered space for individuals to compare and contrast Hinduism and Islam with Christianity. In 1857 Maria Susan Rye, a feminist and a social reformer, wrote an article 'Women in Barbarism' in which she described the status of women in non-Christian countries. To Rye and many of her contemporaries, civilization was judged with reference to Christian practices and values. For example, after summarizing the *Laws of Manu* (an ancient source of Hindu legal guidance), Rye concluded that the depressed status of Hindu women could be attributed to the power of Hindu tradition. Hence, her empathy for the condition of Hindu women had its limits – as long as they remained Hindu, they would be subject to barbarian customs. Christianity and imperial rule offered the only salvation. It also reinforced the superior position claimed by European women. These claims for the superiority of Christianity were not new. For example, in the 1780s, similar sentiments were expressed in the letters that Eliza Fay wrote to her family (Fay 1817).

Another issue raised in these magazines was that of educating Indian women. In particular, emphasis was laid on the efforts made by British women to educate Indian women on issues of sanitation and marriage. Once again, the Hindu religion was depicted as an obstacle to the improvement of Indian women's lives. As readers in *Queen* were informed, 'It is necessary to inculcate in the people a greater knowledge of, and desire for, sanitary improvements. At present time this does not exists, even amongst the best educated classes ... the religious prejudices against cleanliness are so strong, that even the most advanced persons in India are powerless to resist' (*Queen* 22 August 1891, 290). It then reassured its readers that efforts to educate Indian girls on such subjects had already begun.

On the subject of marriage, *Queen* featured in its 'Gazette des Dames' section of 28 September 1878 a reprint of an article previously published in *The Journal of the National Indian Education*. This article reported on the merging of two Indian girls' schools. One was the Bethune School, which was a government-funded institution established in Calcutta in 1849 for the benefit of the children of strict and orthodox Hindus who married their daughters at very early age, thus making them unavailable to receive proper education. The second was the Banga Mahila Bidyalaya, a boarding school for Indian ladies. The report emphasized that this merger would help to educate young Bengali women. Yet *Queen* also stressed that 'the two schools will be kept quite distinct, the feelings of more orthodox Hindus can be as carefully respected as heretofore', thus reminding its readers of the difficulty of balancing British ideas of education for Indian women with orthodox Hindu beliefs.

In keeping with these views of the superiority of British values and institutions, these magazines stressed the important charitable contributions made by British women in India. *Queen*, for example, published several articles that described the works of missionary women and British female doctors and teachers. A typical example was when the Hon Mrs Emily Kinnaird, a regular contributor to *Queen*, described the activities of the Young Women's Christian Association:

> One branch has supplied twelve dozen articles of clothing for the children of an orphanage. Another has collected 135 rupees for the support of a mission school, just at a time when the missionaries were puzzled how to carry it on. Another branch, hearing from a lady doctor of the need for her hospital, undertook to supply the requisite purdahs, quilts, garments, pictures, &c ... (*Queen* 10 October 1891)

Queen enthusiastically supported the charitable works undertaken by Lady Kinnaird and her mission. It wrote: 'Miss Kinnaird is visiting India specially on behalf of mission, and one of the objects she has in view is to start hospitals for Purdah women, under the management of fully qualified medical ladies' (*Queen* 10 October 1891). *Queen* featured several articles and letters from Lady Kinnaird, many of which urged the wives of British civil officials and army officers to join the YWCA in order to help Indian women. She and other women missionaries believed that their organizations would 'prepare [British wives living in India] to take an interest in the missionary effort, which had done so much to open the eyes of the natives to the good of British rule' (*Queen* 6 June 1891, 923). There were also frequent appeals in these journals from women missionaries for donations of pictures, scrapbooks, Christmas cards, toys, dolls, work boxes, wool, and other working materials which could then be distributed in Indian schools. As one appeal noted, these items would then introduce poor families to 'happiness, comforts and refinements of western civilization' (*Queen* 1 August 1891, letter of Mrs Harriet Little, Kohlapur, India dated 15 June 1891).

Queen and *EDM* served as platforms where rationales for increasing involvement of British women in imperial rule were articulated. On the one hand, British women were able to reach sectors of society denied to British men. This was particularly true of medical schools established to educate Indian women on health and sanitation. As one leading article in *Queen* put it when describing Lady Dufferin's scheme to encourage British medical women to come to India, British women 'alone could gain access to the women of the country, and expound the principles of sanitary science to them' (*Queen* 22 August 1891, 290). This editorial urged British women doctors to go to India to help indigenous women.

But this was not mere altruism, as *Queen* acknowledged when it stated that 'England has reaped the benefit of the supply of a want which was felt by India' (*Queen* 10 June 1899, 596). The point was that such schemes offered new opportunities for British women to advance their careers and at the same time act in a manner which associated them with the greater imperial cause.

Just as Indian women were best reached by women doctors, so too would they be best served by women lawyers. As *Queen* recognized, there was a shortage of female legal counsel, which meant that when Indian women sought legal advice, they would have to do so under the constraints of purdah. To quote an article in *Queen*:

> These customs, ordained by caste and conventional usages, are not to be overcome, and therefore, in the interest of Indian women, we can only express a hope . . . that every woman in India may be enabled to obtain legal advice and if requisite, redress by the available means – the consultation of her own sex. (*Queen* 10 June 1899, 956)

EDM and *Queen* also supplied information to readers interested in India about house keeping in the subcontinent through advice columns and articles. These were for the most part written by wives of British civil servants, military officers, missionaries and merchants – individuals who had spent some time in India or were still living in India. By furnishing this type of information, *EDM* not only provided an impression of British daily life in India, but also prepared readers for life in a distant land. Although British society in India was hierarchical, these articles rarely made references to women from the lower classes. Social rankings began with the voyage out to India, and manifested themselves in such mundane things as what to do with the clothes they had worn en route. As 'E.J.' advised in *EDM*, while India-bound memsahibs could wear old clothes during their voyage, on landing they should throw them away or 'give [them] to one of the poor soldiers' wives to wash and keep for herself; [as] many of the poorer wives would consider such a gift quite a boon, and be very thankful for it' (*EDM* March 1878, 188).

In the pages of *EDM* and *Queen*, clothes continued to be a site where the 'otherness' of Indians could be demonstrated. Even in their answers to queries regarding suitable outfits for India and daily life in the subcontinent, contributors made disparaging remarks about those Indian servants charged with the care of clothing, such as *dhobies* (Indian washermen) and *dirzies* (Indian tailors). About *dhobies* one reader calling herself Panjaubee wrote: 'they [*dhobies*] tear and destroy your clothes;

and a self-coloured muslin, trimmed with lace, would have no chance at all when once it has passed through their hands' (*Queen* 10 June 1876). The concern expressed by the 'Panjaubee' memsahib about the *dhobies* was shared by several other memsahibs.[5]

On the other hand, opinions regarding *dirzies* were more ambivalent. Several trusted the workmanship of Indian *durzies*. As commentators claimed, 'if the native tailors have good patterns, they make [clothes] well and reasonably'.[6] But one ex-memsahib advised readers in *Queen* 'that ladies should have instructions at home with a good dressmaker, bootmaker, and milliner; also for gloves, stockings, and veils; and only bring out enough for four months at a time, and send for new ones when required'. She further stressed that it was not wise 'to bring out materials to make up; or ribbons, flowers, and laces to trim with. *Dirzies* can not put any style to anything' (*Queen* 14 December 1895). In the 1870s 'E.J.' wrote in both *EDM* and *Queen* that servants were not bright and could be very slow in finishing any task. This was a point also taken up by another correspondent who reminded readers that the sluggishness of their servants should not prompt people to lose their patience and beat them.

British women's periodicals like *EDM* and *Queen* helped British women to contribute to the development of British national identity by utilizing British women's accounts of life in India to highlight Britain's cultural, religious, racial and moral superiority. These narratives of India consistently presented Indians as culturally and racially inferior, which in turn was used to support the myth of 'British culture as central, stable, and coherent' (Lowe 1991, 109). Through their articles and editorials, these two periodicals underscored the benefits of British rule over India. For example, the lead article in *Queen* on 28 March 1891 insisted that:

> The reforms which had been introduced from time after time, with a firm yet tender hand, by the English Government all met with opposition on the part of the lower and more ignorant part of the population of India. Such were the suppression of the burning of the widows on the funeral piles of their husbands, the immolation of victims under the car of Juggernaut, and the self-inflicted tortures of fakirs; yet these regulations have become part of the law of the land, and hence been accepted by the people, so it will doubtless be with this Act [Child Marriage Act] respecting early child marriage.

Furthermore, journals like the *EDM* explicitly equated nationalism with middle-class domesticity. As *EDM*'s publisher explained when accounting for its title, 'If there is one thing of which an Englishman has just reasons to be proud, it is the moral and domestic character of his countrywomen' (*EDM* 1852, 1) Thus, morality and domesticity became the two pillars upon which Beeton rested his concept of Englishness. Moreover, magazines like *EDM* and *Queen* gave their women authors a new status and a new role as educators and mentors of British women bound for India. Through them, British women became well-informed about their most important possession, India, thus making India part and parcel of their domestic world.

Notes

1. For advice on clothing for the trip, see *Queen*, 14 July 1877, 17 March 1878, 21 October 1882, 24 July 1886, 25 January 1896; for outfits and accessories, see *Queen*, 21 October 1871, 7 July, 24 August 1872, 8 August 1874, 11 March, 2 April, 15 April, 10 June, 16 September, 23 December 1876, 14 July 1877, 17 March, 23 March, 6 April, 7 September, 19 October, 21 January, 21 October 1882, 6 February, 13 February, 20 February, 6 March, 13 March, 20 March, 24 July 1886, 14 December 1895, 25 January, 22 August 1896.
2. *Queen*, vol. 2, 1862, 96; for *Queen's* handling of news, see Beetham 1996, 89–96.
3. See, for example, *Queen* 15 September 1888, 316.
4. *EDM*, vol. 3, 1854–55, 20–4.
5. Regarding *dhobies*, see *Queen* 24 August 1872, 8 August 1874, 14 July 1877, 17 March 1878.
6. *Queen* 21 October 1882; 21 January 1882, 6 February 1886, 20 March 1886.

Works Cited

'An Indian Editor's Rubbish-Basket', *EDM* (November 1871), 274–6.
Beetham, Margaret. *A Magazine of Her Own?: Domesticity and Desire in the Woman's Magazine, 1800–1914*. London, 1996.
Burton, Antoinette. *Burdens of History: British Feminists, Indian Women, and Imperial Culture, 1865–1915*. Chapel Hill, 1994.
Castle, Kathryn. *Britannia's Children: Reading Colonialism Through Children's Books and Magazines*. Manchester, 1996.
Chaudhuri, Nupir. '"Who Will Help the Girls?": Maria Rye and Victorian Juvenile Emigration to Canada', in Rita S. Kranadis (ed.), *Imperial Objects: Victorian Women's Emigration and the Unauthorized Imperial Experience*. New York, 1998.
Cohn, Bernard S. 'Cloth, Clothes, and Colonialism in India', in Annette B. Weiner and Jane Schneider (eds), *Cloth and Human Experience*. Washington, DC, 1989.
Diamond, Marion. 'Maria Rye's Journey: Metropolitan to Colonial Perceptions of Female Emigration', in Rita S. Kranadis (ed.), *Imperial Objects: Victorian Women's Emigration and the Unauthorized Imperial Experience*. New York, 1998.
Diamond, Marion. 'Maria Rye and the *Englishwoman's Domestic Magazine*', *Victorian Periodicals Review* 30 (1997), 5–16.

Fay, Eliza. *Original Letters from India, 1779–1885.* 1817 reprint, New York, 1925.
Ferguson, Marjorie. *Forever Feminine: Women's Magazines and the Cult of Femininity.* London, 1983.
Freeman, Sarah. *Isabella and Sam: the Story of Mrs. Beeton.* London and New York, 1977.
Gellner, Ernst. *Nations and Nationalism.* Oxford, 1983.
Gray, Breda and Louise Ryan. 'The Politics of Irish Identities and the Interconnections between Feminism, Nationhood and Colonialism', in Ruth Roach Pierson, Nupur Chaudhuri with Beth McCauley (eds), *Nation, Empire, Colony: Historicizing Gender and Race.* Bloomington, 1998, 121–38.
Hyde, H.M. *Mr. and Mrs. Beeton.* London, 1951.
Jackson, Peter and Jan Penrose (eds). *Construction of Race, Place and Nation.* London, 1993.
Lowe, Lisa. *Critical Terrains: French and British Orientalisms.* Ithaca, 1991.
McClintock, Anne. 'Family Feuds: Gender, Nationalism and the Family', *Feminist Review* 44 (1993), 61–80.
Parry, Benita. *Delusions and Discoveries: Studies in India and the British Imagination, 1880–1930.* Berkeley, 1972.
Scanlon, Jennifer. *Inarticulate Longings: The Ladies' Home Journal, Gender, and the Promises of Consumer Culture.* London and New York, 1995.
Spain, N. *The Beeton Story.* London, 1956.
'Talk of the Month', *EDM* 3rd series (April 1875).
'Unsanitary Home Life in India', *Queen* (22 August 1891).
Tarlo, Emma. *Clothing Matters: Dress and Identity in India.* Chicago, 1996.
Watkins, C.C. 'Edward William Cox and the Rise of Class Journalism', *Victorian Periodical Review* 15 (1982), 91–3.
White, Cynthia. *Women's Magazines, 1693–1968.* London, 1970.
Yuval-Davis, Nira and Floya Anthias. *Women, Nation, State.* London, 1989.

4
'Half-Caste Bob' or Race and Caste in the Late-Victorian Boys' Story Paper

Kelly Boyd

From the middle of the nineteenth century a new form of periodical literature for young males appeared, the boys' story paper, sometimes referred to as the 'penny dreadful' or 'blood'. The story paper was one of the first forms of mass culture, and was instrumental in helping boys to understand the wider world through tales of adventure. This essay will explore the vision of India in this rapidly expanding form of entertainment for a young male mass audience, with particular reference to the vexed question of caste and racial stereotypes in the late nineteenth century.

Mentioning the boys' story paper today often evokes a nostalgia for empire and the days when Britain's power was global. Like comic books after the Second World War and children's television in the last four decades, they were part of the fabric of growing up in Victorian England, a pleasure shared across the classes. Middle-class parents might have demonized them and judges may have blamed them for juvenile delinquency, but most boys (and many girls) merely saw them as a thrilling diversion (Dunae 1979). Appearing weekly, they were mainly popular with an audience over the age of ten, and to examine these texts today reveals how few concessions were made to the youth of their readership. Although the sentences were kept short, the vocabulary employed was broad, and the narrative structure complex. Unlike the simplified books supplied to today's youth, the Victorian youth was expected to understand much, and the contents of the story papers differed from adult mass market fiction more in the subjects addressed than in language used. The boys' story papers were crammed with stories set around the globe, occasionally peppered with foreign phrases (probably reflecting the writers' public school backgrounds), and, with few illustrations, limited in their visual appeal.

The story paper was made possible in the middle of the nineteenth century following the disappearance of the taxes on knowledge and the invention of new methods of printing which suddenly made large runs of weekly periodicals both possible and occasionally profitable. They trace their descent from two vibrant traditions in British publishing. First, the serialized novel which had developed in the first half of the century, especially as practised by Dickens and G.W.M. Reynolds. This type of serial story, which seduced readers into buying the next instalment, was introduced early on in the boys' story papers. Reynolds in particular had perfected this marketing tool in *Reynolds's Miscellany* (1847–69) (McWilliam 1996). Second, the adventure stories popularly known as 'penny dreadfuls', which capitalized on sensational tales of robbery and derring-do, were a template for the tales of heroes who encircled the globe. 'Penny dreadful' became almost a generic term for these serialized stories, and critics tended to lump all weekly magazines into this category. Some of the early story papers did owe a great deal to the 'penny dreadful' tradition, but the Victorian story paper had not yet hit on the formula of boys' fiction being mainly about boys. The heroes of these early papers were generally young men (and occasionally women), making their way in the world. By the turn of the century there were far more schoolboy heroes in these pages.

The first major publisher of a story paper was Samuel Beeton, whose monthly *Boy's Own Magazine* initially appeared in 1855 with a primarily middle-class target audience. The *Boy's Own Magazine* established the format for the Victorian story paper, one which would be more profitably utilized by publishers like the Religious Tract Society in the *Boy's Own Paper* (1879–1967) and Edwin J. Brett in *The Boys of England* (1866–99) amongst others. Their frequency, size, look, contents and price had stabilized by the 1880s, and by 1900 more than 40 had appeared – although many folded after a year or two. Appearing weekly, they were generally 16 pages of octavo, primarily text. Illustrations ranged from recycled woodcuts (in the more downmarket publications) to six-colour lithographs in Brett's short-run *Boys of the Empire* in 1888. Generally the front page of each issue featured a lively scene from the chief story (to encourage newsagent sales), with smaller illustrations inside. These drawings may have helped readers to imagine other worlds, but due to the tendency of publishers to reuse old illustrations, the pictures might often have only a tenuous relationship to the story, and could as easily convey misinformation about foreign climes as instructive depictions.

Each issue generally included at least one adventure story, usually serial-ized, some ongoing fiction (for example, school stories), and other articles aimed at building the character of the reader. For Beeton's paper this meant short biographies of famous men whose lives were meant as exemplars or warnings to the readers, a feature that would resurface in Brett's *Boys of England* in 1888 in a series about the winners of the Victoria Cross who had fallen in India. Short biographies were a popular form of didactic literature at the time, perhaps due to the influence of Samuel Smiles' *Self-Help* (1859); they offered biographical sketches to demon-strate how hard work could pay off. Both adult and youth periodicals utilized this format.

The readership of the boys' story paper was not limited to the upper echelons of society, but extended to boys of all classes. Although there were one or two titles that focused on an elite readership, most of the proprietors of late-Victorian papers were interested in profit above other considerations. It was a competitive marketplace and most publishers failed to flourish (Rollington 1913, 100). Even the Religious Tract Society, publishers of the *Boy's Own Paper*, inflated their circulation figures and recent scholarship has revealed that their profitability was of limited duration (McAleer 1992). The Religious Tract Society had entered the field in response to many of the criticisms levelled at the early story papers, but found that to compete in the marketplace, it had to adopt the style, content and, to a lesser extent, the attitude of more commercial publishers. Early accounts of the conflict between the first editor of the *BOP* and the Religious Tract Society reveal that the tensions of a religious publisher entering this field were palpable. To focus too much on religion meant that boys would not read the paper, to focus on adventure and imperialism seemed to negate the purpose of entering into the venture (Dunae 1976). Few other religious publishers entered this market, and it was mostly left to individual entrepreneurs to open it up. The most suc-cessful publisher in the field was Brett, who left a handsome estate when he died in 1895 (Springhall 1990, 1994). The *Boys of England*, his most successful paper, published from 1868 to 1898, was priced at two pence. It had an initial weekly circulation exceeding 150 000, rising to 250 000, and a readership that extended from the elite down to the bottom of the social scale (Carpenter 1983, 15, 45–6). Working-class boys often bought story papers second hand or traded them. Because of its wide consumption, the boys' story paper helped to shape how Victorian youth imagined the wider world. Memoirists of all classes evoked the power these tales had on their imagination (Boyd 1991, ch. 6; Richards 1992). And for boys of the working class, in particular, whose access to the hardcover tales of G.A. Henty and W.H.G. Kingston was circum-scribed, they could imbibe imperial dreams repackaged in weekly instal-ments or ripped off by hack writers.

India has long been seen as a place of *Boy's Own* adventure (Richards 1992, 90), and many would assume that tales of the Raj littered nine-teenth-century boys' story papers. But this was not the case; India was curiously absent from these periodicals. The fascination with South Asia as a locale for juvenile fiction in the 'penny dreadful' and its heirs was more a twentieth-century phenomenon. Tales of India dominated hard-cover fiction aimed at a specifically elite audience, but with the excep-tion of several G.A. Henty tales, notably *With Clive in India* (1884), South Asia awaited the artistry of Kipling to bring it home to the middle-class reader. The fondly remembered 'Wolf of Kabul' stories featuring doughty British secret agent Bill Samson and his Himalayan sidekick Chung, who was armed with a cricket bat reinforced with brass metallic bands (his 'Clicky-ba'), were a product of the interwar years, appearing in *The Wizard* in the 1930s. The rarity of Indian settings was a function of several phenomena. First, imperial adventures often opened on a sea voyage, but as most of the action relating to South Asia was land-based, the Navy played only a minor role. This limited its availability for story locales. Naval adventures were a major genre within the boys' story papers, and captured the imagination of many readers during the nine-teenth century when ocean voyages were lengthy and the only mode of travel to most parts of the empire, if not the world. Furthermore, this was the highpoint of the nautical melodrama on the stage (Forbes 1980; Cox 1996). Second, given the focus on military adventure, there were simply not enough proper battles in India of which Britons could be proud. Instead, there was the difficult question of the 1857 Indian Mutiny (as contemporaries termed it), which generally served as the focus of the few tales which did venture onto the subcontinent. This is not to say that this event was not widely discussed elsewhere. In the 30 years following the event over 50 novels took the Mutiny as a theme, as well as numerous plays, poems, histories and personal accounts (Brantlinger 1988, 199–226). Popular novels like Wilkie Collins's *The Moonstone* (1868) opened there. Patrick Brantlinger sees the event as a touchstone for popular attitudes towards race. But these were mostly aimed at an elite adult market. The boys' story papers generally em-ployed battles as a climax of an adventure where the hero could prove his mettle, and often find himself the recipient of some sort of reward. Other battles featured included engagements during the Crimean War, but also great battles of British history, such as Agincourt or Trafalgar.

India just did not offer opportunities for set-piece battles that the English won nobly. Third, there was the reality that much of what happened in India was rather boring administrative duty in which very little possibility for adventure could be found. By the late nineteenth century India, except for certain hotspots like the Northwest Frontier, had been subdued and contemporary battles were few. Where they occurred they might be incorporated into a story, but boys' publishing generally moved swiftly on, and much of the broader discussion on India now focused on how to administer it. This was not the stuff of adventure fiction. Fourth, real-life heroes like Sir Henry Havelock merited short biographies, but were seldom heroes of tales. As Graham Dawson notes in *Soldier Heroes*, Havelock embodied the soldier as Christian gentleman (Dawson 1994, 79–166). However, Victorian story paper heroes were very different from the Havelock model: arrogant and aristocratic, they seldom acted like Christian gentlemen. Indeed, Victorian story paper heroes were generally class warriors bending both the working-class and colonial minions to their will. Havelock rarely featured in the boys' story papers aimed at mass audiences, with the exception of the *Boy's Own Paper*. All these factors combined to mean that India, although exotic, did not seem as effective as other loci for adventure.

There were very few references to India in the boys' story paper until the 1880s. The first volume of the *Boy's Own Paper* in 1879 offered several short features with South Asian settings – for example, a treatment of the 'Afghan Problem' (5–6), which excused brigandage as culturally acceptable to Afghans, although Hindus, they opined, should have known better. It focused on the story of a local bandit chief and how he was eventually persuaded to give up his wicked ways, enlist in the Indian Army and, finally, take up Christianity. Another story in the same volume centred on the pleasures of hunting in India (332–4). Hunting was a recurring topic for inclusion in these papers, often used to valorize elite characters that had few other merits (Boyd 1991, ch.3; Mackenzie 1989). In the next year, *Union Jack: a Magazine of Healthy, Stirring Tales of Adventures by Land and Sea for Boys*, edited by W.H.G. Kingston, serialized G.A. Henty's *Times of Peril: A Tale of India*. Its impact was limited as *Union Jack* never achieved wide sales and had folded by 1883. The title, *Union Jack*, would be revived from 1894 to 1933 in the far more successful Amalgamated Press story paper that featured the adventures of Sexton Blake.

The slow emergence of India into the story papers in the early 1880s was due to several factors. First, after 1857, India had been brought under the direct rule of the government, which inevitably meant that it was more widely discussed. Perhaps even more important, in 1876 Victoria became Empress of India, which legitimated, indeed, almost demanded the recuperation of India as a site of imperial adventure. Finally, the boys' story paper was essentially a conservative cultural form which saw its role as confirming the status quo and, perhaps, inspiring its readers to go into imperial service. India needed soldiers and administrators more than ever with the buffer of the East India Company removed, and story paper publishers wished to validate the importance of the subcontinent in the imperial scheme. However, the scarcity of tales set in India suggests that India was accorded no special position among story paper editors, but cropped up only in an effort to vary the settings of stories. It appeared far less frequently than Canada or even the USA in tales, which suggests that India's grip on the imagination of youthful readers was weak and that few demanded more stories set in the Raj.

When India did appear, it was in one of two ways: through adventure stories and through nonfiction. The latter was notable, because it celebrated the men who had offered themselves in order to solidify Britain's hold on the subcontinent. For example, in 1888 E.J. Brett's *Boys of England*'s feature, 'The Roll of Valour', recounted the stories of men who had won the Victoria Cross during the Mutiny. This was part of a longer series that celebrated patriotism and heroism. This sort of series had two functions. First, and most important, it offered readers short, rousing inspirational stories of British military men, examples for emulation at a time when there were increasing worries about manly behaviour (Boyd 1994; Mangan and Walvin 1987; Roper and Tosh 1991; McLaren 1997; Tosh 1999). This fear about masculinity mainly revolved around the upper-middle classes and the rise of sport in the public schools was one of many methods employed to attempt to masculinize boys in these years. The paradigm these tales offered emphasized bravery in the face of danger and loyalty to the regiment and the crown. Each of the 29 accounts focusing on the Mutiny was constructed as an adventure emphasizing the romantic aspects of warfare rather than the grisly ones. Their ultimate message, a hardly surprising one, was that it was heroic to fight for one's country. This was reinforced by a depiction of the enemy as cowardly and duplicitous. It hardly needs noting that the Raj was assumed to be a good thing; in a period of imperial strength, this conservative form would hardly suggest anything else. The series' second function was more mundane, at least in a publishing sense. As a cycle of short features it was used to pad out the magazine. The space devoted to 'The Roll of Valour' varied from week to week and

Brett had used a similar series in his first volumes in the 1860s: 'How to Become a Great Man' and 'Progress of the British Boy' both carried the same function.

Nonfiction made this point through its valorization of actual heroes, but the fiction of the boys' story paper took exactly the same view, just at greater length and unconstrained by the limitations of actual events. The best examples of this were the famous Jack Harkaway tales initiated by Bracebridge Hemyng (1841–1901) in the 1870s that appeared in *Boys of England*. Louis James has argued that Harkaway and others were 'Tom Brown's Imperialist Sons', and that there is a thin veneer of sadism which runs through these tales, presaged by the bullies like Flashman who appeared in *Tom Brown's Schooldays* (1855) (James 1973; see also Dunae 1977, 1980; Huttenback 1965; Street 1985; Mannsaker 1985; Bristow 1991). James suggests that these tales offered a route from the schoolroom to the role of imperial participant as the public school provided the perfect training for dealing with imperial problems. Jack Harkaway's popularity cannot be understated. Besides eventually getting his own story paper (*Jack Harkaway's Journal for Boys*), there were Harkaway blazers and keychains in an early example of merchandising (Boyd 1991, ch. 3). Harkaway became a template for dozens of other series characters with catchy names and rousing adventures. Yet for our purposes the significant feature of the Jack Harkaway stories is that in his travels he never went to India (although he did visit China). However, other tales repeat many of the attitudes and themes first introduced in the Hemyng stories. A good example is 'Left-Handed Jack on the Plains of India' which appeared in E.J. Brett's *Boys of England* in mid-1891. Left-Handed Jack was a Royal Dragoon and the central character in at least two other tales; the author of the story was anonymous. One-syllable names were popular for heroes, who almost always had some sort of descriptive phrase attached to their sobriquet, like Canadian Jack, Up-to-Date Jack, or Kangaroo Kit in three other concurrent series of stories. Left-Handed Jack himself was a dashing soldier without any close family who was generally popular with his fellow soldiers.

'Left-Handed Jack on the Plains of India' was typical of the few boys' story paper adventure stories set in India. The plot was a standard one, centring on the struggle of the hero to win the love of an attractive young woman, Ada Titmarsh, despite the fact that her father, Sir Septimus, is the villain of the piece. Jack's rival for Ada's affections is Lord Cecil Goldenhurst, brother of an old foe of Jack's. Lord Cecil mistakenly blames Jack for his brother's premature death and hopes to punish him by stealing Ada's affections. This rather formulaic narrative of revenge and love is set in an unspecified regiment serving in Bengal, and it has a rich gallery of Indian characters as well, all negatively portrayed, but worthy of discussion for exactly that reason. The boys' story paper relied on stereotypes as shorthand descriptions and readers of the stories understood these caricatures. Thus most foreigners exhibited some type of flaw, from lazy Irishman to noble Native American (although this latter evolved during the late-Victorian period into the drunken Red Indian). It is worth examining Left-Handed Jack to uncover the variety of negative portrayals in these years. For example, the Rajah of Rampoor and his sister the Maharanee of Almore, a widow generally referred to as Lulu Lal, are both devoted to their own pleasure and are exemplars of oriental laziness and decline. The middle-aged Lulu Lal is also the 'romantic' target of Sir Septimus who eventually marries her for her money and murders her. It can be no accident that her name recalls the *lal bazaar*, a slang term for the red-light district where brothels might be found near army posts (Ballhatchet 1980, 11). This inside joke would have eluded most boy readers, but its inclusion makes the demonization of the boys' story paper by adults who understood the reference more understandable. Other Indian characters include Chorta Baksh, a Parsee soothsayer, a long-bearded 60-year-old who dies in a terrible accident; his servant Ram Dass; Dakka, a toothless forger; Mooghe, a Pathan henchman of Lulu Lal; Syed of Halta, son of Talookdar, the mad Mussulman, who dies after trying to kill Sir Septimus; and Nur Ali, a Sikh Jack is sent to Rampoor to arrest. Needless to say, none are fully rounded characters – they exhibit characteristics like superstitiousness (Chorta Baksh and Ram Dass) or slyness (Mooghe). Some are endowed with certain martial qualities, which fits well with the broader racial stereotypes that had crystallized in the late nineteenth century. Martial race stereotypes had been present in India for some time and shaped recruitment for the Indian Army in the last decades of the nineteenth century (Omissi 1994, ch. 1). These stereotypes are present in this tale in the characters of Mooghe, the Pathan henchman, and Nur Ali, the Sikh; both are endowed with more martial qualities than other characters. But the chief purpose of rendering these characters in this way is to show the bravery and canniness of the hero. Boys' fiction wasted little time on character development – including that of the hero. Instead the tales were more like templates of adventure. The struggles that a hero undertook were never with himself or his conscience, but with evil villains and their lazy henchmen. The Indian characters in 'Left-Handed Jack' were merely racialized versions of English villains and henchmen, applying a different set of stereotypes. The Indian setting was exploited as no more than an exotic backdrop, providing different types of settings for the protagonist's exciting adventures. Perhaps this is most evident in the subplot of Sir Septimus' involvement with Lulu Lal. Even respectable sexual liaisons which included marriage were actively discouraged as likely to cause resentment amongst the local populace (Peers 1998). Of course, neither character is, strictly speaking, under the control of the military, but westerners who transgressed were often cut off from polite society, which was a powerful incentive to conform. 'Left-Handed Jack' functioned as a typical tale of adventure whose greatest task was to convince readers of the adventure that lay ahead for any lad who joined up. A life of excitement awaited any young man who became a soldier, and the most exotic locales awaited him. It also taught its readers to be unthinkingly racist in the way it employed racial categories as shorthand for character failings. This message was not limited to tales with imperial settings, but saturated the Victorian story paper. It was an integral part of the Victorian worldview.

One of the most unusual and informative tales about race set in India was an adventure story, 'Half-Caste Bob; Or, The Hero of our Indian Contingent', a contemporary tale published in Brett's *Boys' Weekly Reader Novelette* in the early 1880s. It is highly unusual and deserves our attention because its hero does not exhibit the racial purity which was characteristic of every other hero of this genre in the period. Bob is a liminal figure, caught to a certain extent between two cultures, and it is his establishment of himself within white British society that makes him an atypical hero. In the remainder of this essay, I will consider the question of race in the boys' story paper, primarily through a discussion of this tale, but within the context of recent writings on the vexed question of racial categories in India.

Attitudes towards race in the context of the Raj were complex. Both Christine Bolt (1971) and Douglas Lorimer (1978) have demonstrated that in Britain there was an elaborate understanding of race as it applied to various groups. By the late nineteenth century, this was not so much a scientific attitude as a cultural one overlain with a bit of science. So in Britain not only were Indians, Africans and the Chinese seen as of a different race, but the Irish and sometimes the Welsh and Scots were referred to in the same way. In the boys' story paper this meant that stereotypes were often applied to each of these groups, and race was deployed as the explanatory mode. This can be clearly seen in the tale of 'Left-Handed Jack' discussed above. Here all the characters were stereotypes including the hero, although the villain's whiteness did not mitigate his treachery. This elastic vision of race had both its advantages and disadvantages in imperial Britain. It meant that a sort of English superiority might dominate, but at the same time it left people who did not precisely fit into one race or another disadvantaged.

The issue of race was complicated for Britons in India by several issues. Bolt argues that the attainments of Indian civilization meant that imperial observers could not adopt as hard a line vis-à-vis Indians as they had towards Africans in Africa. On the scale of acceptability, Indians were seen as several steps above Africans, especially light-skinned (often upper-caste) Indians. She notes the disdain voiced towards dark-skinned South Indians and the admiration for certain groups who manifested some sort of martial skill. This was, of course, complicated by the caste system on the Indian side, and by the class snobbery of the ruling elite.

White people of British origin in India are often subsumed under the blanket term, Anglo-Indian; this merits some discussion as the term had a certain amount of elasticity that affected attitudes towards the half-caste. Often the British ruling class characterized itself as Anglo-Indian (Nadis 1963). This had more to do with their residency and power than any-thing else. But other groups also claimed the appellation and the rights they saw as congruent with it. Chief among them were the group whose descent from both British and Indian forbears placed them solidly neither with the British elite or the subject race. These were the children of liaisons between British and Indian men and women, an expanding group during the nineteenth century, and one which was very aware that its existence on the edge of two cultural groups deeply disadvantaged it. The barriers were both legal and cultural (Hawley 1996).

The legal situation was particularly difficult. In Calcutta, for instance, the presence of an Indian parent automatically excluded one from the benefits of coming under English common law. In the interior, they could be tried under Muslim laws, which many Christian Eurasians found both uncongenial and unfair. This meant that Eurasian marriages might go unrecognized, their children might be branded as illegitimate, and that at their deaths, their wills might not be executed as they wished. Legally, this group was also prohibited from the best offices in the Indian Civil Service, many lower offices in other government departments, and from serving in the military in most capacities. Their disabilities extended to service with semi-independent princes except by special dispensation, which was not very swift in coming. By 1830, these obstacles had inspired a petition to Parliament outlining the groups' grievances and painting the community as loyal subjects who were being poorly treated by the East India Company. Unfortunately, the petition had little effect.

Legal constraints united with cultural ones to limit the opportunities for this sector of the Anglo-Indian community. Half-castes began with a disadvantage because it was generally assumed they were illegitimate. This perception had its roots in the early days of the exploitation of India when it was rare for men to bring their wives with them to the subcontinent. Ronald Hyam (1986, 1990) has argued that many of the men who went out to govern and guard the empire were attracted to the task by the opportunities it afforded them for sexual adventure (for a more nuanced reading, see Berger 1989; Manderson 1997; Bryder 1998; Peers 1998). He notes that most men were prohibited from bringing wives to India – instead they formed what were often long-term liaisons with local women, which Hyam sees as advantageous to both parties. Hyam's assessment of the benefits to each party is controversial, as his viewpoint seems to identify somewhat too closely with the ruling elite and to give as little thought to the consequences of these liaisons as did these men. Both legal restraints on the children of these liaisons and the cultural attitudes of the British community towards them combined to create a class excluded from the advantages of European parentage.

Whether these children were legitimate or not was rather beside the point. Intermarriage redefined the status of one's children, and doomed them to an inferior status within Anglo-Indian society. Boys' educational and employment opportunities were limited, while girls found themselves restricted in the marriages they could probably make. They were not alone in experiencing these constrictions because working-class Britons who had come to India either to work on the railway or as soldiers were also rather circumscribed in their choices.

Working-class Britons differed greatly from the elite military and administrative families often depicted in fiction. They were often seduced into work in India due to the relatively high wages on offer. In the early days, the men arrived without wives and began to marry in India, often taking their wives from the Eurasian community. Here race and class combined to create a subgroup within the Anglo-Indian community who neither fitted with the ruling elite, nor could be treated as Indian workers. David Arnold studied the problems of this subgroup through an examination of the treatment of orphans and vagrants in this period. He revealed the ambiguities of British society in India in their reluctance to challenge categories of race or class when looking after poor whites in times of need. His study of orphans is particularly revealing since it demonstrates that products of unions between Britons and Indians often had a lower status than similarly positioned Hindus and Muslims. This could lead light-skinned Anglo-Indians to try and pass as 'pure' Europeans, which both Arnold and Laura Gbah Bear examine in detail. Race thus becomes even more important than class in defining one's role in this segment of imperial society (Arnold 1979; Bear 1994; Stoler 1992; Manderson 1997).

It should be stressed here that, although much has been made about the fears of illegitimacy, this was not the real issue. Respectability accrued from the right parentage, not from the legal niceties of marriage lines. This is clear from a couple of examples from Kipling's fiction. First, a short story published in 1890: 'Without Benefit of Clergy'. As its title suggests, this tale traces the relationship between a British official, John Holden, and an Indian woman, Ameera. It is a relationship of great love and tenderness, but the protagonist's position means that he cannot consider official marriage to his lover. They have a son, who dies, as does eventually Ameera. Indeed, even their home is swept away by the monsoon, and the hero is left to return to white society, unable to reveal his loss. John McBratney (1990) suggests that this tale is not so much about the exploitation of Indian women as about the 'moral and emotional education of British men'. Furthermore, he sees it as a cautionary tale, warning British men not to be entrapped by the seductions of Indian culture. 'Without Benefit of Clergy' is an interesting story as it acknowledges the existence of sexual liaisons although it inevitably avoids dealing with their implications through the death of Ameera. For most Anglo-Indians, such a relationship with or without benefit of clergy had implications for the partners and their children.

By 1901 and the publication of *Kim*, Kipling was focused on another part of the lower echelons of Anglo-Indian society. Kim is not a half-caste, but the orphan of an Irish soldier, lately of the Sind, Punjab and Delhi Railway, and of a former nursemaid in a colonel's family. Although assumed to be half-caste, he is not, and has the paperwork to prove it, including his parents' marriage lines. This is not the place to analyse *Kim*, but it is important to note the importance of documentation that Kipling provides him with in the first chapter, in order to place his story firmly in a narrative of class and not one of race. Kim is a full-blooded white, and this is as important in the formation of his character as all his adventures.

This should be seen in contrast to the tale of the anonymously authored 'Half-Caste Bob; or, The Hero of Our Indian Contingent', which appeared in Brett's *Boys' Weekly Reader Novelette* around 1883. The series was undated, probably so that issues would retain a longer shelf life. In every issue there is a complete story, and some of the tales may have been published in serial form elsewhere first. At the price of one penny, it would have been affordable for the mass of boys, but would no doubt also have been traded and been available second-hand.

The story is pretty straightforward and is a typical adventure tale with the one exception that its hero (with whom the reader is meant to identify) is a half-caste. At the story's opening Bob Elwyn is the 'almost European' looking 12-year-old son of a young Indian mother (2). Deserted by his English father (who is her husband), Bob's mother dies in the jungle leaving him her marriage licence and his birth certificate and advising him always to cling to the Christian faith. His mother only a few minutes dead, Bob saves a young English officer, Lieutenant Hubert MacPherson, from a tiger. MacPherson helps Bob bury his mother and gets him a posting as a bugler to the Native Army regiment with which he serves. Their friendship grows, especially after Bob rides Mac's horse to victory in a race. Five years later, with Bob now a soldier, and having joined a new regiment, they are posted to Egypt to fight the uprising there. Bob distinguishes himself in battle and wins the Victoria Cross, which Victoria presents to him herself while his regiment is in England. At the same time, he is recognized by his true father who had been called away unexpectedly years earlier and had never successfully traced his son.

Bob clearly inhabits that hazy world of the half-caste, able to distinguish himself with his bravery and military prowess, but forbidden most social contact with Europeans. At the tale's opening he lives with his mother, who is depicted as having a rather stereotypically Indian nature. She is suspicious and fearful for Bob, and her stress on his documents seems rather obsessive. This, however, is typical of much fiction of the period, where denied patrimony and inheritance often played a key role. Bob himself, it is stressed, may not be pure-bred British, but racially it is clear that he could pass and at age twelve he is described as being 'fair almost as a European' (2). His rescue of Lieutenant MacPherson shows his courage, which is a character trait often denied to subject races, and in the following pages of the novelette, he shows his perseverance by his attempts to educate himself in English, Persian and riding. In addition, later it is revealed that he knows Arabic and French as well. This kind of scholarship demonstrates that the European side of his family is the dominant one. Often Indians who study so assiduously are seen as effeminate, but Bob's studies combine with his mastery of riding and his soldiering to prove him an able administrator and exemplar of masculinity. The quality of manliness was much contested in late-nineteenth-century India according to Mrinalini Sinha who has examined the way elites accused educated Indians of effeminacy in an effort to prove them unworthy of self-rule (Sinha 1995, ch. 3).

Bob is taken under MacPherson's wing and is given the cultural context in which he can reach his full potential (the army). However, all of Bob's studies and all his attainment of military skills does not erase the fact that he is a half-caste and thus debarred from full membership in elite British society. This is particularly true where affairs of the heart occur. The story demonstrates this in his relationship with MacPherson's fiancée, Maudie, whose father is commanding officer of the regiment. As MacPherson's young protégé, he sees her often and knows her well. About halfway through the story, the regiment is transferred to Egypt where they participate in the battle of Tel-el-Kabir (1882). Maudie is kidnapped and Bob manages to save her from her Arab captors. She is unconscious, but looking at her calls feelings of love to the surface for Bob. The following passage illustrates the competing feelings within Bob, torn between his attraction for Maudie and his realization that she is forbidden to him.

> 'She breathes!' he said joyfully, 'and apparently is unhurt.'
> Unslinging his water keg, he poured some of its contents into a horn cup, and sprinkled her face, waiting anxiously for her to open her lovely eyes. Conflicting emotions tormented him.
> He had always been fond of this girl—this peri—but until now he never knew how much he loved her.
> 'Maudie, speak to me!' he cried. 'Oh, how I—'
> Placing his hand to his brow, he muttered—
> 'What a wretch I am! I to speak words to her of love. To betray the confidence placed in me by my best friend and benefactor. I could place a pistol to my head, and blow my brains out!'
> How he gazed on her face, that even in its statuesque paleness looked supremely beautiful, and noticed her superb bosom undulating like the sea when stirred by a gentle breeze.
> 'Oh Heaven!' he cried, 'save me from myself; for I feel as if I could press her to my heart, and rain down passionate kisses on her lips.'
> Slowly her eyes opened, and the rosy lids lifted the silken lashes, and with a faint smile, she asked, as she pressed his hand, sending an exquisite thrill through his very soul—
> 'Have we gained the victory, Bob?'
> He smiled in return at her naive question, and replied—
> 'Yes, miss, thanks to you. Drink a little brandy, you will be able then to push on with me.'
> 'Bob, was I dreaming? Didn't I hear you speak to me, or was it mere fancy?'

His face became ashen—steeped to the very lips—fearing that she had guessed at his secret, which had come even upon himself with appalling sadness.

'I spoke, miss, because I thought you were not living—you, so young, and who have made everyone love you. But permit me to help you rise. The enemy may be near.'

She held out both her hands, and he raised her gently, when she kissed him gently, saying—

'Dear Bob, do not think me forward, but henceforth, you shall be to me as a brother, even as Hubert [MacPherson] says you are to him.'

Uncovering his head, he stood bowing before her, and made a solemn vow before high Heaven, never to think of her again but as a dear sister.

Placing her before him on the saddle, he galloped towards the canal, and not a moment too soon, for a numerous body of the enemy's horse appeared in sight.

Several things are noticeable in this passage. First of all, note the formal quality of Bob's diction. Although he speaks correctly, his speech is still somewhat stilted, far more than Maudie's. This might be due to the subject matter and the desire of the writer to show Bob's confusion about his feelings in his diction. But it is more likely that the writer wishes to maintain the reader's knowledge that Bob, no matter how heroic, is still outside society's circle. Second, Maudie's paleness is underlined as a way of emphasizing her whiteness and thus her ineligibility to Bob. Third, the love Bob speaks of is pure, not carnal. There is no question here of Bob's being a sexual threat to her purity, which contrasts greatly to other examples of leering natives. In 'Philip and the Pasha' (ca1880), Lady Eglantine Manvers is kidnapped in Tunis and destined to join the Bey's harem. Although she escapes unharmed, the atmosphere is eroticized and the Arabs are depicted as sexually predatory. Bob's realization of his love for Maudie, on the other hand, affirms his Europeanness as he immediately represses his feelings, notably turning ashen-faced or whiter as he does so. Finally, the scene is rather atypical of a genre that generally did not allow these sorts of emotional interludes. More importantly, if these interludes did occur, the hero would not ultimately be expected to repress his feelings for the girl of his dreams. In most stories, the hero gets the girl. However, Bob's liminal position as a half-caste cannot be ignored. No matter how heroic he is, Maudie is forbidden to him.

Throughout the story, Bob's position on the edge of society is reiterated. Although he has proof of an English father and of his own legitimate birth, this cannot sponge away the fact of his mixed parentage. Like Kipling's Kim, he is essentially an orphan in a society where race is one of the organizing principles. Kim is disadvantaged due to the low status of his parents as well, while Bob is the more typical Victorian hero, a lad who does not really know his father. The tale thus is a conflicted one because it both recognizes the haziness of Bob's position as a half-caste, and also yearns to be a tale of lost patrimony. Like many Victorian heroes, Bob's father is eventually restored to him. Another typical feature of the story is that Bob's father is a member of the ruling elite who has struggled to recover his son, but through no fault of his own has failed.

Bob's father sees him at the ceremony in London where Bob's Victoria Cross is awarded and takes the opportunity to reclaim his son. He explains to Bob that he had been urgently recalled to England due to his father's illness and that his letter explaining the circumstances to Bob's mother had evidently never been delivered. Later he had tried to find them, but had had no luck and he had believed them lost to him forever. As with most Victorian fiction, Bob's father quickly acknowledges him as his legitimate son and the heir to his estates and wealth.

'Half-Caste Bob' is a curious tale as it both confirms the racism of British society in India and denies it. Bob's racial origins continue to dictate his life even after his education and heroism demonstrate his worth as a man. The final paragraph of the story notes that Bob's trip to England will be of short duration and that he will eventually return to India, as an officer. Despite his parentage, India will now be his destiny, a place where his eventual wealth may soften the difficulties of his mixed parentage. However, in many ways this was a radical text, making a spirited, if somewhat obscure, argument for the amalgamation of the legitimate issue of interracial relationships into broader British society. At a time when scientific racism had begun to suggest that intermarriage between the races produced inferior children, this tale suggests otherwise. It pleaded for the half-caste to be taken on his own merit and to be allowed to flourish if he can. The radicalism, of course, stops short of complete incorporation of Bob in that his love for Maudie is denied. Unlike almost every other boys' story paper tale of recovered patrimony, Bob does not marry the object of his affections.

As a hero, Bob is also typical of the genre as he has no faults. Yet, he also differs from other heroes in that he lacks the arrogance of, for example, Jack Harkaway. However, he is an exemplar of manliness – hard working, brave, cheerful and so on. He is meant as a role model for boys reading the tale, but also functions to condemn racism. As such he is less typical of a genre which almost reflexively treated characters of mixed parentage as suspect. Bob, of course, has the added advantage that his father is an English aristocrat, which in these pages implies superior blood and stronger character. For this reason, the tale remains both atypical and extremely revealing about British society. The fact that no other tales have emerged of a similar nature suggests that its message that mixed parentage did not inevitably imply a bad character failed to jibe with wider Victorian opinion. Popular tropes were recycled frequently, but this one appeared just the once, which suggests the tension that the issue of race evoked in Victorian society. In every other way, this tale is a typical one of a dispossessed youth that finds his proper father and succeeds to his patrimony by the end of the tale.

Two other points need to be made about this text. It is unlikely that a half-caste would have been allowed to serve in an Indian Army regiment as from 1795 they had been formally prohibited from doing so except in the capacity of 'fifer, bandsman, drummer, or farrier' (Nadis 1963, 410). Studies of the Indian Army generally do not really address this issue, but suggest that the predominant debate was about martial versus nonmartial races, which implies that half-castes would have been assumed ineligible. The scientific racism of the late nineteenth century saw purity of race as central to strengthening so-called racial characteristics (Omissi 1994, 25–35). There is some evidence of half-castes serving in the Indian Army in the early nineteenth century, but it is limited (Peers 1995, 89). Second, it is doubtful that the author of the tale had much of an idea about the actual workings of the military in India. Most of the military details are quite general and little time is spent on creating the atmosphere of army life except in its most usual form. Reading the tale, it seems like it could be taking place at any military post. This is not surprising as most of the authors who wrote for boys' story papers drew not on their own experiences, but from their readings of other writers – and, of course, their imagination. The details of this narrative do not suggest a deep knowledge of life in the Indian Army.

'Half-Caste Bob' appeared just before the struggles over colonial masculinity which Mrinalini Sinha discusses in her work. In the decade following its publication, she locates a renewed struggle for control in India, waged not through direct action, but through a critique of British governing strategies. Perhaps Bob's isolation as a character reflects the increasingly precarious hold Britain had on India as an organized movement for independence began to take shape. Heroes like Bob belonged to an earlier age of confident rule.

Contrary to the suggestions of many writers, India was not a constant background presence in the boys' story paper (MacKenzie 1984). Although imperial settings did occur, India was not a particularly popular one. As a setting it could not compare to the high seas or more remote historical eras as a location for adventure. Indeed, imperial settings were just that, settings, and they rotated around a variety of locales as editors searched for ways to retell the same basic story over and over again. This did not alter with the coming of the new periodicals from the Amalgamated Press in the 1890s. Weeklies from this press, owned by Alfred Harmsworth, later Lord Northcliffe, would come to dominate the market until after the Great War. Papers like *Marvel* (1893) and *Union Jack* (1894) for the most part eschewed the imperial tale of adventure and specialized in urban thrillers, inspired possibly by the fiction of Conan Doyle. Imperial tales, when they appeared, focused on the white dominions of Canada, Australia and South Africa (Boyd 1994).

The boys' story paper did not provide a wealth of material on India for its readers to enjoy and absorb, but the occasional glimpses it offered were suggestive of wider debates in British society. Adventure tales encouraged dreams of heroism in readers, while accounts of winners of the Victoria Cross suggested that India was a place where respect and honour could be won. A final discourse was centred on race, and a close examination of both stereotypes and the upward mobility of half-caste Bob reminds us that attitudes to race were not invisible in the late nineteenth century. They suffused the literature of the era, occasionally betraying a generosity and inclusiveness, but more often drawing on negative images and reinforcing prejudice. India may not have appeared often in the boys' story paper, but its use as a setting confirmed broader ideas present in British society and alerts us today to the complexity of the imperial moment.

Notes

I would like to express my appreciation of the helpful comments by both the editors, Douglas M. Peers and David Finkelstein, as well as the critical engagement with the essay by Rohan McWilliam.

Works cited

A.U., 'Half-Caste Bob; or, The Hero of Our Indian Contingent', *Boys' Weekly Reader Novelette* 11/103 (ca1883).

A.U., 'Left-Handed Jack on the Plains of India', *Boys of England* 50–51/nos 1272–91 (3 April–14 August 1891).

A.U., 'Left-Handed Jack; or, The Royal Dragoon', *Boys of England* 49 (1890).

A.U., 'Left-Handed Jack; or, The Terror of the School', *Boys of England* 48 (1889).
A.U., 'Philip and the Pasha; or, A Rescue from the Harem', *Boys of England Pocket Novelette* no. 29 (ca1880).
A.U., 'The Roll of Valour: the Indian Mutiny', *Boys of England* 43/nos 1101–40 (23 December 1887–21 October 1888).
Arnold, David. 'European Orphans and Vagrants in India in the Nineteenth Century', *Journal of Imperial and Commonwealth History* 7 (1979), 104–27.
Ballhatchet, Kenneth. *Race, Sex, and Class under the Raj*. London, 1980.
Bear, Laura Gbah. 'Miscegenations of Modernity: Constructing European Respectability and Race in the Indian Railway Colony, 1857–1931', *Women's History Review* 3 (1994), 531–48.
Berger, Mark. 'Imperialism and Sexual Exploitation: a Response to Ronald Hyam's "Empire and Sexual Opportunity"', *Journal of Imperial and Commonwealth History* 17 (1989), 83–9.
Bolt, Christine. *Victorian Attitudes to Race*. London, 1971.
Boyd, Kelly. 'Wait Till I'm a Man: Ideals of Manliness in British Boys' Story Papers, 1855–1940' (PhD dissertation, Rutgers, 1991).
Boyd, Kelly. 'Exemplars and Ingrates: Imperialism and the Boys' Story Paper, 1880–1930', *Historical Research* 67 (1994), 143–55.
Brantlinger, Patrick. *Rule of Darkness: British Literature and Imperialism, 1830–1914*. Ithaca, 1988.
Bristow, Joseph. *Empire Boys: Adventures in a Man's World*. London, 1991.
Bryder, Linda. 'Sex, Race, and Colonialism: An Historiographical Review', *International History Review* 4 (1998), 806–22.
Carpenter, Kevin (comp.). *Penny Dreadfuls and Comics: English Periodicals for Children from Victorian Times to the Present*. London, 1983.
Cox, Jeffrey N. 'The Ideological Task of Nautical Melodrama', in Michael Hays and Anastasia Nikolopoulou (eds), *Melodrama: the Cultural Emergence of a Genre*. New York, 1996, 167–89.
Dawson, Graham. *Soldier Heroes: British Adventure, Empire and the Imagining of Masculinity*. London, 1994.
Dunae, Patrick. 'Boys' Literature and the Idea of Race, 1870–1900', *Wascana Review* (1977), 84–107.
Dunae, Patrick. 'Boys' Literature and the Idea of Empire, 1870–1914', *Victorian Studies* 24 (1980), 105–22.
Dunae, Patrick. 'The *Boy's Own Paper*: Origins and Editorial Policies', *The Private Library* 9/4 (Winter 1976), 123–58.
Dunae, Patrick. 'Penny Dreadfuls: Late Nineteenth-Century Boys' Literature and Crime', *Victorian Studies* 22 (1979), 133–50.
Forbes, Derek. 'Water Drama', in David Bradby, Louis James and Bernard Sharratt (eds), *Performance and Politics in Popular Drama: Aspects of Popular Entertainment in Theatre, Film, and Television, 1800–1976*. Cambridge, 1980, 91–108.
Hawley, Christopher. *Poor Relations: the Making of a Eurasian Community in British India, 1773–1833*. Richmond, 1996.
Huttenback, Robert. 'G.A. Henty and the Imperial Stereotype', *Huntington Library Quarterly* 19 (1965), 63–75.
Hyam, Ronald. 'Empire and Sexual Opportunity', *Journal of Imperial and Commonwealth History* 14 (1986), 34–90.
Hyam, Ronald. *Empire and Sexuality: the British Experience*. Manchester, 1990.

James, Louis. *Fiction for the Working Man, 1830–1850: a Study of the Literature Produced for the Working Classes in Early Victorian Urban England*. London, 1963.

James, Louis. 'Tom Brown's Imperialist Sons', *Victorian Studies* 17 (1973), 89–99.

Kipling, Rudyard. 'Without Benefit of Clergy', in *Black and White*. New York, 1897, 101–38.

Kipling, Rudyard. *Kim*. London, 1901.

Lorimer, Douglas A. *Colour, Class and the Victorians: English Attitudes to the Negro in the Mid-Nineteenth Century*. Leicester, 1978.

MacKenzie, John M. *The Empire of Nature: Hunting, Conservation and Victorian Imperialism*. Manchester, 1989.

MacKenzie, John M. *Propaganda and Empire: the Manipulation of British Public Opinion, 1880–1960*. Manchester, 1984.

Manderson, Lenore. 'Colonial Desires: Sexuality, Race, and Gender in British Malaya', *Journal of the History of Sexuality* 7 (1997), 372–88.

Mangan, J.A., and James Walvin (eds). *Manliness and Morality*. Manchester, 1987.

Mannsaker, Frances M. '"The Dog That Didn't Bark": the Subject Races in Imperial Fiction at the Turn of the Century', in David Dabydeen (ed.), *The Black Presence in Literature*. Manchester, 1985, 112–33.

McAleer, Joseph. *Popular Reading and Publishing in Britain, 1914–1950*. Oxford, 1992.

McBratney, John. 'Lovers Beyond the Pale: Images of Indian Women in Kipling's Tales of Miscegenation', *Works and Days* 8 (Spring 1990), 17–36.

McLaren, Angus. *The Trials of Masculinity: Policing Sexual Boundaries, 1870–1930*. Chicago, 1997.

McWilliam, Rohan. 'The Mysteries of G.W.M. Reynolds: Radicalism and Melodrama in Victorian Britain' in Malcolm Chase and Ian Dyck (eds), *Living and Learning: Essays in honour of J.F.C. Harrison*. London, 1996, 182–98.

Neuberg, Victor. *Popular Literature: a Study and Guide*. Harmondsworth, Middlesex, 1977.

Nadis, Mark. 'British Attitudes Toward the Anglo-Indians', *The South Atlantic Quarterly* 62 (1963), 407–22.

Omissi, David. *The Sepoy and the Raj: the Indian Army, 1860–1940*. London, 1994.

Peers, Douglas M. *Between Mars and Mammon: Colonial Armies and the Garrison State in India, 1819–1835*. London, 1995.

Peers, Douglas M. 'Privates Off Parade: Regimenting Sexuality in the Nineteenth-Century Indian Empire', *International History Review* 20 (1998), 823–54.

Richards, Jeffrey. 'Popular Imperialism and the Image of the Army in Juvenile Literature', in John M. MacKenzie (ed.), *Popular Imperialism and the Military, 1850–1950*. Manchester, 1992, 80–108.

Rollington, Ralph [H.J. Allingham]. *A Brief History of Boys' Journals*. Leicester, 1913.

Roper, Michael and John Tosh (eds). *Manful Assertions: Masculinities in England since 1800*. London, 1991.

Sinha, Mrinalini. *The 'Manly Englishman' and the 'Effeminate Bengali' in the late Nineteenth Century*. Manchester, 1995.

Springhall, John. '"A Life Story for the People"? Edwin J. Brett and the London "Low-Life" Penny Dreadfuls of the 1860s', *Victorian Studies* 33 (1990), 223–46.

Springhall, John. '"Disseminating Impure Literature": the "Penny Dreadful" Publishing Business since 1860', *Economic History Review* 47 (1994), 567–84.

Springhall, John. 'Boys of Bircham School: the Penny Dreadful Origins of the Popular English School Story, 1867–1900', *History of Education* 20 (1991), 77–94.

Stoler, Ann. 'Sexual Affronts and Racial Frontiers: European Identities and the Cultural Politics of Exclusion in Colonial Southeast Asia', *Comparative Studies in Society and History* 34 (1992), 514–51.

Street, Brian. 'Reading the Novels of Empire: Race and Ideology in the Classic Tale of Adventure', in David Dabydeen (ed.), *The Black Presence in Literature*. Manchester, 1985, 95–110.

Tosh, John. *A Man's Place: Masculinity and the Middle-Class Home in Victorian England*. New Haven, 1999.

Turner, E.S. *Boys Will Be Boys: the Story of Sweeney Todd, Deadwood Dick, Sexton Blake, Billy Bunter, Dick Barton et al*. London, 1948.

5
'The Story of Our Lives': *The Moonstone* and the Indian Mutiny in *All the Year Round*

Hyungji Park

Writing in Charles Dickens's periodical *All the Year Round* (*AYR*) in 1862, Sidney Blanchard finds it necessary to mollify his readers near the opening of 'Famine in India':

> We can assure even that particularly uncomfortable person, known as 'the most delicate female', that she may peruse these pages without danger of having her feelings harrowed up by any unpleasant details of suffering such as nature, in a coarse and vulgar way, will make occasionally manifest. (*AYR* 22 February 1862, 519)

Blanchard is at once in jest and in earnest: even as he mocks this fictitious, squeamish female reader, he goes on in his article to oblige her, sanitizing 'nature', often 'coarse and vulgar', into a more palatable art.[1] But Blanchard's opening provokes some curious questions: who, indeed, is this 'most delicate female' who must be protected, what is it that she must be protected from, and what does Blanchard's caveat imply about the editorial boundaries for a 'domestic periodical' like *All the Year Round*? Furthermore, what is at stake in the representation of subjects like India? In a rhetorical move strikingly reminiscent of coverage of the Indian Rebellion of 1857,[2] in which the threatened safety of 'women and children' focused British nationalist outrage against India, here the female reader perusing *AYR* in a Victorian parlour shares such potential victimization with her countrywomen in India. In both cases, rescue is figured as a chivalric protection of endangered femininity. In this essay, I query the representability of India – or rather, the anxiety surrounding such representability – in Victorian writing in the post-Rebellion decade. What

I will propose is that a certain 'master-narrative' of chivalry emerges out of the Rebellion to provide a paradigm for subsequent representations of India in oblique, metaphorical ways. I consider both periodicals and novels by using Dickens's *All the Year Round* and Wilkie Collins's *The Moonstone* (serialized in *AYR* in 1868) as case studies.

The 'representability' of India certainly depends on the medium of publication, ranging from daily journalism to miscellanies anchored in fiction (or what might be called 'domestic periodicals') to novels. Such media represent newsworthy events (the Rebellion, famine in India) either mimetically or 'transformatively', in which the events at hand are imaginatively reshaped for ideological or artistic purposes. By separating, for simplicity's sake, the various media into the poles of 'news' versus 'fiction', three possibilities arise for the two poles' representations of their subjects: (1) both mimetic (news and fiction reflect outside events); (2) one mimetic (news) and the other transformative (fiction); and (3) both transformative. Some forms of realist or historical fiction might fall under option one; option two intuitively fits received categories of news and fiction. Certainly these categories are meant to be unstable groupings, since after all 'fiction' and 'news' both operate as constructed narratives. Coverage of the 1857 Rebellion corroborates the fictionality of these very categories; all forms of coverage – news, fiction, and forms in-between – are involved in legend-making and thus follow the counter-intuitive option three.

The Victorian press, after all, was instrumental in rousing the public to a particular hysteria about the Rebellion through its reporting of breaking news and exaggerated front-line gossip, with the two often indistinguishable from each other. Dailies like the London *Times* were aggressive in their coverage of the events, and yet just as the Rebellion spread, guerrilla-like, around different parts of India, the press's response matched such lack of regulation. With lines of demarcation difficult to ascertain, panicked rumours abounding, and verification of news hard to achieve, Victorian reporting of the Rebellion took on more of the elements of Gothic horror than of balanced journalism with its frequently sensational and contradictory accounts of rape, mutilation and massacre. In one conspicuous example, a clergyman who had written to the London *Times* with a detailed account of the treatment of British women kept hostage, prostituted, and publicly raped, turned out to have been more than a thousand miles from the site of the supposed outrage (Sharpe 1991, 33). Ultimately, the Victorian periodical press became one of most important tools in justifying to the public the immedi- British retaliation against the Indians.

Given such extensive reporting on the Rebellion, one would expect similar engagement in other periodicals like the weekly journals 'conducted' by Dickens. By the time Dickens began *AYR* (on 30 April 1859), he had been running *Household Words* (*HW*) for almost a decade (from 30 March 1850 to 28 May 1859). *HW* was Dickens's mouthpiece during the Rebellion itself, and a few articles dealt, mostly indirectly, with the events. With the end of *HW* caused by a dispute with his publishers Bradbury and Evans, Dickens intended to carry with him his readers, his 'staff of writers', and his own 'strongest energies', from one journal to the other, and repeatedly reassured the public that *AYR* was a continuation of *HW* (*HW* 28 May 1859, 601).[3] By the time of *AYR*, the Rebellion was no longer front-page news, and yet Dickens's intention remained the same during and after the events: he offered his readers a refuge from the onslaught of media coverage about front-line India. What is thus notable about *AYR*'s position on India is its comparative silence.

Accompanied by the slogan 'The Story of Our Lives From Year to Year', each issue of *AYR* opened not with the latest news flash but with a serialized novel, and editorial philosophy emphasized using humour and social commentary to entertain and instruct readers. After all, the slogan emblazoned across the top of every issue of *AYR* heralds the journal's purpose as a *narrativization of experience*. Enter into these pages, Dickens beckons, and reality, or lived experience, will be mediated through fiction, through story-telling: not only is there no 'truth' outside narrative, there is no news outside of fiction. The process of weaving tales out of current events is a domestication of news: Dickens viewed his journals as 'the comrade and friend of many thousands of people, of both sexes, and of all ages and conditions', providing wholesome family fare and light-handed guidance for middle-class households (*HW* 30 March 1850, 1). Yet such domestication did recognize the existence of outside events, that the 'lives' to be turned into 'story' included topics like India and the Rebellion. In fact, the slogan's allusion to Othello carries the recognition that narratives censored for domestic parlours harbour global sources.[4] But such censorship proceeds apace, as can be seen in Dickens's policy and Blanchard's practice, transmuting world events into a material appropriate for the safe haven of the magazine. Thus, with only a scattering of explicit material on India, *AYR* registers the Rebellion through a conspicuous, deliberate absence, with India signalled rather through fears and anxieties about the Empire which implicitly inform the journal's essays.

In what follows, I address how a particularly resonant paradigm arose out of the defining moment of the Rebellion to shape the representation of India for the latter half of the Victorian era. I call into question the possibility of any single 'India in the nineteenth-century media' and focus rather on *imagined Indias* in the Victorian press. Affinities in representation between novels and periodical literature are highlighted by focusing on the contents of *AYR*, particularly around the 1868 serialization of *The Moonstone*. In so doing, I place *The Moonstone* in relation to its contemporary publication context (defined proximately as the other essays in the issues of the periodical in which it was serialized), in the process offering insight into the material contexts for nineteenth century domestic fiction.[5] I turn now to *The Moonstone* before directing more concentrated attention to Dickens's periodical.

Romancing *The Moonstone*

A decade after the Rebellion, *The Moonstone*, the penultimate novel serialized in the first series of *AYR*, ran from 4 January to 8 August 1868.[6] The movement from rebellion to *Moonstone* – historical event to fictional paradigm – is an instance of orientalism in the making. What was sparked by a military conflict became figured in the Victorian imagination as a metaphor for colonial attack on the most sacred and inviolable of domestic spheres. The prevailing rhetoric surrounding the rebellion depicted the Indians as demoniacal in their targeting of British 'women and children', refracting stereotypical concerns with eastern despotism and sexual exploitation through a romance model of damsels in distress. Through such rhetoric in journalism and fiction, the Rebellion widened the rift between colonial and metropolitan spheres: in the simplest terms, the 'Mutiny master-narrative' that emerged posed the victimization of British women by Indian men, a scenario of 'reverse colonization' in which the classic sexualization of the imperial project – West of East – was turned back on the colonizers themselves. Eric Stokes (1986, 1) places the Rebellion within a category of 'movements *sans issue*, leaving no trace except a lasting fear of violence from below'. In this section, I briefly trace the origins and evolution of this imaginative paradigm and then examine in depth one of its most sophisticated examples.

The Rebellion began in May 1857 in Meerut, when a regiment of sepoys (Indian soldiers in the East India Company Army) rejected the new Enfield rifles issued by the British. Cartridges for these rifles needed to be bitten off before use and were believed to be greased with beef or pork fat, taboo to Hindus and Muslims. With fears of the endangerment of caste fuelled by British evangelism, the sepoys refused to use the questionable cartridges, were disciplined for their refusal, and broke into mutiny. The sepoys' defiance, considered to some extent to have converged with civilian disaffection over British rule and general popular resistance, developed rapidly across northern India, persisting in some areas for almost two years. Various elements suggest that the 'Mutiny' enjoyed support beyond the military: for instance, Stokes (1986, 17) notes that mob violence and police defection immediately followed the sepoys' firing upon their officers; Homi Bhabha discusses the circulation of chapatis among the populace after the introduction of the Enfield cartridges (but before the Rebellion itself) as a harbinger of political unrest; Rudrangshu Mukherjee anatomizes the long-term shifts in land governance that may have predisposed the peasantry to support the Rebellion. On the part of the British, the prescribed response to such a threat called for a joint chivalric and nationalistic defence. For one, graphically reported scenes of horror, centred on Cawnpore and Nana Sahib's captivity of British women, provided more fodder for such anxiety than any other incident in nineteenth-century British imperial history. The Hindu leader held hostage about 200 British women and children, and then, in his retreat from advancing European forces, ordered them killed. Amidst widely circulating, graphic stories of sexual atrocities – rape, humiliation, dismemberment – Cawnpore and Bibighar (the site of the subsequent killings) stood figuratively for the victimization of British women, despite evidence that the captive women probably worked at domestic chores and were not sexually molested.[7]

In turn, the rallying cry of protecting 'women and children' strategically functioned to elicit an enraged male defence, and as a useful side effect, this metaphor refigured British men as aggressors rather than as victims, protecting the image of western masculinity. As Jenny Sharpe (1991, 34) notes, 'A focus on the slaughter of defenseless women and children displaces attention away from the image of English men dying at the hands of native insurgents'. Those 'defenseless women', meanwhile, were imagined as victims of the ultimate, unspeakable crime: rape, rendered even more horrible in being inflicted by 'black' men. As a result, the British retaliated swiftly, brutally, and at times hysterically, leading to considerable bloodshed on both sides. Nancy Paxton argues that a shift took place in representations of interracial colonial rape after the rebellion, moving from a Gothic image of European rapists in removed and exotic lands (late eighteenth to mid-nineteenth century) to an 'abrupt transformation ... as English women replace Indian women as the victims' of rape (Paxton 1992, 7). In this reversal of the western imperialist's penetration of a dark feminized continent, 'the category of rape is reserved for English women alone' through selective reporting

(Sharpe 1991, 34). In its aftermath, the Rebellion irrevocably reshaped Victorian attitudes toward its empire into a deep distrust.

The master-narrative that results from the Rebellion, then, figures the British woman as quintessentially the victim – real, imagined, or potential – of the rapacity of eastern men, a threat that directly calls on British men to rally to their defence and a proof of their own masculinity. The resulting novels capitalized on a subject that supplied all the components of pulp fiction – sex, violence, and exotic locales – and numbered at least 50 by 1900 (Brantlinger 1988, 199). Noting that 'the sheer quantity' of such novels 'seems inversely proportional to its quality', Patrick Brantlinger (1988, 199–200) describes such accounts as 'display[ing] extreme forms of extropunitive projection, the racist pattern of blaming the victim [and using]...an absolute polarization of good and evil,...civilization and barbarism'. Predictably, most novels identifiably in the 'Mutiny novel' genre reinforced rather than challenged an ideologically motivated interpretation of the historical event, in an instance of what Edward Said (1993, 12) calls the novel's 'purpose...[in] sustaining the society's consent in overseas expansion'. A wider definition of the 'Mutiny novel' category could include numerous works in which the conflict informs the plots available to Victorian novelists.[8] Furthermore, by scripting international conflict into a chivalric call to arms, the Mutiny narrative causes a further ossification of gendered roles. While in an 1847 novel Jane Eyre could assert that she will 'go out [to the]...enslaved...[and] stir up mutiny' (Brontë 1847, 237), a decade later the image of a mutineering British woman is an oxymoron. Writers like Collins import this anxiety onto metropolitan shores: in scenes from the Rebellion, Anglo-Indian women (British women living in India) are under attack; in domestic Victorian novels, all British women – even those living quietly in Britain – stand at risk.

The Moonstone is, simply put, a monitory tale in which the danger of Indian sexuality is speculatively imported into the country mansions of Victorian society with devastating results.[9] The Moonstone – an Indian yellow diamond of oversized proportions which carries a mythic curse on any unrightful possessor of the stone (held anywhere, that is, other than in the forehead of the Hindu moon-god) – is plundered during the siege of Seringapatam by an Englishman. Upon his death, the plunderer, John Herncastle, wills the diamond to his niece, Rachel Verinder, as her eighteenth-birthday gift in revenge against Rachel's mother; the diamond is delivered to Rachel by her cousin/suitor Franklin Blake, who is unaware of the donor's vengeful intentions. What ought to be a safely domesticated artifact of empire – the diamond – circulates promiscuously (disappearing from Rachel's room on the very night of her birthday party) and prodigally distributes its legendary curse. The Moonstone attracts all sorts of uninvited guests to hover around Rachel: three Brahmin priests seeking to retrieve the diamond, fortune-hunting suitors, insensitive detectives. Gabriel Betteredge – household steward and conservative preserver of family values – sums up the Moonstone's threat as one of reverse colonization: 'here was our quiet English house', he laments, 'suddenly invaded by a devilish Indian Diamond – bringing after it a conspiracy of living rogues, set loose on us by the vengeance of a dead man' (Collins 1986, 67). Such tales of revenge, Betteredge suggests, belong in settings other than English country estates, other than 'in the nineteenth century, mind; in an age of progress, and in a country which rejoices in the blessings of the British constitution' (Collins 1986, 67). The Moonstone enters Victorian society in Collins's novel as a mobile instantiation of the worst western fears of a vengeful, mysterious, fanatical India desirous of redressing the wrongs of British imperialism.

On the night of Rachel's coming-of-age birthday festivities, all interested groups converge on the Verinder family estate, and the party functions as a crucial tableau of the mingling of colonial and domestic spheres. Rachel and the Moonstone – conflated physically and metonymically – are the evening's primary spectacles: with the diamond 'fit[ted]...as a brooch in the bosom of her white dress', Rachel 'was...particularly the centre-point toward which everybody's eyes were directed' (Collins 1986, 100). Rachel's body becomes the site of two jewels: her marriageability (desired by Blake and his rival Godfrey Ablewhite) and the diamond. While the party is in full swing, the Hindu priests arrive disguised as jugglers, 'exhibit their tricks' on the terrace before a delighted Rachel and other party guests, and visually confirm that their diamond is possessed by Rachel before they are chased off the grounds as intruders (Collins 1986, 105). Rachel remains blithely unaware of the Moonstone's curse or of the Indians' significance. Meanwhile, in appropriate chivalric mode, Rachel's self-styled protectors – primarily Betteredge and Blake – huddle together afterwards and invest this scene with horror. 'There she stood', Betteredge narrates, 'innocent of all knowledge of the truth, showing the Indians the Diamond in the bosom of her dress!' (Collins 1986, 106). Transfixed at the thought that the Moonstone on Rachel's bosom is within an arm's reach of its priest-followers, Betteredge figures the scene as a moment of racial as well as erotic voyeurism. Ironically, in expressing such concern about Rachel's visibility, Betteredge imports an Indian cultural custom, likening Rachel's visual availability to a violation of purdah.

In this text, at once a Mutiny narrative and termed 'the first and greatest of English detective novels' by T.S. Eliot (Eliot 1927, 413), the 'mystery' to be solved is not one of 'missing property' but that of 'the vulnerable British woman'. What is at stake is the conflation of Rachel's chastity and the Moonstone, caused by the intrusion of Indian loot into English domestic space. Once the diamond disappears, Rachel herself is suspected of the theft by Sergeant Cuff, and she suddenly finds her reputation compromised, with her chastity as well as her diamond stolen from her. As Blake laments: 'When I came here from London with that horrible Diamond, . . . I don't believe there was a happier household in England than this. Look at the household now! Scattered, disunited – the very air of the place poisoned with mystery and suspicion!' (Collins 1986, 223). The Moonstone tears apart the fabric of the Verinder household, and before events make a turn for the better, Rachel's reputation will remain suspect, she will continue estranged from her lover Blake, and Lady Verinder will die suddenly. Although the Rebellion itself is never named, in making the circulating Indian treasure effectively ruin Rachel, *The Moonstone* betrays an absorption of the Mutiny master-narrative of a British woman's victimization by Indian men or forces.

Yet even as Collins imports this motif of British victimization, the novel's resolution to this imbrication of femininity and empire points to a more complicated relationship to this Mutiny master-narrative. In a categorical shift, the second half of Collins's text becomes a domestic novel with a marriage ending, thus involving a generic as well as ideological reclamation that subsumes the Mutiny/detective plots of *The Moonstone* into a romance plot. In some ways, *The Moonstone* is a female sexual *bildungsroman* that subjects its heroine to an especially arduous course of coming to terms with her adulthood. Rachel's brief period of sexual circulation, between her safer roles as presexual virgin or as secured wife – from her eighteenth birthday on 21 June 1848 to her wedding day on 9 October 1849 – is dangerous and destabilizing, a liminal period punctuated by an encounter with empire. By combining courtship and Mutiny plots, the uncertain period of a woman's sexual availability becomes fearfully exaggerated through a meeting with an Indian diamond, while the courtship solution becomes figured as a chivalric competition among those British men who can rescue Rachel from her compromised position. Marriage, after all, is the all-solving device that disentangles Rachel from the Indian Diamond. And the most suitable executor of that task (that is, the 'detective') is not Cuff – who mistakes the purpose of the investigation when he suspects, rather than protects,

Rachel – but Blake. As it turns out, the Moonstone and India have little to do with the real 'danger' to Rachel, merely serving as metaphors upon which others can hang their evil intentions: the Indian jugglers are innocent; the Moonstone itself leaves Rachel's hands the very evening she receives it. The threats to Rachel, in fact, come from British forces, especially from those who profess to protect her: Godfrey Ablewhite is the Moonstone-thief and desires Rachel for her money; Cuff's imputations damage her reputation; what she sees as Blake's treachery breaks her heart.

Indeed, it is those people and artifacts associated with India that can disentangle Rachel from the plight in which the British men have placed her: the 'truth' is revealed and Rachel's name restored by the ingenuity and expertise of the half-Indian Ezra Jennings, using the imported Eastern drug, opium. Ezra Jennings, born in 'one of our colonies' to a British father and a mother of an unstated other race, is arguably the novel's most noble character and closely allied with Collins himself: besides the authorial power that Jennings mimics in reconstructing an earlier plot in the narrative, the descriptions of his fevered opium-fits are widely considered to be drawn from the author's own experiences (Collins 1986, 420). Yet even as the mixed-race Jennings is crucial to the plot's resolution, his own fate – instrumental, not an end in himself – points to the novel's final reliance on the separation of British and Indian spheres. In fact, although Robert Young states that 'hybridity . . . suggests the impossibility of essentialism', in Jennings's case his heritage seems to reproduce essentialist racial/national difference (Young 1995, 27). Jennings's 'piebald' hair literalizes such differentiation; his hair,

> by some freak of Nature, . . . lost its colour in the most startlingly partial and capricious manner. Over the top of his head it was still of the deep black which was its natural colour. Round the sides of his head – without the slightest gradation of grey to break the force of the extraordinary contrast – it had turned completely white. The line between the two colours preserved no sort of regularity. At one place, the white hair ran up into the black; at another, the black hair ran down into the white. (Collins 1986, 371)

There is no possibility of 'grey': black and white may meet and even run up and down into each other, but the boundary between them, no matter how irregular, is distinct. Whether black and white refer to race or culture (black was his 'natural colour' but he has gained 'white' after years of British living), Jennings's head demonstrates the immiscibility of spheres in Collins's novel; he himself, the racial equivalent of the impermissible 'grey' zone, cannot survive. Pursued by an unspecified but damning accusation from the past – an unnamed, unrelenting taint which smacks not of a particular crime but of a basic English mistrust of the foreign, unfamiliar-looking racial hybrid – he ends in death. While Blake is permitted restitution within metropolitan society, Jennings – his 'darker' double – is never given a comparable opportunity to prove his innocence. Only vicariously through Blake can Jennings achieve exoneration and a union with his beloved 'Ella', a universal 'She'.

Despite Jennings's centrality, the novel's concluding marriage plot is reserved exclusively for the central, and British, pair. Blake, freshly returned from an introspective foreign journey, is now worthy of Rachel's hand, and the couple's union joins family fortunes (the two are only children and first cousins) and restores the foundations of a Victorian society badly shaken by the intrusion of the colonial artifact. All other potential or desired pairings in this novel do not come to fruition: Ablewhite and Rosanna Spearman (the servant-girl in love with Blake) die. Those who cross cultural and national borders – the Brahmin triad and the traveller Mr Murthwaite – operate in a nonheterosexual world. Domestic and colonial spheres are distanced to their original rift, and Rachel settles into married domesticity and maternity while the Moonstone is returned to the Hindu moon-god; indeed, the ritual of the Moonstone's restoration metonymically replaces the traditional narrative closure of the Verinder–Blake wedding. Collins dallies with, but does not endorse, what Anne McClintock might term an 'enlightened hybridity' of the mixing of cultural spheres (McClintock 1995, 10).

Collins's attitude toward the Rebellion and to Britain's empire in general is difficult to assess. One 'periodical context' for *The Moonstone* can be seen in Collins's earlier writings for Dickens's journals, closer in time to the Rebellion, and at first glance these seem to be more directly critical of India. In 'A Sermon for Sepoys' (*HW* 27 February 1858), Collins purports to render an old Indian tale within a frame narrative which equates the sepoys with 'Betrayers and Assassins' (Collins 1858, 247). But the tale that comprises the bulk of the essay rather advocates active participation in life over intellectual philosophizing (and weren't the sepoys action-takers?), while the supposed lesson of the piece – 'The Life that is Most Acceptable to the Supreme Being, is the Life that is Most Useful to the Human Race' – seems hard to read as a condemnation of Indians. In fact, given Dickens's editorial practices, it is possible that Dickens was the one who added the clear moral of the frame. Similarly, in Collins's collaborative novella with Dickens, 'The Perils of Certain English Prisoners', Collins's biographer Catherine Peters writes, 'Dickens wanted to refer indirectly to the Rebellion; the natives were to be seen as treacherous and cunning; and the English, especially the women, as courageous and noble' (Peters 1991, 182). Published on 7 December 1857, as the Christmas extra of *Household Words*, the story transplants the events of the rebellion to a South American island, and its full title didactically elaborates on the 'women and children' theme: 'The Perils of Certain English Prisoners, and their treasure in women, children, silver, and jewels' (see Figure 5.1). The consummate villains of the piece are the 'Sambos' (defined as 'half-negro and half-Indian' and standing in for the sepoys [Collins 1857, 2]) who double-cross their English employers. Again, since Dickens was known to write out explicit instructions for his collaborators on the Christmas numbers (see Stone 1968, Appendices D and E, 661–6), it is difficult to separate out Collins's views from his accession to Dickens's directives, but Lillian Nayder (1992) makes a persuasive argument that Collins's section of the novella (Part 2) is notably less imperialist than are Dickens's sections (Parts 1 and 3). It is unclear how much of *Perils*'s aggressive anti-Indian sentiment can be attributed to Collins, but the express villainy of the 'half-breed', quite different from Ezra Jennings's nobility in *The Moonstone*, is most explicit in the portions of *Perils* attributable to Dickens himself.[10]

In *The Moonstone* itself, Collins is remarkably neutral. India is, on the one hand, the origin of an unrelenting, unsympathetic curse; on the other, it is a site of luxuriant, exotic beauty and power. Moreover, race does not determine either reader sympathy for the various characters nor their moral probity. While the Indian triad commit the only real crime – murder – in a novel full of peccadilloes, they are only replaying Herncastle's bloody acquisition of the Moonstone, and while the English characters see the Hindus as effeminate, cunning and unscrupulous, we as readers also see them in India as noble, self-sacrificial and dedicated. The actual culprit of the case, as we have seen, is the thoroughly hypocritical Ablewhite, whose actions ironize the racial supremacy implicit in his name; meanwhile, the half-Indian Jennings is the paragon of virtue. Although the novel concludes with a separation of metropolitan and colonial spheres that we are expected to welcome, the latter is not subjugated to the former. The Moonstone's fate, after all, is telling. The history of the yellow diamond before it reaches Rachel's hands makes it clear that the Moonstone is meant to stand metonymically for Indian national and Hindu religious sovereignty. Just as India was ruled successively by the Moghul and the British empires, the Moonstone moves

THE PERILS

OF

CERTAIN ENGLISH PRISONERS,

AND THEIR TREASURE

IN WOMEN, CHILDREN, SILVER, AND JEWELS.

THE EXTRA CHRISTMAS NUMBER OF **HOUSEHOLD WORDS.**

CONDUCTED BY CHARLES DICKENS.

CONTAINING THE AMOUNT OF ONE NUMBER AND A HALF.

CHRISTMAS, 1857.

Price
3d.

INDEX.

CHAPTER I.

THE ISLAND OF SILVER-STORE.

IT was in the year of our Lord one thousand seven hundred and forty-four, that I, Gill Davis to command, His Mark, having then the honor to be a private in the Royal Marines, stood a-leaning over the bulwarks of the armed sloop Christopher Columbus, in the South American waters off the Mosquito shore.

My lady remarks to me, before I go any further, that there is no such christian-name as Gill, and that her confident opinion is, that the name given to me in the baptism wherein I was made, &c., is Gilbert. She is certain to be right, but I never heard of it. I was a foundling child, picked up somewhere or another, and I always understood my christian-name to be Gill. It is true that I was called Gills when employed at Snorridge Bottom betwixt Chatham and Maidstone, to frighten birds; but that had nothing to do with the Baptism wherein I was made, &c., and wherein a number of things were promised for me by somebody, who let me alone ever afterwards as to performing any of them, and who, I consider, must have been the Beadle. Such name of Gills was entirely owing to my cheeks, or gills, which at that time of my life were of a raspy description.

My lady stops me again, before I go any further, by laughing exactly in her old way and waving the feather of her pen at me. That action on her part, calls to my mind as I look at her hand with the rings on it—— Well! I won't! To be sure it will come in, in its own place. But it's always strange to me, noticing the quiet hand, and noticing it (as I have done, you know, so many times)

a-fondling children and grandchildren asleep, to think that when blood and honor were up—there! I won't! not at present!—Scratch it out.

She won't scratch it out, and quite honorable; because we have made an understanding that everything is to be taken down, and that nothing that is once taken down shall be scratched out. I have the great misfortune not to be able to read and write, and I am speaking my true and faithful account of those Adventures, and my lady is writing it, word for word.

I say, there I was, a-leaning over the bulwarks of the sloop Christopher Columbus in the South American waters off the Mosquito shore: a subject of his Gracious Majesty King George of England, and a private in the Royal Marines.

In those climates, you don't want to do much. I was doing nothing. I was thinking of the shepherd (my father, I wonder?) on the hill-sides by Snorridge Bottom, with a long staff, and with a rough white coat in all weathers all the year round, who used to let me lie in a corner of his hut by night, and who used to let me go about with him and his sheep by day when I could get nothing else to do, and who used to give me so little of his victuals and so much of his staff, that I ran away from him—which was what he wanted all along, I expect—to be knocked about the world in preference to Snorridge Bottom. I had been knocked about the world for nine-and-twenty years in all, when I stood looking along those bright blue South American waters. Looking after the shepherd, I may say. Watching him in a half-waking dream, with my eyes half-shut, as he, and his flock of sheep, and his two

---

Figure 5.1 Front page of 'The Perils of Certain English Prisoners', from *Household Words*, Christmas 1857.

from Hindu sacred item to Muslim loot (at the beginning of the eighteenth century) and then British plunder (at the end of the century). Meanwhile, the historical model for Collins's Moonstone, the Koh-i-Noor, was gained by the British as a result of the Anglo-Sikh Wars of 1848–49 and ceremonially presented to Queen Victoria in 1850. Within the novel, the Indian jewel is repeatedly threatened with being cut up into several smaller stones, destroying its religious potency but increasing its economic value in an ideal formula for an exploitative British imperialism, but Collins explicitly rejects this option. While it may be unjustified to propose that Collins obliquely enacts the dream of Indian independence through the jewel's return to its Hindu position, the novel's resolution certainly favours a restoration of social equilibrium in both British and Indian societies rather than an imperialist model of conquest and domination.

Part of the difficulty in ascertaining Collins's position arises from the novel's reticence about India. While I have argued that a Mutiny masternarrative structures the very premise of *The Moonstone*, and specific moments in the novel betray debts to popular coverage of the event,[11] the Rebellion itself actually appears nowhere in Collins's text and is, at best, an open secret, unnamed but yet recognizable. At a decade's remove, *The Moonstone* would not be possible without the Rebellion but also profits from the imaginative distance permitted by the hiatus. The enduring transformative legacies from the watershed event were in place – such as the immediate changes in governance (from the East India Company's rule to Crown jurisdiction) and military staffings (an increased ratio of British troops to sepoys). And yet in an intriguing conflation of subject and audience, the chivalric model for anti-rebellion defence becomes transferred into writing about the Rebellion as well. Just as Anglo-Indian women, named and unnamed, entered the annals of history as figures to be protected during the Rebellion, so does Blanchard's 'most delicate female' remain as the presumed audience from whom unpalatable subjects must be shielded. Like other subjects impolite for a middle-class, domestic, and often female readership (money, servants, homosexuality), the Indian Rebellion permeates, transforms, and yet remains unspeakable in *The Moonstone*.

Representing India in *All the Year Round*

In turning to *All the Year Round*, a reasonable assumption would be that the periodical essays evince a more direct engagement with India than does Collins's novel. After all, *AYR* boasted editorials, features on science, history and politics, and numerous other nonfiction categories in addition to fiction. In actual fact, the majority of the essays in *AYR* – aside from a handful expressly on India or the Rebellion – by and large share *The Moonstone*'s silence on the rebellion, echoing the novel's strategies of circumlocution, ellipsis and metaphor. The contents of *AYR* betray the same anxieties about representing India that underlie the Mutiny master-narrative, and also embrace a romance paradigm for protecting the female reader. In this section, I address the range of coverage about India and the Rebellion in *AYR*, to consider what it means to be a domestic periodical that does not talk about the empire. More specifically, I construct my discussion around several narrowing concentric frames: India in the ten-year run of *AYR*, articles on the Rebellion during that time, and then specific articles within the seven-month period during which *The Moonstone* was serialized.

AYR's engagement with India can be loosely grouped into three modes: (1) a serialized anchor novel like *The Moonstone*; (2) nonfictional essays on India written from the perspective of a correspondent or other informant; and (3) essays, fictional or nonfictional, not specifically on India but which harbour prevailing Victorian assumptions about the subcontinent; the latter two groups are the subjects of this section. The essays in category two, which capture a palpable flavour of nineteenth-century India, are authored by contributors ranging from those like Blanchard who wrote from personal experience to, in one case that I found, a self-identified Indian writer who offers his thoughts on how the British should behave in India. In an intervention on the cotton question, the unidentified author of 'Cotton Cultivation in Bengal' (19 October 1861) advocates that India can be turned into a successful cotton supplier for Britain through respect for the native workers, not through imposing imperialist practices. Near the end of the essay, he confesses his race:

> These remarks are written by one of the Hindoo race, who confid-ently hopes and believes that if British capitalists will adopt proper methods for the raising of cotton in India, they will not only be able to invest their capital profitably to themselves, but will also be the instruments of conferring lasting benefits upon the people of the country. (92)[12]

But writers wholly unfamiliar with India could be just as powerful as the more informed writers in shaping Victorian public opinion about the subcontinent (category 3). One unidentified contributor in 1860 laments that '[t]his country seems to consider India, and India alone, as important' (27 October 1860, 69). Professedly writing from a metropolitan perspective, he alludes to the Rebellion in stating that 'We fight for India, with India, in India', and declares that 'we impoverish ourselves (domestically) to pay for the Indian servants who fan our sons who are slowly dying in India, and *of* India', while those sons 'come back sick, with ruined constitutions, from India', harbouring 'tremendously expensive habits' and disrespectful of 'the comparatively unimportant mother country' (69–70; original emphasis). In this proliferation of prepositions – for, with, in, of, from – that describe British relations with India, this writer posits a model of British subjection to a whimsical India. For an audience with limited prior knowledge about India, this paradigm about Anglo-Indian relations derives its power from the unself-conscious simplicity of its inversion of metropole–colony power relations. Thus the idea of India that emerges from a ten-year overview of *AYR* is a composite of accounts stemming from stereotype as well as knowledge. India ranges from being a realistic political entity to a cosmetically re-engineered fiction refracted through a Victorian's imagined India. In either case, readers who relied exclusively on *AYR* for a portrait of India would be in the position of the blind men groping the elephant, receiving fragmentary and contradictory input. To such readers, the subcontinent would be, haphazardly, (1) a producer of cotton; (2) an orientalist site for jugglers and other exotic tricksters; (3) a place that some British men and women, including soldiers, live in, apparently with some difficulty; (4) a land where the native people are disloyal and inscrutable; (5) a habitat for exotic flora/fauna; and, briefly and vaguely, (6) the location of some distant conflict called the Mutiny or the Sepoy Rebellion.[13]

Articles in this last category assume a basic familiarity with the events of the Rebellion. Although most of the direct responses to the rebellion in Dickens's journals naturally came at the end of *Household Words*, *AYR* witnesses the evolution of Rebellion coverage from specific accounts, policy recommendations, and analysis, initially, to fiction and meta-phor.[14] In the first year of *AYR*, 'An Empire Saved' (28 May 1859) and 'European Mutiny in India' (30 July 1859) debate the Rebellion's events and aftermath, with the first essay assessing contributing factors in the conflict (such as technology and regional differences), and the second addressing the post-Rebellion administrative shuffle. When we jump ahead to 1865, the Rebellion is clearly an event of the past: brief allusions can be made without emotion ('Our Colonies', 9 September); and in the next year the Enfield rifle can be cited without connection even to India ('Small Arms', 5 May). In the same year, a retrospective memoir by a man who was a 'very young soldier, newly arrived in India' during the Rebellion, focuses on his personal experiences of pain rather than the political consequences of the event ('Under Fire' 17 February, 125). Blanchard's 'Indian Servants' (27 June 1863) is perhaps the most telling, as it attests to enduring trauma. Blanchard relates the story of a 'native bearer . . . who was a particular favourite, . . . [and] remarkabl[y]' kind to children but who is promptly hanged when '*identified as* a principal agent in the outbreak at Meerut, where, *it seems*, he had *assisted* in slaughtering men, women, and children in cold blood' (417; my emphases). The stock phrase of recrimination – coldblooded 'slaughter' of 'men, women, and children' – is not a particularized accusation but a kneejerk, all-purpose response that overrides all the uncertainties in the case.

Of course, documenting the half-dozen essays on the Rebellion, from among the thousands of articles in *AYR* over a ten-year period, is to emphasize the needles in the haystack. Rather, an imagined India is shaped more potently in the daily routine of essays not overtly on India. I narrow the scope of vision now to a defined set of *AYR* volumes to provide a 'snapshot', as it were, of the periodical as well as to examine closely such uses of India and the Empire. The seven-month period during which *The Moonstone* was serialized offers a meaningful subset of *AYR* as it illuminates parallels between the novel and its publication context.

Between the first installment of *The Moonstone* on 4 January 1868 (volume 19, no. 454) and its last on 8 August 1868 (volume 20, no. 485), about 150 other pieces appeared, including essays, poems, and serialized and non-serialized fiction. Essays were the biggest category in this set (about 110), either first- or third-person, mostly nonfiction, with an accessible, audience-friendly tone, on topics ranging from natural history to historical anecdote, technological innovations to science for the lay-person, cooking suggestions to social criticism, travel accounts to literary humour. While *The Moonstone* was the anchor novel opening each issue, these months saw, in fiction, about ten pieces of short serialized pieces (ranging from two to five installments), about another 20 pieces of short (non-serialized) fiction, as well as the wrap-up of Percy Fitzgerald's novel *The Dear Girl*. Some of the less successful novels in *AYR*, like *The Dear Girl*, would begin as title novels and then be superseded by a higher-profile novel, continuing as a secondary piece until completed. Poetry was also featured in these pages (about a dozen pieces and none of them particularly memorable). The quality of the essays varied but the journal was, by and large, ephemeral; it is fair to say that Collins's novel and Dickens's occasional pieces are the only items still read from these pages. With Dickens on an American tour during much of this time, Dickens himself wrote less than usual, with his contributions during this period limited to *Holiday Romance, George Silverman's Explanation*, and 'A Debt of Honour'.[15] Finally, it must be noted that these seven months demonstrate less attention to the colonies or to foreign lands than is characteristic of the ten-year run of *AYR*, with only two essays explicitly about India. 'My First Tiger' (1 February) is a first-person coming-of-age tale of tiger-hunting in India, while 'In the Indian Archipelago' (9 May) discusses the culture, customs, and religions of the people of Java, Bali, Malay and similar locations.[16]

Within this context, various articles incorporate implied views of India or the empire. I take two examples, one a piece of short fiction and another a natural history essay. In 'Sir John's Troubles', a four-part novella overlapping in its brief serialization with the first installment of *The Moonstone* and sharing Collins's concerns, India stands as a source of sexual suspicion and contamination disruptive to an unsuspecting British society. The plot traces a major-general retired from Indian service (Sir John Milson) who faces the challenge of his career when his best friend Colonel Laber asks him to set up a London establishment – without his wife's knowledge – for Laber's two illegitimate, mixed-race daughters. Milson and Laber are doubles for each other, standing as opposing models for Englishmen's responses to the Rebellion. Sir John is a decorated officer with 'thirty-five years' hard professional work in the East', who has done 'the state excellent service' during the Rebellion, has returned to the metropole without losing 'the faculty of enjoying England and English life' and holding a knighthood and various club memberships (28 December 1867, 66, 69). Laber, meanwhile, whose very name suggests toil in contrast to 'Milson's' hereditary right, remains in India, working to provide for his two daughters (to whom his pension cannot extend): he pays the price of miscegenation through exile from England. These daughters, as the root of subsequent upheaval, corroborate H.L. Malchow's description of 'half-breeds' as seen in the nineteenth century as 'visible reminders . . . [of] a white fall from grace' (Malchow 1996, 177). The resulting plot twists weave a fine line between comedy (white lies, mistaken identities, and sexual guilt imputed to Sir John) and tragedy (his wife Annie suspects and leaves him), but finally document Sir John's tarnishing by India's powerful sexual taint. All is ultimately solved: the secret is revealed, the childless Milsons make Laber's daughters their heirs, and Laber can return to England. As in *The Moonstone*, an Indian past brings transgressive sexual secrets into English space, only to be patrolled through a domesticated ending and reaffirmation of 'family values'.

In a different vein, 'Flies', a humorous natural history essay, fantastic-ally displaces European imperialism onto the world of entomology. The writer proposes that just as 'civilized man is, and always has been, more than a match for the savage', this triumph of 'the Anglo-Saxon and other European races' over 'the aborigines' can be extended to 'the case of house-flies' (4 January 1868, 90). Thus, 'Not only does the European drive away the Maori . . . but . . . the European house-fly drives away the New Zealand fly' (90). In this bathetic analogy between western imperi-alism and natural selection, the writer suggests that the European house-fly has absorbed such supremacy by virtue of proximity: 'Is it that all living things that are much in the society of, or in immediate contiguity to man in a high state of civilization, have their faculties sharpened by the association?' (90). At the other extreme, European house-flies may find themselves outmatched by the exotic Abyssinian seroot which is possessed of a 'terrific' proboscis, one that 'is double, and appears to be disproportioned, being two-thirds the length of the entire insect' (92). The writer continues,

> When this fly attacks an animal or a man . . . it pierces the skin instantaneously, like the prick of a red-hot needle driven deep into the flesh, at the same time the insect exerts every muscle of its body by buzzing with its wings as it buries the instrument to its greatest depth. (92)

This creature carries the kind of oversized sexualized equipment that renders it grotesque but fascinating, rendering pale European versions unable to compete in fleshly matters. The writer concludes in a flourish of zoological xenophobia: 'Better English flies and gnats, better Amer-ican mosquitoes and gallinippers, than such a flying fiend as the Abys-sinian seroot' (92).

But neither 'Sir John's Troubles' nor 'Flies' – essays fairly representative of those published in *AYR* – offer any sense of what is happening in world news from January to August 1868. I began this project piqued by Collins's oblique use of the rebellion in *The Moonstone* and intent on reconstructing the ways in which the contents of *AYR* might have sup-plemented the novel's silence for Victorian readers. After all, it is par-ticularly justifiable in this instance to pose a relationship between the novel and the essays accompanying it: during *The Moonstone*'s serializa-tion, Collins – who had worked intermittently for both *AYR* and *HW* as a staff writer or as an editor – took over some of Dickens's editorial duties while the latter was on his American tour (from November 1867 to May 1868). Thus, in a unique instance in *AYR* for any writer other than Dickens, Collins was reading, editing and selecting the articles that could influence his audience's reading experience of his novel. And yet, despite this connection, my discovery has not been of difference between novel and its context but rather repetition: the *AYR* pages surrounding *The Moonstone* do not fill in such gaps in information – rather, they echo them. What may be expected as an agonistic relationship between a novel and its nonfiction periodical counterparts ends up being more of a collaboration which renders all news as fiction, with Empire metaphorized as sexual currency.

Dickens Inc.

For a weekly journal that ran for ten years, to twenty volumes, with over 600 pages in each volume, *All the Year Round* followed a remarkably consistent editorial philosophy. In his role as a genial but guiding moralist, Dickens intended 'to assist in the discussion of the social questions of the day', claiming 'to bring into innumerable homes, from the stirring world around us, the knowledge of many social wonders, good and evil' (Stone 1968, 26; *HW* 30 March 1850, 1).[17] Contributions were anonymous, and Dickens – in a paternalism ranging from the benign to the tyrannical – accepted responsibility for them all, as was explicitly stated: 'The statements and opinions of this Journal generally, are, of course, to be received as the statements and opinions of its Conductor' (26 December 1863, 419). Dickens follows this line, from an extraordinary note at the end of the run of Charles Reade's novel *Hard Cash*, with a disclaimer: 'But this is not so, in the case of a work of fiction first published in these pages as a serial story, with the name of an eminent writer attached to it.' In Dickens's conclusion – 'I do not consider myself at liberty to exercise that control over his text which I claim as to other contributions' – he grants authorial autonomy to novelists, while asserting control over all other pieces in his journals. In actual fact, his novel-writers were subject to his governing 'guidance' as well. Percy Fitzgerald, one of Dickens's writers and the author of the overly laudatory 1902 *Memories of Charles Dickens*, for one, writes that 'each of the five or six novels I wrote for him [three for *AYR*] was planned and debated with him – the characters, the story as it advanced, the embarrassing tangles which he resolved, the very titles. Then every line almost he revised and corrected' (Fitzgerald 1902, 4), and goes on to document this statement through letters from Dickens. Fitzgerald welcomed such aid; other more sophisticated writers did not. Elizabeth

Gaskell, for one, famously wrangled with Dickens over more than one of her contributions to the periodicals, including *Cranford*, *North and South* and 'A Dark Night's Work'.

Douglas Jerrold, approached to write for Dickens's journals, responded to *Household Words'* rule of anonymity with, 'So I see, . . . for I see Charles Dickens's name on every page' (Fitzgerald 1902, 135) and 'refused to contribute' (see Lohrli 1973, 26). Diversity of opinion was not sought: *AYR* and *HW* were 'Dickens's mouthpiece[s], . . . periodical[s] in which ideas and opinions were advanced, not one[s] in which opposing points of view were debated' (Lohrli 1973, 12). Dickens viewed his journals as vehicles through which he could articulate his views about social issues more overtly than he could in his novels, capitalizing on the wide audience he had gained through the fiction. Oppenlander writes that 'Essentially Dickens sought to publish essays that expressed his point of view about subjects which impressed, intrigued or distressed him . . . His imagination for contriving subjects was boundless, but his time limited, so he farmed out his ideas' (Oppenlander 1984, 35, 36). Dickens's pool of writers thus became extensions of his own pen, writing for him rather than for their own fame. Fitzgerald mocks these young writers (himself one of them), as 'only too eager and apt at imitation. They were even clever enough to pick up a sort of mock Dickensian dialect' (Fitzgerald 1902, 254). This, however, could predictably cause difficulties for other contributors. Oppenlander goes on to say: 'Because he accepted responsibility for what was printed anonymously, he exercised total control over the contributor's text, and felt not only at liberty, but morally obliged to reject what he disagreed with or to change it to suit himself' (1984, 39). Taking his task as editor very seriously, Dickens assiduously corrected virtually all of the writing that went into his journals. 'Editorial revision was extensive – and drastic', as Lohrli (1973, 15) writes: 'Dickens sometimes rewrote articles and stories almost entirely', even changing the endings. Stone (1968, Appendix A, 627–40) reprints Dickens's substantial corrections of an essay for *HW* ('Foreigners' Portraits of Englishmen,' by W.H. Wills and E.C. Grenville Murray). To this day, *AYR* essays are routinely inaccurately attributed to Dickens himself. Louis James advocates reconstructing 'the "holistic" character of a journal, the way in which it possesses a specific identity through the total effect of its contents, tone and style' (James 1982, 110), and with Dickens at the helm of this periodical, it is fair to argue for an editorial consistency, almost a 'corporate identity', governing *AYR*.

In discussing *AYR*'s portrayal of the Rebellion, then, it is appropriate to consider Dickens's personal view of the events in India. Partly conditioned by the fact that his son Walter fought in the Rebellion, Dickens responded with genocidal impulses in his often-cited letter:

> I wish I were Commander in Chief in India. The first thing I would do to strike that Oriental race with amazement . . . [would be] to proclaim to them . . . that I should do my utmost to exterminate the Race upon whom the stain of the late cruelties rested; . . . and was now proceeding, with all convenient dispatch and merciful swiftness of execution, to blot it out of mankind and raze it off the face of the Earth. (Letter to Angela Burdett Coutts, 4 October 1857; *Letters* 459)

Such violent desire for racial extermination lies behind Dickens's own contributions on the rebellion (including *Perils*) and behind his editing of *AYR*. Yet it is telling that Dickens's opinion cannot be readily extrapolated from an overview of *AYR*. Dickens's imperative that the journals serve as domestic companions, as hearthside vehicles of social commentary, prevailed over his vision of the periodicals as vehicles for his opinions. *AYR* and *HW* were, after all, 'to be admitted into many homes with affection and confidence; to be regarded as a friend by children and old people; to be thought of in affliction and in happiness' (*HW* 30 March 1850, 1), and could hardly engage with sensitive political issues of great controversy.[18] Linda Hughes and Michael Lund (1991, 110) propose that the 'temporal and spatial growth of a serial . . . parallels the Victorian principles of empire'. While such structural analogies may be suggestive, in the case of *AYR* the journal disavows any such affinity. For 'Dickens Inc.' – the editorial and writerly apparatus generating *All the Year Round* – empire rather becomes the material for narrative, in nonfiction and other essays as well as in its serialized novels. The Mutiny master-narrative and its romance plot may have originated from a specific event but reflects a prevailing Victorian mode – followed by Dickens and Collins – of securing 'the story of our lives' away from the truly disturbing news of the globe.

Notes

I would like to thank Suzanne Churchill, Adrian Frazier, Lillian Nayder, and the editors of this collection for their readings of and productive suggestions on earlier versions of this essay, and my research assistant Jamie Leahey for work on the statistical survey of *AYR*.

1. Sidney Laman Blanchard wrote about ten essays for *AYR* on India besides 'Famine in India' (22 February 1862), including 'India and Cotton' (13 July 1861), 'Nil Darpan' (9 November 1861), 'Punch in India' (26 July 1862), and 'Yesterday and To-day in India' (17 October 1863). Blanchard was a newspaper editor for several years in India from 1853 onwards, and his essays give a fairly well-rounded picture of Anglo-India. Blanchard focuses primarily on British relations with the Indians, and his attitude ranges from advocacy of India before a British public to sharing that public's racism. Some of his pieces for *AYR* and *Household Words* (*HW*) were later collected in *The Ganges and the Seine* (1862) and *Yesterday and Today in India* (1867).

2. The 1857 conflict has been variously termed the Indian Mutiny, Revolt, or Uprising, and sometimes cited as the first Indian war of independence. Following the editorial policy of this collection, I prefer the term 'Rebellion' to refer to the events, but retain 'Mutiny', as in my title, when referring to a Victorian conception of the rebellion.

3. In fact, Dickens laboured to buy back his copyright to *HW* in order to include its name on the front page of every issue of *AYR*, as the phrase 'With Which is Incorporated Household Words'. While there were some differences between the two journals (*AYR* always opened with a serialized novel; Dickens contributed less to and exercised less direct editorial control over *AYR* because of his increasingly frequent absences from London on reading tours), editorial philosophy and Dickens's intentions did not change between journals.

4. Adapted from *Othello* Act I Scene 3, the phrase borrows from the opening of Othello's speech vindicating his marriage to Desdemona before the assembled Venetian senators. Othello explains that he came to court Desdemona because her father sought his friendship by 'question[ing] me the story of my life/From year to year'. Othello goes on in this speech to enthrall his audience – as he presumably did Desdemona – with tales of 'Cannibals that each other eat, / The Anthropophagi, and men whose heads / Do grow beneath their shoulders'.

5. Serialization, after all, was a common mode of publication for the Victorian novel. Among those novels serialized in *AYR* and *HW* were Collins's *The Woman in White* (*AYR* 1860) and *No Name* (*AYR* 1862–63), Dickens's *Hard Times* (*HW* 1854), *A Tale of Two Cities* (*AYR* 1859), and *Great Expectations* (*AYR* 1860–61) and Elizabeth Gaskell's *Cranford* (*HW* 1851–53) and *North and South* (*HW* 1855).

6. All my references to *AYR* are to the first series, which ran from 30 April 1859 to 28 November 1868. After ten years of *AYR*'s publication, Dickens began a 'new series' (starting a week after the end of the first), so that the multi–volume set would be kept within 20 tomes (longer sets would be harder to sell). For the new series, Dickens made some changes in the journal's format and appearance, and eliminated the 'Extra Christmas numbers'. This second series, begun less than two years before Dickens's death, continued until 1893, with his oldest son, Charles Junior, as editor until 1888.

7. The most recent historical study of the rebellion – Andrew Ward (1996) – focuses on the events at Cawnpore.

8. Some critics suggest that Dickens's view of the French Revolution in *A Tale of Two Cities* (*AYR* 1859) was influenced by the Rebellion (Oddie 1972, esp. 14–15; Brantlinger 1988, 208). Modular units of rebellion narratives can be

found within works such as Arthur Conan Doyle's *The Sign of Four*, in which Jonathan Small's sub-narrative reads as an archetypal racist version of the Rebellion. At the same time, it is not merely incidental that Collins's and Doyle's examples are works of detective fiction. The rise of the detective genre coincides with the height of the British empire, and early examples of the genre, which can be seen as prompted by the need to patrol the new foreign elements within English society, polarize good and evil often along lines of the British versus the foreign. As an essentially conservative genre, detective fiction protects the status quo, restores property, and polices offenders/ challengers to established society.

9.   While John Reed's 1973 article stood for nearly two decades as the only extended treatment of empire and *The Moonstone*, there has been an explosion of articles or book segments on the topic published since 1991. These studies include those by Robert Crooks (1993), Deirdre David (1995, especially 17–20 and 142–7), Ian Duncan (1994), Jaya Mehta (1995), Lillian Nayder ('Robinson Crusoe' 1992), Ashish Roy (1993) and Ronald R. Thomas (1991).

10.   See also Laura Peters's essay, elsewhere in this collection, for a discussion of 'Perils'.

11.   For one, when John Herncastle plunders a dagger with the Moonstone embedded in its handle during the siege of Seringapatam at the novel's opening, the dagger may owe part of its description to the 'sceptre ... inlaid with gems' publicly displayed in London in 1859 and taken at the siege of Lucknow during the quelling of the rebellion (*Art-Journal* 1 June 1859, 195). This exhibition of the 'Lucknow sceptre', advertised as 'of beautiful workmanship ... elaborately fluted ... and enriched with rubies and emeralds', was one of the many public shows about India, including panoramas of the Rebellion, that took place soon after 1857 (195).

12.   While authorship for most of the essays in *Household Words*, the predecessor to *All the Year Round*, is available to us through Anne Lohrli's work on the *HW* Office Book (1973), comparable documentary sources are not extant for *AYR*, and authorship has been determined for only a fraction of *AYR* articles (see Oppenlander 1984). What author attributions I do give for *AYR* and *HW* essays are from Oppenlander and Lohrli, respectively. Since male writers greatly outnumbered female ones among the known contributors to *AYR*, I use a male pronoun in referring to this contributor.

13.   See, for instance, for (1): 'India and Cotton' (13 July 1861), 'Cotton Cultivation in Bengal' (19 October 1861), 'State and Prospects of Cotton' (13 December 1862). For (2): 'Mediums under Other Names' (19 April 1862), 'Shots at Elephants' (29 October 1864), 'Something Like a Conjuror' (11 February 1865). For (3): 'The Englishman in Bengal' (23 February 1861), 'The Great Shoe Question' (28 June 1862), 'Punch in India' (26 July 1862), 'Housekeeping in India' (31 January 1863), 'Something to be Done in India' (26 September 1863), 'Yesterday and To-day in India' (17 October 1863), 'Military Mismanagement' (5 December 1863), 'The Bengal Police' (12 December 1863). For (4): 'Indian Servants' (27 June 1863). For (5): *AYR* contains an extensive natural history series by Sir Emerson Tennent, of about a dozen linked articles, on the fauna in Ceylon (now Sri Lanka), off the southern coast of India. Pieces specifically on India include 'An Ogre' (16 September 1865), and 'Wild-Boar Hunting in India' (28 October 1865). For (6): 'An

Empire Saved' (28 May 1859), 'European Mutiny in India' (30 July 1859), 'Under Fire' (17 February 1866).

14. *HW* articles prompted by the rebellion include 'A Mutiny in India' (15 August 1857, [E. Townsend]), 'Sepoy Symbols of Mutiny' (5 September 1857, [John Robertson]), 'Indian Irregulars' (12 September 1857, [E. Townsend]), 'A Very Black Act' (26 September 1857, [John Capper]), 'Indian Recruits and Indian English' (3 October 1857, [E. Townsend and Alexander Hamilton]), 'Blown Away!' (27 March 1858, [George Craig]), 'At the Siege of Delhi' (3 July 3 1858, [Edgeworth]), 'Perils in India' (22 January 1859, [Henry Morley]), John Lang's *Wanderings in India* series (begins 14 November 1857 and is the lead story of *HW* for its first two installments) and, of course, Collins's own 'A Sermon for Sepoys'. Some of the *HW* essays intervened directly in debates about the Rebellion, in one case recounting the punishment of several mutineers by being blown out of the mouths of cannon ('Blown Away!'). While a few of the articles in *HW* dealt directly with the Rebellion, many of them approach the Rebellion much more obliquely than their titles would suggest. For instance, 'A Mutiny in India' is an account not of 1857 but of an earlier incident; 'Sepoy Symbols of Mutiny' states in its first sentence that lotus-flowers were used as harbingers of rebellion in June 1857, and then goes on to discuss ancient Egyptian symbolism for the lotus-flower.

15. Other contributors in this period included Charles Mackay, George Walter Thornbury, Joseph Charles Parkinson, Malcolm Laing Meason, Henry Morley and George Augustus Sala, as well as Fitzgerald and Blanchard.

16. Other foreign countries figure on occasion. Venezuela is the backdrop for a few essays and short stories (including 'General Falcon' (8 February), 'Major Milligan's Mistake' (22 February), and 'Carabobo' (28 March); China figures in a tale of colonial battle ('Told by a Skipper', 21 March); and 'A Foreign Contract' (22 February) warns of the dangers of foreign investment. Foreign sites closer to home include Italy ('Italian Men and Brothers', 11 January), the Netherlands ('Boy Monsters', 11 January), France ('The French Press', 18 January), Russia ('The Russian Peasantry', 18 April, 'Among Russian Peasantry', 8 April), and Hungary ('The World's Wages: An Hungarian Story', 25 April).

17. In subject matter, Dickens considered as his scope 'every nation upon earth' (*HW* 30 March 1850, 1). In 1866, some eight years into the run of *AYR*, Dickens described his journal as 'a collection of miscellaneous articles interesting to the widest range of readers, consisting of Suggestive, Descriptive and Critical Dissertations on the most prominent topics, British and foreign, that form the *social history* of the past eight years' (my emphasis; quoted in Fitzgerald 1913, 240). Because *AYR* was simultaneously published in America, such an 'international' readership made Dickens careful to leaven any aggressively 'local' (that is, British) points of view, especially during the Civil War. Dickens's domestication of news was a result of publishing exigencies as well as intent: printing arrangements with the American publishers, who required advance plates, dictated that each issue of *AYR* went to press two weeks before its publication date, limiting the journal's engagement with current events, and Dickens had to '[reject] good papers if he thought the subject matter would lose topicality by the publication date' (Oppenlander 1984, 38).

18. Alternative titles that Dickens considered before settling on 'All the Year Round' included such domestically inflected possibilities as 'Household Harmony', 'The Hearth', 'Home', 'Home Music', 'English Bells', and 'Good Humour' (26 January 1859 letter to Collins, reproduced in Hutton 1892, 90–1). Dickens's emphasis on the middle-class nature and 'wholesomeness' of his periodical argued against the inherited association in the world of periodicals between 'cheap' and 'disreputable'. Richard Altick (1957, 347) writes that the 'great importance [of *HW*] is that through the excellence of its contents and the prestige of Dickens' name it helped to break down further the still powerful upper-and middle-class prejudice against cheap papers'. For a brief history of Dickens's position in relation to such periodicals, see Oppenlander (1984, 18–22, 28–9). Stringent editorial control as well as careful screening of contributors guaranteed wholesome fare for a family journal. Fitzgerald expresses astonishment that 'Boz should have admitted to a family journal a writer whose orthodoxy was suspect, and whose 'free thought' was likely to leaven her writings', none other than the 'free-thinking' Harriet Martineau (1913, 271, 270).

Works cited

Altick, Richard. *The English Common Reader: a Social History of the Mass Reading Public 1800–1900*. Chicago, 1957.

Bhabha, Homi. 'By Bread Alone: Signs of Violence in the Mid-nineteenth Century', in *The Location of Culture*. London, 1994, 198–211.

[Blanchard, Sidney Laman]. 'Famine in India', *All the Year Round* (22 February 1862), 519–23.

[Blanchard, Sidney Laman]. 'Indian Servants', *All the Year Round* (27 June 1863), 416–20.

Brantlinger, Patrick. *Rule of Darkness: British Literature and Imperialism, 1830–1914.* Ithaca, 1988.

Brontë, Charlotte. *Jane Eyre.* 1847. Reprinted New York, 1987.

Collins, Wilkie. *The Moonstone.* 1868. Reprinted London, 1986.

Collins, Wilkie. 'A Sermon for Sepoys', *Household Words* (27 February 1858), 244–7.

Collins, Wilkie and Charles Dickens. *The Perils of Certain English Prisoners, Household Words* (Christmas 1857), 1–36.

'Cotton Cultivation in Bengal', *All the Year Round* (19 October 1861), 91–2.

Crooks, Robert. 'Reopening the Mysteries: Colonialist Logic and Cultural Difference in *The Moonstone* and *The Horse Latitudes*', *Lit: Literature, Interpretation, Theory* 4 (1993), 215–28.

David, Deirdre. *Rule Britannia: Women, Empire, and Victorian Writing.* Ithaca, 1995.

Dickens, Charles. *The Letters of Charles Dickens.* ed. by Graham Storey and Kathleen Tillotson. vol. 8 (1856–58). Oxford, 1995.

Doyle, Sir Arthur Conan. *The Sign of Four.* 1890. Reprinted in *Sherlock Holmes: Selected Stories.* Oxford, 1980, 67–205.

Duncan, Ian. '*The Moonstone*, the Victorian Novel, and Imperialist Panic', *Modern Language Quarterly* 55 (1994), 297–319.

Eliot, T.S. 'Wilkie Collins and Dickens'. 1927. Reprinted in *Selected Essays.* New York, 1964, 409–18.

Fitzgerald, Percy. *Memories of Charles Dickens*. London, 1902.

'Flies', *All the Year Round* (4 January 1868), 88–92.

Hughes, Linda K. and Michael Lund. *The Victorian Serial*. Charlottesville, 1991.

Hutton, Lawrence (ed.). *Letters of Charles Dickens to Wilkie Collins 1851–1870*. London, 1892.

James, Louis. 'The Trouble with Betsy: Periodicals and the Common Reader in Mid-Nineteenth-Century England', in Joanne Shattock and Michael Wolff (eds), *The Victorian Periodical Press: Samplings and Soundings*. Toronto, 1982, 349–66.

Lohrli, Anne. *Household Words: a Weekly Journal 1850–1859 Conducted by Charles Dickens*. Toronto, 1973.

McClintock, Anne. *Imperial Leather: Race, Gender and Sexuality in the Colonial Contest*. New York, 1995.

Malchow, H.L. *Gothic Images of Race in Nineteenth-Century Britain*. Stanford, 1996.

Mehta, Jaya. 'English Romance; Indian Violence', *The Centennial Review* 39 (1995), 611–57.

Mukherjee, Rudrangshu. *Awadh in Revolt 1857–58: a Study in Popular Resistance*. Delhi, 1984.

Nayder, Lillian. 'Class Consciousness and the Indian Mutiny in Dickens's "The Perils of Certain English Prisoners"', *SEL: Studies in English Literature* 32 (1992), 689–705.

Nayder, Lillian. 'Robinson Crusoe and Friday in Victorian Britain: "Discipline", "Dialogue", and Collins's Critique of Empire in *The Moonstone*', *Dickens Studies Annual* 21 (1992), 213–31.

Oddie, William. 'Dickens and the Indian Mutiny', *Dickensian* 68 (1972), 3–15.

Oppenlander, Ella Ann. *Dickens' All the Year Round: Descriptive Index and Contributor List*. Troy, New York, 1984.

Paxton, Nancy L. 'Mobilizing Chivalry: Rape in British Novels about the Indian Uprising of 1857', *Victorian Studies* 36 (1992), 5–30.

Peters, Catherine. *The King of Inventors: a Life of Wilkie Collins*. London, 1991.

'Real Mysteries of Paris and London', *All the Year Round* (27 October 1860), 69–72.

Reed, John R. 'English Imperialism and the Unacknowledged Crime of *The Moonstone*', *Clio* 2 (1973), 281–90.

Roy, Ashish. 'The Fabulous Imperialist Semiotic of Wilkie Collins's *The Moonstone*', *New Literary History* 24 (1993), 657–81.

Said, Edward W. *Culture and Imperialism*. New York, 1993.

'Sir John's Troubles', *All the Year Round* (28 December 1867, 4 January 1868, 11 January 1868), 66–72, 84–8, 105–8.

Sharpe, Jenny. 'The Unspeakable Limits of Rape: Colonial Violence and Counter-Insurgency', *Genders* 10 (1991), 25–46.

Stokes, Eric. *The Peasant Armed: the Indian Revolt of 1857*. ed. C.A. Bayly. Oxford, 1986.

Stone, Harry (ed.). *Charles Dickens' Uncollected Writings from Household Words 1850–1859*. 2 vols. Bloomington, Indiana, 1968.

Thomas, Ronald R. 'Minding the Body Politic: the Romance of Science and the Revision of History in Victorian Detective Fiction', *Victorian Literature and Culture* 19 (1991), 233–54.

Ward, Andrew. *Our Bones Are Scattered: the Cawnpore Massacres and the Indian Mutiny of 1857*. New York, 1996.

Young, Robert J.C. *Colonial Desire: Hybridity in Theory, Culture and Race*. London, 1995.

6
'Double-dyed Traitors and Infernal Villains': *Illustrated London News*, *Household Words*, Charles Dickens and the Indian Rebellion

Laura Peters

> The British press in India was an arm of power... There was not a newspaper writer or conductor who was not as ready to fight with his sword as with his pen in support of the supremacy of his race and country throughout the entire peninsula, or who would have breathed a word that might have weakened the hands of the Government in a crisis so awful. [The press enhanced] British spirit and patriotism for keeping up the heart and stirring up the enthusiasm of the people in support of Law and Order. The press in a righteous and popular war is like the trumpeter or the standard bearer in an army: it both inspires courage and keeps it up to the mark, not of mere duty, but of zeal and devotion. (*Illustrated London News* 12 September 1857, 286)

Lord Canning's implementation of the Press Restriction Act in India in 1857 was greeted with astonishment and surprise by the British media in India and in Britain. The extract above is a response from an editorial in the *Illustrated London News* (hereafter *ILN*) to the Act. In its defence of the role of the press, the editorial articulates several discourses which were not only emotive but hegemonic; namely, the press is an arm of power and its editors would fight to ensure racial supremacy. In addition, the press would help to identify the foe in order to whip up popular support for power and inspire a zealous courage within the troops. What the *ILN* does not acknowledge overtly is the role that the media plays in the production of the event and how it seeks to determine the political course of events. In his work, *Covering Islam*, Edward Said argues for the role of the media and its journalists in the construction of a political agenda around historical events. The resultant coverage is 'misleadingly full. [It] has licensed not only patent inaccuracy but also expressions of unrestrained ethnocentrism, cultural and even racial hatred, deep yet paradoxically free-floating hostility' (Said 1981, xi). This dialectic produces a 'word politics [which] sets up situations, justifies actions, forecloses options, and presses alternatives on the other' (Said 1981, xvi).

How the Rebellion in India was mediated by the press in Britain, and how Dickens was influenced by and contributed to this mediation is the central concern of this chapter. More specifically, this chapter will explore the extent to which Dickens was not only dependent on coverage in papers like the *ILN* for political subjects for his own periodical, *Household Words*, but also how Dickens narrativized the events of the Rebellion in his section of the short story 'The Perils of Certain English Prisoners and Their Treasure in Women, Children, Silver and Jewels' ('Perils'), co-authored with Wilkie Collins, and which ran in the 1857 Christmas issue of *Household Words* (reproduced as Figure 5.1 in this volume). By using the events of the Rebellion as a base for his narrative in 'Perils', Dickens too acted as an arm of empire in his reproduction of the values being consolidated in the mediation of the event. He was also contributing to a public debate sparked by the rebellions in India but which quickly expanded to consider Britain's role in empire. While most scholarship on the coverage of the Indian Rebellion refers to *The Times*, *Lloyd's Weekly*, *Reynold's News* and *the Morning Post* (Byrne 1957; Hutchins 1967; Dawson 1994), I have chosen to concentrate on the relatively unexplored links between the *ILN* and Dickens. Others have discussed Dickens's 'Perils' in the past; their focus, however, has been either on his links to other journals such as *Punch* and *The Times* (Oddie 1972), or on exploring how Dickens appealed 'to the racial hatred generated by the Indian Mutiny in order to solve the problem of class conflict and alienation in the British rank and file' (Nayder 1992, 700–1). But there is a more interesting case to be made for examining links between Dickens, his work and the *ILN*. Dickens was reading the *ILN* regularly at this time; he chose to publish his correction to a review of his work, 'A Curious Misprint in the Edinburgh Review' in the *ILN* on 8 August 1857 – at the same time as the newspaper was publishing extensive editorials and survivors' accounts of the Rebellion. I shall consider 'Perils' in this context, first identifying the role played by editors and the press in constructing a response to the Indian Rebellion, then exploring the ambiguity surrounding the identification of the official enemies and heroes of this historical event, and finally analysing the consolidation of imperial power that occurred in periodical mediations of the events.

The role of the press

'A Very Black Act' appeared in the 26 September 1857 issue of *Household Words* [hereafter *HW*]. Written by John Capper, a British editor of a provincial paper in India, it complained of the newly imposed censorship on the print media in India. The rationale for the censorship allegedly lay in the publication, by Bengali and Persian newspapers, of a proclamation by the King of Delhi offering to remunerate deserters from the British army. Capper's objections lay not in whether such censorship was justified, but in the universality of the censorship which, he argued, levelled 'the white European to the depths of the black Asiatic' (Capper 1857, 293). In seeking to distinguish himself, Capper argued that he had willingly undertaken the increased scope of the editor's role in India as 'the duties of armed volunteer, policeman, special messenger, and anything else required by the state at this critical juncture' (Capper 1857, 293). What is of interest in this article is this frank revelation that the press was not only an arm of empire but was directly involved in the policing of empire in India. The fact that Dickens chose to run an article which revealed the imperial role of the British editor in India raises interesting questions. How did Dickens view his role as editor in Britain? Did he identify his role as imperialist in nature? Did he draw parallels, even unconsciously, between the imperial role of the British editor in India and his own role as editor in Britain? Certainly, Capper's analysis of the situation in India in 'A Black Act' is one Dickens shared, particularly in its articulation of and emphasis on the treachery of the 'natives', the incompetence of the colonial administration, and the ill-treatment meted out by British society to its own soldiers.

The active mediation and production of the event by the press gave it an imperial role. The *ILN* offered a frank analysis of the domestic role of the press in the Rebellion when it argued that it had an obligation: to expose errors of the past in order to prevent their recurrence; to act, in other words, as a medium through which both 'men of authority' and parliamentary candidates could address the public and offer 'general enlightenment'. Contributions were especially welcome from both soldiers and civilians whose firsthand experience would enable much of what formerly seemed unaccountable in the mutiny to be made 'intelligible' by revealing for the readers 'the real springs of the machinery of revolt' (*ILN* 12 September 1857, 257). The manifesto of general enlightenment to which this editorial referred was akin to that of *HW*, the weekly periodical edited, or 'conducted' rather, by Dickens. However, the overall function of the press was to contribute to the general enlightenment by imparting knowledge – a knowledge which was constructed, as this article will argue, according to certain discourses of savagery and civilization, of orientalized degeneracy and of national identity – all of which helped to consolidate a hegemonic power. In the colonial discourse structuring this coverage it is possible to identify the workings of the rhetoric of empire which sought to establish authority through 'the demarcation of identity and difference' as a mode of 'legitimising [...the coloniser's] own position in the colonial community' (Spurr 1993, 7). 'Perils' can be read in this context as a moment of intersection between journalism and literary practice, an intertextual cultural exchange which also worked to legitimize attitudes to empire.

Identifying the enemy and the hero

Before considering 'Perils' it is necessary to examine the context from which it arises – namely the coverage of the rebellion in the *ILN* and *HW* and the discourses informing each. From the earliest coverage there was an ambivalence towards the identification of the enemy and the hero. Initially, the enemy was perceived to be among the colonial administrators rather than the indigenous peoples; contributing to the general enlightenment of the British public did not initially take the form of blind patriotism in either the *ILN* or *HW*. From the onset of the crisis in India well into the revelations of the alleged massacres, both journals were critical of government mismanagement and incompetence, arguing that they had contributed to, if not created, the current situation in India. On 1 August 1857 the *ILN* ran an editorial in response to the Indian rebellion in which it argued that the Rebellion currently shocking the nation was 'long since predicted and foreseen'. It attributed the rebellion to the behaviour of 'raw youths' of the British army who control a 'splendid army...formed from the most aristocratic, exclusive, and high-spirited of the natives'. These same raw youths were accused of being 'ignorant even of their drill' and abusive in referring to 'the natives – proud and sensitive high-caste Brahmins as "niggers" with whom it was degrading to associate' (*ILN* 1 August 1857, 105–6). The concerns expressed here were further developed in 'Errors of Indian Policy', an editorial run on 22 August 1857, which called for a 'radical reform' of military, administrative, social and political relations after the Mutiny has been put down in order to 'retain India' (*ILN* 22 August

1857, 185). The editorial argued that insensitivity to Indian language and, more importantly, indigenous religions by the British officers in command had allowed 'greased cartridges' to be used by the indigenous soldiers – one of the initial reasons cited for the Rebellion. E. Townsend's short story, 'A Mutiny in India', which appeared in the 15 August 1857 issue of *HW*, was equally scathing of the English commanders in India. The fictional English commander, Daintry, was presented as typically representative of military commanders 'born five hundred years too late [... the product of] an old-fashioned education; that is to say, he wrote badly, spelt worse, and, as a matter of choice read not at all'. Townsend's piece ended with the Rebellion in the regiment being suppressed, but not before Daintry had been killed. The conclusion of the story was the most critical: it argued that the hushing up of the affair, in the form of 'a foolish punctilio' restricting the press, would only ensure more disastrous ramification by preventing the exposure of 'the true causes of the rottenness of our Indian civil and military system' (Townsend 1857b, 154–6).

Likewise, early coverage in the *ILN* was at pains to stress that the cause of the general malaise in the military ultimately rested with those in command. Each month the paper carried a litany of tales of poor judgement and mismanagement that often costed lives. There was the death of General Handscombe which occurred when, misjudging the seriousness of the Rebellion, he rode up through burning bungalows to the battle lines of the 71st 'in the hope that his presence and speech might have the effect of bringing the mutineers to reason' (*ILN* 8 August 1857, 150). He was killed on the spot. General Hewett was arrested for not acting soon enough to quell the Rebellion when in command at Meerut: it was alleged that as a result of his inaction women and children had died (*ILN* 8 August 1857, 150). Major-General Lloyd was removed from his command for his 'culpable neglect' (*ILN* 26 September 1857, 322). The general dissatisfaction with the governing of India culminated in a petition by the British inhabitants of Calcutta and of the Presidency of Fort William in Bengal to the Queen for the recall of Lord Canning, a point widely reported in the British press. The petition charged that 'all the calamities, the results of the spread of the mutiny, were directly attributable to the blindness, weakness, and incapacity of the local government of India, [... which was] full of weakness and vacillation'.[1] The petition echoed the widespread concern articulated in the *ILN*, *HW* and elsewhere in response to the Press Restriction Act; one of its claims was that the Act was 'systematically used by the Governor-General and his Council for the intimidation of the press, the suppression of the truth, and of every discussion, or expression of opinion, unfavourable or unpleasant to Government' (*ILN* 21 November 1857, 515). Ultimately, the *ILN* did not hesitate to use the incompetence displayed in the governing of the periphery as a means of criticizing the home government in England; it warned that the government should not repeat the same mistakes in India that it had made during the Crimean War (*ILN* 5 September 1857, 234).

However, alongside this persistent, overt media criticism of the colonial government was a simultaneous questioning of the nature of those who were governed in India, a questioning which shed light on contemporary imperial theories of civilization and barbarism. This questioning fed into larger anxieties about the British empire. It is possible then to identify a shift in the coverage from a residual dissatisfaction about the Crimean War and worries about the quality of people sent out to govern colonial outposts to an emerging anxiety about the state of the British empire and the nature of those to be governed. In reconsidering how India, indeed the whole British empire, was to be governed, an underlying question was raised on whether indigenous peoples, as 'a conquered race', could be governed in the same manner as 'Lancashire', or indeed if it was possible to 'transform the nations of the whole world into models of Great Britain' (*ILN* 8 August 1857, 185). The paradox or ambivalence structuring this media questioning and coverage is one moment in the rhetoric of empire which Spurr (1993, 7) usefully identifies as the moment of 'preparation for the domestication of the colonised and as a moral and philosophical precondition for the civilising mission'. As the Indian Rebellion of 1857 escalated, the conclusion the media drew was that it was a mistake to rely on 'fatherly justice and wisdom' (*ILN* 8 August 1857, 185) and to allow the 'natives' to govern themselves as if they were 'Englishmen' rather than governing them by the 'strong arm and inflexible will which are alone fitted for Orientals' (*ILN* 12 September 1857, 258). The *ILN* also lamented giving freedom of the press to the people of India, allowing Indian peoples to hold offices in court, and doing away with military discipline. A policy of British settlement in India was presented as the ultimate solution for counteracting the 'Hundreds of millions of dark-skinned men' who threatened 'the one dominant Christian power' (*ILN* 3 October 1857, 334). As these media sources perceived it, a substantial British settlement would ensure 'a large infusion of the Anglo-Saxon element' to raise, 'by the indirect operation of the European race...the native population...above the influence of a corrupt half-civilisation' and thus ensure 'freedom and progress' (*ILN* 31 October

1857, 426). The insistence on such an absolute, essential difference was a mode of colonial control; the insistence was a method of denying those with a constructed racialized difference the same political rights enjoyed by those falling in the category of sameness. Thus, the periphery was to be governed by the metropole, but only those in the metropole and British expatriates in the colony were to enjoy the power of government.

In asserting both that the oriental race only recognized the spectacle of power, and that the European race was needed to raise the native population above their current corrupt half-civilization, the *ILN* operated a discourse of degenerate barbarism combined with exotic excess which was 'orientalist' in nature. This is easily discernible in the coverage of the Rebellion; Delhi was constructed as 'a city steeped in . . . the revolting feculence of Eastern debauchery, and ever the rally-point of mischievous cabals or dangerous intrigues' (*ILN* 8 August 1857, 147). Representations of indigenous peoples removed from British control painted a picture of a degenerating race, such as the 'Bengal Sepahees, who, from good and valiant soldiers, have, through the instrumentality of wild fanaticism and their own worse passions...become converted... into miscreant thieves and murderers' (*ILN* 8 August 1857, 186). This degeneracy discourse was not unique to *ILN*. An article in *HW* by E. Townsend, entitled 'Indian Irregulars', queried whether natives should be commissioned at all as officers in view of contemporary perceptions of native commissioned officers as 'a set of worn-out, puffy, ghee-bloated cripples' (Townsend 1857a, 244). Likewise, in 'Indian Recruits and Indian English', co-authored by E. Townsend and Alexander Hamilton, the English spoken by Indian recruits was described as an eruption of 'barbaric words from dialects spoken by those hundred and eighty millions who eat rice and worship idols', and cadets were compared unfavourably to ape tribes (Townsend and Hamilton 1857, 321–2). Even indigenous allies of the British troops did not escape the discourse of racial superiority: the 5 September issue of *HW* refers to the 'Ghoorkahs' (*sic*), important allies of the British forces, as 'gallant Lilliputians' who look like 'so many monkeys . . . humanised by that sudden burst of unaffected grief' (Robertson 1857, 243). In the face of such harsh portraits of degeneracy, barbarism and animalistic behaviour, the Rebellion came to be viewed as a 'war of colour and creed against civilisation and Christianity; a united revolt of the Eastern against Anglo-Saxon power' (*ILN* 5 September 1857, 251). Alongside the 1 August *ILN* coverage of the parliamentary debate in which Disraeli argued for the rebellion to be considered in terms of a national revolt, in *HW* of 5 September, the writer of

'Sepoy Symbols of Mutiny', John Robertson, compared the Rebellion to a religious insurrection, thus raising the spectacle of another Holy War.

These moments offer good examples of the Rebellion being both covered in the press and mediated through the rhetoric of empire, as when the *ILN* advocated the domination of the indigenous peoples because it insisted they were 'slavish, superstitious, treacherous, and ungrateful'. It was such qualities which seemingly composed the 'true Mahommedan type [King of Awadh] – bloodthirsty, vindictive, selfish and dissolute, and unrelenting' for whom 'absolute, uncontrolled, and unadulterated power' is needed to subdue 'Asiatic barbarism' with 'European civilisation' (*ILN* 12 September 1857, 257). These quotations highlight an underlying racial stereotype which assumed that, left to their own devices, the 'natives' would degenerate into barbarism. It was a process in which the colonizer created the colonized in order both to subject the colonized and to construct a desired self-portrait (cf., Memmi 1990, 121). In addition, the assertion that the civilizing influence was only effective if it was rigorously policed reveals a larger anxiety about the British empire as a whole, namely, if this rebellion were victorious it might spread to other parts of the empire. The anxiety is that the empire would disintegrate into a spectacle of widespread murderous barbarism.

With such a clearly defined enemy in the indigenous peoples a hero was needed. In sharp contrast to these representations of degenerate barbarity was the representation of the disciplined heroism of both the British forces and their allies. Reports started appearing which narrated the tales of 'Englishmen', full of 'mettle', daring to confront 40 000 'well-disciplined troops' with 3400 men and suffering only minimal losses.[2] Although the *ILN* made it abundantly clear that British forces in India relied on loyal indigenous forces to win, the main focus of its coverage was one which stressed the heroism of British men and women in India by testifying to the 'indomitable spirit on the part of our countrymen, and . . . our fair countrywomen' in the face of 'wholesale butcheries' and 'foul indignities'. This line of coverage continually stressed the 'courage, patience, good judgement and temper' (*ILN* 29 August 1857, 210) of the British forces. This discourse of British heroism culminated in an *ILN* editorial on 3 October 1857 which talked of the 'PLUCK' of the men and women as not only the best of British character but as the basis for racial superiority – 'the possession of every quality – physical, mental, or moral – which raises one man or one race of men to the pre-eminence over another' – over that 'ineffable villain' Nana Sahib (*ILN* 3 October 1857, 329).

Consolidation of imperial power and the construction of a national identity

For the audience in the metropole and British communities in India, the discourse of pluck and dutiful valour quickly conflated with a discourse of national identity to consolidate a national hegemony. To map this it is necessary first to extend the contextualization to a consideration of the public mood. Although the Rebellion in India garnered widespread coverage, it was the news of the raping and killing of women and children that caught the popular attention, making it one of the primary concerns of the day. However, it is important to note that these reports were by no means accurate. In fact, some British historians from 1865 (George Trevelyan) onwards asserted that these alleged rapes did not occur during the Rebellion in 1857. Rather, as Nancy L. Paxton (1992, 6) argues, the allegations of Indian men raping English women

> emerged at a particular crisis point in the British rule of India and performed specific ideological work... this narrative naturalized British colonizer's dominance by asserting the lawlessness of Indian men and, at the same time, shored up traditional gender roles by assigning to British women the role of victim, countering British feminist demands for women's greater political and social equality. In short, texts which focus on the rape of English women by Indian men were used to mobilize literary traditions about chivalry in service to the Raj.

In the more general context of media coverage of wars, it is important to note that the demonization of the enemy through stories of the raping and murdering of women and children is a constant thread right up to the present. More specifically, however, in the nineteenth and early twentieth centuries this type of coverage in Britain sought to consolidate imperial power and to construct a national identity based on a notion of superiority. Thus, during this time, such coverage formed part of the larger project of policing imperialism. As Philip Taylor (1995, 165) argues, 'Military success appeared to prove British racial superiority over inferior peoples, and this myth was perpetuated in a variety of media, from newspapers to novels, from parades to postcards, from school textbooks to societies, from board-games to biscuit tins'. Such propaganda worked to disseminate imperial values – the combination of 'military adventure, racial superiority and exotic locations' was an appealing one (Taylor 1995, 165). During the Rebellion, then, media coverage worked to ensure that British forces defeated the Indian 'mutineers' through whipping up public support and indignation; it was committed to the projection of racial and national superiority.

Thus, as a result of the alleged atrocities reported in the media, public concern over the Rebellion was intense; the Rebellion quickly outstripped 'the darkest period of the Crimean campaign' for creating a shared feeling of indignation across all classes. 'Every British heart, from the highest to the humblest of the land, glows with honest wrath, and demands justice, prompt and unsparing' noted the *ILN* (5 September 1857, 235). Such was the concern for the victims of the Rebellion that a meeting was convened on 25 August 1857 at the Mansion House by the Lord Mayor to raise money for suffering British men, women and children in India. The resolutions passed at this meeting are of interest in signalling the popular mood regarding the Rebellion and its causes. Although there were hints at the meeting of an awareness that maladministration by the East India Company likely contributed to the Rebellion,[3] this was overshadowed by more general feelings of outrage and calls for vengeance. A 'gallant Admiral' talked of feeling 'even hatred and contempt towards those who had been the cause of the terrible outbreak. It made his blood boil.' Despite his age the same Admiral vowed to 'render assistance with his blood or with his sword'. The general conclusion of the meeting was that the Rebellion was a religious war waged against Christians; it also voiced a general desire to link this rebellion with other indigenous rebellions and acts of resistance. While calling for punishment adequate to the offence, Mr Justice Haliburton claimed that the outrageous conduct of the 'red devils' in British North America was child's play compared with the outrages committed in India (*ILN* 29 August 1857, 214). Overall, the public mood was such that the 5 September issue reported that recruiting agents met with great success and 'nearly all the recruits have enlisted with a desire to get out to India and to avenge their murdered countrymen' (*ILN* 29 August 1857, 243). By 31 October the Indian relief fund had raised in excess of £165 000. 'Loud and prolonged cheering' in the theatres and other places of amusement and 'immense excitement in all parts of the metropolis' greeted the news of the recapturing of Delhi (*ILN* 31 October 1857, 426).

As the *ILN* started to write of the responsibilities which 'devolve upon us as one of the greatest Powers in the world, having neighbours in every hemisphere, and ruling over countless millions of men, of all colours and races, and of every possible diversity of thought, habits, manners, and modes of faith' (*ILN* 29 August 1857, 209), it is possible to identify the consolidation of imperial power as the discourse of heroism and that of a people under siege elides into a discourse of national identity. It is interesting to note the neat hegemonic shift as the tone of the coverage changes from one criticizing mismanagement in the administration of India to one criticizing Indian administration in terms of an excess of 'humanity and generosity', which too early assumed 'the good faith and gratitude of the Asiatic soldiers' (*ILN* 5 September 1857, 235). India is now constructed as a place of battle between 'the mild and beneficent rule of Christian England' and the 'ruthless barbarism of the Mahommedans'. As such it became the backdrop for a variety of tensions and questions of home rule then under discussion in Britain. One good example was when the *ILN* overtly stoked Anglo-Irish tensions by claiming the Dublin *Nation*'s coverage of the rebellions was treasonous in the 'rabid delight' it drew from the suffering of English men and women. It also accused the *Nation* of having impugned the courageous character of the British forces through its claims that 'the brave Britons have run'. As a result, the *ILN* was quick to assert that 'the spectacle of heroism which one and all have exhibited since the outbreak of the mutiny has been well calculated to impress the world with admiration of the British character' (5 September 1857, 238). These skirmishes in the media served as warnings of the much larger Imperial issues at stake as a consequence of failure to suppress the Indian rebellion.[4]

On one level, what was sought was a victory in India to restore Britain's prestige, in order to reverse the damage done to the national image after the Crimean War (*ILN* 26 September 1857, 305). Overall, the possibility of victory in India both contributed to the restoration of a tarnished national reputation abroad and served to mobilize British society around notions of heroism and vengeance. As the *ILN* put it, 'The whole country has become martial; and thousands and tens of thousands of gallant men would think it a privilege to have a shot at the sepoys, and become the instruments of Heaven for the punishment of such red-handed, black-haired villains as Nana Sahib and his accomplices' (*ILN* 26 September 1857, 305).

This coverage of the Rebellion and Dickens's role in this coverage was a forerunner to the more systematic official propaganda that emerged during the First World War; even before this, Rudyard Kipling officially wrote as a propagandist during the Boer War. However, unlike the coverage of the Rebellion, the overt criticism of the government's handling of aspects of the First World War was missing in part because of the passing of the 1914 Defence of the Realm Act. This Act prohibited the publishing of any news that might cause 'disaffection' amongst the civil and military sectors of Britain and her allies (Sanders and Taylor 1982, 9). Instead, the literary community secretly started to work as propagandists for the British High Command, publishing pamphlets, works of fiction and poems which constructed the myth of the Germans as 'Prussian Ogres' and 'Beastly Hun' (Taylor 1992, 180). In direct contrast to the coverage of the Rebellion, these writers, through their insistence of the cheerfulness of the British troops and the 'incisive and efficient generals' (Buitenhuis 1989, xvi), obfuscated the appalling conditions and the often inept leadership. However, like the coverage of the Rebellion, these propagandists not only ensured popular support for the British role in the war (and therefore, initially at least, ensured a ready supply of volunteers) but some of the writers enlisted in the fighting forces. Thus, Dickens's role in the mediation of the events of the Rebellion prefigured the larger, more co-ordinated role played by literary figures in the mediation of the First World War. In both there was a concerted effort to: demonize the enemy; assert racial superiority; and fetishize woman as an icon of purity who needed protection by the chivalrous ally from the rapacious enemy. It is not surprising then that the calls to hang Nana Sahib and to raze Delhi in the latter part of the Rebellion were echoed in the calls to 'Hang the Kaiser' and 'Make Germany Pay' (Sanders and Taylor 1982, 162) at the end of the First World War.

Responses to the Rebellion

The *ILN*, unlike other newspapers at the time which called for vengeance, argued for British troops carrying out 'JUSTICE; – no more and no less. They will be soldiers and not executioners'; with the exception of wishing an example be made of Nana Sahib taking the form of being 'tied up to the nearest tree, as an example of British justice upon the murderers of women and children' (*ILN* 5 September 1857, 237–8). However, this call for justice must be interrogated because it included for the *ILN*, if thought ultimately necessary, a razing to the ground of Delhi.

> If, in the estimation of our Generals on the spot, it be necessary for the security of our power . . . that the great Mahommedan city of Delhi should be razed to the ground, and salt strewn upon the site of its mosques and palaces, no cry . . . of cruelty that may arise from the ultra-humanitarians, 'who live at home in ease', will prevent or retard, consummation.

It ended with an insistence on the distinction between revenge which was 'Asiatic' and justice which was the response of the 'Englishmen' (*ILN* 19 September 1857, 281–2).

The *ILN* was not alone in calling for a razing of Indian cities – among the supporters of the razing of Delhi was Lord Ellenborough, who had been Governor-General of India during the 1840s. Given the context of the coverage in other papers at the time, the *ILN* may be said to have been rather moderate. However, justice was perceived to be done in India when executions of the rebels began; these executions took place, often without trial, either by hanging, shooting or blowing the rebels from the mouths of cannons. The latter method met with great approval in the British expatriate community. As early as 22 August the first reports could be found in the *ILN* of British forces putting to death captured rebels by blowing them from mouths of cannons. The *Peenha Observer* argued on 27 August that the mutineers should be punished by 'hanging, drawing, and quartering – on a gallows raised so high over the Royal Palace at Delhi that the 'Great Exhibition should be witnessed by all the country round'. The 12 September issue reported British troops arriving and taking 'a terrible revenge...shooting down the natives like pigeons, and hanging them on every tree' (*ILN* 12 September 1857, 258), while the 26 September issue described a punishment invented by a British officer which involved high-caste Brahmins having to clean the blood from the building where the women and children were slaughtered – an act which would cause the Brahmins to lose caste – before they were hanged. Indeed, long after the Rebellion was quelled *HW* was still running articles on executing people by blowing them from the mouths of cannons. On 27 March 1858 George Craig's piece entitled 'Blown Away!' offered a survey of different cultural methods of capital punishment, highlighting the method of blowing from the mouth of a cannon which he claimed was an ancient Hindustani custom. The article justified this as a response to the Rebellion on the grounds that the mutineers had allegedly 'planned the destruction of every European – man, woman, and child – on the island of Bombay' (Craig 1858, 349). It even offered an eyewitness account of such an execution.[5] However, ultimately the article recommended the abolition of this form of execution – not on the grounds of its cruelty and inhumanity – but because 'India has become so familiarised to the spectacle, that it excites little or no dread' (Craig 1858, 350). Thus, as a military execution, it had too much dignity and was not painful enough. In the conception of punishment as a spectacle which must excite dread, it is possible to identify the workings of what Foucault terms the spectacle of the scaffold in which the public execution has 'a juridico-political function. It is a ceremonial by which a momentarily injured sovereignty is reconstituted' (Foucault 1991, 48). The public execution was thus an 'emphatic affirmation of power and ... of intrinsic superiority' (Foucault 1991, 49) on the part of the British who, having put down the Mutiny, sought not only to avenge alleged atrocities but to restore the power of the colonial administration. The punishment of execution by being blown from the mouth of a cannon functioned in the same way as the hanging, drawing and quartering that Foucault described: both were calculated not only to assert power but as ceremonies of punishment were 'an exercise of terror' along the line Foucault proposes in *Discipline and Punish*.

When this method of punishment ceased to provoke this terror, the final stance taken by the *ILN* coverage was an advocacy of extermination: it wished that the Indian mutineers 'had not only been disarmed but exterminated' (*ILN* 3 October 1857, 330) (see Figure 6.1). This discourse of extermination was a product of earlier rabid media coverage that had unproblematically alleged that 'Children have been compelled to eat the quivering flesh of their murdered parents, after which they were literally torn asunder by the laughing fiends who surrounded them' (*The Times* 17 September 1857, 9) and that 'Parents ... were made to swallow portions of the flesh cut from the limbs of the children, and afterwards burnt over a slow fire' (Byrne 1957, 295–6). These allegations are now known to be false, but at the time served effectively to mobilize British society around a discourse of extermination. Thomas Macaulay described 'an account of that dreadful military execution at Peshawar – forty men blown all at once from the mouths of cannon, their heads, legs, arms flying in all directions – [being] read with delight by people who three weeks ago were against capital punishment' (Hutchins 1967, 85). British media coverage was fairly unanimous at this point in calling for vengeance in the form of extermination: *Lloyd's Weekly* called for 'vengeance upon the fiends'; *The Times* and *The Morning Post* advocated 'the extermination and rooting out from the face of the earth the Mohammedan and Brahminised demons who have committed crimes on British women and maidens too horrible to name'; and the *Newcastle Chronicle* advocated 'vengeance ... sharp and bloody, [They should be] exterminated as if they were so many wild beasts' (Dawson 1994, 65).

Echoes of this inflammatory rhetoric can be found in Dickens's infamous letter of 4 October 1857 (written the day after the *ILN* editorial advocated extermination) to Angela Burdett-Coutts in which he took the strong arm, inflexible will discourse to its logical, 'proto-fascist'

EXECUTION OF MUTINEERS AT PESHAWUR: BLOWING FROM THE GUNS, ETC.

Figure 6.1   'Execution of Mutineers at Peshawar: Blowing from the Guns, etc.' from *Illustrated London News*, 3 October 1857, p. 333.

(Tambling 1995, 189) conclusion: Dickens's answer to rebellion was genocide.

> I wish I were Commander in Chief in India. The first thing I would do to strike that Oriental race . . . should be to proclaim to them, in their language, . . . that I should do my utmost to exterminate the Race upon whom the stain of the late cruelties rested; . . . to blot it out of mankind and raze it off the face of the Earth. (Dickens 1937–8, 350–1)

It is during these cries for vengeance that 'Perils' was written.

'Perils' as a mediation of the Rebellion

In the coverage of the Rebellion in the *ILN* and *HW* it is possible to identify key issues such as: the imperial role of the editor and of the press; a unanimous early criticism of the government and military commanders responsible for India; the construction of British heroism and national identity based on discourse of civilization and barbarism which depends on a notion of racial superiority and an orientalized degeneracy; and a discourse of justice which quickly collapses into one of extermination. These are the key overriding issues which structure Dickens's section of 'Perils' and offer a good example of Dickens's reliance on journalistic coverage as a source of political information. In this context, it is possible to read 'Perils' as a narrativization of what was being reported in the *ILN*.

Dickens consciously entered the colonial arena through his popular fiction and short stories. In 1853, the same year that his 'The Noble Savage' appeared in *HW*, Dickens wrote: 'a nation without fancy, with some romance, never did, never can, never will, hold a great place under the sun' (Dickens 1853). For Dickens, imaginative stories and cultural products were not only rejuvenating influences but could be seen to contribute to national greatness in a mode similar to that of the press. Likewise, Dickens's intention for 'Perils' to mediate a response to the Rebellion are apparent in his comment to Benjamin Webster in November 1857 that he hoped the newly finished 'Perils' would light 'up all the fire that is in the public mind at this time' (Oddie 1972, 7). In 'Perils', then, it is possible to see Dickens simultaneously in the dual role of imperial editor for *HW* and imperial author. 'Perils' reconstructed the events of the Rebellion and perpetuated a certain interpretation of these affairs.

Dickens's intention to stoke the fires of empire can be read as an attempt to reconcile inner discontents to (and perhaps his own discontentment with) the imperial project. Dickens was critical of the governing of outposts of empire and the contempt for which he holds these governors[6] was evident in the portrait of self-important buffoonery in the figures of Mr and Mrs Pordage in 'Perils', the self-styled Commissioner of the colony in the story.

Yet, on the other hand, Dickens was not in agreement with the line of criticism which suggested that the behaviour of the British provoked the Rebellion. In 'Perils', Dickens took issue with the line of argument most clearly apparent in the piece printed on 1 August in the *ILN* attributing the Rebellion to the behaviour of 'raw youths' of the British army who were placed in control of 'the most aristocratic, exclusive, and high-spirited of the natives [who are] proud and sensitive high-caste Brahmins' (*ILN* 1 August 1857, 105–6). Significantly, in 'Perils' Dickens never attempts to represent the native peoples as 'splendid' and 'aristocratic'; rather they are infantile, animalistic and fiendish. In contrast, the raw youths, in the form of Gill Davis, Harry Charker and Tom, are disciplined, and well versed in their drill. Other key representatives include an abusive Sergeant Drooce who nevertheless dies valiantly for duty's sake and Captain Carton, the officer in command, who inspires Gill's eternal admiration.

More specifically, Dickens's conscious emphasis in 'Perils' on the selfless heroism of the marines, particularly Gill and Harry, and their devotion to a British society which has ill used them was part of Dickens's self-proclaimed project to celebrate 'without any vulgar catchpenny connexion or application, some of the best qualities of the English character that have been shown in India' (Dickens 1937–8, 889). This celebration was in keeping with what both the *ILN* and 'A Very Black Act' determined was needed by the state at this critical juncture. On a personal level, Dickens believed in the best qualities of the English in India – or in other colonies for that matter – as evidenced in his encouraging his son Walter to go to India in July 1857 at the age of 16 to be a soldier in the 26th Native Infantry. On a public level, 'Perils' was received in the spirit that Dickens intended; on 24 December 1857 *The Times*, in its review of 'Perils', acknowledged Dickens's success in highlighting 'the salient traits so recently displayed by his countrymen and countrywomen' during the Mutiny (Oddie 1972, 4).

An area of media coverage that provided source material for Dickens's desire to represent these 'best qualities' of the English was what I term 'survivor' letters: eyewitness accounts, often by soldiers, recounting their experience of the rebellion. 'Perils' was not only written as a personal account of a Royal Marine, Gill who survived a rebellion in South America, but it also resonates with the descriptions and themes found in the survivor letters. I will give one such example. On 12 September the *ILN* published a letter written in Allahabad on 20 June 1857 by a British soldier.

> I had gone to bed and was just falling asleep, when I was aroused by a rolling fire of musketry (close to my bungalow) in the Sepoy lines ... The Sepoys were murdering their officers and attacking the treasury. Just then a fearful shout, the yelling of a thousand infuriate fiends, burst forth into the still night, accompanied by the shrieks of the poor young officers who were being cruelly murdered. Stream after stream of fire blazed up as the wretches set fire to the bungalows.
>
> It is impossible for me now to go through incident after incident of that fearful night. The Sepoys broke open the gaol and let loose 4000 convicts. These fiends, excited by opium and drink, burst over the place and burnt all our bungalows ... Both my pistols snapped when the time came to use them, and I feel sure that they had been tampered with by my own servants, men that I had had for years, and treated with great kindness. The rascals took my watch, which was under my pillow when the row commenced. (*ILN* 12 September 1857, 275)

In this brief account one can identify some crucial similarities between this 'survivor' letter and Dickens's 'Perils'. In the survivor letter, the soldier was attacked while asleep, the compound was burned to the ground and its inhabitants brutally murdered. 'Perils' not only recounted that the Fort was 'set ... in flames' but suggests the motivation for doing so was to 'roast us alive: which was one of their favourite ways of carrying on' (Dickens 1987b, 63). Second, in the survivor letter the attackers were depicted as demons, fiends and convicts – the last description referring to the widespread release, or self-liberation, of thousands of prisoners during the rebellion. A report printed in the *ILN* claimed that 3000 prisoners had freed themselves at Allahabad alone and were 'committing all sorts of outrages' (*ILN* 8 August 1857, 147). In 'Perils' the rebels were comprised of

> barbarous Pirates, scum of all nations, headed by such men as the hideous little Portuguese monkey, and the one-eyed English convict ... The worst men in the world picked out from the worst, to

do the cruellest and most atrocious deeds that ever stained it? The howling, murdering, black-flag waving, mad, and drunken crowds of devils that had overcome us by numbers and by treachery? (Dickens 1987b, 66)

Third, in the survivor letter the treachery was experienced on a personal level due to the duplicity of 'trusted' servants – for example, the tampered guns and the theft of the watch – while in 'Perils' the 'artful savage' (Dickens 1987b, 162) had managed to render all the powder and personal cartridges unserviceable. Dickens plays on the latter point – the level of personal treachery – in order to develop the central line that 'you can never trust a native'. In 'Perils', while Christian George King is 'showing all the little colony, but especially the ladies and children, how fond he was of them, how devoted to them, and how faithful to them for life' (Dickens 1987b, 175), he is also plotting with the Pirates to murder them. Likewise, the minute Gill decides 'If ever a man, Sambo or no Sambo, was trustful and trusted, to what may be called quite an infantine [*sic*] and sweetly beautiful extent ... it was that Sambo Pilot, Christian George King' (Dickens 1987b, 176), he is haunted and comes to learn of his artful treachery.

The survivor letters also bear witness to the heroism of British women who endeavour to protect their children in the face of certain death, a point which Dickens also emphasized. In a letter to Morley on 18 October 1857, Dickens stated that 'I wish to avoid India itself; but I want to shadow out, in what I do the bravery of our ladies in India' (Dickens 1937–8, 891–2). A survivor letter on 22 August offered a heroic portrait of the wife of the Sergeant Major at Neemuch who managed to kill two rebels before she died defending her children. Likewise the 12 September issue of the *ILN* printed a letter written by an officer's wife dated Agra 29 June which told of being deserted by her servants and left to '[wander] about in the night in momentary peril of our lives ... the bungalows were in blood-red flames ... and the shrieks of the mutineers made us quake' (*ILN* 21 September 1857, 275). However, she owed her life to the endeavours of 'natives', not the least of whom was a maharajah. The 24 October issue carried by far the most harrowing account of the atrocities suffered by one woman who, while lying injured, has to witness the murder of her children by the rebels. It was a heart-rending account, yet this woman ultimately also owed her life to the endeavours of various 'natives'. In 'Perils' Dickens makes much of the calm resourcefulness of the women, who were 'steady and busy' (1987b, 186) in the fort before the attack and the bravery of the women during the attack. Furthermore,

Miss Maryon shields Gill three times from attacks that would have meant certain death; Mrs Venning manages to strike a pirate while protecting her granddaughter before she falls, 'shot by his pistol' (Dickens 1987b, 191). Dickens obfuscates entirely the vital role of the indigenous people in aiding the British.

Other correspondents' reports used certain words and phrases that then became key words resonating throughout Dickens's short story. One such report of 8 August told of the rebels who 'became the assassins of their own officers' and then commenced 'burning the church and every bungalow in the place, and looting the treasury'. Throughout the Rebellion, the emphasis of the rebels was as much on the looting of the treasury as it was on the murdering of women and children. Indian papers stressed that they believed the real cause of the Mutiny was a 'lawless desire for plunder . . . [by] a set of undisciplined scoundrels, who were ready to shoot them [their officers] or to cut their throats if they stood in the way of their realising it' (*ILN* 8 August 1857, 147). Dickens links these two in his title when he refers to the 'treasure in women, children, silver and jewels'. Dickens uses the word treasure metonymically to symbolize the value of women and children in the imperial mission. Perhaps the single most important incident for British sensibilities during the Rebellion was what was referred to in the 22 August issue of the *ILN* as the 'ghastly picture of rapine, murder, and loathsome cruelty worse than death' (*ILN* 22 August 1857, 202), which described the massacre of 132 women and children ordered by Nana Sahib. The massacre commenced with Sahib's treachery and brutality in slaying them on the very rafts which he agreed to provide to allow them to escape. The survivors were then taken to the parade ground. It is a detail that Dickens does not miss; the initial treachery in 'Perils' centres around the disabling of the boats. Also, numerous reports described the mutineers, especially Nana Sahib, as a 'double-dyed traitor' and a 'villain' (*ILN* 5 September 1857, 243). In 'Perils', Gill describes Christian George King as a 'double-dyed traitor and a most infernal villain' (Dickens 1987b, 182).

Although the intertextuality between 'Perils' and the survivor letters signals itself, it is at those points where 'Perils' perhaps quite consciously differs from these 'survivor' letters that it is possible to identify Dickens's own imperial project. Gill, unlike the soldier from Allahabad, is woken by a dream vision and an inner knowledge rather than a direct attack: therefore, he is not caught napping but discovers the treachery through alertness and a good soldier's instinct. Gill does not flee the fighting or the attack but stays to defend the women and children in the fort; he displays a valour and determination that is greatly acclaimed. It can be

read as an endeavour to undo, or to rewrite, the inability of British soldiers to protect their women and children in India. Most crucially, the
multicultural composition of the forces fighting on the British side is an
aspect that Dickens conveniently obfuscates in 'Perils', although not in
HW. The survivor letters of British soldiers often referred to the debt
they owed to loyal indigenous people – whether aiding British soldiers
in the defence of a fort or helping them to escape.

In fact Dickens's representation of the indigenous population, in the
form of Christian George King, is most objectionable and is informed by
an underlying discourse of civilization and barbarism based on a notion of
degeneracy or 'reverse' evolution. Not content with describing Christian
George King's movements as spasmodic and unnatural (as if he has not
evolved into flowing motions), Christian George King nods 'as if it was
jerked out of him by a most violent hiccup – which is the way with
those savages', and his speech is a 'very objectionable kind of convul-
sions'. Ultimately, Dickens animalizes Christian George King: he runs at
'a wolf's trot'; he is 'barbarous' or 'barbarian'; he 'cluck[s]'; he speaks
in a 'low croak'; and he clings to Gill's leg in battle like a 'serpent'. The
final image is not only of 'a Traitor and a Spy' but an 'animal . . . [who
is] Shot through the heart . . . [and covered with] slime' (Dickens, 1987b,
170–205). This clucking and croaking bears a strong resemblance to
Dickens's nonfictional writing on 'The Noble Savage' in *HW* in 1853, in
which Dickens refers to the notion of the Noble Savage as 'an enormous
superstition' which is in reality 'a savage . . . to be civilised off the face of
the earth' – a 'howling, whistling, clucking, stamping, jumping, tearing
savage' whose absence is 'an indispensable preparation for the sowing
of the very first seeds of . . . humanity' (Dickens 1987a, 467). Ultimately,
'Perils' also revealingly revels in an excess which far surpasses these
survivor letters. This excess alerts one not only to the fear of the other
embedded within colonial desire, but also to the imaginative response
to the threatening nature of empire. By representing British forces and
colonialists as heroic and full of valour and trustworthiness, Dickens
ensures a clear identification and destruction of the threatening enemy
and a reaffirmation of national and masculine myths.

In the final analysis, Dickens shared a common concern that the
Rebellion could spread throughout the empire. This concern was
expressed most succinctly in an editorial of the *ILN* of 1 August which
argued that 'Every day that Delhi remains in the hands of the mutineers
is a day of peril to British power. Its possession . . . is an incentive to
rebellion' (110). The possible loss of empire not only threatened
national mythology but had economic and political ramifications. The

fear was that with the 'empire in the East ... imperilled', British 'prestige' and 'supremacy' among the European nations was also at risk (*Lloyd's Weekly*, 6 September 1857, 6). The resonance of the peril at hand is utilized in the title of the short story. It is possible then to read, as Patrick Brantlinger does, Dickens's location of the tale in Central America (what Dickens refers to as the West Indies) as an extension of the idea of rebellion to other parts of empire by equating East Indians, native Indians and Africans with each other and therefore implying that all 'natives' are untrustworthy (Brantlinger 1988, 207). This is also an interesting prefiguration of the Morant Bay rebellion and the Governor Eyre question which would involve Dickens eight years later. Dickens's underlying comment can be identified in the protagonist Gill's warning to 'trust no Sambo, and, above all, if he could get any good chance at Christian George King [CGK], not to lose it, but to put him out of the world' (Dickens 1987b, 184).[7]

This hard-line advocacy of a brutal putting down of rebellion echoed the agitation within the media to rule through fear. As an *ILN* editorial of 22 August argued, 'The spectacle of power is that which we should exhibit ... Asiatics differ not simply in religion, but in blood, from Europeans. They worship Power. They understand the strong arm, the inflexible will, the unrelenting determination' (*ILN* 22 August 1857, 186). In 'Perils', Gill is characterized by the Maltese leader of the rebellion as 'determined'. In addition, the final dark and menacing exhibition of Christian George King after his death, not only evokes the spectacle of lynching, but reflects the determination of Captain Carton, the officer who shot him. The hanging narrativizes the *ILN's* desired fate for Nana Sahib – namely the 'rope, not cold steel of the bullet' (*ILN* 5 September 1857, 235). If the Rebellion was a religious war, as was generally perceived, then Dickens was clear to emphasize in 'Perils' that the idyllic paradise had been purged of its demon, enabling the colonizers to revel in the Garden of Eden and the sailors to claim a spiritual reward: 'we went out of the gate too, marching along the level plain towards the serene blue sky, as if we were marching straight to Heaven' (Dickens 1987b, 207).

Dickens's concern with the situation in India did not cease after the publication of 'Perils', rather it developed into a more moderate stance. In addition to specialized articles, *HW* continued to run the series 'Wanderings in India', written by John Lang, which maintained its criticism of the governing of India until the series' conclusion at the end of February 1858. Among its narrative concerns were: the litany of broken promises to loyal soldiers (Lang 1857–8, 15); the imbecility of the commanding officers (Lang 1857–8, 64); the ambiguity between not establishing whether India should either be governed in India or in England (Lang 1857–8, 92); and the widespread corruption within the justice system (Lang 1857–8, 181). In addition a separate article, 'A Sermon for Sepoys', written on 27 February by Wilkie Collins, tackled the contentious issue of the conversion to Christianity – the 'taming [of] the human tigers in that country by Christian means' (Collins 1858, 244). It concluded with the maxim that a life most acceptable was that which was most useful to the human race which, it claimed, was 'Surely not a bad Indian lesson, to begin with, when Betrayers and Assassins are the pupils to be taught' (Collins 1858, 247).

What this chapter has attempted to do, then, is to map the intersection of political, journalistic and literary discourses which emerged from the same crisis and combined to mediate the same structure of feeling. All contribute to the cultural debate surrounding the Rebellion; all carry within their forms similar political and ideological agendas. In short, all participate in the 'word politics' to which Said refers. Dickens too enters this word politics as journalist, editor and author.

Notes

1. By this time Lord Canning was known as 'Clemency' Canning, both in India and in Britain, because he was considered to be 'soft' on rebels (Oddie 1972, 5).
2. What is interesting to note is the frank admission in the press of the indebtedness of Englishmen to their indigenous allies, 'the wild forces of the Gheend Rajah', the 'gallant little Ghoorkahs' and the 'tall [bloodthirsty] Affghans ... [who swipe] off both ... legs with ... a scimitar' (*ILN* 8 August 1857, 147). As late as 3 October 1857, reports were being published in the *ILN* of entire native regiments, such as the 31st at Saugor, headed by native officers, with no Europeans, who attacked, routed and defeated 'rebel countrymen' (*ILN* 3 October 1857, 331). It is important to note this as it does offer a certain qualification of the construction of racial types discussed and will come to bear on the construction of national types discussed later in this piece.
3. For example, 'Mr. Jones, amidst some interruption, suggested that if the East India Directors would refrain from spending £3000 or £4000 a year in feasting, they would soon obtain a goodly sum towards alleviating the distress now existing in India' (*ILN* 29 August 1857, 214).
4. One of the perceived consequences of not suppressing the Indian Rebellion was that there would be more trouble in the constituent parts of Great Britain – particularly Ireland. It is important to note the similarities in the construction of the character of the indigenous peoples in India and those in Ireland in newspapers at the time.
5. The following is an excerpt of an eyewitness account of an execution by blowing from the mouth of a cannon:

As the hour of five struck, the stillness became awful; every feeling and faculty was strung to its utmost tension, and the beating of hearts became audible. The spectacle was one of quiet horror; there being none of that excitement which is to be met with at a public execution in any other part of the world. The natives of India are not a demonstrative race, and they looked on with an appearance of stolid indifference. The handful of stern and determined Europeans had, moreover, over-awed them, and there was but one feeling predominant – fear . . . The word 'Fire!' rang out clear as a clarion-note from the lips of Capt. Bolton. Next moment, the earth shook as if a volcano had opened at our feet. The guns were enveloped in thick clouds of smoke, through the white wreaths of which little particles of a crimson colour were falling, thick as snow-flakes. The particles were the prisoners blown into atoms.

When the smoke cleared, a score or two of half-naked men, each with a broom and a small basket, were scattered over the plain. They were the sweepers, picking up the fragments for internment, and robbing the crows of their morning repast. As the sun dipped in a sea of gold the artillery limbered up, the military marched to their lines, and the crowd dispersed.

Those who witnessed the impressive scene will never forget it. The Europeans were scarcely one to a thousand – in fact, they could hardly be seen amongst the myriads of Asiatics; but all appeared as cool and confident as if they had been at a review in Hyde Park. (Craig 1858, 349–50)

6. Dickens had a well-documented aversion to the rise of the bureaucracy and the civil servant. In his novel *Little Dorrit* (written 1855–7) Dickens offers a withering portrayal of the Circumlocution Office as a model of 'how not to do it'. The fact that Dickens chooses to staff the Circumlocution Office with a family called the Tite Barnacles reveals the parasitic nature of these civil servants; they are to be read as a drain on the 'ship of state'.

7. The Morant Bay rebellion can be seen as a pivotal moment for Dickens. Earlier in the century, Dickens was vehement in his support for the abolitionists. However, by the time of Morant Bay in 1865 Dickens's own attitudes towards people of colour had changed. He no longer believed in the noble savage or the nobility of other races (as evidenced by his article, 'The Noble Savage' written for *Household Words* in 1853); the Jamaican uprising only served to underline, for Dickens, that indigenous peoples needed to be ruled by force. In England at the time, Governor Eyre's brutal suppression of the Morant Bay rebellion split the public into those who thought that he should be brought back to England and tried for murder and those who felt his actions were justified. What is not often discussed is the fact that Dickens sided with the latter while his close friend Wilkie Collins sided with the former. For a fuller discussion of the issue, see Catherine Hall, *White, Male and Middle-Class*. Cambridge, 1992.

Works cited

Brantlinger, Patrick. *Rule of Darkness: British Literature and Imperialism, 1830–1914*. Ithaca, 1988.

Buitenhuis, Peter. *The Great War of Words: Literature as Propaganda 1914–18 and After*. London, 1989.

Byrne, F. 'British Opinion and the Indian Revolt', in P.C. Joshi (ed.), *Rebellion 1857: a Symposium*. New Delhi, 1957, 290–8.

Capper, John. 'A Very Black Act', *Household Words* (26 September 1857), 293–4.

Collins, Wilkie. 'A Sermon for Sepoys', *Household Words* (27 February 1858), 244–7.

Craig, George. 'Blown Away', *Household Words* (27 March 1858), 348–50.

Dawson, Graham. *Soldier Heroes: British Adventure, Empire and the Imagining of Masculinities*. London, 1994.

Dickens, Charles. 'Frauds on the Fairies', *Household Words* (1 October 1853).

Dickens, Charles. Letter to Angela Burdett-Coutts, in *Charles Dickens, Letters*, ed. Walter Dexter, 3 vols. Bloomsbury, 1937–8.

Dickens, Charles. 'The Noble Savage', *Household Words* 1853, reprinted in *Uncommercial Traveller and Reprinted Pieces*. Oxford 1987a, 467–73.

Dickens, Charles and Wilkie Collins. 'The Perils of Certain English Prisoners and Their Treasure in Women, Children, Silver and Jewels', *Christmas Books*, Oxford 1987b, 161–208.

Foucault, Michel. *Discipline and Punish: the Birth of the Prison*. trans. by Alan Sheridan. London, 1991.

Hall, Catherine. *White, Male and Middle Class*. Cambridge, 1992.

Hutchins, F.G. *The Illusion of Permanence: British Imperialism in India*. Princeton, 1967.

Lang, John. 'Wanderings in India', *Household Words* (1857–8).

Memmi, Albert. *The Coloniser and the Colonised*, trans. by H. Greenfeld. London, 1990.

Nayder, Lillian. 'Class Consciousness and the Indian Mutiny in Dickens's "The Perils of Certain English Prisoners"', *Studies in English Literature* 32 (1992), 689–705.

Oddie, William. 'Dickens and the Indian Mutiny', *The Dickensian* 8 (1972), 3–15.

Paxton, Nancy L. 'Mobilizing Chivalry: Rape in British Novels about the Indian Uprising of 1857', *Victorian Studies* 36 (Fall 1992), 5–30.

Robertson, John. 'Sepoy Symbols of Mutiny', *Household Words* (5 September 1857), 228–32.

Said, Edward. *Covering Islam: How the Media and the Experts Determine How We See the Rest of The World*. London, 1981.

Sanders, M.L. and Taylor, Philip M. *British Propaganda During the First World War, 1914–18*. Basingstoke, 1982.

Spurr, D. *The Rhetoric of Empire: Colonial Discourse in Journalism, Travel Writing and Imperial Administration*. London, 1993.

Tambling, Jeremy. *Dickens, Violence and the Modern State: Dreams of the Scaffold*. London, 1995.

Taylor, Philip M. *Munitions of the Mind: a History of Propaganda from the Ancient World to the Present Era*. Manchester, 1995.

Townsend, E. 'Indian Irregulars', *Household Words* (12 September 1857a), 244–6.

Townsend, E. 'A Mutiny in India', *Household Words* (15 August 1857b), 154–6.

Townsend, E. and Hamilton, Alexander. 'Indian Recruits and Indian English', *Household Words* (3 October 1857), 319–22.

7
Narratives of Progress and Idioms of Community: Two Urdu Periodicals of the 1870s[1]

Javed Majeed

An overview

The background to this chapter draws upon Imdad Sabri's magisterial three-volume study of the Urdu press in nineteenth-century India, *Tārīkh-e ṣaḥāfat-e urdū* (1953–63). Sabri lists some 1572 Urdu periodicals of varying duration. For each periodical, he supplies the date of the first issue, the place of issue, the names of the owner and manager (*mohtamim*) of the press concerned, as well as the name of the editor. For most (but not all) of the periodicals he tells us how often they were issued, and he sometimes gives the date when the periodical ceased publication. Furthermore, each volume of his study contains a preface detailing the location of copies of periodicals in a variety of archives and libraries, as well as an appendix listing the periodicals covered in each volume. The existence of those periodicals for which copies do not survive are detailed on the basis of notices and reviews in the surviving copies of other periodicals, which Sabri often cites in full, giving full references in terms of pagination and the dates of the issues in which these reviews and notices are to be found. However, the bulk of Sabri's study consists of very useful excerpts of varying length from a wide range of periodicals, as well as biographical sketches, again of varying length, of some of the editors and owners of the presses concerned. This helps to make his lengthy three-volume study (altogether amounting to some 2000 pages) an indispensable, not to mention impressive, primary and secondary source.

Here I will concentrate on two periodicals, both of which were consulted in the Oriental and India Office Collections, British Library. One of these is *Mufīd-e ʿām* ('General usefulness'), a twice-monthly journal published in Agra. I will concentrate on one year of this periodical, namely the issues from 1 March 1869 to 1 March 1870. The second periodical, *Aligarh Institute Gazette* (hereafter *AIG*) was published from Aligarh every two weeks with an English-Urdu section, and an Urdu only supplement. Here I concentrate on the Urdu supplement for the year 1875.

A number of interesting issues arise from focusing on and comparing *Mufīd-e ʿām* and the *AIG*. Firstly, there is the question of what sort of relationship these periodicals have with the British Indian state. Also of importance is how these periodicals pictured the state and their own interactions with it. Answering such questions helps us to understand how, to adapt Habermas' phraseology (Habermas 1989, 43), the Urdu periodical press became an object for itself to reflect upon, and how it read and debated about itself. However, this is not to suggest that the bourgeois public sphere in Europe as delineated by Habermas was reproduced in pre-colonial or colonial India (on the differences between the two societies, see Bayly 1996, 181–2, and from a different perspective, Chatterjee 1994, 75).

Secondly, it repays examining how the styles and registers of Urdu used relate to the ideological concerns of these periodicals. I argue that these ideological concerns focus on grappling with narratives of progress and corresponding idioms of community. These two themes are interrelated. Thus, the way a periodical interacted with and pictured the colonial state was, to some extent, reflected in the style of Urdu it used.

In his study of the Urdu press, Sabri (1953–63) does not arrive at any general categories regarding the nineteenth-century periodicals he surveys. However, by way of background to this essay, I have collated and analysed the information in his work to make some general points. First, as mentioned above, for most (but not all) of the Urdu periodicals he surveys, Sabri tells us how often they were issued. Of those whose frequency of issue he notes, the majority (some 460) were issued weekly. Around 287 were issued monthly, 87 were issued every two weeks, 23 were issued thrice monthly, 23 were dailies, 13 were issued twice a week, one was a biannual publication, and one was an annual publication. Secondly, the contents of the majority of nineteenth-century Urdu periodicals were generally eclectic. In this regard, the contents of *Mufīd-e ʿām* are typical. Every issue I examined for the year 1869–70 followed the same format in terms of an article on the virtues of learning (*faẓīlat-e ʿilm kī bayān men*), which sometimes extended to pieces on women's education, then official news regarding the Department of Public Instruction under the title '*Sar rishta-ye tāʾlīm*', followed by articles on agriculture, a history of sages and philosophers (*'Ḥukamā-ye falāsifa kī qadīm tārīkh'*), a history of former Indian kings (*'Tārīkh-e bādshāhān-e salaf'*), inspirational verse (*'Ash 'ār ābdār-e naṣīḥat-āmez va 'ibrat-khez'*), a table listing the local prices for a variety of agricultural goods, an abridgement of the government gazette (*'Khulāṣa gavarnmanṭ gazaṭ'*), and finally an abridgement of Urdu and English papers (*'Khulāṣa akhbārāt-e urdū va angrezī'*). To a certain extent, the eclectic nature of Urdu periodicals such as the *Mufīd-e 'ām* combined what C.A. Bayly has described as 'the Indian form of "treasury of learning" with that of the British compendia of useful knowledge' (Bayly 1996, 235).

However, Sabri also mentions a number of periodicals whose scope is more restricted. Collating his information once again, we find some 69 periodicals that would come under the generic heading of *guldasta*, literally a 'nosegay of roses'. These were literary journals containing selections of poems, accounts of poets' gatherings and competitions (*mushā'ira*), and biographical sketches of important poets, past and present. We also find some 28 legal journals, and some 72 religious journals, of which 12 had a Christian orientation, 40 addressed Islamic issues, and 30 were Hindu in orientation, representing the views of specific bodies such as the *āryā samāj* or a caste association or a *sabhā* [assembly or society].[2] Thus, whilst the majority of the Urdu periodicals cannot be subsumed under one category alone – including the two periodicals examined in detail here – there were some periodicals which had a clearly defined focus.

It is important to remind oneself of the difference between Urdu in the nineteenth-century Indian landscape and Urdu in contemporary South Asia. Today, exclusive connections between Urdu and South Asian Islam are seen as self-evident. However, these connections were yet to triumph in the India of the 1860s and 1870s. Although the Hindi–Urdu controversy does have an increasingly important presence in the periodical press from the 1860s onwards, the fact remains that a significant number of editors and proprietors of Urdu periodicals were not Muslims. As mentioned above, Sabri lists the names of the proprietors and editors of Urdu periodicals, and putting this together from his three volumes, we find that some 287 of the proprietors and editors mentioned were non-Muslims, for some of whom Sabri includes biographical sketches. This impression is reinforced by the official reports on vernacular newspapers and periodicals, which list the names of editors and proprietors of Urdu journals. Thus in the 1873 report for the Northwestern Provinces, for example, 45 periodicals are listed – 32 Urdu, 2 Urdu–Hindi, and 11 Hindi. Of the Urdu periodicals, 11 of the proprietors and 15 of the editors are also non-Muslims (*Selections* 1873, 526–8). Much of this has to do with fact that Urdu was the official court language of the Northwestern Provinces, but none the less, there is evidence to support C.R. King's approach to the Hindi–Urdu controversy in terms of the processes of assimilation and differentiation (King 1994; see also Dalmia 1997). Using the terms of King's analysis, in the periodical press of the 1870s and earlier, although there are some signs of differentiation between Urdu and Hindi in terms of religious identity, these signs are still very much on the margins. In part, at least, this is clear from the existence of what might be called Hindu-oriented publications in Urdu mentioned above, but it is also clear from such Islamic-oriented publications as the monthly *Koh-e ṭūr* ('Mount Sinai'), which was first issued in Gujranwala in December 1866. This periodical contained translations of the Quran, as well as traditions relating to the prophet Muhammad, but its owner was a non-Muslim, Divan Chand (Sabri 1953–63, 2: 268).[3]

Furthermore, most of the Urdu periodicals reflect the more flexible polyglot landscape of nineteenth-century India in terms of the wide range of styles and registers which these periodicals drew upon before the increasing standardization and differentiation of languages. A small number of Urdu periodicals also contained sections in the devanagari script, as well as sections in both the devanagari script and in English.[4] There is also one example of an Urdu periodical in roman script. This was a Methodist paper, the *Kaukab-e 'īsawī* ('Star of Jesus'), issued twice a month in Lucknow from May 1868 onwards (Sabri 1953–63, 2: 393).[5] Small though these numbers are, these examples are significant in that they reflect a readership that was able to move between the Perso-Arabic and devanagari scripts, and they also indicate that script itself had yet to become a powerfully articulated symbol of a communally charged linguistic identity (for which, see Brass 1974, ch. 3).

Narratives of progress

Robert Nisbet has argued that during the period 1750 to 1900 'the idea of progress reached its zenith in the Western mind in popular as well as scholarly circles. From being one of the important ideas in the West it became the dominant idea.' He goes on to say that this period also saw the 'secularization' of the idea of progress; as a historical process it was detached from its previous relationship with God, making it a historical process 'activated and maintained by purely natural causes' (Nisbet 1980, 171–2). To a certain extent, this idiom of progress was used by the British Indian state as part of its legitimizing rhetoric, the idea being that it required the intervention of this state in Indian history in order to set it on a progressive path. Thus British rule in India was seen by some liberal thinkers, such as John Stuart Mill, as embodying the forces of progress, and so as playing out a narrative of history as progress (Mill 1858, 91–160; Mill 1861, 142–453; see also Bearce 1961, 282–5).[6]

In official reports on the Indian language press, this kind of view is reflected in the sort of language used and the recurrence of certain formulae, in which development is expressed in terms of a list of factors with a hidden causal link. Thus, in the Report for 1869, both the development of female education and of the 'vernacular' press are presented in terms of 'signs of progress' that have occurred under the patronage of the state (*Selections* 1870, 224). Indeed, sometimes, as is the case here, the interest the Indian-language press took in the development of education for women is seen as a measure of its maturity (ibid., 224–5).

It is with the signifying of these signs of progress and possible alternatives that the Urdu periodical press is concerned. On one level, both the periodicals examined here appear to mimic and participate in the colonial state's idiom of progress, but on another level the style of Urdu in which this idiom of progress is formulated is sometimes interrupted by other styles associated with pre-existing idioms or poetics. This intertwining of styles, or the interaction of different stylistic arenas, is eloquent of the ambivalences surrounding the Urdu periodical press's engagement with the notion of progress. These ambivalences were also evident in the poetic works of the period, such as Altaf Hussain Hali's *Musaddas madd o jazr-e islām* ('Musaddas on the flow and ebb of Islam') of 1879 (for which, see Hali 1997). They are also indicative of what Habermas, in another context, called the 'tension-charged field' between state and society in which 'authority and publicity confronted each other' (Habermas 1989, 73). It was in just such a tension-charged field that the Urdu periodical press had to negotiate its own trajectory.

The *AIG* was strongly linked to the Aligarh movement. Broadly speaking, the Aligarh movement represented the interests of an Urdu-speaking elite and service gentry (both Hindu and Muslim) in late nineteenth-century India. Its aim was to enable these groups to adjust to the new realities of British power after the traumatic suppression of the Indian Rebellion of 1857. The rhetoric of the movement focussed on education reform, which saw fruition with the establishment of the Muhammadan Anglo-Oriental College in 1875 at Aligarh (for a history of this movement, see Lelyveld 1978 and Hali 1901). At first glance, the *AIG* seems to have had close links to the state and its idiom of progress. Thus, to give just one example, in its issue of 22 January 1875 it reports on the visit of a European official, Sir John Strachey, to the Institute, and includes the text of his speech which he delivered in Urdu. This speech sets out an agenda for replaying an enlightenment narrative of progress in India, in which all the signs of progress are gathered together in pseudo-causal linkages (*AIG* 22 January 1875, 50–6).

The visit of a high-ranking official to the Aligarh Institute points to the high degree of patronage the Aligarh movement received from the government (Lelyveld 1978, 135–41). Official reports on Indian-language papers frequently cite or refer to passages from the *AIG* as important examples of what one report called, referring to this periodical itself, 'the progress party' (*Selections* 1873, 518).[7] The Report for 1872 also points out that the *AIG* has the highest circulation in the Northwestern Provinces (381 copies), but of these 381 copies, the government itself bought 100 copies – native Indians accounted for only 191 subscriptions (*Selections* 1873, 516, 526–7; the remaining copies were sent to European subscribers). The same report also points out that the *AIG*'s circulation had fallen from the previous year's total of 462 copies. This was due to the reduction in the number of copies taken by the government, which was once again indicative of the importance of government patronage to the survival of this periodical (*Selections* 1873, 516). One appendix to the *Report on the Progress of Education for 1870–1871* lists the Scientific and Literary Societies for the Northwestern Provinces. The Aligarh Institute comes top in terms of its subscriptions and also in terms of receiving the largest amount of money from the government – almost half as much as the next society down the list. Furthermore, the description of the Institute's purpose closely mirrors the language of progress in Sir John Strachey's speech, but this is also true of the other 16 societies listed (*Report on the Progress of Education* 1871, 3–6).

All editors must have been aware of the yearly reports compiled by the government on the Indian-language press, and this might be in part responsible for the invocation of the trope of progress in a wide variety of periodicals of different standing, from the *Mufīd-e ʿām* to the *AIG*. Such invocations were often there to help win government subscriptions, as well as perhaps lessen the likelihood of falling foul of Act 25 of 1867 for the Regulation of Printing Presses and Newspapers, and Act 27 of 1870 which covered seditious writings defined as 'attempts to excite feelings of disaffection to the Government' (Burns 1940, 262–9). Furthermore, the government was also an important source of information. Every issue of *Mufīd-e ʿām* included three sections, one a summary of items from the *Government Gazette*, another a summary of news relating to the Department for Public Instruction, and the third a listing the prices for a variety of agricultural produce. This last section drew its information from the *Government Gazette for the North Western Provinces*, which was issued in English, Urdu, and Hindi, and contained frequent supplements listing 'prices current in the chief stations in the North-Western Provinces'. Usually 17 locations were listed, along with the prices of 22 agricultural products, such as different types of wheat, sugar, rice, and so on. (For example, see the Supplement to the *Government Gazette, North-Western Provinces*, 8 January 1869, and also for 20 January, 3 February, 8 February, 13 February, and so on.)

Thus, *Mufīd-e 'ām* incorporated parts of the official paraphernalia of administration and government regulations as part of its news function. It also contained reports on the proceedings and meetings of 'reform' societies such as the Sosā'iṭī rafāh-e khalāiq-e āgra (the Society for the welfare of the inhabitants of Agra) in its issues of 15 June, 1 July, 1 August and 1 October 1869, the Anjuman-e taḥzīb-e kānpūr (the Society for the edification of Kanpur) in its issue of 15 September 1869, and the Anjuman-e aḥbāb-e maqām-e muzaffarpūr (the Society of the Friends of Muzaffarpur) in its issue of 1 December 1869. Historians such as David Lelyveld have highlighted the growth of debating societies and Literary and Scientific Associations in late-nineteenth-century India (Lelyveld 1978, 80–1). Here one aspect needing to be highlighted is the way in which the state's official reports, the debating and reform societies and groups, and the press itself formed a circle of readers, reinforcing and reading each other in ways which underpinned the narrative of progressive reform in the public sphere. The signs of progress alluded to in official reports included not just the development of the 'vernacular' press, but also the growth of reform societies, while many of these reform societies also subscribed to each other's journals, and saw themselves, along with government, as patrons of the press. (For example, see *Mufīd-e 'ām* 1 September 1869, 16 thanking the Anjuman-e Banāras for its subscription for a year.) Meanwhile, the press published and publicised the aims and proceedings of these societies, many of which included accounts of visits and speeches by government officials. In some ways, the press acted as a conduit between different groups, as when the *Mufīd-e 'ām* for 1 August 1869 reported on correspondence between the Majlis-e anjuman-e nanītāl and the Majlis-e rafāh-e khalāiq-e āgra, which outlined issues of progressive reform centring on women's education which both groups needed to discuss together. Four items for discussion were suggested: whether women's education should be conducted at home or in schools; who was to supervise their education; which books should be included in the curriculum; and who should take and supervise their examinations (*Mufīd-e 'ām*, 1 August 1869, 15).

However, there are significant ways in which this self-reinforcing circle of a progressive idiom is interrupted in *Mufīd-e 'ām*. First, in every issue there is a section on increasing the produce of land which reads like an instruction manual. To all intents and purposes, this is cast in a scientific, utilitarian mould, with a discussion of different types of soil and fertilizer, methods of horticultural practice from sowing seed to weeding, irrigation, suitability of plants for a variety of soils, crop rotation, together with diagrams of different agricultural implements and instructions on how to use them. However, in the issue of 15 March 1869, after discussing a variety of types of soil, the writer accounts for the mixture of soils in every region in terms of the Biblical and Quranic story of Noah's flood. It was the effect of the flood, the author claims, which left the otherwise separate types of soil so intermingled (*Mufīd-e 'ām* 15 March 1869, 4). In other words, legend and myth are used as explanations alongside language which is of a scientistic cast.[8]

This blending of myth or legend with scientistic discourse indicates how the incorporation of the narrative of progress in *Mufīd-e 'ām* had not resulted in oppositions of fact and fiction, myth and history, or magic and science, so characteristic of European narratives of progress. Thus, the section entitled *'Khulāṣa akhbārāt-e urdū va angrezī'* (a summary of Urdu and English newspapers) often contains news in the sense familiar to western observers today – that is, an account of verifiable events in specific localities at specific times. However, interspersed with this are news accounts which refer to magical happenings, without any hint on the part of the editor that they are discontinuous with news in the sense mentioned above. Thus, in the issue of 1 March 1869, the news section contains an item on how a spring had been discovered in Swat, which has magical healing properties (*'chasmā-ye āb-e shifā'*) (*Mufīd-e 'ām* 1 March 1869, 16). Similarly, in the issue of 15 July 1869 the report on the building of the Suez canal mentions the discovery of a magical tree (*'Darakht-e 'azīm us-shān'*), under which Jesus and Mary supposedly rested on their way to Egypt from Canaan (*Mufīd-e 'ām* 15 July 1869, 13). There are a number of other stories of a similar flavour recounting magical or miraculous happenings, alongside more mundane news items.[9] In fact, the reports on the wonders of technology fit in with these reports on magical happenings.[10] They become an extension of such magical events. Rather than conflicting with the magical world, technology becomes a part of it.

Similarly, *Mufīd-e 'ām* has a section in every issue entitled *'Tārīkh-e bādshāhān-e salaf'* or the history of former kings. This is mainly an account of the early Muslim dynasties of medieval India, but the first excerpt in the issue of 1 March 1869 begins with an account of the pillar at the fort of Allahabad, and the place of worship underneath the fort which is called pattāl purī. This contains an everlasting tree called 'akhai bar', that will last until qiyāmat (the day of judgement). Noteworthy here is the mixture of Hindu and Muslim elements, with the reference to an immortal tree in Hindu legend and the allusion to Quranic teleology. The author then goes on to describe the engravings on the pillar in 'hindī' script, which have not been fully deciphered by the British, along with engravings by the Mughal emperor Jahangir, listing the names of his ancestors in Persian (*Mufīd-e ʿām* 1 March 1869, 8–9). What the author is referring to here is one of Asoka's pillars, in the temple at the confluence of the Ganges and Jumna, and its inscriptions. The inscriptions are indeed extended by engravings in Persian by Jahangir listing his ancestors (*Imperial Gazetteer of India Provincial Series: United Provinces and Oudh* 1908, 1: 19, 24, 11: 78–9, and Fuhrer 1891, 127–30).

Thus, a history of Muslim kings begins with Hindu legend and mythology underpinning the location of the fort. There is a sense of layers of history reflected in the engravings on the pillar stretching from Asoka to Jahangir, but there is no hint of any conflict between the layers of what amounts to a palimpsest. Indeed, throughout the *Mufīd-e ʿām* all rulers, whether Muslim, Hindu or British, are in fact treated as part of a continuum, and as belonging to a category of their own which has little to do with everyday life. The editor uses a variety of terms for the British, ranging from 'sarkār' (chief, master) in the issue for 1 January 1870, to 'bādshāh' (king) in the issue of 1 July 1869. Furthermore, the author of the piece in the 1 March issue refers to a Colonel Kyd, who repaired the structure and converted it from a palace into a military fort. In the *Imperial Gazetteer*, Colonel Kyd is noted as having pulled down the pillar in 1798 (Fuhrer 1891, 130). In other words, the author also weaves into his renditions of annals and chronicles of the medieval period references to more recent times. He begins with a specific locality, the seat of government for the Northwestern Provinces and Awadh, and his historical narrative begins with the sacred confluence of rivers, a mythological tree, and a historical pillar. Interwoven into this account of a sacred Hindu locale are citations from the Quran and Hadith that again are simply part of the author's eclectic repertoire. The different strands of this narrative have yet to be communalized, while the elements of myth, legend and history are conflated, rather than distinguished from one another.

Indeed, the narrative of progress in *Mufīd-e ʿām* is sometimes absorbed into larger cultural narratives. At the very least, it becomes simply another layer in an already layered notion of progress. Thus, every issue of *Mufīd-e 'ām* examined for the year also has a section entitled '*Faẓīlat-e 'ilm kī bayān men*' or 'On the virtue of learning'. This section repeatedly paints the picture of an alternative moral economy, in opposition to the power and wealth of worldly rulers. The style is gnomic, containing aphorisms and maxims in Persian and Arabic, most of which refer to the conduct of daily life and the intuitive moral rules that should be followed in our dealings with each other. In other words, this section in *Mufīd-e 'ām* is a popular version of the tradition of *adab* literature. This was a species of polite literature, medieval in origin, whose polished sense of artifice reflected its concern with the codes of behaviour and values that should underpin personal development. Barbara Metcalf (1984, 2) has usefully characterized *adab* literature as reflecting 'a high valuation of the employment of the will in proper discrimination of correct order, behaviour, and taste'. In this regard, it is perhaps interesting to note that Imdad Sabri begins his monumental study of the Urdu periodical press by arguing that the history of Urdu *adab* is not complete unless it incorporates a history of Urdu journalism (*ṣaḥāfat*) so that he sees journalism of the type represented in the periodical press as a subcategory of *adab* literature (Sabri 1953–63, 1: 20).

However, alongside this popular rendition of the traditions of *adab* literature, *Mufīd-e 'ām* also contains strong elements of popular wisdom literature, reflected in the aphoristic style of much of the paper. Every issue examined here also contains a section entitled '*Ḥukamā-ye falāsifa kī qadīm tārīkh*' (the ancient history of philosophers and sages), which consists of the anecdotes and sayings of Plato, Pythagoras, Aristotle and other Greek philosophers. The 'Report on the vernacular press, N.W.P' for the year 1869 comments on this part of *Mufīd-e 'ām* thus: 'That part of the paper devoted to the memoirs of the ancient Greek philosophers is interesting and worth perusal' (*Selections* 1871, 432–3). This section is quite clearly an example of Graeco-Arabic gnomologia, translated into Urdu. This body of Arabic literature, dating from the ninth century, consisted of collections of ethical sayings and anecdotes ascribed to Greek philosphers (Gutas 1975, 1986, 15–36). This section of *Mufīd-e 'ām* clearly indicates that this literature had been transmitted to India, but the present author is unable to shed any light on the means by which it was transmitted. There is no space here to do a detailed comparison of the anecdotes and sayings of Greek philosophers in *Mufīd-e 'ām* with similar Arabic texts edited and translated by Dmitri Gutas. However, there is one major difference: as is to be expected, *Mufīd-e 'ām* is more eclectic in its use of sources. It works Biblical and

Quranic anecdotes into its history of the Greek philosophers in a way which is not to be found in the Arabic literature examined by Dmitri Gutas. Thus, in the issue of 1 March 1869, the author writes of Aristotle's meeting with the Prophet Elias (*Mufīd-e 'ām* 1 March 1869, 6), while in the issue of 15 March 1869, the editor explains how Pythagoras learnt natural philosophy from Solomon, and how Greek knowledge was transmitted to pre-Islamic Iran through one of the Persian kings, of *Shāh nāma* fame, who conquered Greece, and brought back with him Socrates and Hippocrates (*Mufīd-e 'ām* 15 March 1869, 5). Furthermore, the maxims and aphorisms of Greek philosophers are supplemented by citations from the Persian classical poets, Sa'di and Hafiz (*Mufīd-e 'ām* 1 May 1869, 2). These elements give an indication of how one body of popular wisdom literature developed through a variety of accretions in an Indian context.

To sum up the argument so far, *Mufīd-e 'ām* demonstrates how an eclectic tradition of popular wisdom literature, which reads in this case like an Urdu version of Graeco-Arabic gnomologia, persisted into late nineteenth-century India. The gnomic sayings and aphorisms, drawn from cultural reserves pre-colonial in origin, have more weight in *Mufīd-e 'ām* as a whole than the rather fragile signs of the European narrative of progress. There is an idiom of self-improvement in *Mufīd-e 'ām*, but it is fashioned from elements of popular wisdom literature, and/or from the framework and style of thinking of ethical treatises represented by such earlier medieval works as Nasir ud din Tusi's *Akhlāq-e nāṣirī* ('The Nasirean Ethics'). The diction used by progressive societies and periodicals draws on the vocabulary and conceptual framework of this literature, so that the idiom of progress simply becomes part of a much more powerful pre-existing polite literature of moral self-improvement, as well as popular wisdom literature in a gnomic style. To give an example, in *Mufīd-e 'ām* virtually all the societies it reports upon use the phrase '*tahzīb-e akhlāq*' in the summary of their aims. The aim of the '*Anjuman-e tahzīb kānpūr*' is reported to be the *tahzīb-e akhlāq* of the people of that locality (*Mufīd-e 'ām* 15 September 1869, 16). Similarly, in an article on the necessity of women's education, one of the aims is defined as '*akhlāq kī tahzīb*' (*Mufīd-e 'ām* 1 January 1870, 2). Furthermore, the phrase is also used to describe the section in the periodical which contained excerpts from the works of poets (*Mufīd-e 'ām* 1 May 1869, 16). The phrase '*tahzīb-e akhlāq*' is quite clearly drawn from Persian literature on ethics and moral conduct. This phrase is the title of the first section of the *Akhlāq-e nāṣirī*. This treatise, which first appeared in 1235, has been described by G.M. Wickens (1964, 9) as the 'best known ethical digest to be composed in medieval Persia, if not in all medieval

Islam'.[11] Wickens translates the phrase to mean 'The Correction of Dispositions', and, in many ways, this is the founding category of the treatise as a whole. As Tusi argues, he is concerned with the science of how the human soul can acquire a disposition 'such that all its acts, proceeding from it by its will, may be fair and praiseworthy' (ibid., 35).

It is important to remember that texts such as these were still part of a Hindu–Muslim heritage in late-nineteenth-century India. The official report of 1869 on 'Books submitted to government by native writers' contains a detailed account of a treatise in ethics in Urdu of 150 pages by a 'Pandit Kashee Nath' (*Selections* 1870, 3: 47–57). The report describes its contents as 'Mahomedan [*sic*] moral science and etiquette, arranged and epitomized for use in Hindoo and Mahomedan [*sic*] families and schools'. The manuscript is also described as a compilation of moral science and etiquette, drawn from three important Persian works, the *Akhlāq-e nāṣirī*, the *Akhlāq-e jalālī*, and the *Akhlāq-e moḥsinī*. The report then goes on to say that the 'author assumes without hesitation the suitability of the system to Hindoo and Musalman alike'. It adds that 'most Hindoo gentlemen in the Upper Provinces have made these works the subject of study' (ibid., 47–8).

An interrupted new style

Thus, a reading of Urdu periodicals shows that the European narrative of progress becomes an extension and refashioning of pre-existing idioms. However, the colonial state and some periodicals, such as the *AIG*, attempted to define a new style of Urdu which would form an appropriate vehicle for the message of European progress. The *AIG*, in its issue of 19 February 1875, has a long piece discussing how it self-consciously used a certain style of Urdu, because it fits in better with its message of reform and progress. The ideal it strived for was plain, unadorned prose, in contradistinction to the ornate, polished style of belles lettres (*inshā*). The article lists the qualities of prose that the *AIG* tries to embody, namely transparency (*ṣafā'ī*), accuracy (*durustī*), and plainness (*sādagī*). These qualities stand in opposition to the devices of metaphor, simile and rhyme used in the tradition of ornate prose writing which results in a regard for words alone rather than for their meaning (*AIG* 19 February 1875, '*Taraqqī-e'ilm-e inshā*' ['The development of belles lettres'] 121–3).

There is a clear overlap between the qualities of prose the *AIG* tries to foster and the qualities of writing that official reports try to encourage through their patronage. For example, the author of the 'Report on vernacular newspapers and periodicals published in the North-Western provinces during 1869', draws a similar distinction between 'plain grammatical Oordoo' with a 'simple and forcible style', and rhyming prose with its emphasis on sound rather than sense, its inaccurate use of words, and its disregard for the 'conventionalities of Grammar'. The latter negative qualities characterized the Urdu manuscripts which were submitted to the government for prizes (and needless to say, failed to win any prizes), while the former qualities were embodied by such texts as Nazir Ahmad's *Mirāt ul-'urūs* ('The Bride's Mirror') which was successful in winning the prizes that the government offered (*Selections* 1870, 219–20).[12]

The state intervened in the stylistic arena, using its patronage to foster certain stylistic qualities, and discourage others. Furthermore, the official reports on Indian-language newspapers, and a number of the periodicals themselves, also point to the way in which the state encouraged the use of articles written in a certain style as part of the school curriculum. The state attempted to foster a certain style of Urdu as part of its education policy in the Northwestern Provinces. In the 'Report on the vernacular newspapers and periodicals' for 1872, Kempson discusses the educational benefits of government patronage for the Indian language press. He avers to 'the extension which is insensibly given to the vocabulary of teachers and pupils, and their power of expression', and he adds that 'This is a matter of some importance now that written examinations are likely to demand a higher tone of exactness' (*Selections* 1873, 513). The report later cites with approval the proposal of an Indian scholar that 'the best selections in Urdu, according to current usage, for use in schools would be a selection of articles from Native newspapers' (ibid., 521). In the 'Report on vernacular newspapers and periodicals for 1869', the reason for the withdrawal of government patronage for the Hindi version of the *Muir Gazette* is given as the 'want of ordinary care shown by the editor in making his paper really useful to the schools as a correct model of Hindee' (*Selections* 1870, 216; see also 236 on the necessity of a well-edited 'nagree or Urdu paper' for schools). The question of a reformed stylistics, which both the state and the *AIG* addressed, therefore involved not just an engagement with the European narrative of progress, but also a concern with the didactic aspects of educational policy. In some ways, this may have been a continuation of the useful knowledge movement of the 1830s and 1840s, which also tried to link the spread of such knowledge with the development of an appropriate idiom in Urdu (Bayly 1996, 219–20).

However, this reformed stylistics and the Urdu of the official gazette itself was an unstable construct. I have shown elsewhere how the East India Company's administrative English in the first half of the nineteenth century drew in part on the preceding Persian language of the Mughal administration, incorporating Persian terms in Roman script often without elucidating them (Majeed 1995a). So, too, the different styles of Urdu in the first Urdu newspaper of Delhi, the *Dehlī urdū akhbār*, can be characterized in terms of how some sections incorporated terms from English, and how some, for example those reporting the diary of the Mughal court, consisted of ornate Urdu closely tied to Persianate models of polished prose (Faruqi (ed.) 1972, 8–9).[13] Similarly, in the Urdu version of the official gazette for the Northwestern provinces, while the majority of terms for departments have Urdu equivalents, some have to be transcribed rather than translated. These include the terms 'police' and 'stamp' (*Gavarnmaṇṭ gazaṭ mumālik-e maghribī va shimalī* 7 July 1869, 27: 472, 473).

In some ways, it is the theme of translation that dominates Sir John Strachey's speech in the *AIG*, referred to above. This speech offers India a package of progress, which includes popularizing Western sciences and arts ('*maghribī 'ulūm va funūn*') into the languages of India. Quite literally, therefore, the subject of Sir John Strachey's speech is the translation of modernity into Indian languages, and indeed the bulk of the speech draws attention to the Institute's efforts to translate 27 works on a variety of subjects from English into Urdu. What is interesting here are the terms Strachey uses for these subjects. Some, such as political economy, are transcribed, rather than translated, into Urdu, while other terms, for example mathematics, use Arabic terms that had been absorbed into Urdu, in this case, ''*ilm-e riyāẓī*' (*AIG* 22 January 1875, 50–6). This combination of transcription and the usage of terms already existing in Urdu, albeit in the speech of a British official, is just one manifestation of the theme examined here, namely the way in which Urdu periodicals could call upon pre-existing terms and resources to envisage their own versions of progress.

More importantly, even the *Aligarh Institute Gazette*, with its self-conscious attempt to purge itself of rhetorical polish and complex stylistics, cannot rid itself completely of this heritage. There are a number of occasions when its reformed stylistics are interrupted by the very style it tries to jettison. Thus, in the issue of 29 January 1875, an article praising the simple style of another paper (the *Atālīq-e hind* or 'The Mentor of Hind') itself uses a series of complex metaphors to express that praise, in which the discursive world of the paper is compared to the saplings in a walled garden bringing forth variegated fruit in the fullness of time (*AIG* 29 January 1875, 73). In the same issue, the progress of another paper, the *Hindū Parkāsh*, is also expressed through a series of metaphors relating to childhood and adolescence (ibid., 73 – I discuss these metaphors more fully below.)

In contrast to the *AIG*, the style of *Mufīd-e 'ām* covers a wide variety of registers, from the administrative Urdu of government orders and notifications, to rhyming prose or *musajja'*.[14] But what is particularly significant here is the way in which articles of scientific and technological import are interrupted by rhetorical devices or styles untamed by the state's attempt to reform Urdu prose. For example, in the issue of 1 September 1869, there is a discussion on the rotation of crops and sowing of seeds, which is interrupted by four lines of Persian combining two metaphors, one of pearl divers and the other of a rose garden (*Mufīd-e 'ām* 1 September 1869, 4). In other words, there is a sudden switch from the Urdu of the instruction manual to the Persian of metaphors. Similarly, in the issue of 15 November 1869 the language of horticultural instruction is again interrupted by the polished artifice of metaphor. The context here is a discussion of irrigation and provision of water for crops, where those benefactors who provide wells for villages will be rewarded by the 'saplings of their good names blossoming and spreading so that the rose-bushes of their attributes will remain verdant in the four meadows of the world' (*Mufīd-e 'ām* 15 September 1869, 4).

The ways in which these two Urdu periodicals grappled with the European master-narrative of progress were reflected in the styles of Urdu within each periodical, with different styles being played off against each other. One of these styles was the reformed prose patronized by the state, but this was often interrupted by the rhetorical artifice of earlier traditions of writing, which resisted integration into state-patronized stylistics. In part this may have been due to the sophistication and depth of these earlier traditions of writing. Francis Pritchett's illuminating work on these earlier poetic systems carefully reconstructs and explicates the rhetorical practices of these traditions for a modern readership, for whom, especially in translation, such practices can superficially appear as 'flowery' (Pritchett 1994, 63–122; see also Shackle 1996).

Idioms of community

Despite these differences between *Mufīd-e 'ām* and the *AIG* in terms of style, there was one overwhelming area of similarity, which consisted of the way in which the category of community was itself conceived. The arrangement of news in both periodicals shows no clear sense of foreign and Indian news, so that the boundaries between *desh* and *pardesh* are vague. There are no separate sections for foreign and local news, rather items from each are cited in no particular order in the same section.

This lack of any clear distinction points to the way in which identities and their boundaries were as yet not clearly formed. So, too, a diversity of terms are used to refer to the category of community and location, such as 'qaum', 'mulk', 'ahl', 'waṭan', and 'vilāyat', which are employed in varying senses. The word 'qaum' is used to refer to religious community (the 'qaum' of Muslims and 'qaum' of Hindus), as well as rank, as for example the term 'sharīf qaum' is used to refer to high ranks, both Muslim and Hindu, in north Indian society. So in the *AIG* of 1 January 1875, the word 'qaum' is used to refer to Hindustanis generally (that is, north Indians), while in the issue of 29 January 1875, the same term is used to refer to the upper ranks in Hindustani society (*AIG* 1 January 1875, 10–11, 29 January 1875, 79).[15] The range of terms for community in the *Mufīd-e 'ām* are more various, and include the term 'ahl', which is used with reference to the inhabitants of India ('ahl-e Hind'), as well as with reference to Muslims and Hindus (*ahl-e islām and ahl-e hunūd*) (*Mufīd-e 'ām* 1 March 1869, 2, 1 August 1869, 2, and 15 October 1869, 2). The term 'qaum' is also used to refer specifically to caste (*Mufīd-e 'ām* 1 October 1869, 13 where an item appears referring to a marriage advertisement in a Calcutta newspaper placed on behalf of two women of the Brahmin and Kayasth 'qaum').

It is clear that in this period these terms have yet to acquire a restricted range. There is no clear sense of a hierarchy of identities or loyalties, nor any self-conscious effort, as there was later in Muhammad Iqbal's work, to articulate any such hierarchy (Majeed 1995b). The only words which have strong connotations are the words 'Hindustan' and 'Hindustani', which are quite clearly cross-communal. The term Hindustani seems also to be a class category, referring to the service gentry trained in Persian and Urdu, both Hindu and Muslim. In fact, both periodicals are committed to maintaining ranks in north Indian society. In the case of the *AIG*, in particular, where the European master narrative of progress comes through more clearly, this narrative in no way undermines the distinctions of rank. Moreoever, in contrast to the unclear distinction between *desh* and *pardesh*, the distinctions between ranks in society are taken to be self-evident. We might even say that the syncretistic culture of this Hindu–Muslim gentry is in part held in place by the belief in the importance of rank to the functioning of society. Both periodicals carry articles, some taken from other papers such as the *Hindū Parkāsh* (*AIG* 12 February 1875, 107–8) and some written by their own editors, expressing anxiety about the possible undermining of distinctions of rank in society by the colonial state. These anxieties cluster around three main issues: first, the fact that the colonial legal system does not take into account the rank of the accused when he is of high rank (see *AIG* 29 January 1875, 74–5 on the treatment meted out to the ruler of Baroda); secondly, because of this insensitivity to rank in British Indian law, the lower orders now behave as though they are equals to higher orders (this is reinforced by anecdotes about some everyday incidents in Aligarh and Agra); (*Mufīd-e ʿām* 1 May 1869, 15–16) and thirdly, the seating arrangements in railway carriages fail to make enough allowances for the niceties of rank among passengers (*Mufīd-e ʿām* 15 October 1869, 13–14).[16] This last anxiety is suggestive in that railways might also undermine the specific sense of a Hindustani identity, even while bringing together different parts of the 'desh' as a whole. Indeed, the image of a network of railways becomes apposite for the dialectic of difference and sameness that seems to characterise this sense of a ranked society.

Habermas' argument is useful in this context as a point of contrast. Part of Habermas' critique of the notion of publicity consists in showing how the public of eighteenth- and nineteenth-century Europe was imagined to be formless (he calls it the 'fiction of the *one* public'), although in practice it was structured by qualifications of property and education (Habermas 1989, 56, 85). However, in the Indian periodicals examined here the public is imagined as having a clear hierarchy based on rank, and this further complicates the press's own sense of critical publicity, in so far as it was easier for the European press to take on a representative role on the basis of an imagined formless public. Here the whole issue of public representation becomes fraught with questions of difference, not just vis-à-vis the British, but also with reference to ranks and distinctions within one's own community. In a sense, these periodicals, and perhaps the Indian-language press as a whole, replay, within the context of an Indian community, what Chatterjee has called the 'rule of colonial difference' (Chatterjee 1994, 16–27). This might also be related to the press's playing of the European narrative of progress. Its filtering of this narrative was highly differentiated and layered, both in terms of social categories and the pre-existing symbolic and cultural resources it drew upon.[17] Some examples of this differentiated view extended to a concern with the way Hindustanis are perceived and stereotyped by others. The *AIG* of 1 January 1875 refers to an article in the *Times* on the Khan of Khera and the Nawab of Awadh, which unfavourably contrasts their rulership with that of the British state. The author takes it on himself to defend what he calls the Hindustani *qaum*, by arguing on number of levels simultaneously, which is indicative of his awareness of the complexities of the issues at stake. On the one hand, the article agrees that British principles of government are in fact superior to Hindustani principles of government; on the other hand, the author also argues that each country has the right to its own system of government, and therefore the best solution in this case is for the Princely States to adapt British systems of government as they see fit, with the press playing a role as a repository of information and as counsellor to the rulers (*AIG* 1 January 1875, 10–11).

The *AIG* contains two other articles which engage with stereotyping, one in the issue of 29 January 1875, and the other in the issue of 12 February 1875. The first attempts to rebut British stereotyping of Hindustani society by arguing that caste as a principle of social organization is in fact superior to the principle on which English society is based, namely class, which is founded on wealth alone. Furthermore, 'excommunication' from one's caste group ('*zāt uthānā*') is no different from the way individuals in England are debarred from society if they are in disgrace. It then goes on to suggest that the highest classes in English society behave in much the same way as the lowest ranks in Hindustani society. At the same time, the article also argues that these lower castes have maintained a cohesion amongst themselves which almost makes them self-regulating entities, and that 'sharīf' groups, both Hindu and Muslim, have not maintained such a cohesion, with the result that their conduct remains unregulated and their prestige declines (*AIG* 29 January 1875, 79–80; for an excellent discussion of the term *sharīf* see Sheikh 1989, chs 1 and 3).

This contradictory argument works on a variety of levels. Overall, the defence of rank in Hindustani society involves using lower castes as both exemplars and foils, so that the upper castes are rebuked for failing to live as close to the ideal of caste as the lower castes do, while English upper classes are condemned for using a practice of governing their members which is similar to that of Hindustani lower castes. This simultaneous idealization and degradation of lower castes when defending the hierachical society of Hindustan against British stereotypes is eloquent of the different fronts on which the Urdu periodical press reflected upon its own structure of society in the light of its engagment with the colonial state. To adapt Partha Chatterjee's (1994) terms of argument, the article in the *AIG* attempts to negotiate both bourgeois claims of equality and the colonial strictures on caste which were used to deny Indians nationhood, while at the same time reinterpreting the hierarchy of Hindustani society in terms of its ability to maintain social cohesion. There is also a hint of reconstructing caste groups as embodying practices of self-regulation in which elements of self-government may be incipient.

However, at the same time as drawing analogies between Hindustani caste and English class, to the detriment of the latter, the *AIG* is also at pains to point out the limits of such analogies. Thus, in the issue of 19 February 1875, the author discusses the problem of translation and the incorporation of words from other languages. In this context, he points to categories for which there is no equivalent in the English language by arguing that the term 'sharīf' and the term gentleman are not equivalents. This is because the term 'sharīf' can only be understood in terms of its relationships to other categories of rank in Hindustani society (*AIG* 12 February 1875, 107–8). As the press reflects upon its position and the structure of its own society *vis-à-vis* others, the language of colonial difference converges with the language of caste difference, and at the same time as analogies are drawn, the limits of those analogies are also called into attention.

David Washbrook has explored how Indians remained trapped in those categories of the Raj which they sought to challenge, and how these categories were underpinned by a 'sociology of multiple ethnicity' (Washbrook 1982). The *AIG* of 12 February 1875 has another piece taken from the *Hindū Parkāsh* in which the author in part challenges the very idea of a stereotype. The article argues that it is impossible to believe in any general qualities belonging to a 'qaum', since a 'qaum' is made up of so many individuals, each with different qualities, from which one cannot infer general national characteristics. The author is keen to argue that the stereotype of the British as honest and honourable is no more reliable than the stereotype of Hindustanis as dishonest and dishonourable. He also explains some stereotypes as arising from misperceptions of the environment in which people live; thus the view of Kashmiris as dirty is misplaced because although Kashmiri towns are dirty, the inhabitants themselves are clean. The problem is that the government in question does not fulfil its civic duties. However, at times the author also rebuts stereotypes by invoking other stereotypes; for example, he argues that some say Englishmen are brave because they eat meat, but Marathas do not eat meat, yet they are brave (*AIG* 12 February 1875, 107–8). The concern with stereotypes has much to do with the typologies on which European notions of race rested, (for which see Banton 1987) but it is also connected with the hierarchy of rank in India itself. All this is part of an attempt to defend Hindustanis against colonial strictures while redeploying a language of difference to shore up Hindustani society itself. At times this means both challenging the very language of stereotyping, while using that language to rebut specific instances of stereotyping.

The young and the old

Sara Suleri has pointed to the images of youth and old age that characterized Edmund Burke's rhetoric on India, and especially to the recurring
figures of the youthfulness of colonialism and of India as the locus of all
things ancient (Suleri 1992, 32–3). The Urdu periodical press also used
images of youth and childhood to characterize itself. For example, the
AIG describes the *Hindū Parkāsh* as in its early stages like a fragile infant,
unsure of life, suddenly rising up into a healthy fullness of youth
('shabāb') (*AIG* 29 January 1875, 73–4). Elsewhere images of infancy
and old age are combined, as, for example, when the paper reflects
upon its own project to reform Urdu stylistics. It describes Urdu poetry
of the eighteenth and early nineteenth centuries as beautiful, but analogous to the stories that a toothless old crone recites to children to
send them to sleep (*AIG* 19 February 1875, 122). This characterization
of the Urdu press and Urdu literature both as on the verge of death and
as infants yet to learn to speak, expresses well the press's own ambivalence towards the European narrative of modernity. This narrative renders India both helpless infant and helpless old crone – that is, both
anachronistic and as having to learn the lessons of modernity, just as a
child has to learn how to walk and talk (for some characterizations of
Indians as childlike in imperial ideologies, see Metcalf 1995, 25, 192,
199, 229–30). However, the image is fraught with ambiguity. To be both
old and young *vis-à-vis* the colonial state is to suggest both wisdom and
possible displacement as the youth matures and takes the place of its
parent.

In a sense, what is missing in the metaphor is the figure of the Indian
parent. The *AIG* also contains the image of the missing or unknown
parent. Thus, the issue of 19 February 1875 deals with some adverse
comments by other newspapers on itself. The *AIG* replies by likening the
situation to two boys (born of the same mother) insulting each other's
mother (*AIG* 19 February 1875, 125–6). The question of old age, infancy,
and the missing or unknown parent can be read on another level too.
Like Kipling's Kim himself, the press is unsure of its lineage and identity.
It is half colonial sahib and half Indian vagrant, and in part this derives
from its role as intermediary between state and society. This is clearly
how the colonial state conceived of the Indian language press – namely
as an intermediary with qausi-representative functions. This view is
expressed repeatedly in official reports on the Indian-language press.
For example, the report on 'Vernacular newspapers and periodicals,
published in N.W.P during 1869' expresses the hope that the Indian-

language press will become a 'valuable auxiliary to the Government in giving currency to authentic information, as well as eliciting loyal discussion on measures in contemplation, and on the administration generally' (*Selections* 1870, 235; see also *Selections* 1873, 513, 521). This view is echoed by *Mufīd-e ʿām* in two articles on the press, which define the raison d'être of the Indian-language press in terms of its role as intermediary and as representative of both colonial government and Indian society (*Mufīd-e ʿām* 1 July 1869, 2, 6). In some ways, the Urdu press appears to have continued the functions of those powerful Indian figures of the 'Indian ecumene' who saw themselves as mediators between people and government in the territories of the East India Company (Bayly 1996, 180). Central to the Indian-language press's sense of itself is this attempt to negotiate the difficult zone between colonial state and society. This might also explain many of its ambivalences. Unlike the public arenas studied by Sandra Freitag (1989, 1991), the Urdu-language press in this period did not see itself as constituting an alternative world of moral authority to the institutions of the colonial state. Rather its authority derived from its intermediary position in the tense field between state and society. Furthermore, the press also saw itself as of mixed lineage, in that in reflecting upon itself, it clearly draws attention to its affinity with the role of the '*akhbār navīs*' or news writer in the Mughal empire (*Mufīd-e ʿām* 1 July 1869, 6; see also *Selections* 1871, 426–8 on an article in another paper on this topic, and Fisher 1993 on the office of the *akhbār navīs*).

Thus, the image of childhood/old age and the absent parent can also be read as the press's own sense of its mixed lineage. On the one hand, it inherited and developed the role of the *akhbār navīs* in Mughal India, yet on the other hand it was patronized and watched over by the colonial state which itself looked upon the Indian-language press and 'native' public opinion as a parent might look upon the growth of a child. The press's intermediary position in the tension-charged field between the colonial state and Indian society was also reflected in its ambivalence towards Indian rulers, and then later the Princely States. Secondary sources make it clear that from the early nineteenth century onwards the Urdu periodical press was critical of Indian rulers. At the same time, such publications were sympathetic to Indian rulers in their dealings with the East India Company and, later, the British government (Khan 1991, 51–2). However, Bayly (1996, 200) has suggested that in pre-1857 India, Indian rulers discouraged the use of the printing press because it threatened their authority. And there were cases of outspoken editors in princely states being persecuted by the authorities there (Khan 1991,

235, 267, 295ff.). It is not surprising therefore that the Urdu press contains both sympathetic and negative images of Indian rulers and princes. An example of this complex attitude is to be found in the *AIG* of 1 January 1875, 29 January 1875, and 12 February 1875, which deal with the deposition of the Maharajah of Baroda. There is a delicate rendering of the whole question of loyalty in the context of British India, and in some ways there is even a redefining of the parameters of loyalty in the colonial context (see Bayly 1994, 12, 21 for a re-examination of the question of loyalty in this context). The articles steer a course between supporting the deposition of the Maharajah while criticising the inadequacy of the British legal representation accorded to him. However, the Urdu periodical press's ambivalence to the Indian princes is probably also the other side of its ambivalence to the colonial state itself. The shoring up of princely India by the British Indian state might also be evidence of the latter's own contradictory stance on modernization (Metcalf 1995, 72–4, 191–3, 197–9; see also Washbrook 1981 for a critique of the British Indian state's stance on modernization).

The issue here is basically one of a tussle between the press and the princes for the role of authoritative representative of Indian society. One indication of this occurs in the *AIG*, which argues that the decision as to the worth of Indian princes should be made in newspapers and periodicals (*AIG* 1 January 1875, 10). There is a sense here in which the press continues an earlier indigenous discourse on the rights and duties of kings, and the moral limits of their rule (for which, see Bayly 1996, 180, 204–8). Habermas has argued that before the development of the public sphere in Europe, the nobleman's personage displayed and embodied authority in his cultivated personality. The staging of publicity linked to this personage involved personal insignia, demeanour, and forms of address (Habermas 1989, 7–13). It was the assimilation of courtly culture by bourgeois humanism that laid the foundation of the bourgeois public sphere in Europe (ibid., 13–19). In similar fashion, the ambivalence of the Urdu periodical press towards Indian princes is linked to the manner in which the latter are their rivals for claiming the authority of representative publicity. The public representation of authority by the princes' courtly ritual and their very persons were at odds with the burgeoning role of the press as spokesperson for both colonial state and Indian society. Furthermore, news had yet to become a commodity in this period, with the result that the news sections in Urdu periodicals drew heavily upon other periodicals and papers. This is true for the news sections in both periodicals examined here, where extracts are cited along with the paper from which they are taken. This exchange of news between papers lends the Urdu press the character of a collaborative enterprise in this period, as it steered its course between the princely and British states and Indian society.

Conclusion

By way of conclusion, I want to sketch out two avenues of exploration that this short study of the nineteenth-century Urdu periodical press has open up.

First, when considering the development of realist literature in Hindi and Urdu from the late nineteenth century onwards, it is important to remember that the language of social realism was first constructed in the Indian-language press. Subsequent Indian literary expressions in the genres of the short story and the novel reworked and fed off this language for their own purposes. Similarly, we can read the growth of progressive literature in the twentieth century in terms of a genealogy that included the 'progressive' stances of the Urdu periodical press from at least the 1850s onwards – and perhaps even earlier if one thinks of Ram Mohan Roy's Persian paper of the 1820s, *Mirāt-ul Akhbār* (for this paper, see Sabri 1953–63, 1: 52–8).

Secondly, the way the Urdu periodical press grappled with the European narrative of progress and appropriated that narrative might also shed light on such later notions of the self as Muhammad Iqbal's *khudī* or selfhood (for which, see Majeed 1993). Modern Indian categories of self need to be understood in the context of all the tensions and ambivalences surrounding the narrative of progress. This would apply also to categories of self and narratives of development in texts such as Nehru's *The Discovery of India* (1946). In many ways, the Indian-language press in its engagement with the state and Indian society, in its reflection upon its own role and pedigree, and in its drawing upon pre-existing cultural and symbolic resources as it grappled with the notion of progress, paved the way for these later definitions of selfhood and the narratives in which they were embedded.

Appendix: Nineteenth-century periodicals in Urdu of a Hindu or Sikh orientation

(Source: Imdad Sabri, *Tārīkh-e ṣaḥāfat-e urdū*. References are to the volume and page numbers of his study.)

1. *Benāras Gazette*, first issued 1845, weekly, editor Gobinder Gonāth. Contained translations of shastras and other Sanskrit literature. In both devanagari and Perso-Arabic script. (1: 264)
2. *Al-navāj va nuzhat ul arvāḥ*, Agra, first issued December 1848, weekly, editor Jawāhir Lāl. Included a supplement of renditions of Hindu mythology and doctrine. (1: 349–56)
3. *Victoria Paper*, Sialkot, first issued 1853, weekly, editor Munshī Dīvān Chand. Contained articles on doctrinal matters relating to Hinduism. (1: 461–2)
4. *Ṣubḥa-e ṣādiq*, Madras, first issued 1860, three times monthly, editor Abdur Raḥmān Shaffāf. According to de Tassy, this contained criticisms of practices seen to be in conflict with the shastras. (2: 149)
5. *Mufīd ul inām*, district Farakhabad, first issued 1860, weekly, editor Munshī Shankar Sarūp Najāt. Contained 'recommendations to help women resist conversion to Christianity'. (2: 152)
6. *Bhārat akhand amrit*, Agra, first issued 1864, dedicated to reform of 'Hindu' social and religious practices on the basis of a correct interpretation of the Vedas. (2: 188)
7. *Gyānī patrikā*, Lahore, first issued 1 June 1865, editor Pandit Makandar Rām. The title page contained a notice in Persian of its contents, informing the reader that the periodical contained translations of ancient Sanskrit literature. In both devanagari and Perso-Arabic script. (2: 197–8)
8. *Mangal samāchār*, Aligarh, first issued 1870, monthly, editor Munshī Piyāre Lāl. Contained essays on shastras. (2: 351)
9. *Makhzan mahābhārat*, Agra, first issued 1871, twice a month, with a title page in Persian reading 'consisting of details of the birth of the earth and heaven, humans and animals and angels etc., and ways to attain eternal heaven . . .'. (2: 419)
10. *Kāyasth samāchār*, Lucknow, first issued 1872, twice a month, editor Lāla Gokul Prashād. Represented the interests of the *Kāyasth* community. (2: 445–6)
11. *Nādir ul akhbār*, Mangir, first issued 1872, weekly, organ of the Mangir Brahmo Samaj. (2: 447)
12. *Murāsala-e kashmīr*, Lucknow, first issued August 1872, monthly, represented the interests of the Kashmiri pandit community. 56 pages were in Urdu and two in Hindi. (2: 455–60)
13. *Hindū parkāsh*, Amritsar, various possible dates for first issue but sometime in 1873, editor Rajab Ali, issued under the direction of Lāla Gaur Makandar Rāe, organ of the Committee of dharam sabhā Amritsar. In Perso-Arabic, devanagari, and gurmukhi. (2: 513–16)
14. *Hādī ḥaqīqat*, Lahore, first issued in 1873, twice a month, publisher Babū Keshab Chandar Sen, organ of Brahmo Samaj. In both Urdu and Hindi. (2: 516)

15. *Hindū bāndhū*, Lahore, first issue 1 April 1875, monthly, owner Pandit Shiv Narāyan Agnihotrī, purpose defined on its title page as the revival of the 'Hindu qaum' on the basis of a correct interpretation of Sanskrit texts. (2: 545–6, title page cited in full)
16. *Āryā samāchār*, Meerut, first issue January 1879, monthly, issued under the supervision of Munshī Kalyān Rāe, organ of the Arya samaj. (3: 146)
17. *Sabhā kapurthalā*, Kapurthala, weekly, first issued in 1879 under the direction of Divan Mithar Dās, president of the dharam pardayenī, editor Munshī Barkat ʿAlī Shaukat. (3: 147)
18. *Dharam jīvan*, Lahore, first issued 13 January 1883, edited and supervised by Pandit Shiv Narāyan Agnihotrī and Prabh Bāvī Satyanand Agnihotrī, organ of Qaumī sanyās dharam. (3: 242–55, includes long excerpts from this periodical)
19. *Sukhdāik sabhā*, Rawalpindi, first issued January 1883, edited and supervised by Hari Chand Sahnī and Boṭāmal ānand, organ of Birādarī Bharochian. (3: 292–3)
20. *Indar parast prakāsh*, Delhi, first issued in June 1883, weekly, owned by Pandit Jīnī Prashād. (3: 300)
21. *Qaumī Kāyasth Nigam Omāyān*, Lucknow, first issued in January 1884, monthly, edited by Lāla Debī Prashād. (3: 332–3, 343)
22. *Gaur Kāyasth*, Allahabad, monthly, edited by Munshī Sadan Lāl. (3: 370)
23. *Āryā Darpan*, Shahjahanpur, first issued in January 1878, monthly, edited by Munshī Bakhtāvar Singh, paper of the Arya Samaj. (3: 129)
24. *Desh Upkārak*, Lahore, weekly, editor Rāe Sālig Rām, supervised by Pandit Har Gopāl, branch of the Arya press. (3: 317)
25. *Āryā Mitar*, first issued 1 January 1884, in memory of Swami Dayanand, editor Bāvā Narāyan Singh, supervised by Munshī Kānshī Rām. (3: 319)
26. *Āryā Patar*, Bareilly, monthly, first issued January 1884, published by Lāla Rāj Bahādur, secretary of the Arya Samaj, in both Urdu and Hindi. (3: 319)
27. *Āryā Gazette*, Firozepur, weekly, first published 15 July 1888, published under the supervision of Munshī Gobind Lāl. (3: 410)
28. *Kāyasth Reform Association*, Agra, monthly, first published January 1887, edited jointly by Narāyan Prashād and Babu Har Gobindnāth. (3: 454–55)
29. *Āryā Patar*, Bareilly, monthly, editor Ḥakīm Raghbīr Sahāe Baryān, Arya Samaj publication. (3: 681)
30. *Āryā Musāfir*, monthly, Jalandhar, editor Mahāshay Wazīr Chand, organ of Arya Sabha, Punjab. (3: 744–47)

Notes

1. This article was presented at a seminar in Birkbeck College, University of London in June 1997. I am grateful to Shruti Kapila, Sudipto Kaviraj, Bhaskar Mukhopadhyay, Christopher Shackle, Radhika Singha and Ravi Vasudevan for their comments on that occasion. I am also grateful to John Cooper for his suggestive criticisms and help, and to Martin Moir and Saleem Qureishi for their help in the India Office Library. This article is dedicated to the memory of John Cooper whose kindness, courtesy and learning will be missed by many.

2. For details of these, see the Appendix at the end of this chapter. On the character and role of the sabhā, see Bayly (1996, 187).
3. Sabri also cites detailed extracts from an Urdu periodical entitled *Makhzan mahābhārat*, which was first published in Agra in 1871. Its title page was in Persian reading 'consisting of details of the birth of the earth and heaven, humans and animals and angels etc., and ways to attain eternal heaven . . .' (2: 419).
4. Some examples of these are to be found in the Appendix.
5. This paper later changed its name to *Kaukab-e Hind* or the 'Star of India'.
6. But for a telling analysis of the contradictions in the state's modernizing stance vis-à-vis Indian society, see Washbrook (1981, 649–721).
7. For other references to the *AIG*, see 'Vernacular Newspapers and Periodicals, Published in N.W.P during 1869', in *Selections from the Records* (Allahabad: Government Press, 1870) 218, 225–6, 'Report on the Vernacular Press, N.W.P', in *Selections from the Records* (Allahabad: Government Press, 1871), 317, 325–6, 377, 380, 414–17, 417, 431 and 'Report on the Vernacular Newspapers and Periodicals published in the North-Western Provinces during 1872', in *Selections from the Records* (Allahabad: Government Press, 1873), 516, 517, 518, 524.
8. For another example, see *Mufīd-e ʿām*, 'Ḥālāt-e qadīma kī taḥqīq bazarīʾa sayyāron ke', on a Russian observatory that might be used to locate Noah's ark, 1 September 1870.
9. For example, see *Mufīd-e ʿām*, 'hikāyet-e ʿajīb' on a boy saved from a flood by a snake, 15 July 1869, 14, issue of 1 November 1869, on the miraculous punishment of an individual who violated the sanctity of Hussein's tomb, 1 November 1869, 14, and on the sudden irruption of a reservoir of water at a location in Australia, 15 November 1869, 11.
10. For example, *Mufīd-e ʿām*, 'nau ījad gārī', on a self-propelled vehicle, 1 August 1869, 12, 'daryā-ʾī gārī' on a 'buggy' that travels on water, 1 September 1869, 13.
11. For an abridged version of the Persian text, see *Akhlāq-e nāṣirī* (Teheran: Intishārāt-e Tus, n.d).
12. See also 'Report on the Vernacular Press, N.W.P' in *Selections from the Records of Government, North-Western Provinces* (Allahabad: Government Press, 1871) 4: 393 which approvingly cites the view of an Indian periodical on Nazir Ahmad's novel: 'a model of plain, eloquent, and idiomatic Oordoo style' with useful 'moral instruction and didactic pieces interspersed through it'. For an excellent piece on Nazir Ahmad's novel, amongst others, see C.M. Naim (1984).
13. Faruqi's edition is a useful compilation of excerpts from the *Dehlī urdū akhbār*. For one example of the incorporation of English terms, see the issue of 9 February 1840, where one section carries the title transcribed into Urdu from English 'polītīkal ḍīpārṭmanṭ'. The same issue carries the regular section on the diary of the Mughal king, entitled 'Ḥuẓūr-e wālā' ('the exalted presence'), which is a heavily Persianized piece of prose.
14. For examples of rhyming prose in *Mufīd-e ʿām*, see 15 April 1869, 16 which consists of an advertisement for another paper, 15 May 1869, 16 describing the hot weather in Agra, 1 July 1869, 16 describing the effect of heat and cholera on Agra, 15 July 1869, 16 on rainfall in Agra, 1 August 1869, 13 on

the heat in Dera Ismail Khan and 16 on rainfall in Agra, and 1 December 1869, 2 in which part of an article on good conduct is in rhyming prose. For some interesting examples of both news items and notices of papers in rhyming prose, see Sabri (1953–63, 2: 193–4, 226–9, 234–5, 281).

15. See also the issues of 12 February 1875, 107 where the term is used to refer to the British and Indians as different peoples, 111–12 where the term 'mulk' is used for countries, and 104–6 where the term 'qaum' is used in the general sense of peoples. There is an obvious analogy between the slipperiness of this term and the term 'jāt', for which see Chatterjee (1994, 221–3).

16. Earlier, a more specific interest in the workings of British Indian justice centred on the trials of those who were accused of participating in the 1857–58 Rebellion. Sabri cites excerpts from Urdu periodicals which contained detailed accounts of these trials. For some examples, see Sabri (1953–63, 1: 508, 2: 71–5, 139–45, 161, 164–6, and 223).

17. It is important to note here that the British state in the 1870s held the view that there was no homogeneous public in India, but the assumptions underlying this view were somewhat different from those in the Urdu periodical press examined here (Burns 1940, 280–8, and for some comments, Chatterjee (1994, 24–6)).

Works cited

Aligarh Institute Gazette. Aligarh, 1875.

Banton, Michael. *Racial Theories.* Cambridge, 1987.

Bayly, C.A. 'Returning the British to South Asian History: the Limits of Colonial Hegemony', *South Asia* 17 (1994), 1–25.

Bayly, C.A. *Empire and Information: Intelligence Gathering and Social Communication in India, 1780–1870.* Cambridge, 1996.

Bearce, G.D. *British Attitudes towards India 1784–1858.* Oxford, 1961.

Brass, Paul. *Language, Religion, and Politics in North India.* Cambridge, 1974.

Burns, M. *The Indian Press: a History of the Growth of Public Opinion in India.* London, 1940.

Chatterjee, Partha. *The Nation and its Fragments: Colonial and Postcolonial Histories.* Delhi, 1994.

Dalmia, V. *The Nationalization of Hindu Traditions: Bharatendu Harishchandra and Nineteenth Century Banaras.* Delhi, 1997.

Faruqi, Khwaja Ahmed (ed.). *Dehlī urdū akhbār.* Delhi, 1972.

Fisher, Michael. 'The Office of the akhbār nawīs: the Transition from Mughal to British Forms', *Modern Asian Studies* 27 (1993), 45–82.

Freitag, Sandra B. *Collective Action and Community. Public Arenas and the Emergence of Communalism in North India.* Berkeley, 1989.

Freitag, Sandra B. 'Introduction' to *South Asia*, special issue on *Aspects of 'the Public' in Colonial South Asia* 14 (June 1991), 1–13.

Fuhrer, A. *The Monumental Antiquities and Inscriptions in the North-Western Provinces and Oudh.* Allahabad, 1891.

Gavarnmaṇṭ gazaṭ mumālik-e maghribī va shimalī (for 1869). Allahabad, 1870.

Government Gazette, North-Western Provinces (for 1869). Allahabad, 1870.

Gutas, Dmitri. *Greek Wisdom Literature in Arabic Translation: a Study of the Graeco-Arabic Gnomologia.* New Haven, 1975.

Gutas, Dmitri. 'The Spurious and Authentic in the Arabic lives of Aristotle', in Kraye, Jill, W.F. Ryan and C.B. Schmitt (eds), *Pseudo-Aristotle in the Middle Ages: the Theology and Other Texts*, London, 1986, 15–36.

Habermas, Jurgen. *The Structural Transformation of the Public Sphere: an Inquiry into a Category of Bourgeois Society*. Translated by Thomas Burger with the assistance of Frederick Lawrence, 1962; Oxford and Cambridge, 1989.

Hali, Altaf Hussain, C. Shackle and J. Majeed (eds), *Hali's Musaddas: the Flow and Ebb of Islam*, Delhi, 1997.

Hali, Altaf Hussain. *Ḥayāt-e Jāved*, 1901; Lahore 1986.

Imperial Gazetteer of India, vol. 5. Oxford, 1908.

Imperial Gazetteer of India Provincial Series: United Provinces of Agra and Oudh. Calcutta, 1908, vol. 1.

Imperial Gazetteer of India Provincial Series: United Provinces of Agra and Oudh. Calcutta, 1908, vol. 11.

Khan, Nadir Ali. *A History of Urdu Journalism 1822–1857*. Delhi, 1991.

King, C.R. *One Language, Two Scripts: the Hindi Movement in Nineteenth Century North India*. Delhi, 1994.

Lelyveld, David. *Aligarh's First Generation: Muslim Solidarity in British India*. Princeton, 1978.

Majeed, Javed. 'Putting God in His Place: Bradley, McTaggart, and Iqbal', *Journal of Islamic Studies* 4 (1993), 208–36.

Majeed, Javed. '"The jargon of Indostan": an Exploration of Jargon in Urdu and East India Company English' in Peter Burke and Roy Porter (eds), *Languages and Jargons: Towards a Social History of Language*, Oxford, 1995a, 182–205.

Majeed, Javed. 'Pan-Islamism and Deracialisation in the Thought of Muhammad Iqbal', in Peter Robb (ed.), *The Concept of Race in South Asia*, Delhi, 1995b.

Metcalf, Barbara Daly (ed.). *Moral Conduct and Authority: the Place of Adab in South Asian Islam*. Berkeley, Los Angeles, and London, 1984.

Metcalf, Thomas R. *Ideologies of the Raj*. Cambridge, 1995.

Mill, J.S. 'Memorandum of the improvements in the Administration of India during the Last Thirty Years (1858)', in John M. Robson, Martin Moir and Zawahir Moir (eds), *Writings on India by John Stuart Mill*. Toronto, 1990.

Mill, J.S. 'Considerations on representative government (1861)', in Wollheim Richard (ed.), *John Stuart Mill. Three essays*. Oxford, 1975, 142–453.

Mufīd-e 'ām. Agra, 1869–70.

Naim, C.M. 'Prize-winning Adab: a Study of Five Urdu Books Written in Response to the Allahabad Government Gazette Notification', in Barbara Daly Metcalf (ed.), *Moral Conduct and Authority: the place of Adab in South Asian Islam*, Berkeley, 1984, 290–314.

Nisbet, Robert. *History of the Idea of Progress*. New York, 1980.

Pritchett, Francis. *Nets of Awareness: Urdu Poetry and its Critics*. Berkeley, 1994.

'[Report on] vernacular newspapers and periodicals, published in N.W.P during 1869', in *Selections from the Records of Government North-Western Provinces*. Allahabad, 1870.

'Report on the vernacular press N.W.P [for the year 1870]', in *Selections from the Records of Government, North-Western Provinces*. Allahabad, 1871.

'Report on the vernacular newspapers and periodicals published in the North-Western provinces during 1872', in *Selections from the Records of Government, North-Western Provinces*. Allahabad, 1873.

Report on the Progress of Education in the North-Western Provinces for 1870–71. Allahabad, 1871.

Sabri, Imdad. *Tārīkh-e ṣaḥāfat-e urdū.*, 3 vols. Delhi, 1953–63.

Shackle, Christopher. 'Settings of panegyric: the secular qasida in Mughal and British India', in Stefan Sperl and Christopher Shackle (eds), *Qasida Poetry in Asia and Africa.* Leiden, 1996, 1: 205–48.

Suleri, Sara. *The Rhetoric of English India.* Chicago and London, 1992.

Sheikh, Farzana. *Community and Consensus in Islam: Muslim Representation in Colonial India, 1860–1947.* Cambridge, 1989.

Tusi, Nasir ud Din. *Akhlāq-e nāṣirī.* 1298. Teheran, n.d.

Washbrook, David. 'Law, State and Agrarian Society in Colonial India', *Modern Asian Studies* 15 (1981), 649–721.

Washbrook, David. 'Ethnicity and Racialism in Colonial India', in Robert Ross (ed.), *Racism and Colonialism.* Leiden, 1982, 143–81.

Wickens, G.M. *The Nasirean Ethics.* London, 1964.

8

'Strange Medley[s]': Ambiguities of Role, Purpose and Representation in Kipling's *From Sea to Sea*

John McBratney

It is sometimes overlooked that Rudyard Kipling, the prolific poet, short story writer and novelist, began his writing career as a journalist in India. From 1882 to 1889, he worked as an assistant editor for the Lahore *Civil and Military Gazette* (see Figure 8.1). In November 1887, having established his talents as a journalist, he was transferred to the larger, more influential sister newspaper at Allahabad, the *Pioneer*, for which he worked as an assistant editor and special reporter. In March 1889, he embarked on a steamship voyage to London, during which he carried out his final assignment for the *Pioneer*, writing a series of sketches about his stops in Southeast and East Asia and North America. Thus ended his 'seven years' hard' as a professional newsman.[1]

Of the work he published during his Indian years, Kipling is best known for the short stories and verse he wrote, with startling frequency, for the *Gazette*, *Pioneer* and other Anglo-Indian papers.[2] Yet he obviously also produced a great deal of straight journalism. Although much of it in Lahore was the routine output of a sub-editor, at Allahabad he was allowed to choose his tasks with greater freedom. For the *Pioneer*, he travelled on special assignment to various spots in India, reporting his impressions in several series of sketches. These represent his most extended, substantial and lively contributions to Anglo-Indian journalism.

Much of his travel through India occurred on two main trips. In November–December 1887, he journeyed to the Native States of Rajasthan; the sketches that ensued, titled 'Letters of Marque', appeared between 14 December 1887 and 29 February 1888 in the *Pioneer* and the *Pioneer Mail*. Next, in January–February 1888, he toured eastern India, visiting Calcutta, the railway workshops at Jamalpur, the coalfields at

CIVIL AND MILITARY GAZETTE.

New Series }
No. 2,523 }

LAHORE, WEDNESDAY, FEBRUARY 11, 1885.

{ Vol. X.

LIST OF CONTENTS.

TELEGRAPHIC INTELLIGENCE.

[Reuter's Telegrams.]

THE WAR IN THE SOUDAN.

REINFORCEMENTS FOR EGYPT.

London, Feb. 9.

The 3rd battalion, Grenadier Guards; the 1st battalion, Coldstream Guards, and the 2nd batta-

---

THE FRANCO-CHINESE WAR.

(From our own Correspondent.)

Colombo, Feb. 9.

The China Mail of the 27th ultimo confirms the latest news of the French preparations for a strong advance on Tamsui. Further reinforcements have reached Kelung; bringing the number of the troops up to 3,500, besides 1,000 sailors and marines. Admiral Courbet states that, with this force, he will march to Tamsui. On January 15th, the French attacked the Chinese outpost adjoining the town, and met with a stout resistance. The enemy fought obstinately, and drove back 300 French regulars who lost 50 men. The accounts, which come through French sources, are unreliable. It is believed that the Chinese muster very strong along the road to Tamsui; and that the French met with a stubborn resistance during January. Large reinforcements, with arms and money, have been poured into Formosa.

The publication of the proclamation of neutrality at Hongkong has incensed the French, who talk of reprisals, and say that they will search all British vessels. On the blockade of the Canton river, the Chinese fleet rendezvous at Shanghai, preparatory to breaking the blockade at Formosa. The ships and guns are effective, but the crews and officers are demoralised; as the sailors are being taught drill by English words of command mixed with German words. Great efforts are being made to pour reinforce-

---

Private Letters from Wady Halfa, which lies on the Nile just below the Second Cataract, state that there is an immense amount of sickness there—principally typhoid.

The command of the 2nd battalion, West Riding (76th) Regiment, vacant on the 25th instant, goes to Lieutenant-Colonel T. T. Hodges, whilst the vacant lieutenant-colonelcy will, in all probability, go to Major Tidmarsh, at present with the 1st battalion at Rawal Pindi.

The services of Major A. Gasetle, 4th Punjab Infantry, have been placed at the disposal of His Excellency the Commander-in-Chief, for employment on special duty in Bluchistan, in connection with Colonel Sandford's survey of the routes between Peshin and the Punjab.

A resum of the 21st Punjab Native Infantry, at Rawal Pindi, shot a Lance-Havildar of the same regiment, on the morning of the 9th instant. Death was instantaneous, the bullet passing through the brain. Nothing is known concerning the motive for the deed. The murderer was immediately secured.

Major-General Cameron, who succeeds

---

material. There was a falling off in the importation of Government arms and ammunition, and stationery. Turning to exports, we find that the total for the first three quarters of .883 was over Rs. 60,37,00,000 ; whereas that for the nine months ending in December last, was less than Rs. 56,31,00,000. This decrease is largely accounted for by the falling off in the wheat trade. In the nine months, India exported less than Rs. 4,85,00,000 worth of wheat ; against over Rs. 7,99,00,000 in the same months of 1883.

A little more than a year ago, three occurred in the small town of Bahawalpur, in the Rohtak district, a robbery which is now famous, not only from the fact that it was accompanied with murder, but also because at least two of the perpetrators, Amir Khan and Mufti, were the prominent members of the most formidable class of criminals we have at present to deal with ; namely, the Pathan. Amir Khan was, in fact, the leader of a gang once numbering some twenty members, but happily now almost extinct. He combined in himself the qualities of great pluck, ferocity, and a very fertile

Giridih, and the government opium factory at Ghazipur. This trip yielded four series of sketches – 'The City of Dreadful Night', 'Among the Railway Folk', 'The Giridih Coal-Fields', and 'In an Opium Factory' – published in various papers associated with the *Pioneer* between 18 February and 26 September 1888. The letters describing these two tours were included, along with sketches from his 1889 ocean voyage and some fiction, in *From Sea to Sea*, first published in two volumes in 1899. The writings from the two trips offer glimpses of a variety of Indian locales including eastern and western India; the Native States and British India; and, within Anglo-India, commercial society and the civil services. In the letters about these tours, he adopts a wide repertoire of personae, from official to bohemian, that suggests the ambiguity both of his relation to respectable Anglo-India and of his purposes in visiting these locales. These ambiguities of role and purpose produce contradictory representations of India that hint at Kipling's particular and Anglo-India's general anxiety about knowing and ruling India.

The opening of 'Letters of Marque' offers a preview of Kipling's project in *From Sea to Sea*; it also reveals the fissures that threaten to split that endeavour apart:

> it is good for every man to see some little of the great Indian Empire and the strange folk who move about it. It is good to escape for a time from the House of Rimmon – be it office or cutchery – and to go abroad under no more exacting master than personal inclination, and with no more definite plan of travel than has the horse, escaped from pasture, free upon the countryside.[3]

The narrator begins with an air of confidence, but several ambiguities already belie that mood. The 'good' of this sight-seeing mixes recreation for a hard-working servant of the Raj and instruction in the nature of the land he and his fellow Britons govern. His peregrinations will take him through the complacently known ('the great Indian empire') by way of the mysterious unknown ('strange folk'). The traveller worships in the House of Rimmon but also wishes to escape its confining 'office [and] cutchery [court-house]'.[4] Any attempt to unravel these ambiguities must begin with a look at Kipling's sense of his role as a reporter.

Englishman, globe-trotter, loafer

The issue of role is best seen against Kipling's uneasy allegiance to his newspaper audience. Both the *Civil and Military Gazette* and the *Pioneer* were important semi-official journals that catered to an Anglo-Indian readership.[5] As the youngest civil servant in the Lahore station and a mere assistant editor at the *Gazette*, Kipling stood near the bottom of the social pecking order enshrined in the Warrant of Precedence. At the *Pioneer*, he enjoyed greater prestige, in part because he held a more powerful position and in part because, through his vivid writing and his family's social accomplishments, he became a member of Viceroy and Lady Dufferin's inner circle of acquaintances (Carrington 1955, 64–5).

Yet his social status remained suspect in the eyes of many. In the midst of Kipling's bright success, 'Simla', according to Dennis Kincaid, 'remained cold. The fellow was clearly a bounder' (Kincaid 1938, 230). If the upper echelons of government were suspicious of Kipling's lampoonings of officialdom, middle-rank civil servants were delighted. He addressed much of his work to these men, whom he called 'the Sons of Martha', the obscure, ordinary officials and military officers who did the bulk of the hard work of empire (Kipling 1939, 380–1). Yet he was not always comfortable with this group of officials and soldiers either. Though he admired their talent, pluck and industry, he was frustrated by the monotony of their talk and the complacency of their vision. In a May 1888 letter to Edmonia Hill, he wrote, 'I have returned to the old wearying, Godless futile life at the [Allahabad] club – same men, same talk, same billiards – all *connu* and triply *connu* ...' (Kipling 1990, 1: 171). Throughout his career as a journalist, he seemed an insider-outsider to official life. Though privy to the deepest gossip and latest news at Simla, he was often disdained by its residents. Though he sympathized with the 'Sons of Martha', he at times felt remote from their habits and views.

The letters collected in *From Sea to Sea* suggest a writer who deliberately exploits his ambiguous relation to his readers. On the one hand, he often identifies with them, calling himself, generically, the 'Englishman'. On the other hand, he relishes deeply his freedom from his office mates: 'It is good to be free, a wanderer upon the high-ways, knowing not what to-morrow will bring forth' (15: 92). Beyond officialdom, he encounters the antitheses of the 'Son of Martha' in two types: the globe-trotter and the vagabond. In imaginatively tacking among the three figures of 'Englishman', tourist, and tramp, Kipling fashions, in fascinating ways, his own flexible sense of role as a journalist.

His most complicated relationship involves that favourite object of Anglo-Indian scorn: the globe-trotter. He especially condemns the touring Briton for his self-proclaimed mastery of things Indian: 'By the time that an Englishman has come ... to India, he can – these eyes have seen him do so – master in five minutes the intricacies of the "Indian Bradshaw", and tell an old resident exactly how and where the trains run' (15: 4). As much as he disdains the globe-trotter, however, he realizes that, once he has left his newsroom, little separates him from the common tourist. As he departs the House of Rimmon, he lapses into 'a state of mind which, for his sins, must be the normal portion of the Globe-trotter – the man who "does" kingdoms in days and writes books upon them in weeks' (15: 3–4). Kipling devises two main strategies to distance himself from the globe-trotter.

First, he takes pains, in a time-honoured way, to distinguish himself as a *traveller* from the globe-trotter as a mere *tourist* (Buzard 1993, 80–154; Fussell 1980, 39). The distinction begins with a different attitude to the textual: the tourist relies on his guidebook; the traveller, though he may carry one, is quick to set it aside. On his visit to Chitor, the journalist remarks, 'Objects of archaeological interest are duly described in an admirable little book of Chitor which, after one look, the Englishman abandoned. One cannot "do" Chitor with a guide-book' (15: 108). The globe-trotter's absolute dependence on his Baedeker results in his continually misreading it and the India it describes: 'He "reads up" – to quote his own words – a city before he comes to us, and, straightway going to another city, forgets, or, worse still, mixes what he has learnt...' (15: 12). The tourist falls into interpretive confusion because he lacks experience of the country – an experience the Anglo-Indian would seem to have in deep reserves.

But experience is a tricky guide, as a comparison of the Anglo-Indian with the tourist implies: 'There is, if a work-a-day world will believe, a society [of globe-trotters] entirely outside, and unconnected with, that of the Station – a planet within a planet, where nobody knows anything about the Collector's wife, the Colonel's dinner-party, or what was really the matter with the Engineer' (15: 30). A grasp of the intricacies of station gossip hardly qualifies as the kind of understanding that would make sense of the states of Rajasthan. This ironic salute to his comrades betrays, on one level, Kipling's characteristic ambivalence toward his readers. On another level, it bespeaks the author's sense of his own ignorance, for he belongs to the station, too. Throughout his journeys, Kipling hints that he lacks any adequate experience on which to base his observations. He calls himself variously an 'amateur Globe-trott[er]' (15: 34), 'an Anglo-Indian Cockney' (15: 58), 'a babbling and a gushing enthusiast' (15: 108), 'the uninitiated' (15: 126), an 'Up-country innocent' (16: 368), and 'Ignorance' personified (16: 383).

If Kipling refuses to rely, like the globe-trotter, on a garden-variety Baedeker, he inevitably falls back on some guide to ground his observations.

He chooses the *Ur*-text of all English narratives about Rajasthan: James Tod's *Annals and Antiquities of Rajasthan, or the Central and Western Rajput States of India* (1829–32). Tod's historical research, conducted intermittently over a span of 17 years while a soldier and diplomat among the Rajputs, represents one of the most detailed, comprehensive monographs about an Indian people ever assembled by a Briton.[6] Yet Kipling's reliance on Tod reveals its own species of uncertainty. In his references to his predecessor, he confesses to a sense of having come too late to appreciate the genuine appeal of the heroic Rajputs. The cities of Amber and Chitor are dead: Jaipur, Udaipur, Jodhpur and Boondi are flourishing, but in Kipling's view they are all (except perhaps for Boondi) blighted by modernization. Ironically, Tod, too, was tardy, having arrived in Rajasthan to find a defeated people whose glory lay in their past. Kipling's dependence on Tod, thus, puts him at two removes from the presence of the Rajput past. He instinctively knows this. When he writes of Rajasthan's ancient greatness, he does so in the form of tales, thus levelling history to story with ironic effect. He realizes finally that, as a traveller, he is little different from the tourist; he may read a better guide, but he shares with the globe-trotter a belated relation to the foreign confirmed by their mutual reliance upon texts that mediate that relation.

But Kipling refuses to accept without a struggle a place among the ranks of the mere globe-trotter. To differentiate himself anew, he employs a second strategy that will have a profound impact on his vision of his journeys' purposes and his depictions of India. This strategy is to *play* at being a tourist. He speaks of being 'settled into his part' (15: 5) as a traveller and of its being 'pleasant to play at Globe-trotting' (15: 10). This ploy allows him to place some distance between himself and the tourist who continues to view himself unselfconsciously. Thus set apart from both the Anglo-Indian bureaucrat and the globe-trotter, he enjoys a liminal position between their societies that yields him an awareness of the factitious conventions that order both. Indeed, he is aware of the fictionality of all social role and agency, freeing him to adopt a dizzying array of masks.[7] This vertiginous role-playing is a complex matter that touches, on the one hand, Kipling's bicultural upbringing in India and, on the other, the new understanding of culture as performative articulated by anthropologists like Franz Boas and Bronislaw Malinowski and fiction-writers like Conrad and Kipling.[8]

The polymorphous journalist delights most in the kind of personae that allows him to engage in a sort of boyish slumming.[9] On these jaunts, he impersonates that other antithesis of the 'Son of Martha', whom he variously describes as 'the vagrant traveler' (15: 35), the 'loafer' (15: 35), 'the wanderer' (15: 92), the 'tramp' (15: 124) and the 'enviable and unshackled vagabond' (15: 136).[10] As a loafer, Kipling relishes reconnoitering existences off the tourist's beaten track: 'A perverse taste for low company drew the Englishman from the pavement – to walk...up a side-street, where he assisted at a quail-fight and found the low-caste Rajput a cheery and affable soul' (15: 16). He goes on to rub shoulders with the agents of Anglo-Indian banks, whom he lumps together in the 'brotherhood of the Pauper Province' (15: 49): the 'bagmen travelling for the big English firms' (15: 124); the 'mixed crew' who are 'Bummers, land-sharks, skirmishers for their bread' (15: 135); and a story-telling *chowkidar* [watchman] in Boondi. Yet Kipling enjoys his roadside associations not so much for their camaraderie as for the amplitude of self they nourish. He assumes the standing of the tramp to earn himself the most flexible entrée into the varied ways of life he meets.

A description of the 'set of the day' on his last evening at Boondi sums up the attractions of loaferdom:

> This moment of change can only be felt in the open and in touch with the earth, and once discovered, seems to place the finder in deep accord and fellowship with all things on earth. Perhaps this is why the genuine loafer, though 'frequently drunk', is 'always polite to the stranger', and shows such a genial tolerance towards the weaknesses of mankind, black, white, or brown. (15: 215)

The paean is certainly heartfelt, yet lest we be fooled by its sentiment, it is followed immediately by 'a desire to see a fellow-subject' (15: 215) from the Anglo-Indian cantonment. The sudden shift in allegiance from tramp to official carefully frames Kipling's tribute to vagabondage, reminding us that he only plays at the 'genuine loafer' in 'deep accord and fellowship with all things on earth'. He improvises at loaferdom because his sinking low allows him, in springboard-fashion, to launch himself imaginatively outward through a range of different parts: Englishman, globe-trotter, and tramp. This striking of attitudes accounts for the strange mixture of tones – from grand self-abasement to cynical knowingness to lofty prophecy – that we encounter here (and elsewhere) in Kipling's youthful work. It also explains the odd blend of purposes that guides his journalistic writing about India. How this medley accords with the goals of empire – goals that would seem too utilitarian to permit the flippancy of either globe-trotting or tramping – remains to be studied.

Freedom within broad limits

As his shuttling among the figures of official Anglo-Indian, tourist and vagabond suggests, Kipling's roles might be divided between official and bohemian. These different kinds of agency suggest contrasting purposes – a contrast we recall from the opening of 'Letters of Marque': 'It is good for every man to see some little of the great Indian Empire . . . It is good to escape for a time from the House of Rimmon.' Do these divergent purposes – survey and escape – mutually exclude each other, or are they compatible with some larger authorial aim? What relation do these endeavours have to the ends of empire?

Kipling's 'see[ing] some little' of the empire seems clearly congruent with his official duties as a reporter for the *Pioneer* and with the agenda of a Raj interested in consolidating its claim to rule India. As a lens through which stay-at-home Anglo-Indians might vicariously observe the Indian empire, Kipling writes with the eye not just of a reporter but of an amateur ethnographer, hoping to give his audience a larger sense of the many cultures that make up the far-flung Raj. The latter part of the nineteenth century saw the institution, under Denzil Ibbetson, W.W. Hunter, H.H. Risley and others, of the voluminous surveys, gazetteers, glossaries, and censuses that described and categorized the various peoples of the Indian subcontinent. These efforts led Anglo-Indian administrators to 'pigeonhole', in Bernard Cohn's word, the diversity of ethnic and social types of India in distinct, fixed cultural categories (Cohn 1968, 15).

Kipling saw himself producing an impressionistic version of these researches. The journalist-ethnographer parses the social structure of the 'River of Life' (5: 198) he meets upon the highways; and whether he describes the peoples of the Rajput States, the railway employees at Jamalpur, the mining supervisors at Giridih, or the policemen in Calcutta, he describes the world of each as a discrete cultural whole, distinctive in its history, beliefs, dress, gesture, and speech.[11] Udaipur 'governs itself in its own way, and is always in its own way, which is by no means ours, very happy' (15: 65). The reporter writes of the special 'Genius of the Place' (15: 107) at Chitor. Like the census-takers, he is also fond of making comparisons among these different cultural groups, often with an eye to martial qualities that might serve the Raj:

> The Rahtor, who comes of a fighting stock, is a fine animal, and well bred; the Hara, who seems to be more compactly built, is also a fine animal; but for a race that show blood in every line of their

frame, from the arch of the instep to the modelling of the head,
the financial . . . class of Rajputana appears to be most remarkable.
(15: 185)[12]

Though they are not as crudely described, Anglo-Indians also come in
for pigeonholing. Like many nineteenth-century ethnographers and
historians of British India, Kipling 'Indianizes' them, seeing them as
members of a caste. The political agents and professionals who serve the
Princely States are 'men who bear the hat-mark on their brow as plainly
as the well-born native carries the *trisul* of Shiva. They are of the same
caste as the toilers on the Frontier' (15: 71). At Jamalpur, 'The railway
folk, like the army and civilian castes, have their own language and life,
which an outsider cannot hope to understand' (16: 377). Like the ethnographer, the reporter sometimes seeks to place his survey of cultural
types within a quasi-scientific structure. In the motley assembly at the
Sailors' Home in Calcutta, he finds a veritable 'ethnological museum . . .
[of] specimens' (16: 322).

The figure of the 'ethnological museum' is significant. Kipling was
the son of an archaeological museum curator. He was drawn to and
admired museums; the Jaipur Museum, with its '"South Kensington"
cases – of the approved pattern' (15: 39), draws a rave review. Kipling's
ethnological museum represents one example from the range of orientalist institutions and practices (census, library, archive, collection,
museum, durbar and colonial exhibition) that Edward Said and others
identify as powerfully central to the European attempt to discipline the
'disorder' of Asia under a regime at once epistemological, cultural, economic, and political.[13] In that museum, miscellaneous peoples were isolated as exhibits, reduced to their essences by labels, arranged in cases
that imposed order upon their shifting variety, organized as knowledge
of a putative completeness and finality, and objectified in a way both to
signify and enable western domination. Foucault observes that such
archaeologies of knowledge are immensely productive – a productivity
that, in Kipling's case, is simultaneously discursive and political.[14] In
this regard, Kipling mimics Tod. *Annals and Antiquities* was meant to
serve as a historical reference to help British officials 'arbitrate with justice
in their [the Rajputs'] national disputes' and thereby preserve these
states as a 'defence' against enemies to the West (Tod, 'Author's Introduction' 1920, 2: lxviii). In his own idiosyncratic way, Kipling also
intended to educate his official readers about types and castes, both native and British, about whom they knew little and whose acquaintance
would assist them in governing India.

If Kipling's official role as reporter-*cum*-ethnographer is clearly consonant with the goals of empire, his role as bohemian seems patently to oppose, even subvert, imperial ends. The gusto with which the vagabond rhapsodizes about life on the road – its closeness to nature, easy pace, haphazard plan, less than respectable company, and freedom – might seem to mock the purposes of officialdom. Yet the loafer's mode of seeing India constitutes a way of mastering India as efficacious as the ethnological reporter's. The key to his efficacy lies in his assumed lowliness, as the 'set of the day' at Boondi reveals: in that moment, the vagabond reporter feels that his commonness puts him 'in touch with the earth' and 'in deep accord and fellowship with all things on earth'. Like the others he meets at the bottom of the social scale, he touches the putative essences of place and person. The idea expresses Kipling's romantic belief in the power of the weak – the child, the drunkard, the low-caste Indian, the vagrant Briton – to see into the life of things. In 'Letters of Marque', this power includes uncanny knowledge of imperial economic and political practices. To cultivate this power, he recommends that an agent training for the Intelligence and Political Department don a 'pair of sack breeches and old hat' and tramp 'on the Road' through Rajasthan: 'he might gain an insight into the tertiary politics of States – things less imposing than succession-cases and less wearisome than boundary disputes, but very well worth knowing' (15: 136). In his last epistle in 'Letters of Marque', Kipling puts his peroration on Indian revenue collection in the mouth of 'an intelligent loafer' (15: 220).

The vagabond reveals his usefulness even when his interests seem less than practical – indeed, disinterestedly aesthetic. Throughout his career, Kipling, the bard of work, confessed his uneasiness at the frivolity of the writer. Among the railwaymen at Jamalpur, he sees himself as an 'outsider', a mere 'writing-man, who plays with shadows and dresses dolls that others may laugh at their antics' (16: 388). The touring writer appears particularly ludicrous when seen against the figure of the late nineteenth-century flâneur whom he resembles.[15] Kipling's itinerant artist is a peculiarly Anglo-India flâneur – a combination of touring scene-painter out of an Anglo-Indian tradition of the picturesque and peregrinating aesthete out of a Victorian tradition beginning with the Pre-Raphaelites and culminating in the decadents.[16]

Kipling had close ties to the nineteenth-century aesthetic movement in Great Britain. His father, a skillful architectural sculptor, was influenced by the Pre-Raphaelites and the arts-and-crafts movement. One of his uncles was Edward Burne-Jones, and William Morris sometimes visited his family when Kipling was young. In those moments in *From*

Sea to Sea in which the reporter indulges in Pre-Raphaelite scene-painting, he often acknowledges his debt to his artistic forbears. He genuflects before Ruskin (15: 41) and sings of the sunset 'amid a circle of Holman Hunt hills' (16: 186). His palette shows the aesthete's preference for gorgeous, recherché colours: 'The bathing-ledge at the foot of the [Udaipur] City wall was lighted with women clad in raw vermilion, dull red, indigo and sky-blue, saffron and pink and turquoise...' (15: 69).

It may seem odd to pair 'Kipling' and 'aesthete' in the same breath. Indeed, critical discussion of the late-Victorian period conventionally opposes the 'Arties' and the 'Hearties', the decadence of Wilde and Beardsley and the counter-decadence of Kipling's imperialism and Shaw's socialism. But as early as 1913 Holbrook Jackson defined an important link between fin de siècle art and empire:

> It [decadence] is a demand for wider ranges, newer emotional and spiritual territories, fresh woods and pastures new for the soul. If you will, it is a form of imperialism of the spirit, ambitious, arrogant, aggressive, waving the flag of human power over an ever wider and wider territory. And it is interesting to recollect that decadent art periods have often coincided with such waves of imperial patriotism as passed over the British Empire and various European countries during the Eighteen Nineties. (1976, 64)

Recent studies of the late-Victorian period have echoed Jackson in observing the ways in which the decadence and empire-building were coupled in unexpected ways (Brantlinger 1983, 115, 126, 136–7; Hennegan 1990, 194). Kipling bears out the connexion. Despite his jibe at Wilde's coterie in 'In Partibus', the poet of empire represents a swaggering, hyper-masculine cousin of the 'long-haired things/In velvet collar-rolls' (quoted in Carrington 1955, 142).[17]

In 'Letters of Marque', the aesthetic Kipling sometimes indulges in the decadents' 'form of imperialism of the spirit'. He writes literally about capturing a scene in words: 'Not often does a reach of the River of Life so present itself that it can without alteration be transferred to canvas. But the Treasury of Boondi... stood complete and ready for any artist who cared to make it his own' (15: 198). He sings: 'It is good, good beyond expression, to see the sun rise upon a strange land and to know that you have only to go forward and possess that land – that it will dower you before the day is ended with a hundred new impressions and, perhaps, one idea' (15: 164). Kipling's dowry of 'impressions' and 'idea[s]', caught in the picture and song of the bohemian aesthete, is here analogous to the archive of observations assembled by the ethnographer-reporter. Both figures catalogue India as a way of 'possessing' it more firmly, both for themselves and for their official readers. Though the vagabond may seem free of the constraints that trammel the serious journalist, he is none the less bounded, protected and guided by the Raj the official journalist represents. Kipling describes the Sahib miners at Giridih as providing for their Indian employees 'freedom within broad limits' (16: 423). British India affords the footloose journalist an equally generous compass, within the limits of its institutional and ideological authority, to create multiple identities freely and, out of these personae, to generate knowledge useful to it.

'Letters of Marque' is thus aptly titled. According to the *OED*, such letters are 'a license to fit out an armed vessel and employ it in the capture of the merchant shipping belonging to the enemy's subjects, the holder of letters of marque being called a privateer or corsair...'. Though western and eastern India are not precisely enemy territory, they are none the less subject to the licence of a private, freelancing writer to 'capture' cultural and aesthetic property in promotion of imperial rule. The government allows Kipling to play the roles of ordinary Englishman, globe-trotter, serious reporter and vagabond aesthete not only to signify the amplitude of its power to contain multitudes but also to generate, by means of his pen, discourses of varied strands, both ethnographic and aesthetic, which weave together to gird an empire. Indeed, Kipling's structure of plural personae amounts to a private counterpart to the imperial museum, his collection of self-identities mirroring the colonial archive in its method, motive, and power.[18] Whether as sober newsman or tramping artist, Kipling places himself and a diverse India in order; as he 'possesses [himself and] the land', the Raj also secures its paramountcy over the subcontinent.

But the diverse cultures of India are not so easily possessed. Homi Bhabha (1985) observes that the text of the colonizer, riven as it is by its own ambivalences, at once fails to constitute a unified, authoritative body of knowledge about its subject and opens itself up to appropriation and resistance by the colonized. What is true of the colonizer's text is true also of his and Indian subjectivities. While Kipling's unsettled persona can be subsumed, organized, and roughly stabilized within the broad limits of empire, it tends to come apart on the trickier ground of its encounter with Indian subjects. To this unstable side of Kipling's and the Raj's project, seen in the newsman's ambiguous representations of India, we now must turn.

Strange medleys

We have seen how the shifting, even schizoid nature of Kipling's journalist identity can be made to do useful work, of a discursive and ideological kind, for the British Indian empire. However, that benefit is gained at the cost of a fundamental contradiction: the polymorphous regime of the reporter's persona stands at odds with the rigidly particularized matrix of knowledge he produces. The world he describes is ontologically divided against itself. The journalist is permitted to don different guises in improvising a plural identity, but the objects he is studying, particularly Indians, are allowed no such freedom. Their identities are fixed, demarcated and ordered within the sequences of knowledge that make up the 'ethnological museum'. Or so the journalist wishes to believe.

Kipling, as a latter-day 'paternalist' in the tradition of Thomas Munro, John Malcolm, Mountstuart Elphinstone and Charles Metcalfe, was enamoured of the image of the authentic 'native' – the romantic dream of the indigene largely untouched by western civilization (Metcalf 1994, 24–7; Stokes 1959, 8–25). He is at times delighted by the Rajput States because of their freedom, relative to British India, from contamination by western notions of progress. Boondi comes in for special praise because, unlike Jaipur with its drains, Udaipur with its State Engineer, and Jodhpur with its 'energetic doctor', it 'has none of these things' (15: 179–80). Instead, 'It is a beautifully lazy city, doing everything in the real, true, original native way . . .' (15: 181).

Yet there is nothing really 'true' or 'original' about Boondi, as the reporter himself elsewhere reveals. He lauds a Boondi doctor for 'the happy, indolent fashion that must have merits which we can not understand' (15: 184), yet those merits derive from a training in western medicine, as the doctor himself makes clear. The journalist desires the 'original native way', yet declares that 'The population of Boondi seems more obviously mixed than that of the other States' (15: 186) – a mixture to which recent, migrant peoples have added their members. Where does one find an 'original' native in this miscellany? While the reporter is willing to apprehend his belatedness as a tourist, he resists recognizing the anachronism implicit in his idea of an original native. Moreover, while he revels in the freedom of creating his own chameleon subjectivity, he denies the possibility or, when he does behold it, the validity of the native as mixed. How can this be?

The reason lies in the power of the hybrid native, particularly the anglicized Indian, to transgress the limits of his identity and agency as defined by the parameters of Anglo-Indian knowledge. Kipling believed in the concept of the racial type developed by physical anthropologists of the mid-nineteenth century.[19] He found the type attractive because it implied that individual races were essentially distinct from each other and unchanging. The idea of such distinctions inevitably suggested the notion of a permanent racial hierarchy, a hierarchy that served to justify the rule of superior Anglo-Saxons over lesser races. To this concept of empire, hybridity was a clear threat. According to conventional racial thinking, 'miscegenation' between members of different types usually produced unviable or sterile offspring, thus preserving distinctions among races. Yet in some instances, racial hybridity was seen to engender a monstrous vitality that elided hard-and-fast racial differences.[20] In his letters to the *Pioneer*, cultural, as opposed to biological, mixture seems to flourish with a horrific vigour. Jai Singh made Jaipur into a 'marvel' of political and cultural order, but 'Later on came a successor, educated and enlightened by all the lamps of British Progress, and converted the city of Jey Singh into a surprise – a big, bewildering, practical joke' (15: 14). The reporter's mixed emotions are clear: 'The result of the good work is that the old and the new, the rampantly raw and the sullenly old, stand cheek-by-jowl in a startling contrast' (15: 14). 'Big, bewildering'; 'rampantly raw'; 'cheek-by-jowl' – all these suggest a 'strange medley' (15: 14) of cultures that is large, dangerously vital, hard to control, and uncomfortably intimate.

The threat of social cross-fertilization points to an even graver menace: the danger of *political* hybridity embodied in the anglicized Indian nationalist. Kipling warns of this danger most vehemently in 'The City of Dreadful Night', in part a harangue levelled at British Calcutta's encouragement of native self-government. As he listens to a debate about the Municipal Bill, he shudders at the 'cant' uttered by a Bengali politician: 'We planted it and it grew – monstrous as a banian. Now we are choked by the roots of its spreading so thickly in this fat soil of Bengal' (16: 309). The monstrosity is defined here by its power to grow, encroach and suffocate. It suggests an indigenous force that, having assimilated British ways ('That torrent of verbiage is Ours' [16: 309]), now thrusts itself upon the Anglo-Indian to the point of stifling him.

The letters in *From Sea to Sea* are punctuated by moments in which the Indian – or worse, some hybrid of British and Indian – threatens to inundate, entomb or incorporate the Anglo-Indian. In 'Letters of Marque', the reporter descends into the Gau-Mukh (Cow-Mouth) at Chitor and there feels as if the springs at the bottom 'would continue to pour water until the tank rose up and swamped him, or [as if] some of the stone slabs would fall forward and crush him flat' (15: 114). This moment is a brilliant pastiche of 'imperial gothic', produced by a self-conscious aesthete thrilling to *frissons* of horror before the exotic.[21] Yet the mask of the parodist melts away in 'The City of Dreadful Night'. As in the Gau-Mukh scene, the reporter descends, on a Dantesque journey, into the deepest circle of an Indian hell, a Calcutta brothel in which he finds again the threat of incorporation. Here, however, the menace comes not from the indigenous but from a cross of native and British in the form of a Eurasian prostitute: 'she – the widow of a soldier of the Queen – has stooped to this common foulness in the face of the city, she has offended against the White race' (16: 348). In both the plunge into the Gau-Mukh and into inner-city Calcutta, encroachment is rendered in terms of an eroticism that threatens to elide the boundary between Indian and Briton. By the guttering spring, the reporter finds the lingam, 'the loathsome Emblem of Creation' (15: 114). In the Calcutta slums, he encounters the sign of an even more 'loathsome', because blatantly miscegenetic, sexuality. Yet the danger of the cross-racial is not so much sexual as cultural and political; indeed, the sexual signifies the cultural (the westernization of India) and the political (the extension of democratic rights to the English-educated Indian intelligentsia). Through miscegenation, India threatens to assimilate the Briton to itself, thereby growing beyond its essence as defined by British ethnology and, in a reversal of British possession of India, engrossing the Anglo-Indian within a creation partly British in origin and design. Such ironies are repugnant and frightening to the servant of empire; they are an offence 'against the White race'.

In *Kim*, Kipling wrote: 'All India is full of holy men stammering gospels in strange tongues; shaken and consumed in the fires of their own zeal; dreamers, babblers and visionaries: as it has been from the beginning and will continue to the end' (1987, 80). But this image of an eternally unchanging India is a figment of the idealizing paternalist imagination. In *From Sea to Sea*, the journalist was able to exploit the ambiguity of his colonial situation to fashion, with vivid ingenuity, a plural identity. By multiplying the points of view he brought to bear upon the India he saw in his journeys, he was able to compose a rich picture of the western and eastern subcontinent. Wherever he went, he looked to isolate the discrete, 'original' essence of each society he encountered, building up an ethnological museum to house pieces of an India his readers might not have known. Yet he denied to the Indian 'pieces' the very power to invent hybrid versions of themselves that he himself exploited.

He denied it for good reason. By refusing to acknowledge that Indians could transgress against the limits of their 'essential' natures to enact mingled identities out of the scripts of different cultures, he denied them the capacity to learn from the west and, by transforming European values in distinctively Indian ways, to grow in new political directions that would inevitably challenge British rule. What he failed to realize was that the ambiguities in the colonial situation that allowed him to recreate himself were also available to Indians to invent themselves anew. In his fond envoy to Boondi, he celebrates 'The utter untouchedness of the town . . . Read Tod, . . . and the spirit of the place will enter into you and you will be happy' (15: 214). He cannot see that Tod 'touched' Boondi, that he himself has 'touched' it, and that, while the genius of the place was penetrating these Britons' hearts, the 'spirit' of the British was entering Boondi as well, triggering a metamorphosis that Kipling could witness only with anxiety for the future of British rule.

Notes

1. 'Seven Years' Hard' is the title of ch. 3 of Kipling's posthumously published memoirs, *Something of Myself: For My Friends Known and Unknown* (1937). This chapter describes his years as a journalist in India. The most informative overview of these years is found in Pinney (1986). For further information about Kipling's newspaper career, see Carrington (1955, 43–119).
2. 'Anglo-Indian' is a term that is bound to cause confusion. Before the twentieth century, Britons used it to refer to their compatriots living and working in India. With the 1911 Census, however, the term came to designate those persons (formerly called 'Eurasians') who were of mixed British and Indian descent (Lewis 1979, 127n2). However, the former use of 'Anglo-Indian' persisted until 1947. To avoid confusion, I use the term in the former sense.
3. Kipling (1899, 15: 3). All subsequent quotations from *From Sea to Sea* will be cited internally.
4. In 2 Kings 5, Naaman, a Syrian general, was cured of leprosy when he bathed in the River Jordan as the prophet Elisha commanded. Although he wished to convert to Judaism, this change was complicated by his necessary return to Syria, where, at his king's bidding, he would have to continue worshipping the pagan deity Rimmon. For this sin, he requested the Lord's pardon, which Elisha granted. Kipling often alluded to India as the House of Rimmon, where the British served among 'alien' gods.
5. In the words of its own credo, 'The object of the *Civil and Military Gazette* [was] to make [it] a faithful and conscientious advocate of the true interests of the services, civil and military, in India, watching all that affect[ed] those interests for good or evil' (quoted in Barns 1940, 277). The *Pioneer* was an even more powerful advocate of and conduit for official views. Through its contacts with junior members of the Secretariat and its highly paid official contributors in every Simla department, the paper earned a reputation for being 'the first with the news' (quoted in Barns 1940, 269).

6. See *The Dictionary of National Biography* and William Crooke (1920, 1: xxv–xliv), for details of Tod's life and work. For a recent study of Tod's *Annals*, see Inden (1990, 172–6). For an incisive response to Inden, see Peabody (1996).
7. According to Vasant Shahane (1973, 16), Kipling used about 25 different pseudonyms in his journalism – a clear testimony to his malleable sense of persona.
8. For a fascinating discussion of the advent of the new, 'ethnographic' understanding of culture, see Clifford (1988, 92–113).
9. In this respect, he anticipates the boy Kim, who is something of a journalist, with 'a lust to go abroad . . . and discover news' (Kipling 1987, 209).
10. The reporter's antecedents are clear. As a literary figure, he harks back to the *picaro* of Nashe, Defoe, and Smollett; Byron's Childe Harold and Don Juan; Whitman's loafer at his ease; and Twain's boy-adventurers lighting out for the Territories. As a newsman, he recalls the 'vagabondage' of the bohemian reporters, especially George Augustus Sala, of the mid-century *Illustrated Times* (quoted in Wiener 1986, 64). With these progenitors, he shares social mobility and contact with a miscellaneous humankind.
11. Although in some ways opposed to their assumptions and methods, Kipling shared with proponents of indirect rule a basic anthropological premise: that the proper 'units of study' ought to be 'small-scale cultural formations . . . treated as integrated and complete social systems' (Feuchtwang 1973, 99).
12. Compare with Mr Thomson's description of the Gakkhars: 'Physically [they] . . . are not a large-limbed race, but they are compact, sinewy, and vigorous. They make capital soldiers, and it has been stated on good authority that they are the best light cavalry in Upper India' (quoted in Rose 1970, 2: 276).
13. Said (1978, 141). In Indology, the most incisive and influential scholar of the ways in which colonial forms of knowledge promote imperial power has been Bernard Cohn (1983, 1996). For other discussions of the relationship between imperial power and knowledge, see Inden (1990, 33–48); Metcalf (1994, 113–59); Mitchell (1992); and Richards (1993, 11–44).
14. One could choose any discourse from the variety of discursive formations Foucault treats to illustrate the relation between archaeologies of knowledge and their productive power. Consider, for example, 'the archaeological description of "sexuality"' (Foucault 1972, 193). In *The History of Sexuality*, he writes:

> And these discourses on sex did not multiply apart from or against power, but in the very space and as the means of its exercise. Incitements to speak were orchestrated from all quarters, apparatuses everywhere for listening and recording, procedures for observing, questioning, and formulating. (1978, 32–3)

15. For a discussion of the nineteenth-century French *flâneur* as a student of culture mediating 'between aesthetic vision, on the one hand and ethnographic inquiry, on the other' (122), see Ferguson (1993). The journalist Kipling, I will argue, also combines aesthetic and ethnographic methods in his construction of culture.

16. For commentary on the picturesque tradition in Anglo-India, see Amur (1983); and Suleri (1992, 75–110).
17. For commentary on Kipling's ties to the aesthetic movement, see Bloom (1987); Caserio (1987, 119, 124); Ford (1965, 62–5); Goonetilleke (1988, 20); Green (1965, 82); Le Galienne (1971, 329); Paffard (1989, 39); and Scott (1971, 310).
18. James Clifford (1985, 240) observes:

> The history of anthropology needs to accommodate a perspective on col-lecting that embraces both a form of Western subjectivity and a changing set of powerful institutional practices. The history of collections (not lim-ited to museums) is central to an understanding of how those social groups that invented anthropology have *appropriated* exotic things, facts, and meanings. ('Appropriate': to make one's own, from the Latin, *proprius*, proper, property.)

> Collection under these circumstances, I am suggesting, need not be limited to appropriation of 'exotic others', but could include possession of unusual versions of the (western) self. Both kinds of collection are tactics within a single strategy of domination.

19. Observing a black American, Kipling writes: 'I turned and saw by the head upon his shoulders that he was a Yoruba man, if there be any truth in ethnological castes. He did his thinking in English, but he was a Yoruba negro, and the race type had remained the same throughout his generations' (1899, 16: 75). Kipling's notion of racial fixity echoes the theories of Robert Knox, the leading proponent of the racial type among physical anthropologists in mid-nineteenth-century England. See Knox's *The Races of Men* (1862).
   At times, Kipling found the idea of type confining. Much of his most vital fiction is, in one sense, a protest against the ironclad demands of race. Mowgli, Kim and others liminal characters in his fiction, seek to enact hybrid identities beyond the constraints of received ideas of race. Yet this freedom is given only to Britons and only under certain circumstances; Indians, with the arguable exception of Hunder Chunder Mookherjee in *Kim*, are denied this right.
20. For analysis of the many, often contradictory strands of scientific discourse on racial hybridity, see especially Young (1995, 6–19). For other treatments of hybridity in its shifting racial and cultural forms, see Bhabha (1985); 'Hybridity' (1995); Malchow (1996, 167–237); and McClintock (1995, 65–71, 300–2).
21. For an illuminating discussion of the imperial gothic, see Brantlinger (1988, 227–53). For a rich study of the gothicization of race in relation to domestic society and Empire, see Malchow 1996. For analyses of Kipling's descent into the Gau-Mukh, with its evocation of the erotic and the uncanny, see Sullivan (1993, 19–21); and Wurgaft (1983, 137–8).

Works cited

Amur, G.S. 'In Search of the Picturesque: John Lang's *Wanderings in India and Other Sketches of Life in Hindostan*', in H.H. Anniah Gowda (ed.), *The Colonial and the Neo-Colonial Encounters in Commonwealth Literature*. Mysore, 1983, 49–62.

Barns, Margarita. *The Indian Press: a History of the Growth of Public Opinion in India.* London, 1940.

Bhabha, Homi K. 'Signs Taken for Wonders: Questions of Ambivalence and Authority under a Tree Outside Delhi, May 1817', *Critical Inquiry* 12 (1985), 153–64.

Bloom, Harold. Introduction to *Rudyard Kipling.* Harold Bloom (ed.), *Modern Critical Views.* New York, 1987, 1–7.

Brantlinger, Patrick. *Bread & Circuses: Theories of Mass Culture as Social Decay.* Ithaca, 1983.

Brantlinger, Patrick. *Rule of Darkness: British Literature and Imperialism, 1830–1914.* Ithaca, 1988.

Buzard, James. *The Beaten Track: European Tourism, Literature, and the Ways to Culture, 1800–1918.* Oxford, 1993.

Carrington, Charles. *Rudyard Kipling: His Life and Work.* London, 1955.

Caserio, Robert L. 'Kipling in Light of Failure'. *Grand Street* 6.1 (1986). Reprinted in Harold Bloom (ed.), *Rudyard Kipling.* 117–43.

Clifford, James. 'Objects and Selves – An Afterword', in George Stocking Jr. (ed.), *Objects and Others: Essays on Museums and Material Culture. History of Anthropology, vol. 3* Madison, 1985, 236–46.

Clifford, James. *The Predicament of Culture: Twentieth-Century Ethnography, Literature, and Art.* Cambridge, MA, 1988.

Cohn, Bernard S. *Colonialism and Its Forms of Knowledge: the British in India.* Princeton, 1996.

Cohn, Bernard S. 'Notes on the History of the Study of Indian Society and Culture', in Bernard S. Cohn and Milton Singer (eds), *Structure and Change in Indian Society.* Chicago, 1968, 3–28.

Cohn, Bernard S. 'Representing Authority in Victorian India', in Eric Hobsbawm and Terence Ranger (eds), *The Invention of Tradition.* Cambridge, 1983, 165–209.

Crooke, William. Introduction. James Tod. *Annals and Antiquities.* 1:xxv–xliv.

Ferguson, Priscilla Parkhurst. 'The Flâneur and the Production of Culture', in Ann Rigney and Douwe Fokkema (eds), *Cultural Participation: Trends Since the Middle Ages.* Amsterdam, 1993, 109–24.

Feuchtwang, Stephen. 'The Colonial Formation of British Social Anthropology', in Talal Asad (ed.), *Anthropology and the Colonial Encounter.* London, 1973, 71–100.

Ford, Boris. 'A Case for Kipling?', *Scrutiny* 11.1 (1942). Reprinted in Elliot L. Gilbert (ed.), *Kipling and the Critics.* New York, 1965, 59–73.

Foucault, Michel. *The Archaeology of Knowledge and the Discourse on Language.* 1971. Trans. A.M. Sheridan Smith. New York, 1972.

Foucault, Michel. *The History of Sexuality Vol. 1, An Introduction.* Trans. Robert Hurley. New York, 1978.

Fussell, Paul. *Abroad: British Literary Traveling between the Wars.* New York, 1980.

Goonetilleke, D.C.R.A. *Images of the Raj: South Asia in the Literature of Empire.* New York, 1988.

Green, Roger Lancelyn. *Kipling and the Children.* London, 1965.

Green, Roger Lancelyn (ed.). *Kipling: the Critical Heritage.* New York, 1971.

Hennegan, Alison. 'Personalities and Principles: Aspects of Literature and Life in *Fin-de-Siècle* England', in Roy Porter and Mikúlâs Teich (eds), *Fin de Siècle and Its Legacy.* Cambridge, 1990, 170–215.

'Hybridity', in Bill Ashcroft, Gareth Griffiths and Helen Tiffin (eds), *The Post-Colonial Studies Reader.* London, 1995, 183–209.

Inden, Ronald. *Imagining India*. Oxford, 1990.
Jackson, Holbrook. *The Eighteen Nineties: a Review of Art and Ideas at the Close of the Nineteenth Century*. 1913. Reprint. Atlantic Highland, NJ, 1976.
Kincaid, Dennis. *British Social Life in India, 1608–1937*. London, 1938.
Kipling, Rudyard. *From Sea to Sea*. In *Writings in Prose and Verse of Rudyard Kipling*. Outward Bound Ed. 2 vols (15, 16). New York, 1899.
Kipling, Rudyard. *Kim*. 1900–01. London, 1987.
Kipling, Rudyard. Letter to Edmonia Hill. Lahore, [9–11] May 1888, in Thomas Pinney (ed.), *The Letters of Rudyard Kipling*, 1: 171. Iowa City, 1990.
Kipling, Rudyard. 'The Sons of Martha'. 1907. In *Rudyard Kipling's Verse*. Definitive edn. Garden City, NY, 1939.
Knox, Robert. *The Races of Men: a Philosophical Enquiry into the Influence of Race over the Destinies of Nations*. London, 1862.
Le Gallienne, Richard. 'Kipling's Place in Literature', *Munsey's Magazine* 68 (1919). Reprinted in Roger Lancelyn Green (ed.), *Kipling: the Critical Heritage*. 327–31.
Lewis, Robin J. *E.M. Forster's Passages to India*. New York, 1979.
Malchow, H.L. *Gothic Images of Race in Nineteenth-Century Britain*. Stanford, CA, 1996.
McClintock, Anne. *Imperial Leather: Race, Gender and Sexuality in the Colonial Contest*. New York, 1995.
Metcalf, Thomas. *Ideologies of the Raj*. Cambridge, 1994.
Mitchell, Timothy. 'Orientalism and the Exhibitionary Order', in Nicholas Dirks (ed.), *Colonialism and Culture*. Ann Arbor, 1992, 289–317.
Paffard, Mark. *Kipling's Indian Fiction*. New York, 1989.
Peabody, Norbert. 'Tod's *Rajast'han* and the Boundaries of Imperial Rule in Nineteenth-Century India', *Modern Asian Studies* 30.1 (1996), 185–220.
Pinney, Thomas. Introduction. *Kipling's India: Uncollected Sketches, 1884–88*. New York, 1986, 1–26.
Richards, Thomas. *The Imperial Archive: Knowledge and the Fantasy of Empire*. London, 1993.
Rose, H.A. (comp.). *A Glossary of the Tribes and Castes of the Punjab and North-West Frontier Province*. 1917. Based on the *Census Report for the Punjab, 1883*, by Sir Denzil Ibbetson, KCSI, and the *Census Report for the Punjab, 1892*, by Sir Edward Maclagan, KCIE, CSI, 3 vols. Reprint. Patiala, 1970.
Said, Edward W. *Orientalism*. New York, 1978.
Scott, Dixon. 'Rudyard Kipling'. *Bookman* (London) 5.18 (1912). Reprinted in Roger Lancelyn Green (ed.), *Kipling: the Critical Heritage*. 308–17.
Shahane, Vasant. *Rudyard Kipling: Activist and Artist*. Carbondale and Edwardsville, IL, 1973.
Stokes, Eric. *The English Utilitarians and India*. Oxford, 1959.
Suleri, Sara. *The Rhetoric of English India*. Chicago, 1992.
Sullivan, Zoreh T. *Narratives of Empire: the Fictions of Rudyard Kipling*. Cambridge, 1993.
Tod, James. *Annals and Antiquities of Rajasthan, or the Central and Western Rajput States of India*. 1829–32. Reprint. William Crooke (ed.). 2 vols. London, 1920.
Tod, James. 'Author's Introduction to the Second Volume of the Original Edition', *Annals and Antiquities* 2: lxvii–ix.
Wiener, Joel H. 'How New Was the New Journalism?', in Joel Weiner (ed.), *Papers for the Millions: the New Journalism in Britain, 1850s to 1914*. Contributions to the Study of Mass Media and Communications, 13. New York, 1986, 47–71.

Wurgaft, Lewis D. *The Imperial Imagination: Magic and Myth in Kipling's India.* Middletown, CT, 1983.

Young, Robert J.C. *Colonial Desire: Hybridity in Theory, Culture and Race.* London, 1995.

9

Representing the Technology of the Raj in Britain's Victorian Periodical Press

A. Martin Wainwright

Not far from Hardwar, where the Ganges descends onto the plains of northern India, is the city of Rurki. It is the site of India's first engineering college, established in 1848, and the entrance to the Solani River Aqueduct, completed in 1854. The aqueduct, which crosses rapids at the entrance to the Ganges Canal, was the longest in the world at the time of its completion. In order to celebrate its and the Canal's completion, the Government of India placed two magnificent stone lions at its entrance and held a religious ceremony near the carvings on the morning of 8 April 1854 (Stone 1984, 40–3). Nine years later, William Simpson captured the entrance to the aqueduct in his watercolour painting, 'View of the Ganges Canal'. The same scene, from a slightly different angle, appeared as a print in the *Illustrated London News* (*ILN*) when the Canal opened.[1] Both renditions show the two lions guarding the entrance to the aqueduct with snow-capped Himalayan peaks lining the distant horizon (see Figure 9.1). As if challenging the sentiment of Percy Bysshe Shelley's 'Ozymandias', these lions appear to proclaim the permanence of western technology, particularly amid the supposed backwardness of the East. Indeed both renditions of this scene highlight the contrast between western and eastern technological prowess by juxtaposing a factory in the background and Indian travellers using antiquated forms of transport in the foreground. The *ILN*'s version contrasts a steam-powered river boat with the more primitive oar and sailing vessels that Indians used to ply the waters.

Both renditions of this scene capture the two assumptions that justified the Raj in the minds of many Britons. One was that technology would bring unlimited progress for the betterment of humankind. The other

185

Figure 9.1 'Opening of a new bridge at Travancore' and 'View of the Ganges Canal', from the *Illustrated London News*, supplement, 5 August 1854, p. 117.

was that westerners, particularly Britons, were the best suited to introduce this technology to the non-western world.

The British press of the day did not hesitate to make explicit in writing
what was implicit in art. 'This stupendous work is hailed by the people
of India as one of the grandest improvements yet affected by European
civilisation and enterprise', proclaimed the *ILN*. *Blackwood's Edinburgh
Magazine* even published a poem to honour the Canal's inauguration
ceremony, a Christian service of thanksgiving attended by British
administrators and engineers and their Indian servants:

> Years hence, some aged man may say –
> Of those who stand to-day
> By the glad baptism of your youngest born; –
> Where from his fruit-grove, far around
> He eyes the green and affluent ground: –
> 'I stood among them on that shining morn,
> I saw the ruler of the land
> Let loose the waters with an easy hand;
> The river vainly idolised of yore
> Now first her servants blessed;
> The white-topped mountains never bore
> Us benefit before,
> Till taught by those wise strangers of the West.'
> (*Blackwood's Edinburgh Magazine*, October 1854, 475)

This verse reveals several assumptions about the role of western technology that many Victorians held and frequently expressed in their periodicals. First, technology was a primary means of progress. Second, the
western introduction of technology in India was an unmitigated benefit
to the indigenous population. Third, the belief systems of India not
only led its inhabitants away from God, their superstitious characteristics
hindered Indians from advancing to the level of civilization that Europeans and their descendants had attained. Finally, these three assumptions justified Britain's occupation of India as a means of bringing the
material benefits of modern technology, unfettered by erroneous cultural
taboos, to the inhabitants of the subcontinent. Although space does not
allow an exhaustive study of the topic here,[2] a sampling of journals and
newspapers from 1850 to 1914 demonstrates that these assumptions
permeated the periodical press's coverage of India.

That the periodical press had a significant impact on perceptions of
the educated classes, there can be little doubt. Recent scholarship indicates

that the 'circulation of periodicals and newspapers was larger and more influential in the nineteenth century than printed books' (Vann and VanArsdel 1994, 3). For popular dailies and weeklies, such as the *Times*, the *Manchester Guardian*, and the *ILN*, we know enough about their circulation to conclude that they were read widely among the upper and middle classes, from which came the people most likely to influence the imperial relationship between Britain and India (Ellegârd 1971, 2–22). But the trade journals portraying technological innovations were probably no less influential. For the professions supporting such advances, journals were by far the most important form of communication. Circulation statistics for professional and trade journals remain elusive, in part because the editors refused to release the figures – a practice which Ruth Richardson and Robert Thorne describe as 'mindless secrecy' (Richardson and Thorne 1994, 60). Nevertheless, the sheer volume of publications and accompanying advertisements in the natural and applied sciences indicates an avid readership with a voice in business, education and politics. Journals such as the *Builder*, the *Engineer*, *Engineering*, the *Mark Lane Express* (*MLE*) and the *Journal of the Royal Agricultural Society* were the major journals in architecture, engineering and agriculture and shaped the way that these professions developed. Indeed, as the contributors to *Victorian Periodicals and Victorian Society* have aptly demonstrated, journals bore a major responsibility for the emergence of professions in the modern sense during the late nineteenth century (Vann and VanArsdel 1994, 5–6). Although it is impossible to identify specific subscribers, engineers who worked in India would almost certainly have read these journals or been exposed to their ideas. In some cases, the engineers most involved in the introduction of western technology to India wrote the articles describing what they had achieved. Sir Arthur Cotton, for instance, devoted much of his career to irrigation projects in southern India, and Horace Bell worked as a senior engineer on India's railways. Other contributors were scholars, such as Sir Wolseley Haig, who co-edited the *Cambridge History of India*, and Sir William Wilson Hunter, who published biographies of British rulers of India.

Equally important was the extent to which Indians read these journals. Here again, circumstantial evidence suggests that Indian elites, at the very least, were exposed to the ideas presented in British journals. Because so many of the authors who wrote on India had worked there themselves, connections between journalism in India and Britain were numerous. For instance, one of the contributors cited in this essay, Sir Roper Lethbridge, was also an editor of the *Calcutta Review*. Another, Juland Danvers, was a member of the Northbrook Indian Society, which catered to Indians living in England. Indeed, the presence of Indian students in late-Victorian and Edwardian Britain, many of them studying the applied sciences, probably formed an important link whereby the ideas presented in British journals could be transmitted to India. Indian contributions to the *Indian Magazine and Review*, the monthly journal of London's Indian National Association, reveal sentiments similar to those published in other journals covered in this essay. Furthermore, Indian journals, whether aimed at a specific audience, such as the *Calcutta Review*, or catering to a profession, such as *Indian Engineering*, often had British editors and were clearly based on British counterparts. In some cases these Indian journals suffered from competition with British journals sold in India (Chaudhuri 1996, 178–81).

The press's portrayal of the application of western technology in India was based on the underlying faith in material progress in any setting. Martin Weiner has demonstrated that many British intellectuals continued to be suspicious of machinery throughout the nineteenth century (Weiner 1981, 11–84). Nevertheless, few writers in the Victorian and Edwardian press disputed the long-term benefits of technological innovation. Such optimism characterized the periodical press, whose coverage of the subject varied according to the focus of the journal. Technical journals, such as *Engineering*, the *MLE* and the *Journal of Science* were inherently favourable toward technology. Journals and newspapers aimed at the lay reader, however, covered technology only if it was dramatic. The subject appeared either in connection with disaster or as the promise of material and spiritual benefits.

It is not surprising, therefore, that some of the press's greatest panegyrics to technology accompanied the Great Exhibition in 1851, one of the first great media events focusing on the applied sciences. Claiming that 'in the history of nations, as in that of individuals, physical facts always take precedence of, and are the forerunners of moral and spiritual facts', the *ILN* accompanied its coverage of the Great Exhibition with predictions that technology would improve the world spiritually as well as materially. Listing numerous areas of technological advance over the preceding hundred years, it argued:

> The workers of the world having shown each other how they can work . . . will learn, that if co-operation be good in this respect, it may be good also in another. They have exhibited in concert; the next step will be to work in concert, not alone in physical, but in moral and religious work. When they take *that* step a new era will begin, and Utopia will no longer be an idle dream, but will take the form and substance of a possible fact. (*ILN* 10 May 1851, 392)

Implicit in this passage is the assumption that the 'workers of the world' are of the western world, since in 1851 Europe and North America virtually monopolized the production and implementation of the technology to which the article refers. But, as the article made clear, this monopoly did not prevent the rest of humankind from taking part in the soon-to-be-realized 'Utopia'. The writer went on to describe the wares of other lands exhibited in the Crystal Palace, and its first subject was India. For India was 'perhaps the land in which there is more "future" for our commerce and manufactures than any other'. The reason was technology: 'Railroads have commenced there, and before long a double railway route through Europe, with the electric telegraph, will make Calcutta nearer to us in time than Berlin was a century ago' (*ILN*, 10 May 1851, 392).

India had one of the largest exhibits in the Crystal Palace. It occupied 'both sides of the eastern end of the Western Avenue entering on the transept' and comprised a 'collection which is an exhibition in itself'. India's imposing presence at the Exhibition served three purposes: it reminded visitors of the vast wealth that modern technology could tap in the subcontinent; it demonstrated the potential benefits that Britain could bring to other lands through technology; and it provided a contrast between the advanced technology of the West and the traditional technology of the rest of the world (*ILN*, 10 May 1851, 392).

Just as India's exotic conditions were an excellent subject for the Great Exhibition, so they provided ideal settings for technological themes that justified depiction through words and pictures in the press. In this sense India was a worthy topic of coverage regardless of any didactic motive that accompanied reportage on these themes. Since India and technology individually offered scenes that even in black-and-white lithograph must have been a feast for the eyes of Victorian readers, the *ILN* frequently combined its coverage of the two. *Engineering* did the same through words and drawings, albeit in a more prosaic fashion. The 'Notes on India', which appeared in every edition of this journal, attest to the interest that India sparked in the imaginations of members of technical professions. India was so fascinating because it presented topographical, climatological and cultural challenges on a far larger scale than did Britain. At the time of its construction, the Ganges Canal was three times longer than the next largest irrigation system in the world. Similarly, the railway descent of the Eastern Ghats was one of the world's most complex engineering projects in its day.

Three reasons accounted for the massive scale of these projects. First, India's topography often demanded it. To build a railway from Bombay to Madras required the traversing of terrain with which British railway

engineers never contended at home. Second, because British administrators were spread thinly across the subcontinent, it was easier to
supervise the construction of a few big projects than many smaller ones.
Thus the East India Company built a massive irrigation canal rather
than a series of tanks on the plateau between the Jumna and the Ganges.
Finally, because they reflected the stature of the British Raj as the heir to
the Mauryans and the Mughals, large engineering projects better served
as reminders of British authority and power than did smaller ones.

British engineers could develop techniques in India that made their
efforts at home seem simple by comparison. So great was the magnitude
of India's challenges that for some irrigation engineers, such as Captain
Proby Cautley and Sir Arthur Cotton, there was little to learn from the
experiences of projects in Europe. The *Builder* warned civil engineers
headed for India of 'the difficulties and peculiarities that must be contended against'.

> Trains of loaded elephants on railways drawn by bullocks, ever recur-
> ring use of sunshades and punkahs; mighty inundations sweeping all
> before them; immense trees imbedded [*sic*] in rivers to the great
> increase in the dangers of navigation; vast deposits of silt choking up
> canals and rivers; boat-bridges; constant liability to the inroads,
> attacks, and devastation of a seemingly inconsiderable, but in reality
> insidious enemy it is impossible to exterminate: the white ant, are but
> a few of the local novelties quite unconnected with the puzzling dif-
> ferences in building materials available, which of course present a still
> more important study to be mastered. (*Builder* 2 November 1867, 794)

Nineteenth-century India was therefore, according to Daniel Headrick,
'a laboratory of hydraulic engineering and a school from which this
knowledge spread to other lands' (Headrick 1988, 196). Bruce Hunt
(1997, 312–15) has taken this assertion further, arguing that the imperial
context played a vital role in shaping some technologies, because without
the challenge of empire, many of the techniques developed to meet it
would have been unnecessary. These triumphs of technology were obvious
material for the periodical press, as were the failures.

Journalists eagerly covered the surmounting of these obstacles. One
such account, however accurate, of the construction of the Cauvery
Falls hydroelectric dam was worthy of a novel by H. Rider Haggard:

> Hilly jungles infested by tiger, panther, and bear had to be spanned,
> and herds of wild elephants to be combated before telegraph posts,

carrying six strands for copper wire, could be set up. The machinery had to be dragged thirty miles from the railway station to the works by elephants and the long-horned white draught bullocks for which Mysore has long been famous. Another and even greater enemy fought by Captain Joly de Lotbinière, the Canadian officer who initiated and executed the enterprise, was the widespread superstition that the god of the sacred Cauvery would annihilate all who tampered with the stream. Labour was consequently most difficult to obtain, and it was only by the greatest tact and ingenious explanation that the work was able to proceed. Cholera and malaria, always deadly in the riverbeds, particularly when freshly dug, also proved an obstacle. (*ILN* 26 July 1902, 14b)

It was, however, the railway that exercised the Victorian and Edwardian imagination the most. The entire enterprise owed its existence in part to the press's influence. In the 1840s the *Times* and the *Economist* joined the textile and railway industries in pressuring the East India Company to guarantee 4.5–5 per cent profits to the companies that developed India's railways. Indian railways served a number of important functions for Britain and the Raj. They enabled the Raj to deploy troops rapidly, but most importantly they opened up areas of the subcontinent's interior that had hitherto been economically useless for British entrepreneurs. The Government of India enticed British engineers with offers of free transport and salaries double those that they would have earned at home. These engineers faced challenges unknown in Britain. The subcontinent's mountains required tunnels longer than any in Britain, and its flood-prone rivers called for bridges greater than the world had hitherto seen. Most impressive of all, however, was the descent of the Great Indian Peninsula Railway from the Deccan Plateau to the Coromandel Coast by way of the Bore Ghat. This stretch of line, completed in 1863, required 25 tunnels, six viaducts, and stations at which trains would reverse their direction in order to negotiate the precipitous cliffs of the Eastern Ghats.[3]

The Bore Ghat descent was the scene of dramatic railway disasters which Victorian journals eagerly described. When in 1867 a viaduct on this section of track collapsed, the *ILN* depicted the rubble and *Times* criticized the Bombay Presidency for not maintaining standards in the system (*ILN* 21 September 1867, 312, and *Times* 6 September 1867, 8). A train crash at a reversing station two years later prompted what was for the time a lurid reference in the *ILN* to the accident having 'mutilated the unfortunate occupants [of the train] in the most horrible manner' (*ILN* 6 March 1869, 238 and 248).

The press's concentration on railways was evident even in the rare discussion of road construction, which engineers carried out 'with all gradients and curves suitable for railways, so that in the event of a railway being thereafter considered advisable along any such line, the road already formed would be found suitable for that purpose' (*Engineering* 9 November 1866, 361). The *ILN* covered the construction of railways, especially their bridges, in detail. Work on the Calcutta–Delhi line was the focus of a two-page pictorial display crowded with elephants, camels, 'natives' dancing, and a pontoon bridge (*ILN* 7 June 1851, 538–9). Another article, on the Great Indian Peninsula Railway, depicted the railway running through a variety of impressive scenery (*ILN* 8 July 1854, 4).

The challenges of India also influenced the structure of trains. Long journeys required innovations in accommodation, which the press covered enthusiastically. In an article accompanying diagrams of carriages on the Great Indian Peninsula Railway, the *Railway Gazette* (12 January 1906, 348E) described amenities, such as ladies' cloakrooms, that it suggested British railways should imitate. Railways were also the focus of efforts to combat that most pervasive impediment to travelers in India: heat. *Engineering* (24 September 1874, 238) published seven plans for railway carriage cooling systems long before the invention of air conditioning. The Prince of Wales' visit to India (1905) occasioned the construction of luxury carriages that pioneered the use of electric fans (*Railway Gazette* 26 January 1906, 12).

Implicit in these reports, however, whether of the triumphs or the failures of western technology, was the inferiority of the East. Disasters associated with transport or engineering may have illustrated the need for caution as British engineers harnessed the forces of nature. But the assumption that western society was uniquely capable of improving India was rarely left in doubt. The Victorian understanding of Indian society and culture formed the necessary backdrop to the press's portrayal of the subcontinent's indigenous technology. For Victorians, India was a land of extremes: of sun-scorched plains and snow-capped mountains, of fabulous wealth and dire poverty, of sublime philosophers and blind superstition, and of ancient knowledge and primitive technology. Just as Victorian editors of popular journals only included in their periodicals what appeared to be remarkable about technology, so they usually covered India either for its exotic appeal or for the ways in which its study tended to elevate the esteem that Britons held for their own culture.

The press often combined these two elements in the same article. In its coverage of the Great Exhibition, for instance, the *ILN* emphasized

the antiquity of Indian manufactures in its description of 'Indian toys –
probably exactly the same kind of toys that Indian children played
with when British children were sold in the slave market of Rome, or
even when Alexander the Great defeated Porus and crossed the Hindus
[*sic*].' Yet the same article also reminded the reader that Indian technology had advanced no further than ancient times in its reference
to 'pottery...of the form found in ancient Egyptian and Etruscan
remains' (*ILN* 10 May 1851, 392). A similar contrast appeared in the
Builder's report on public works in India in 1873. The article begins by
asserting that, contrary to popular belief in Britain, 'India *has* an engineering history, marked by works whose usefulness may vie with the
works of any other nation'. In fact the major thrust of this report is an
appeal to British engineers 'to do what the Hindoo [*sic*] did in a most
efficient manner in many parts of the country...that is store water all
over it' (*Builder* 8 November 1873, 889). In making this argument, however, the article proceeds to dismiss all other aspects of Indian technology as virtually useless:

> The ancient engineering works of India in the south are, with the
> exceptions of the [water storage] tanks, neither very numerous nor
> well executed....In Central India, and towards Bombay, we have
> many curious works, but not very instructive in an engineering point
> of view; such are the tombs of the Ghond Kings at Chanda, the forts
> of Gawilghur and Narnulla. (*Builder* 8 November 1873, 889)

The article had a higher opinion of 'ancient Mohammedan rulers [who]
left us noble examples of architecture' (*Builder* 8 November 1873, 889).
Nevertheless, concluding that 'the history of native engineering in
India as regards the Hindoo is not brilliant, but it was useful', the writer
left little doubt that although British engineers might learn something
from their indigenous predecessors, their presence on the subcontinent
was necessary for its continued progress.

It was difficult to ignore totally the achievements of indigenous technology. The textual and archeological work of 'orientalist' scholars and
the incidental information acquired through surveys of the land provided ample evidence of earlier achievements in transport and industry.
The trade journals, less overtly ideological in their focus than the popular
press, frequently gave a nod to indigenous technology and occasionally
devoted an entire article to it. *Engineering* devoted two pages in a 1912
edition to evidence of ironmongering in ancient India (Graves 1912,
644–6). In 1867 the *Journal of Science* pointed to 'proof that attention

had once been given to the construction of roads, in the fine avenues of trees, which in some districts measured several hundred miles in length' (*Journal of Science* January 1867, 23). Writing for the *Journal of the Royal Agricultural Society of England*, Sir George Birdwood, a former professor of botany at Bombay University and a well-known proponent of Indian culture, referred to Indians as 'the most industrious and patient agriculturalists ever evolved by any known division of the great Aryan race, and blessed with a civilisation ... essentially identical with Greece and Rome' (Birdwood 1893, 859). Eighteenth-century European descriptions of India were replete with observations such as these, and the editors of Victorian technical journals were probably aware of them.[4]

Nevertheless, for many Victorians and Edwardians, including those who wrote in professional and trade journals, India's technological lag behind western countries was a direct result of its culture. In this belief journalists and authors of the late nineteenth century reflected the long-established ascendancy of the policies of social improvers, such as the utilitarians who governed India in the 1820s and 1830s, over 'orientalists' who had dominated public policy in the late eighteenth century. Late-Victorian and Edwardian writers also exhibited thinking that resulted from a shift in perception that Michael Adas identifies as occurring in the eighteenth century. Whereas European observers of the sixteenth and seventeenth centuries had criticized Indians for their supposed spiritual ignorance (evidenced by their practice of Islam and Hinduism rather than Christianity), their British counterparts in the nineteenth and twentieth centuries highlighted Indian culture's technological and scientific ignorance (Adas 1989, 4–14).

The assumption that India's cultural flaws caused its technological inferiority was present even among those who praised certain aspects of Indian culture. Writing for the *Journal of the Society of Arts* (*JSA*) in 1886, C.H. Baden-Powell, a Punjab judge and specialist on the Indian land system, praised the 'aesthetic' value of Indian handicrafts. Noting the appearance of mills on the subcontinent, he lamented the imminent demise of India's traditional crafts. Yet Baden-Powell managed to turn this into a backhanded compliment of Indian culture by attributing the preservation of Indian handicrafts to 'the (fortunate) Oriental slowness to change, and a sort of non-inventiveness and lack of desire for novelty, which marks most Indian races' (Baden-Powell 1886, 709). Moreover, he neglected to mention the damage that these crafts had already suffered under British authorities more interested in developing consumer markets in India than protecting its indigenous manufactures.

Nowhere was the press more adamant about the shortcomings of India's indigenous technology than concerning agriculture. A reader of the Victorian or Edwardian periodical press might be pardoned for believing that the main reason for Britain's occupation of India was the prevention and amelioration of famine. For this was the aspect of British rule that most frequently appeared in print. The British press deemed Asian rulers to have been wholly inadequate at controlling famine. In a diamond jubilee retrospective on the Raj written for the *Imperial and Asiatic Quarterly Review*, Sir Roper Lethbridge, a former education administrator in India, stated succinctly an assumption that the Victorian press frequently expressed about India's indigenous rulers:

> In the olden time, under Native rule, it is of course obvious that no organised action for the relief of Famine was possible, for the organisation did not exist. Consequently, when crops failed, the people died like flies; and the survivors, when the famine was past and gone, had more land than they knew what to do with – and increased and multiplied again until they were again decimated either by famine or by pestilence, or yet more frequently by war or civil disturbance. (Lethbridge 1897, 2–3)

None of Lethbridge's criticisms were of Indian technological capabilities. Rather they focused on the perceived, inherent disorganization, ignorance and violence of Indians as an ethnic group. These supposed cultural, and possibly biological, flaws condemned Indians to endless Malthusian cycles of overpopulation and famine. The technological solutions to this curse, the article implied, were simply beyond the capacity or even the understanding of Indians.

When the press covered indigenous Indian technology, it emphasized its inadequacy to deal with India's problems, especially relating to famines. More important, however, were the frequent claims that India's religions discouraged technological innovation. Writing for the *MLE*, Harold Cox, the economist and former lecturer at Aligarh University, expressed frustration over the role of Hindu taboos in preventing the acceptance of substitutes for fertilizers:

> It is difficult for a European to understand how people who do not mind patting dung with their hands into cakes to be used as fuel in cooking their food, should yet regard it as defiling to them to spread bone manure. But there are a good many other Hindoo [*sic*] notions which are utterly unintelligible to Europeans. (Cox 1887, 568)

Muslims fared no better than Hindus in the pages of Victorian and Edwardian journals. For if the caste system prevented Hindu society from material progress, the warrior ethos forestalled technological advances in Muslim societies. Writing for the *JSA*, Sir William Lee-Warner, secretary of the India Office's Political Department, declared:

> Despite all the brilliant achievements of the Mohammedan builders of empire, and the legacies of the great Akbar, of which British administrators know the lasting value, the sword was never sheathed... Numerous were the victories of war, but those of peace were few, and in the clash of arms histories of the Indian peoples could not be written. (Lee-Warner 1900, 214)

That Britain too engaged in warfare throughout the nineteenth century is implicit in the list of conquests that Lee-Warner includes in the article (Lee-Warner 1900, 225). But it never occurs to him that this fact in any way places British rulers on a moral plane similar to that of their Muslim predecessors.

Victorian readers learned the disastrous results of the Muslim warrior code. In his analysis of famines under Muslim rule, written in 1901 for the *Imperial and Asiatic Quarterly Review*, Wolseley Haig, Officiating Deputy Commissioner in the Hyderabad Assigned Districts, began with the assertion that 'we have no practical lessons to learn from the famine policy of Oriental monarchs of the Middle Ages'. He went on to emphasize the credulity of Islamic rulers, the first famine being 'attributed by Muslim historians to the Divine displeasure at the slaying of a holy man', and their brutality through digressions about gruesome tortures and executions (Haig 1901, 10).

Even where evidence of extensive technological development existed the Victorian and Edwardian press tended to argue that the characteristics of the population led to its underutilization. This assertion reflected a social construction of science which has been the subject of extensive study.[5] An 1874 article in *Engineering* declared that the 'past reveals to us India under native rule covered from north to south and from east to west with works of irrigation, the remnants and traces of many of which still exist'. But, the writer argued, the indigenous population had not only failed to improve on millennia-old technology, it had allowed this legacy to deteriorate. The causes were not difficult to isolate. With a nod to 'political changes and revolutions', the writer focused on 'the natural tendencies of the races inhabiting these countries to allow anything, buildings, houses, clothing &c., to fall into decay from habitual neglect'.

Imagine a district overturned by war or political or civil discord upon the return of the inhabitants... to their lands, they, if Orientals, do not combine to reconstruct, or repair their reservoirs or branch canals so as to keep the whole of their lands under irrigation; on the contrary, they bow to fatality, and using such an amount of water as the damaged or decayed works still furnish, irrigate perhaps a tenth part of their lands. (*Engineering* 28 August 1874, 155–6)

Thus the imposition of western technology through imperialism became a self-validating mission, since the apparent achievements of earlier civilizations in India only demonstrated their inadequacy. The very decision of Victorian and Edwardian journals to use technology as a criterion for measuring the values of a culture was itself a product of western values. As Donald MacKenzie has pointed out: 'Not only the production of new ideas but also the process by which these are accepted or rejected can be affected by social factors' (MacKenzie 1981, 3). In this case, the social construction of technology in the imperial context disallowed the possibility of past technological prowess in non-European cultures already deemed to be inferior.

The vast majority of British journalists writing on India considered its civilization to be markedly inferior to that of the West. But many writers assumed the gap to be cultural rather than biological. Indians might have childish beliefs and their often violent actions might betray a lack of temper that the supposedly more mature civilization that ruled them maintained. But if, according to the British press, Indians could not develop advanced technology on their own because their culture was not sufficiently developed, then it was Britain's mission to develop it for them and even to pass on some of this knowledge. As a writer for *Engineering* optimistically (and condescendingly) proclaimed of Indians in 1886, 'Although the people are not robust yet they are patient and enduring, and can be taught new processes if the work be conducted with care and with due regard to their prejudices and religious opinions' (*Engineering* 5 March 1886, 229).

In the almost unanimous opinion of Victorian and Edwardian journalists the inability or unwillingness of Indians to develop their own advanced technology justified Britain's occupation of the subcontinent. Even when the application of western technology to exploit India's resources obviously served Britain and its empire, the press of the day argued that India benefited too. According to Wyndham R. Dunstan, Director of the Scientific and Technical Department of the Imperial Institute, the reason for mining India's coal deposits was to make them 'available for use all over India, and for export to the principal ports of the Eastern World' (Dunstan 1902, 371).

Harold Cox's 1887 *MLE* report on a model farm near Kanpur is typical of the rhetoric that accompanied such assertions. He wrote of the 'vivid impression' the farm left on his mind 'of the work which England is through her agents doing in the East, a work which, when every allowance is made for blunders numerous and mixtures of motive, we must allow is a noble work'. Comparing the technological relationship of the West and India to that of the prince and the princess in *Sleeping Beauty*, Cox wrote, 'India has slept long, but at length the prince has arrived to awaken her. Already the courtyard is astir with the whirr of western activity, and within the prince is shaking off her sleep and preparing to spring to new life' (Cox 1887, 1162).

This analogy reveals much about British assumptions surrounding their occupation of India and transfer of technology to the subcontinent. It combines nineteenth-century romanticism and the cult of chivalry with faith in progress and the potential of technology. Furthermore, it portrays India (and Indians cumulatively) as a woman awaiting the guiding hand of Britain, a man. Given the prevailing attitudes of the day, portraying Indians in the role of women was probably even more damning than portraying them as children. With appropriate guardianship and tutelage, male children could, after all, grow up to be adults participating fully in society. Women, on the other hand, were deemed incapable of running their own affairs and needed the constant companionship of men to operate in the public sphere. Recent scholarship has demonstrated that such imagery was popular in the colonial discourse of this period.[6] The obvious intent of the model farm was to teach Indians techniques that would allow them to increase their own agricultural production. Even the farm's superintendent was an Indian. But the article left no doubt that such technology transfers were a benefit of and reason for British rule. The author took pains to remind the reader that Kanpur, the site of the model farm, was thirty years earlier the scene of the 'horrible massacre of Europeans by Nana Sahib' (Cox 1887, 1161).

In the immediate aftermath of the Rebellion of 1857–58, the *ILN* had been more explicit. Declaring that 'the natives at large have essentially benefited by the change of masters', the writer on an article on railway bridges contrasted the achievements of earlier rulers with those of the East India Company, with the former clearly falling short:

It is true we do not erect temples to idolatry, nor huge tombs, nor lofty fortresses; but we have done far more: we have done our best, amidst enormous difficulties and obstructions, to give the people education and a wholesome administration of justice; we have constructed roads and canals, built bridges, introduced steam navigation and improved agriculture . . . (*ILN* 18 September 1858, 254)

Nevertheless, because 'much more had to be done', the article's author predicted that with the war's end 'great works of peace will be actively begun'. Among these works was 'railway construction for India', which 'notwithstanding the late distracted state of that country, is progressing with great rapidity here' (*ILN* 18 September 1858, 254).

Since the transfer of technology played such a prominent role in the realization of the Victorians' ostensible mission in India, it is not surprising that periodical literature frequently featured technology and India together. The *Imperial and Asiatic Review*, which regularly covered Indian themes, often emphasized technological development on the subcontinent. But even in journals that had no inherent reason to publish articles on either, the two themes often appeared together: thus the appearance of these topics in periodicals as varied as the *Athenaeum*, *Blackwood's Edinburgh Magazine*, the *ILN*, the *Saturday Review* and the *Times*.

The articles in these journals were virtually unanimous in their portrayal of technology as a gift that British administrators and engineers were giving to India in order to improve its standard of living. A review of Alfred Deakin's *Irrigated India* published in the journal *Athenaeum* described the Raj as 'a wise and benevolent despotism' whose administrators deserved praise for 'their devotion to work for the welfare of the people' through the introduction of western technology and the creation of public works (*Athenaeum* 15 April 1893, 475).

This theme permeated regular reports of technological achievement in India. The agricultural benefits of technology were prominent. A series of articles in *Engineering* began with the assertion that the 'irrigation works of Northern India . . . contribute most materially to its prosperity' (*Engineering* 6 April 1888, 141),[7] and a letter to the *Asiatic Quarterly Review* praised the Raj's encouragement of earth sciences, the main objective of which was 'to increase the food supply of the people of India and [develop] its mineral wealth' (Brown 1903, 182–93). The press expressed similar confidence in other public works. An article in *Engineering* pointed out that the remodelling of Madras harbour had considerably increased the capacity of seaborne trade into the city (*Engineering* 19 April 1912, 528), and the *ILN* carried a full-page, aerial-view drawing of a 1145-acre land reclamation proposal for Bombay. The caption underneath explained that 'unless the scheme is carried out the growth and prosperity of Bombay will be seriously hampered: rents will go up, and there will be much over-crowding' (*ILN* 29 November 1913, 890) *Engineering* also hailed the construction of the Jehlum River Hydro-Electric Power Plant as the result of the Raj's 'broad-minded policy in developing the latest possibilities of the immense and valuable country...for the welfare and enlightenment of the native inhabitants' (*Engineering* 19 January 1906, 103).

In this context, the development of communications was seen as an essential accompaniment to the war against famine. As a writer in *Engineering* observed in 1866:

> It is in vain that irrigation works are extended, if means be not at the same time afforded for transporting the surplus produce of land to other districts; thus it is that we have so often witnessed the occurrence of disastrous famines in one part of India, and people dying by thousands from actual starvation, whilst almost in the adjoining districts the abundance of the harvest has been such that grain is almost a drug in the bazaar, the want of internal communications alone preventing the superabundance of one district from supplying the wants of the other. (*Engineering* 9 November 1866, 361)

The railway soon came to be seen as essential to Britain's mission in India. Writing for *Cornhill Magazine*, Juland Danvers, the Director of Indian Railways, listed its services to the inhabitants of the subcontinent:

> They [the railways] have developed the resources of the country; they have added to its military strength; they have stimulated trade; they have improved the material and social condition of the people; they have helped the missionary and the schoolmaster; and, in times of scarcity, have saved the lives of a starving population. (Danvers 1869, 79)

But the missionary influence of the railway was not limited to the transport of 'the missionary and the schoolmaster'. The railway was itself a missionary of social and technological enlightenment as the *ILN* proclaimed in its report of the inauguration of the first passenger rail service on the subcontinent: 'The superstitions of the ages seemed to melt away as the gigantic reality of steam and mechanism passed before their [Indians] wondering eyes' (*ILN* 4 June 1853, 436). Danvers argued that the railway was helping to eliminate one of India's most ancient social curses, for 'a high caste will rather submit to the indignity of sitting cheek-by-jowl with his own servant than pay the extra cost of a second-class fare' (Danvers 1869, 68–9). Even the *Indian Magazine and Review*, a journal contributed to and read widely by Indian elites in Britain and at home, asserted: 'Railways have been justly regarded as among the most important of the civilizing agencies which are promoting social progress in India' (*Indian Magazine and Review* October 1872, 191).

The preponderance of glowing reports on the reshaping of India through western technology could not completely muffle the claims of some critics that Britain's presence on the subcontinent was harming more than helping its indigenous population and that better government rather than better technology was the solution. Much of the criticism was apparent only through the rebuttals that these journals carried. One such article arose from W.S. Caine's assertion in the House of Commons that the most recent Indian famine resulted from the British government's 'rack-renting' of the peasantry through land revenue.[8] In a blistering attack on his speech, the *Saturday Review* accused critics of the Raj of being 'would-be Parnells' who held out the 'tempting bait' of rental reductions 'to the loyal classes who have refused to dance to their piping'. The anonymous writer painted a picture of British efforts against famine almost entirely in technological terms: 'The Indian Government has called into existence a system of canal irrigation for which no parallel can be found in the history of the world. Surveys and inquiries have been repeatedly directed to ascertain all possible sources and areas of extension' (*Saturday Review* 8 February 1902, 167). If famines continued to occur in spite of these Herculean applications of technology, then the fault lay not with the benevolent administrators of the Raj but with 'the thriftlessness of the national character' with which they contended. The 'true remedy' was 'the promotion of education, . . . the expansion of manufacturing industries, the advancement of agricultural efficiency and the limitation of [indigenous elites] to encumber and alienate rights over land', in short, the triumph of western culture, characterized by technology and order, over eastern culture, characterized by 'thriftlessness' and chaos (*Saturday Review* 8 February 1902, 167).

Criticism of technology transfers tended to dispute the method rather than the competency of the British authorities who applied technology. In 1855, Arthur Cotton, former Chief Engineer of Madras and responsible for some of southern India's most spectacular irrigation projects, warned against developing railways at the expense of canals. The former, he claimed, incorrectly as it turned out, could 'not convey the quantity of goods required . . . [nor] at the low price required'. Writing for *Macmillan's*

Magazine, Herbert Wood, an engineer working for the Government of India, gave a sympathetic reprise of Cotton's assertions after a particularly bad famine in 1877 (Wood 1878, 236–56). In a remarkable inversion of the usual arguments for technology, Horace Bell, a former Senior Engineer for Indian Railways, argued in 1901 that because the development of railways in India lowered the price of exporting grain from the subcontinent, it actually exacerbated famines by discouraging the stockpiling of foodstuffs during years of plenty. His proposal was to restrict the export of grain (Bell 1901, 291).

Occasionally, however, a writer conceded mismanagement and even greed among British administrators. Criticism of the East India Company was common after the Rebellion of 1857–58. Journalists often blamed the Company for contributing to the poverty of Indian peasants. A *Journal of Science* article implied that the poor repair of India's roads was a temporary phenomenon brought on by the collapse of the Mughal empire and perpetuated by the indifference of early East India Company administrators (*Journal of Science* January 1867, 22–3). An article in the *MLE* discussed the 'mischievous results of the Permanent Settlement of Lord Cornwallis in Bengal in 1793', as a result of which rents rose dramatically and 'the unfortunate ryots [agriculturalists], defrauded of their right to fixity of tenure in their holdings, were beyond endurance'. In spite of resulting famines, the article argued, 'nothing was done to remedy this gigantic blunder made by their British rulers' until the aftermath of the Rebellion (*MLE* 8 January 1883, 37). Criticisms of the East India Company after its demise did not, however, question Britain's current technological mission in India.

Only rarely did the periodical press publish material that questioned Britain's ability ever to rule India better than, or even as well as, its indigenous rulers. When such material appeared, it inevitably involved a debate over the effectiveness of the application of western technology in India. Birdwood's review in the *Journal of the Royal Agricultural Society* attributed India's slowness of material progress to the 'foreign, ill-considered, impractical, and fruitless education we [the British] have enforced through our political ascendancy on the people of India'. The result was that 'of every thousand educated natives in India, only four have received any form of technical instruction' (Birdwood 1893, 859–60). Similarly, in an address to the London branch of the National Indian Association published in the *Indian Magazine and Review*, Lakshmidas R. Sapat, a teacher from Kutch, complained about the British insistence on using English as the sole medium to instruct Indian students in the applied sciences:

We may well ask with what chances of success the Finsbury Technical Institute, or any school of that kind, would work in England if the sons of artizans [*sic*] before entering it were, after finishing their ordinary elementary course (science excluded), required to go through a five years' course of French or German, and if one of these languages were introduced as a medium of instruction in such institutions. (*Indian Magazine and Review* July 1900, 174)

More dramatic was the published debate following a paper in the *JSA* which extolled 'the material progress of India under the Crown' (Hunter 1893, 337). Disputing the paper, H.M. Hyndman argued that the infusion of modern technology into India was for the purpose of serving British elites, rather than Indians:

[Indians] were asked to congratulate themselves on the extension of railways, but these railways were owned by Englishmen, and from them an enormous revenue was drawn to this country from the people of India... Such a drain was never known in the history of civilisation as was now being taken from the impoverished people of India, and with no real benefit to the working people of England. (Hunter 1893, 341)

As for famines, 'they had been worse under [British] rule than under any previous rule of which there was any record' (Hunter 1893, 341). Publication of such views, however, was the exception, and it merely highlights the tendency of the Victorian and Edwardian periodical press to accept uncritically the notion that Britain's occupation of India was a necessary, if often unappreciated, act of British benevolence.

Some aspects of the Victorian and Edwardian press's coverage of technology in India may seem familiar to the modern reader. The exotic allure of India drew many journalists to juxtapose in picture and words the familiar (such as western technology) with the wholly unfamiliar (such as jungles and elephants). Where the Victorian and Edwardian press differed from that of today was in its confident assumption that the introduction of western technology justified British rule in India. This assumption was born of the conviction that western technology had the power not only to transform society but to transform human moral behaviour. Thus the transfer of technology from Britain to India transcended the level of mere economic necessity to become a sacred mission in the view of many Victorian and Edwardian journalists. Public works of irrigation and communication became the physical manifestations of more abstract concepts, such as efficient government and the rule of law, which supposedly made British culture so superior to India's and made British occupation necessary for the good of the subcontinent's inhabitants. Two world wars, the threat of nuclear destruction, and the collapse of Europe's empires have made western journalists more circumspect about the benefits of western technology. As Adas has pointed out, the belief in technology as an important means of improving underdeveloped societies continues. But the modern version of that belief does not argue that western powers must rule a society in order for it to benefit from western technology. Furthermore, it is in the United States, strengthened more than demoralized by the cataclysms of the early twentieth century, that the faith in technology as a cure for material and social ills persists so strongly (Adas 1989, 402–18). In Britain the use of the spread of technology as a major justification for imperialism faded with the era of formal empires. In this sense, journalism merely reflected contemporary prevailing attitudes.

In one respect, however, the Victorian and Edwardian periodical press revealed something to the British public of which it may not have been aware. The press showed that India, for all its apparent backwardness, was extending the limits of western technology. As a result it was in India rather than Europe that some of the greatest innovations in large-scale engineering occurred. In this sense India became a technological centre worthy of news coverage in its own right.

Notes

1. Simpson's watercolour resides in the India Office Library and Oriental Records. Its most recent publication is on the dust cover of the *Cambridge Illustrated History of the British Empire*, ed. by P.J. Marshall (Cambridge, 1996). The print in the *Illustrated London News* is in volume 25 (5 August 1854), 117. Its artist is anonymous.
2. This essay focuses exclusively on journals and newspapers published in Britain. It does not examine the portrayal of medical technology, a topic covered elsewhere in this book.
3. See Daniel R. Headrick, *Tools of Empire: Technology and European Imperialism in the Nineteenth Century*. New York, 1981, 180–90 and idem, *The Tentacles of Progress: Technology Transfer in the Age of Imperialism, 1850–1940*. New York, 1988.
4. See the collection of eighteenth- and early-nineteenth-century European observations of evidence of Indian technology in Dharampal (ed.), *Indian Science and Technology in the Eighteenth Century: Some Contemporary European Accounts*. Delhi, 1971.

5. For further discussions of the social construction of science and technology in the imperial context, see Deepak Kumar (ed.), *Science and Empire: Essays in Indian Context, 1700–1947*. Delhi, 1991; and John M. MacKenzie (ed.), *Imperialism and the Natural World*. Manchester, 1990. Examples of this literature for the hard sciences include Donald A. MacKenzie, *Statistics in Britain, 1865–1930: the Social Construction of Scientific Knowledge*. Edinburgh, 1981, and Lewis Pyenson's three books: *Cultural Imperialism and Exact Sciences: German Expansion Overseas, 1900–1930*. New York, 1985; *Empire of Reason: Exact Sciences in Indonesia, 1840–1940*. Leiden, 1989; and *Civilizing Mission: Exact Sciences and French Overseas Expansion, 1830–1940*. Baltimore, 1993. For the social construction of colonial science through museums, see Gyan Prakash, 'Science "Gone Native" in Colonial India', *Representations* 40 (1992), 153–78; and Susan Sheets-Pyenson, 'Civilizing by Nature's Example: The Development of Colonial Museums of Natural History, 1850–1900', in Nathan Reingold and Marc Rothenberg (eds), *Scientific Colonialism: a Cross-Cultural Comparison*. Washington, DC, 1987, 351–77.
6. See Mrinalini Sinha, *Colonial Masculinity: the 'Manly Englishman' and the 'Effeminate Bengali' in the Late Nineteenth Century*. Manchester, 1995. Chivalric imagery was not confined to the colonial relationship. It was used extensively among the middle and upper classes of Victorian and Edwardian Britain to describe and circumscribe gender relations and duties as well as social and political missions. See Mark Girouard, *Return to Camelot: Chivalry and the English Gentleman*. New Haven, 1981; and Paul Fussell's discussion of what he terms 'high diction' in *The Great War and Modern Memory*. New York, 1975, 21–3.
7. The rest of the series can be found in the following editions in vol. 45: 4 May 1888, 423; 18 May 1888, 473; 8 June 1888, 555; and 22 June 1888, 607.
8. See *Parliamentary Debates* 4th series, 102 (3 February 1902), 266–328. Caine had served in 1890 as a delegate to the Indian National Congress in Calcutta.

Works cited

Adas, Michael. *Machines as the Measure of Man: Science Technology and Ideologies of Western Dominance*. Ithaca, 1989.
'Agricultural Engineering in India – No. I.', *Engineering* 45 (6 April 1888), 341.
Baden Powell, B.H. 'Indian Manufactures from a Practical Point of View', *Journal of the Society of Arts* 34 (14 May 1886), 708–21.
Bell, Horace. 'Railways and Famine', *Journal of the Society of Arts* 49 (15 March 1901), 290–305.
Birdwood, George. 'The Improvement of Indian Agriculture' (book review of John Augustus Voelcker, *Report on the Improvement of Indian Agriculture*), *Journal of the Royal Society of Agriculture* 3rd series 4 (30 December 1893), 859–60.
Brown, George. Letter entitled 'Scientific Research in Relation to Economic and Agricultural Development in India', *Asiatic Quarterly Review* 3rd series 15 (January/April 1903), 182–93.
'Changing Sea into Land: the Bombay Reclamation Scheme', *Illustrated London News* 43 (29 November 1913), 890.
Chaudhuri, Brahma. 'India', in J. Don Vann and Rosemary T. VanArsdel (eds), *Periodicals of Queen Victoria's Empire*. Toronto, 1996, 175–200.
'Civil Engineering in India', *Builder* 25 (2 November 1867), 794–6.

'Communications in India. II – Roads', *Engineering* 2 (9 November 1866), 361.

'Cooling Railway Carriages', *Engineering* 18 (24 September 1874), 238.

Cotton, Arthur. 'On Public Works for India, Especially with Reference to Irrigation and Communications', *Journal of the Society of Arts* 3 (27 April 1855), 397.

Cox, Harold. 'Agriculture and Peasant Life in India', *Mark Lane Express* 57 (2 May 1887), 568.

Cox, Harold. 'An Indian Government Model Farm', *Mark Lane Express* 57 (12 September 1887), 1161–2.

Danvers, Juland. 'Indian Railways', *Cornhill Magazine* 20 (July 1869), 68–80.

Dunstan, Wyndham R. 'The Coal Resources of India and Their Development', *Journal of the Society of Arts* 50 (21 March 1902), 371–407.

Ellegård, Alvar. *The Readership of the Periodical Press in Mid-Victorian Britain.* Goteborg, 1957.

'Fall of a Viaduct on the Great Indian Peninsula Railway', *Illustrated London News* 51 (21 September 1867), 312 and 'India', *Times* 25 (6 September 1867), 8.

Graves, H.G. 'Further Notes on the Early Use of Iron in India', *Engineering* 10 May 1912, 644–6.

'The Great Indian Peninsula Railway Disaster', *Illustrated London News* 54 (6 March 1869), 238 and 248.

'The Great International Exhibition', *Illustrated London News* Exhibition Supplement to 18 (10 May 1851), 391–2.

'The Great Indian Peninsula Railway', *Illustrated London News* 25 (8 July 1854), 3–4.

Haig, Wolseley. 'Some Historical Indian Famines', *Imperial and Asiatic Quarterly Review* 3 (January/April 1901), 9–34.

Headrick, Daniel R. *The Tentacles of Progress: Technology Transfer in the Age of Imperialism, 1850–1940.* New York, 1988.

Hunt, Bruce J. 'Doing Science in a Global Empire: Cable Telegraphy and Electrical Physics in Victorian Britain', in Bernard Lightman (ed.), *Victorian Science in Context.* Chicago, 1997, 312–33.

Hunter, William Wilson. 'The Progress of India Under the Crown', *Journal of the Society of Arts* 41 (24 February 1893), 329–45.

'Indian Famine and English Quacks', *Saturday Review* 93 (8 February 1902), 166–7.

'Indian Intelligence', *Indian Magazine and Review* 22 (October 1872), 191–2.

'Iron Working in India', *Engineering* 41 (5 March 1886), 229.

'Jhelum River Hydro-Electric Power Installation in British India', *Engineering* 81 (19 January 1906), 103.

Lee-Warner, William. 'Our Work in India in the Nineteenth Century', *Journal of the Society of Arts* 48 (2 February 1900), 213–28.

Lethbridge, Roper. 'India in the Sixtieth Victorian Year', *Imperial Asiatic and Quarterly Review, and Oriental and Colonial Record* Series 3 (July/October 1897), 1–9.

MacKenzie, Donald A. *Statistics in Britain, 1865–1930: the Social Construction of Scientific Knowledge.* Edinburgh, 1981.

Madras Harbour: the Remodeling and Equipment. Review in *Engineering* 93 (19 April 1912), 528.

'The Means of Transit in India', *Journal of Science* 4 (January 1867), 22–33.

'Methods of Education in India', *Indian Magazine and Review* 355 (July 1900), 169–83.

'New Rolling Stock on the Great Indian Peninsula Railway', *Railway Gazette* 3 (12 January 1906), 348E.

'On Defective Irrigation in India', *Engineering* 18 (28 August 1874), 155–6.

'Opening of the First Railway in India', *Illustrated London News* 20 (4 June 1853), 436–8.

'The Opening of the Ganges Canal', *Blackwood's Edinburgh Magazine* 76 (October 1854), 475–6.

'Power Transmission in India', *Illustrated London News* 121 (26 July 1902), 14b.

'Prince of Wales' Tour in India', *Railway Gazette* 4 (26 January 1906), 12.

'Public Works Reform in India', *Builder* 31 (8 November 1873), 889–90.

'Railway Bridges for India', *Illustrated London News* 33 (18 September 1858), 254.

Richardson, Ruth and Robert Thorne. 'Architecture', in J. Don Vann and Rosemary T. VanArsdel (eds), *Victorian Periodicals and Victorian Society*. Toronto, 1994, 45–61.

'Science', *Athenaeum* 3416 (15 April 1893), 475–6.

'Sketches in India: Railway from Calcutta to Delhi', *Illustrated London News* 28 Second Supplement (7 June 1851), 538–9.

Stone, Ian. *Canal Irrigation in British India: Perspectives on Technological Change in a Peasant Economy*. Cambridge, 1984.

'Tenant-Right in India', *Mark Lane Express* 53 (8 January 1883), 37–8.

Vann, J. Don and Rosemary T. VanArsdel (eds). *Victorian Periodicals and Victorian Society*. Toronto, 1994.

Weiner, Martin. *English Culture and the Decline of the Industrial Spirit*. Cambridge, 1981.

Wood, Herbert. 'Famines and Floods in India', *Macmillan's Magazine* 37 (January 1878), 236–56.

10
The Army in India and the Military Periodical Press, 1830–98

T.R. Moreman

Historians have devoted remarkably little attention to the specialized weekly, monthly and quarterly military journals which were published in Britain and India during the nineteenth century, despite the fact that they represent an untapped mine of information about the Army in India and on colonialism in general. This is hardly surprising, however, as until comparatively recently the Indian Army has not attracted the attention it deserves from either military or imperial historians considering its importance as the final arbiter of European rule (see Omissi 1994 and Heathcote 1995). Throughout the nineteenth century the military played a pivotal role in the development and maintenance of the colonial state, bolstering the British regime from internal threats as well as safeguarding it against foreign invasion. Units of the British Army and until 1858 the East India Company's (EIC) own locally recruited armed forces, divided between the presidencies of Bengal, Bombay and Madras, encountered military problems very different from those experienced in Europe or other colonies requiring them to quickly to adapt their organization, equipment and training to suit local conditions. The Company's army was a distinctive military response to the demands of imperial rule in India. While British battalions followed the normal European pattern, the Company's forces included several regiments of European rank and file and a much larger number of regiments of Indian sepoys (from *sipahi*, a Persian term for soldier) under the command of British officers. Sepoy regiments, carefully organized, trained and equipped so as not to offend the caste, ethnic and religious sensibilities of their Indian officers, NCOs and other ranks, formed the mainstay of the Indian Army and particular care was always taken to ensure that they would be both militarily effective and loyal to the colonial regime. Following the 1857–58 Indian Rebellion the size of the

British component of the Army in India increased, yet they were still outnumbered by the radically reorganized sepoy regiments of the Indian Army (now directly controlled by the Crown). Many officers took a keen interest in Indian military affairs given the size of the armed forces committed to ensuring colonial rule. In a recent article, Douglas Peers (1997) has identified various mid-Victorian periodicals, such as *Blackwood's Magazine, Edinburgh Review, Fraser's Magazine, Mofussilite, Delhi Gazette, Calcutta Review* and *Meerut Universal Review*, in which officers expressed their interests and opinions about the Indian Army. This important study provides a valuable starting point for those interested in the Army in India, although he only briefly mentions various specialized military periodicals in which officers wrote and debated about their own profession. The peculiar professional needs of the far-flung British garrison formed the subject of a series of editorials, articles and debates conducted within the pages of these specialized professional periodicals during the nineteenth century. This chapter will identify those military journals that dealt with Indian military affairs in Britain and India during the mid and late nineteenth century and assess how India was represented in their pages. In particular, it will focus on an influential late-Victorian periodical – the *Journal of the United Service Institution of India*. It will then conclude by examining how the military and media functioned together by tracing how the concept of 'martial race' was discussed and developed in the pages of a series of representative articles.

The specialized military press first emerged as a distinct form of media following the end of the Napoleonic Wars. It was expressly targeted at a fairly narrow audience – active or retired members of the British and East India Company's armed forces – although occasionally such periodicals were read by members of the general public interested in military affairs (Tucker 1994, 62). The press reflected and in part contributed to the emerging professionalism of the British armed forces by providing officers with a valuable forum for professional discussion, as well as a means for agitating for reform in the organization, equipment and training of the British Army (see Strachan 1985). Many periodicals were comparatively short-lived, such as the *Royal Military Calendar, British Military Library* and *British Army Despatch*, but others proved more enduring. They all occasionally covered Indian affairs. Perhaps the most important of these commercial military periodicals was the *Naval and Military Magazine* launched in 1827 (later renamed the *United Service Magazine*, then the *United Service Magazine and Naval and Military Journal* before seeing in the twentieth century as *Colburn's United Service Magazine*). Two weekly newspapers – the *Naval and Military Gazette* (1833–86) and

United Service Gazette – also thrived and during the 1880s were joined by other weeklies such as the *Broad Arrow* and various illustrated journals. These monthly and weekly periodicals contained lively editorials, columns of 'naval and military intelligence' and correspondence from their readers. During the early nineteenth century they included personal memoirs, anecdotes and semi-fictional stories of wide appeal to their readership, as well as a steadily increasing number of articles on more serious military subjects for naval and army officers.

Their treatment of British troops serving in India or the EIC's army was comparatively limited, however, due to the generally dismissive attitude of British service officers (apart from those who had served in India) towards the EIC's Bengal, Bombay and Madras armies. With its garrison of 20 000–30 000 Europeans plus up to ten times as many sepoys, India was one of the most common destinations for the officers and men of the British Army. Yet while many saw service in India, few thought that India had much to offer by way of professional training, especially when compared to what was happening in Europe (Strachan 1997). Indeed, many almost paradoxically believed that nothing of military importance could be learnt from their fellows who commanded Indian troops or from campaigns in the subcontinent against non-European troops. Most contributions about India were letters and articles submitted from officers serving in the local garrison. To the British public and most officers, India was a strange, distant land of little direct interest, apart from when major military operations involved considerable British service troops (Reader 1988, 42). This limited interest in India was reflected in commercial periodicals, such as the *United Service Magazine*, where the articles and letters that did appear dealing with the subcontinent were mostly anecdotal or frequently romanticized tales of derring-do frequently intended to secure income and personal advantage for their authors. This was even more apparent in the pages of the semi-official press, periodicals produced by retired and serving officers which were officially independent of the army and navy though strong unofficial ties existed. They enjoyed considerable editorial independence and did debate controversial issues though they were careful to avoid polemic and hence took care to locate such debates within a professional context. Articles were generally confined to accounts of major campaigns in Sind or the Punjab or to some calamitous event that galvanized interest, such as the operations in Afghanistan (1839–42) or the Indian Rebellion of 1857. During the late nineteenth century coverage gradually increased as the British garrison grew in size to around 66 000 officers and men, covering more specialized subjects such as the recruiting of the Indian

Army or strategy in Asia. However, the total number of articles on India in journals like the *United Service Magazine* still paled in comparison with those on Europe, and in a good year there might be at most ten articles out of the 50 or so annually published.

The institutional or semi-official periodical press, run mostly by retired officers working in independent organizations loosely affiliated to the military, that begun publication in the 1850s, had a better coverage of India. Perhaps the most important periodical was produced by the United Service Institution in London, originally formed in 1831 as a naval and military library and museum for officers from the Army, Navy and Marines, Yeomanry and the EIC's Land and Sea Forces (Altham 1931, 237 and see also Welch 1998). In 1839 it was renamed the United Service Institution, reflecting the involvement of officers from all services, but despite considerable interest a lack of funds prevented publication of a journal by the initially struggling institution. A £400 grant from Lord Panmure – the Secretary of State for War – and the remittance of taxation on its premises finally allowed the launch of the first edition of an in-house periodical published in 1857 by W. Mitchell & Sons of 39 Charing Cross Road. Publication began in an environment conducive to interest in military affairs following the disasters of the Crimean War and the Indian Rebellion. In his opening address to the first edition of the *Journal of the United Service Institution*, Colonel James Lindsay outlined the aims of both the Institution and this new venture:

> All other professions have establishment for imparting professional knowledge . . . In the learned and scientific societies of the country, naval and military science has been hitherto neglected and unrecognised; it is the promise of this Institution to fill that vacancy . . . In the Journal or the Proceedings we propose to print the lectures, or an abstract of lectures, and the discussions which take place. The numbers will be issued three or four times a year, and sent to all members serving in other parts of the country and in the Colonies. They will contain every information connected with the Institution . . . In this manner we hope, by giving officers a *quid pro quo*, by making the Institution practically useful by promoting and encouraging information which must be beneficial, to obtain the hearty concurrence of the officers of several services. (Lindsay 1857, 4–5)

Two years later this periodical became the *Journal of the Royal United Service Institution* (*JRUSI*), following the award of a Royal Charter. Unlike existing commercial titles containing material of general interest to the wider paying public, its contents were specifically devoted to military topics of perceived professional importance to serving officers. Articles, contributed by active service or retired officers, reflected the diverse tasks carried out worldwide by the British armed forces and Royal Navy. They included discussions of contemporary European warfare, colonial campaigns, tactics, and military organization as well as short papers discussing recent military inventions and their impact on the battlefield. Following an initial burst of interest in 1857–58 – when some 33 000 troops from the home army helped suppress the Indian Rebellion – considerably less attention was paid to representations of Indian military affairs. Indeed, discussions of conventional warfare dominated the *Journal* during the late nineteenth century, reflecting the preoccupation of British military thought with operations against a European opponent (see Bailes, 1980). This is hardly surprising given the broad range of tasks on which the British armed forces were engaged. On occasion, however, articles dealt with Indian military subjects such as strategy and the military geography of Central Asia, land and sea communications with the subcontinent, specialized rifle corps for service on the Northwest Frontier, transport and supply and recent campaigns on the frontiers. During the 1880s and 1890s the number increased as concerns about the defence of the Northwest Frontier against Russian attack gained wider credence. In 1885 the organization of the British component of the Army in India was carefully examined in the influential *JRUSI* prize-essay competition (inaugurated in 1878), normally sponsored by senior officers and accordingly widely read, which discussed whether a proportion of the British troops should be localized solely for duty on the subcontinent (see Browne 1885). Many essays were won by officers of junior rank who were given thereby an opportunity to express views on topics normally ignored by the British Army. In 1887 Captain Charles Callwell, for example, argued that important lessons could be learnt from colonial 'small wars' (including those fought in India) of lasting value to the British Army (Callwell 1887). This article marked an important step in Callwell's career, for he was later acknowledged as the British Army's leading theoretician of colonial warfare throughout the Empire and became a major contributor to other service periodicals. Normally, however, treatment of Indian subjects was confined to general accounts of the native army as a whole that were primarily intended to familiarize British service officers with Indian defence problems.

Other more specialized semi-official professional military journals also dealt with Indian military affairs. In 1858 the Royal Artillery Institution at Woolwich, with financial support from the Board of Ordnance, published the first volume of its *Minutes of the Proceedings of the Royal Artillery Institution* covering the period 1848–57. This included a series of articles dealing with India, though they were primarily concerned with technical issues connected with the organization, equipment and training of Royal Artillery batteries. Occasionally the *Proceedings* included articles dealing with broader issues, such as recruiting for the Indian Army or military operations in tribal territory bordering Afghanistan.

The Royal Engineers similarly published their own periodical after 1870 at Chatham. The monthly *Royal Engineer's Journal* was sold 'for circulation among the officers of the Corps of Royal Engineers only', and was published in a tabloid form very different from that published by the gunners, reflecting its emphasis on mundane in-house day-to-day corps affairs. It too dealt occasionally with India. In 1879, for example, several articles discussed the equipment required for service in Afghanistan. It was complemented by the more technical *Professional Papers of the Corps of Royal Engineers* whose annual volumes began publication in 1837. These circulated scientific and professional information to officers serving around the globe, but were also available on the general market.

The publication of specialized military periodicals was not confined to Britain. Many British officers participated in scientific and military societies during the early nineteenth century in Bengal, Madras and Bombay who also wished to find an outlet for their opinions and write about professional military issues of direct relevance to their careers (Peers 1995, 12–13). The appearance of such journals in India in the 1830s coincided with a spectacular growth of Anglo-Indian publishing in general which was matched by growing interest in India in Britain. Unsurprisingly, these journals were more representative of Indian military affairs than those produced in Britain, although they were comparatively few in number.

In 1833 *The East Indies Service Journal and Military Magazine* was launched at Calcutta edited and written largely by Joachim Haywood Stocqueler (a pseudonym adopted by Joachim Heywood Simmons) – editor of the *Calcutta Englishman* and *Bengal Monthly Sporting Magazine* – to test whether a potential market existed for a military periodical. In the preface to the first edition he pointed out:

> The British Army has found material for a press of its own – and, in conjunction with the navy, at this moment supports a copious monthly, and two voluminous weekly publications devoted almost entirely to the consideration of military matters ... Gentlemen, the

organ of the British Army is not your organ. Your interests are not only habitually neglected in the English UNITED SERVICE JOURNAL, but too often opposed from motives of unworthy and unmerited partiality. Your appeals for redress find no echo there – your reputation is neither supported nor enhanced by honorable statements of your present condition, nor details of your past glories. (Stocqueler 1833, ii)

An annual subscription of Rs 16 was charged for this quarterly, which was distributed throughout India to subscribers including the Governor-General, the Commander-in-Chief, officers ranging in rank from major-general to lieutenant and various regimental Book Clubs and societies. As a profit-making enterprise this journal had to entertain as well as educate, a fact reflected in the language and substance of many of its articles. *The East India United Service Journal* played an important role in disseminating information on professional issues to the widely scattered garrison, bringing officers into contact and providing an important forum for expressing opinions on military questions of particular relevance to the EIC's own armed forces and the regular British garrison (see K-X O-X 1836, 219–20). Articles covered such diverse subjects as: regimental histories, biographies of Indian officers, discussions on the organization of locally raised units, sketches of recent campaigns such as the assault on Bhartpur in 1826, as well as more mundane details such as births, deaths, marriages and General Orders issued by the military authorities. It proved so popular that officers and regimental book clubs requested it should be produced more frequently. Accordingly after July 1833 it became a monthly publication. By 1838 the *East India United Service Journal* had incurred considerable financial losses, however, primarily due to the late payment of subscriptions, as well its inability to obtain sufficient new material from contributors (Anon. 'Notice to Readers' 1838, I). Although a quarterly edition of the *East India United Service Journal* appeared in July, it was forced to cease publication in April 1839. A similar fate awaited the *East India Magazine and Military Review* published at Calcutta by R.C. Lepage & Sons in 1853. In the opening section the editor observed:

In presenting the first number . . . to the Officers of Bengal, Madras and Bombay, the Editor feels it is his duty to tell them plainly that without their literary assistance and support, he will be, he must be powerless; that any individual talent, any amount of personal industry must fail in the attempt to give the Indian Armies a Military periodical worthy of them, unless the Officers themselves will guide it with their experience, and assist it with their talents. (Anon. 'Editorial' 1853)

The first volume contained articles discussing the Indian medical services, the commissariat services in the three presidencies, volunteering, furlough regulations and the Bengal Military Fund as well as a section of correspondence. Despite the editor's initial optimism, it soon failed as a commercial venture and ceased publication after only one volume had appeared.

The Army in India lacked a professional periodical of its own during the controversial deliberations about its future which followed the Indian Rebellion, a debate which resulted in the deployment of a considerably larger proportion of regular British troops and the reconstitution of the Indian Army on very different ethnic lines. It was not until 1871 that the most significant military periodical published in India during the nineteenth century was launched. Whilst on leave in England during 1867, Colonel Charles MacGregor visited the United Service Institution at Whitehall and was soon convinced that a similar forum for professional debate was required both to educate and enable British officers to discuss and write about professional issues specifically affecting the Army in India (MacGregor 1888, 329; Kale 1988, 408–9). The United Service Institution of India (USII) was founded at Simla in late 1870 for the 'promotion of Naval and Military art, Science and Literature'. It was closely modelled on its 'parent' at Whitehall with membership open to all Army, Royal Navy and Volunteer Corps officers serving in India, as well as any other gazetted Government officials, upon payment of a joining fee of Rs 5 and an annual subscription of the same amount. Although 'United Service' formed part of its title, the distance from the coast and the small size of the naval presence on the East Indian Station meant few naval officers ever joined.

From its inception the USII enjoyed powerful patronage from senior British and Indian service officers. The Earl of Mayo (the Governor-General in Council) served as its main patron, while the commanders-in-chief of the Bengal, Bombay, Madras armies and the Royal Navy on the Indian station acted as vice patrons. On 31 May 1871 General Sir Robert Napier – the Commander-in-Chief in India – addressed the inaugural meeting of the USII which had already enrolled 350 members. To make it representative of the entire Army in India the adjutant-generals from Bengal, Madras and Bombay nominated members of the governing body. The newly elected Council, headed by Major-General A. Huyshe, accordingly consisted of officers from all over India, although in practice it was dominated by officers serving at Army Headquarters at Simla. Corresponding Members were appointed at cantonments throughout India to collect subscriptions, arrange lectures and debates, forward articles and to communicate with the Council at Simla. Branch institutions also opened at the large cantonments at Agra, Secunderabad and Darjeeling, where lectures were also held by groups of officers keenly interested in professional issues. By the end of 1871 the USII's first annual report recorded that 800 members had joined the Institution which closely followed the rules and conventions of the RUSI (Trousdale 1985, 29). Most were officers of field rank, captain to lieutenant-colonel, although a handful of subalterns and a larger number of more senior officers also joined the new USII.

The publication of a journal, similar to that produced by the RUSI, for the 'instruction and information of Army and Navy', was one of the USII's immediate aims, so as to give it as wide an appeal as possible to British officers deployed across the length and breadth of the subcontinent. Although produced at Simla, it was intended to be representative of the armed forces in India as a whole rather than just favouring the Bengal Army and the adjutant generals from each presidency were asked to collect articles suitable for publication. In the preface to the first edition, the editor noted:

> It is equally open to all to make use of the Journal and Papers, and Lectures from wherever sent will meet with equal attention: indeed it is hoped that the Institution will tend to smooth over all local, regimental or departmental prejudices, and induce every one to pull heartily together to one great end – the good of the service. (Preface, 1871)

However, in practice this was never fully achieved since the large number of officers in the dominant Bengal Army greatly outnumbered those serving in other presidencies and as the journal was based in the Bengal Presidency, officers on that establishment generally ran the Institution.

In May 1871, the *Proceedings of the United Service Institution of India* was launched, published under the authority of the Council and printed by Erasmus Jones of 5 & 6 Indian Street, Simla. To tide the organization over initial difficulties with the periodical, the Adjutant General was approached, with Lord Napier's support, for permission to employ official printing presses to produce the journal and free postage to distribute it to its members. Although these requests were refused, the Governor-General sanctioned a grant-aid of Rs 150 per month with effect from 1 July

1871 to cover costs – subject to withdrawal should the USII fail in its set objective.[1] This new journal was qualitatively different from those periodicals published in Britain in that it dealt specifically with topics concerning the Army in India, including articles on such varied subjects as the uniforms, the organization, equipment and despatch of overseas expeditions from the subcontinent, and the equipment of troops on active service. Unlike commercial periodicals, it did not have to entertain and was able to concentrate on strictly professional issues. It was intended this new venture would be published on a monthly basis or as often as practicable depending on the number of articles and notices submitted by British and Indian service officers. Both the form and contents of *Proceedings* were modelled closely on that published by the Royal Artillery Institution, containing original papers on military subjects, reports of lectures and ensuing discussions, opinions of members on previous articles, translations of selected articles in foreign military periodicals, short notices on professional subjects, notices of important military inventions, correspondence on professional subjects and finally occasional papers. Papers were initially solicited on a range of military topics concerning the Army in India: the formation of a transport department, military telegraphs and signalling, the organization of the Native Army, the defence of the Northwest and Northeast Frontiers, lessons taught by warfare in India or against 'undisciplined' enemies, mountain warfare, the aid available from India in event of war against France, Russia or Prussia, and tactics and training.

The *Proceedings* quickly established itself as the house journal of the army in India, a journal truly representative of the professional needs of the garrison (Brief 1979, 34). It attracted articles originally delivered as lectures at Simla and branch institutes across India and, during the 1870s, it featured work on a range of issues including recent military innovations, signalling, narratives of recent operations, military law and the education of Indian officers. Many papers discussed conventional warfare so as to keep officers abreast of how military developments in Europe were revolutionizing the conduct of conventional warfare during the mid and late nineteenth century. These articles were not submitted with any expectation of payment and were written by authors who were mostly regimental officers of the rank of captain to lieutenant-colonel seeking to advance their profession rather than their own self-interest. To encourage thought and discussion a Gold Medal was presented to the USII by Sir Henry Durand (a founding member) in 1872. This was awarded to the author of the best paper printed each year on a subject judged by the Council most useful to the army in

India. Lieutenant-Colonel Frederick Roberts – a rising star – was awarded the first Durand Medal, for arguing that Camps of Exercise were urgently needed in India to study the lessons of the 1870–71 Franco-Prussian War. Topics were set each year by the Council – usually including the Commander-in-Chief – and normally reflected pressing issues affecting the Army in India, to the extent that they provide a useful barometer of changing interests in military affairs in India (Sharma 1970, 536). In 1883 the title of the *Proceedings* was changed to the *Journal of the United Service Institution of India*, although in form the periodical remained largely unchanged. To cover mounting printing and distribution costs the official grant was increased in November 1883 to Rs 3,000 per annum.[2] This allowed the USII to appoint a permanent paid secretary who, in addition to his post in the quartermaster general's department, edited the journal. Moreover, to record discussions following lectures a reporter was also employed whose notes were then edited and printed in the journal for its growing readership. By 1 January 1893 the membership of the USII had risen to 783 officers, ranging in rank from lieutenant to the commander-in-chief in India – General Sir Frederick Roberts. Readership of the journal had also expanded to include subscribers from various military departments of the Government of India, regimental institutes, sergeants' mess libraries, soldiers' libraries, volunteer corps, clubs and institutes where it was read by members of the civilian community. Other copies were sent to Britain and some overseas as far afield as the United States of America. Membership and readership continued to increase up to the turn of the century. On 1 January 1899, for example, the *JUSII* was circulated to 89 life members, 900 ordinary members and was sent to 45 regimental or other institutes where each copy was probably read by a large number of additional officers and some British NCOs.

The Indian periodical military press published, as has been outlined, articles on a range of subjects of professional interest to serving British officers. However, several recurrent topics appeared in the pages of the military periodical press during the nineteenth century. Foremost amongst these were discussions of recruiting and 'martial race' ideology, a key colonial ideological construct that by the late nineteenth century dictated the recruitment of the Indian Army. To illustrate how the military and media functioned together, this section of the chapter will focus on several representative articles dealing with officers' views and opinions on martial race and recruitment that appeared in both Britain and India.

When it was first raised, the Indian Army displayed no real preference for specific ethnic groups, enlisting any men from the precolonial military labour pool willing to enter British service in the Bengal, Madras and Bombay armies (Metcalf 1998, 126). The ranks of the Bengal Army (the largest), however, were quickly filled by large numbers of high-caste Brahmins and Rajputs from Awadh. The military authorities quickly established a fixation on race and difference between themselves and their Indian troops, in part to explain why so many Brahmins and Rajputs had enlisted. From the 1820s racial characteristics rather than caste exerted an important role in determining military organization in India, especially after doubts arose about the loyalty and reliability of Indian sepoys following the First Burma War and Barrackpore Mutiny (latter on again in the 1840s) (Peers 1991, 545–6). In a series of anonymous articles in the commercial press, written largely in response to ill-informed criticism by British service officers about the loyalty and reliability of Indian troops, Brahmins and Rajput troops were vigorously defended and depicted as more martial than other recruits in the Native Army. Indeed, they formed the prototype for the theory of the martial races. Foundational stereotypes were formed for groups that enlisted in the ranks, with alleged differences between races accentuated and highlighted in this literature. According to one anonymous officer in an article contributed to the *United Service Journal*, Rajputs were a 'high-minded and brave race', Sikhs were 'slow-witted' but formidable soldiers and Muslims particularly courageous, although this characteristic was ascribed to religious fanaticism (Anon. 1836). Muslims were less popular as sepoys for other reasons. As one officer noted in 1845: 'The Mahomedans are good soldiers, though they seldom become so attached to the service as Hindoo, and their private conduct is much less moral, and their private habits much more prone to dissipation' (Anon. 1845, 240). To make their point writers used exotic language and romanticized imagery to describe their men in contributions to military periodicals intended both to inform and entertain a paying readership. For example, the same author also discussed Rajputs:

> The Bengal Infantry ... consist[s] principally of Rajpoots, a race distinguished amongst the military tribes, and who are brought up from the cradle with a love of arms. If they do not attend to the labours of husbandry, the sword, spear, and shield are still their companions; and whatever his pursuits may be in civil life, the Rajpoot never neglects his martial exercises; and every sentiment, every action of the man is marked by the expression and bearing of the soldier. They have a high sense of honor, and will bear neither slight nor insult; and though deficient in that energy which marks the European

character, they have a passive courage which enables them to cope with danger in whatever form it may encounter them. (Anon. 1845, 240)

Difference between Europeans and Indians was implicit in such articles, with British officers and other ranks regarded as inherently better than sepoys in such key military attributes as bravery, leadership, initiative and resourcefulness. Racial characterizations and the cult of the officer portrayed British officers as morally and physically superior: a view that had become entrenched by the end of the century.

Such representations of Indian sepoys and their supposed martial attributes built upon existing indigenous perceptions, which had already been fashioned into a hierarchical ordering of Indian society. This process had already occurred by the third decade of the nineteenth century as Indian communities were 'partly compartmentalised, characteristics . . . assigned, and the process of ranking was slowly underway' (Peers 1997, 129). British officers displayed a marked preference for sepoys drawn from the landed peasantry, with agricultural or pastoral backgrounds, that were physically fit, inured to hard work, morally strong and, perhaps most importantly, were willing to enlist in British service. In many respects the often romanticized language used to describe such men was similar to that used to depict Scottish highlanders, another allegedly martial race.

The 1857 Indian Rebellion made race an even more powerful determinant of the recruitment of the Indian Army, as it underwent root-and-branch reform in an effort to create a loyal and militarily effective fighting force. In the 1860s ethnic groups from northwestern India, who had supported the British in their hour of need, progressively replaced most of the remaining Rajputs and Brahmins in the ranks of the Bengal Army. This established new patterns of military collaboration. As a result of the Indian Rebellion, the need to know and understand the culture, religion and supposed characteristics of newly introduced Sikh, Pathan and Punjabi Muslims took on a new significance to British India. Difference between Indians and British officers and soldiers still remained a key item of faith. Yet coverage of the Indian Army in the commercial and new semi-official military press in Britain was strangely limited and no counterpart existed in India where officers could express an opinion. On occasion articles did appear in the British press using romanticized language similar to that used to describe sepoys before 1857–58. For example, Vincent Eyre, a retired major general, in a *JRUSI* article in 1868 that discussed the use of Indian regiments outside the subcontinent depicted Sikhs as the 'bravest, hardiest, and the most formidable' of Indian troops (Eyre 1868, 87).

Following the publication of the *Proceedings of the United Service Institution* in 1871, the military and the periodical press worked in closer co-operation and the number of articles discussing recruiting and developing martial race ideology increased, in some cases at the direct request of the military authorities. In the first volume, 'Goorkha' (1871) sketched the history of the enlistment of men from Nepal and carefully catalogued the 'castes, tribes, peculiarities and habits' of Gurkha troops for his fellow officers with the aim of facilitating recruitment and assisting day to day running of regiments. As David Omissi (1994) has shown, many regimental officers were keenly interested in finding better troops for their units, especially men from northern India. As Lieutenant-Colonel G. Hunter Thompson, officiating commandant of the 19th Punjab Infantry, wrote in an article published later that year:

The Bengal Native Infantry is at present composed of nearly every class and caste of natives from Peshawar to Assam. It is true that the present recruiting regulations prohibit the entertainment of inferior classes, still many of the regiments require a deal of weeding, and the army would be a far more serviceable one, were its ranks confined to the following classes, *viz*, Pathans. Sikhs, Punjabee Mussulmen, Ghoorkhas and Rajpoots. (Hunter-Thompson, 1871, 5)

Several other important articles appeared in the *Proceedings* during the 1870s that discussed the 'soldierly qualities', 'military proclivities' and 'fitness for service' of Sikhs, Dogras, and other ethnic groups from the Punjab and northern India. While these articles still used labels and stereotypes that would have been familiar to readers before the Indian Rebellion, a more scientific tone was evident in the writings in this in-house journal, with distinct military skills and characteristics that reflected perceived military needs of the day especially prized. In an 1872 article discussing Sikhs, Captain H.C. Price, second in command of the 1st Sikh Infantry, discussed their religion, their 'races and castes', the area they inhabited and also their ceremonial customs. Regarding their particular attributes, Price observed:

The national character is a fine one, and produces admirable military materials. Although capable of showing élan and vivacity when the occasion requires it, the Sikhs are rather steady, earnest and stubborn than impetuous; better fitted for deeds requiring unflinching resistance than those requiring dash; better suited for holding a position than attacking one. They are undoubtedly brave . . . They possess a strong feeling of independence, are straightforward and manly, genial in disposition and not quarrelsome. They have a good deal of self-esteem, and, for Orientals, a fairly high standard of honour. They are faithful and true to the salt of the Government they are serving, and seldom show insubordination. (Price 1872, 68)

In comparison, Dogras, according to Lieutenant-Colonel J.J.H. Gordon of the 29th Punjab Infantry in a similar article, were: 'As soldiers . . . not remarkable for daring or impetuous bravery, but are valuable for quiet, unflinching courage, patient endurance of fatigue, and for orderly and well conducted habits' (Gordon 1873, 43). Later that year Captain E.W. Pitcher, in an article discussing the military tribes and races of the Punjab and Northwestern Frontier, criticized Pathans for being 'impatient of strict discipline, slovenly and careless in their dress, unsteady on parade, much addicted to gambling, reckless in their expenditure, and free livers'. Yet despite these glaring disqualifications for military service, he went to praise skills in hill fighting, a growing commitment for the Indian Army, that were highly valued (see Moreman 1998). 'On service . . . they are perfect skirmishers, bold, active, and intelligent, but unless well led are apt to get out of hand; they will undergo any amount of hardship, seldom knock up, and are capital foragers' (Pitcher 1873, 51).

These contributions to the *Proceedings*, written by serving regimental officers, were an important starting point for the more detailed ethnographic mapping of the Indian Army and the wider dissemination of information about 'martial races'. They considerably augmented existing information about Indian troops available to newly commissioned subalterns, officers exchanged between regiments and members of the British Army stationed in India for the first time. Indeed, several had originally been prepared specifically at the direction of the commander-in-chief, to inform officers about the 'class characteristics' – language, culture and background – of their men to improve man management and the interior economy of regiments.[3]

The Second Afghan War and increasing perception of a Russian 'threat' to British India were instrumental in bolstering belief during the 1880s that northern India races were innately superior in fighting skills to others in the subcontinent. In particular, ethnic groups from the Madras Presidency were singled out for criticism as environmental and climatic factors were increasingly employed to explain suitability for military service. Not all officers accepted this view. Some staunchly defended men under their command from southern India in articles that challenged the official line. In the *Proceedings* in 1881, for example, Lieutenant-Colonel F.W. Tyrrel, commanding officer of the 37th Grenadier Regiment of Madras Infantry, staunchly defended Telingas, Tamils, Brahmins, Rajputs, Marathas and Muslims from southern India. He portrayed the Telinga sepoy as a 'gentle and inoffensive individual, very clean in his dress and person, and generally well behaved'. He went on: 'The best Telinga recruits ... are those obtained from agricultural districts; sturdy rustics, accustomed to follow the plough' who were 'quiet, docile and clean' but also 'densely stupid' (Tyrrel 1881). The latter qualification for recruitment mirrored in some respect those assigned to men from northern India, but this and the handful of other articles dealing with Madras troops had little impact in terms of changing official policy which was now dictated by senior officers from the Bengal Army. Such dissenting articles are significant in demonstrating, however, that a lack of consensus existed amongst British officers in India on martial race discourse, but the supporters of the Madras Army were now in a distinct minority. By the late 1880s, the result of the 'Punjabization' of the Indian Army was a military machine organized on the basis of caste and ethnicity that drew its manpower from an increasingly narrow range of Indian communities from northern India. As Major-General J.J.H. Gordon explained in a 1888 *JRUSI* article about the Bengal Army:

> Two-thirds ... are recruited from Northern India and Nepal, and one-third from the North-West Provinces ... The chief among them are the Hindoo classes of the Sikh and the Dogra Rajput of the Punjab, the Gurkha of Nepal, and the Brahmin, Rajput and Jat, and other Hindoo classes of the north-west, while of the Mahommeddans there are the Pathan border tribes of Northern India, the Punjabi, and the Hindostani classes. All are of the peasantry class, of good physique, hardy, enduring, and courageous. There is no lack of them. The military spirit still lives among them, our service is popular, and they come forward freely to enlist. (Gordon 1888, 311–12)

However, the position regarding recruitment was not so promising as this officer in Britain believed.

The *JUSII* was at the forefront of the ongoing professional debate about 'martial race' and recruiting during the 1890s, as growing difficulties were experienced in finding sufficient 'first class' recruits to fill Indian regiments. As the availability of manpower from recognized fighting classes declined, so efforts to create a detailed ethnology of recognized warlike races (to exploit their manpower) and identify new sources of martial recruits intensified. In an 1890 article Colonel F. Lance pointed out that recruiting problems were being experienced and observed: 'We must now look for the flower of the native army among peoples who have more recently come under our rule, and whom the blessings of the "pax Britannica" have not yet enervated as well as tranquilised.' Several potential sources of new manpower were identified by this officer, who characterized them in language reminiscent of stereotypes already established for other martial groups. Baluchis, for example, were described as 'extremely hardy, and of very fair physique' (Lance 1890, 387, 389). Yet in the discussion following this lecture other, more prosaic, reasons were advanced by several senior officers for falling recruitment – in particular, competition from various colonial corps and a combination of declining wages and status.

The military authorities worked hand-in-hand with the editors of the *JUSII* to provoke discussion, gather new information and invite ideas from regimental officers about martial races and recruiting. In 1891 the Council of the United Service Institution (which included several senior Bengal Army officers) set the title: 'Our recruitment grounds for the future for the Indian Army. In view of the obtaining the best material for our soldiers, the "pax Britannica" having reduced the warlike spirit of some races which have hitherto supplied our native armies, by inducing their youth to lay aside the sword for the ploughshare', for its annual prize essay competition. Later that year three essays contesting this view, written by regimental officers, appeared in the journal, noting potential new sources of manpower, as well as means of fully exploiting sources of men from recognized 'martial races' in India. An increasingly 'scientific' approach was taken in this literature, one which eschewed the romanticized language and colourful imagery employed by writers in commercial military periodicals earlier during the century at a time when the aim had been to entertain as well as inform. In the prize essay Lieutenant F.G. Cardew exhaustively catalogued and assessed the races and classes currently enlisted in each presidency's army, before recommending whether they should be enlisted in the future. Jats, for example, were described as a 'hardy agricultural people, of exceedingly fine physique, entirely free from caste prejudices, brave in war and readily amenable to discipline'. With regard to Sikhs he noted: 'Of the virtues of the Sikhs, his value as a soldier, and his military traditions, it would be superfluous here to speak; everybody knows them, and knows too that they exist now as well as they did thirty years ago.' Cardew concluded that dedicated recruiting officers were necessary to enlist better recruits and that ample reserves of manpower were available in India, including the inhabitants of independent tribal territory on the Northwest Frontier (see Cardew 1891).

The supposed martial characteristics of smaller tribal sections and subdivisions of various hitherto overlooked ethnic groups were carefully charted by other contributors. Lieutenant-Colonel M.J. King-Harman, an officer serving in the 2/4th Gurkha Rifles, depicted Yusufzai Pathans, for example, as 'swaggering, blustering bullies . . . [they] look very well in uniform, but they have small hearts. and are most unreliable and treacherous as a rule' (King-Harman 1891, 163–4). In the third prize essay Lieutenant E. Barrow directly attacked the idea that Indian races were losing their fitness for military service which was a key element of martial race theory:

> At all events it is contrary to common sense to suppose that the children of Khalsa warriors who fought at Chillianwalla, or the grandchildren of the sepoys who fought under Lake, have lost all their moral characteristics, while their physical attributes remain to all seemingly unchanged. We may not now get the cream of Indian manhood, but that is entirely due to other causes which money can control, and not to any appreciable reduction in warlike spirit. (Barrow 1891, 175)

These important articles represented the first systematic examination of recruiting carried out in the periodical press and attracted much professional interest. While it is difficult to establish any direct linkage with the *JUSII* competition, in 1891–92 the military authorities appointed District Recruiting Officers for each of the main martial races to improve the recruiting system.

The appointment of District Recruiting Officers and improvements in the pay and status of sepoys did not bring to an end to interest in martial race and the recruitment of the Indian Army. A succession of officers, who contributed articles to the *JUSII*, remained concerned that sufficient good quality men would not be forthcoming for the native army. For example, Lieutenant H.L. Showers (1891) suggested that Bhils of Meywar should be recruited and three years later Lieutenant-Colonel M.J. King-Harman (1894) suggested that Malaya should be regarded as a possible source of recruits. A continuing belief in the shortcomings of the current recruiting system and the declining martial attributes of some ethnic groups was evident again in 1897, when the Council of the United Service Institution directed entrants in its prize essay competition to identify manpower for the Indian Army outside the subcontinent based on the assumption that reserves of Indian martial manpower had been exhausted. In the prize essay Captain G.F. Napier, for example, identified Chinese, Pathays and other non-Indian races as sources of fighting material for Indian regiments (Napier 1897). A marked improvement in the quality and quantity of information about specific 'martial races' was reflected in the essay contributed by Captain George Ranken, who charted in detail the recruiting potential of various trans- and cis-border Pathan tribes, sections and sects (see Ranken 1897). This essay was a direct result of his tour of duty as District Recruiting Officer, Pathan District 1892–95, a position that had enabled him to study and gather detailed information about trans- and cis-border Pathans who were a widely recognized 'martial race' increasingly viewed as providing an untapped reserve of manpower for Punjab regiments. As well as greatly improving the quality of Official information available to officers, other District Recruiting Officers later produced detailed caste handbooks of the Indian Army that described in elaborate detail the ethnology, culture and religious practices of Indian ethnic groups based on personal study over several years. While these handbooks constituted the authoritative source of guidance on individual martial races, the service press, however, remained into the next decade an important medium for professional discussion of those Indian races not yet covered in official sources and elaborating further on perceived differences between Indian races.

The development of a military press catering expressly for British officers had considerable significance in terms of the growth of professionalism in the Indian Army and the study of local defence problems. Perhaps unsurprisingly, the India constructed and negotiated in the specialized professional military press was always viewed narrowly in terms of the military problem its control presented, with security always a paramount concern. This discourse reveals much about attitudes towards India amongst officers belonging to both the British and Indian services, eager to further their own careers in the subcontinent. A comprehensive survey of the contents of the military periodicals identified in this chapter indicates that very different approaches were taken in representing India between those produced in Britain and the subcontinent. The spasmodic and limited coverage of Indian affairs in periodicals published in Britain ensured they had little influence on the Army in India, other than acquainting British service officers and a small proportion of the public with the unique difficulties encountered by imperial troops on the subcontinent. Most editors confined their coverage to general discussions of Indian military affairs that appealed to a paying readership or the problem of imperial defence in a wider imperial context. This disinterest, however, appears almost paradoxical given that the 'one overriding imperial mission' of the late-Victorian Army was the defence of the Northwest Frontier of India against a perceived Russian 'threat' (Spiers 1992, 274). It is easy, however, to identify the reasons. Despite the fact that one-third of the army was deployed in India following the Indian Rebellion, most British service officers were dismissive of the Indian Army. Most knew little about India and cared even less despite the expansion of British control in India and operations along its frontiers during the late nineteenth century. The professional outlook and perspectives of the regular British and Indian armies also conflicted and it must be remembered that India was only one – albeit large – commitment for the British armed forces.

The emergence of a distinctive Anglo-Indian military press resulted from the fact that Indian subjects were generally ignored in journals produced in Britain. It also reflected a search for professional status and recognition by officers of the Indian Army, and the development of a military professionalism tailored to colonial military requirements in the subcontinent as distinct from that developed in Britain which primarily looked towards European experience. Although obvious interest was displayed by British officers in Indian military affairs in the early nineteenth century, it must be remembered that the early commercial periodicals published in India suffered considerable difficulties in maintaining enough paid subscribers to make them financially viable. It is clear that the *JUSII* would probably have suffered a similar fate to its predecessors if it had not secured powerful patronage and, more importantly, a sizeable financial contribution from the Government of India. The early commercial Indian periodicals also had to reflect commercial realities, in terms of publishing articles on diverse subjects and by being written in literary styles that would appeal to a paying audience. As this essay has demonstrated, the *JUSII* proved the most detailed, substantial and enduring of Indian military periodicals with its contents dominated by articles discussing the organization, equipment and training of the Indian Army ignored elsewhere. It was instrumental in fostering professionalism in the army in India during the late nineteenth century and allowed officers of the British and Indian services to express their own opinions and debate upon various narrow professional military, as opposed to political, topics directly affecting the garrison.

Those articles that regularly appeared discussing recruitment and the martial qualities of Indian sepoys, indicated how important this subject

was to the colonial military. British officers needed to know and understand the religion, culture, traditions and social organization of their
sepoys to facilitate control of their regiments and identify new recruits.
Following the publication of the *JUSII*, the military and the media
worked very closely, with certain articles dealing with the characteristics
of Indian sepoys initially written at the deliberate request of senior
officers. The *JUSII* thus acted as a means of promoting and disseminating
official views, although other articles containing opinions in direct conflict with official policy also appeared in its pages. Perhaps the closest
examples of co-operation between officialdom and this periodical were
the prize essay competitions, in which senior officers used the *JUSII* to
stimulate discussion of key issues concerning the Indian Army. The
majority of articles dealing with martial race reflected the common
assumptions prevailing in British society about the subcontinent, but
they also made an important contribution in gathering and disseminating new knowledge about India and its inhabitants. The Indian Army
always formed a major cultural interchange between European and
Indian society, although its interpretations of Indian society were
coloured by racist and ethnocentric perceptions (Peers 1995, 12–13).
Foundational representations created by officers writing in the military
press in the 1830s and 1840s, which helped articulate and codify martial
race theory, were later developed and widely disseminated by the *JUSII*
to their successors throughout India. In the long term, the military representations of Indian martial races that first appeared in journal articles
were incorporated into imperial discourse when official caste handbooks
were published by the military authorities at the turn of the century.
While the latter assumed an authoritative position, the military press
remained an important means into the next century for British officers
to write about issues affecting the recruitment of Indian regiments –
and in particular to identify potential new sources of manpower for the
Indian Army up to the outbreak of the First World War.

Notes

1. Major-General A. Huyshe, President of the Council of the United Service
   Institution of India, to the Adjutant-General, received 31 May 1871, and Colonel H.K. Burne, Secretary to the Government of India, Military Department,
   to the Adjutant General, 3 July 1871, P/605, Oriental and India Office Collections, British Library [hereafter OIOC].

2. Council of the United Service Institution of India to the Adjutant General in India, and Lt.-Col. A. Crookshank, Offg. Deputy Secretary to the Government of India, Military Department, to the Adjutant General in India, P/2086, OIOC.
3. See Maj.-Gen. F. Thesiger, Adj. Gen, to Officers Commanding certain Regiments of Native Cavalry and Infantry, 7 March 1874, Ms.Eur.F.114/5(4), Napier Papers, OIOC.

Works cited

Altham, E. 'The Royal United Service Institution 1831–1931', *Journal of the Royal United Service Institution* 76 (1931), 235–45.
Anon. 'The Indian Army No. 3', *United Service Journal* 1836.
Anon. 'The Military Constitution of our Indian Empire', *United Service Journal* (1845), 416.
Anon. 'Notice to Readers', *East India United Service Journal* 12 (1838), i.
Anon. 'Editorial', *The East Indian Army Magazine and Military Review* 1 (1853), 1–2.
Bailes, H. 'The Influence of Continental Examples and Colonial Warfare upon the Reform of the Late Victorian Army' (PhD, University of London, 1980).
Barrow, E.G. 'Our Recruiting Grounds of the Future for the Indian Army', *Journal of the United Service Institution of India* 20 (1891), 173–92.
Brief, D. 'The Punjab and Recruitment of the Indian Army 1846–1918' (MPhil, Oxford, 1979).
Cardew, F.G. 'Our Recruiting Grounds of the Future for the Indian Army', *Journal of the United Service Institution of India* 20 (1891), 131–56.
Eyre, V. 'The Sikh and European Soldiers of our Indian Forces', *Journal of the Royal United Service Institution* 11 (1868), 86–103.
"Goorkha". 'Notes on the Goorkhas', *Proceedings of the United Service Institution* 1 (1871), 17–32.
Gordon, J.J.H. 'The Dogras', *Proceedings of the United Service Institution of India* 3 (1873), 31–43.
Gordon, J.J.H. 'The Native Army of Bengal: Its Constitution, Organization, Equipment, and Interior Economy', *Journal of the Royal United Service Institution* 32 (1888), 311–28.
Heathcote, T.A. *The Military in British India: the Development of British Land Forces in South Asia 1600–1946*. Manchester, 1995.
Hunter-Thompson, Lt.-Col. G. 'On the Constitution, Equipment, Pay, &c., of the Bengal Native Infantry, with suggestions for reform', *Proceedings of the United Service Institution* 1 (1871), 5–7.
Kale, B.D. 'Major General Sir Charles MacGregor: a Profile', *Journal of the United Service Institution of India* 68 (1988), 407–12.
K.-X. O-X. 'An Invocation to Members', *East India United Service Journal* ns 27 (1836), 42–6.
King-Harman, M.J. 'Our Recruiting Grounds of the Future for the Indian Army', *Journal of the United Service Institution* 20 (1891), 157–72.
King-Harman, M.J. 'Malay as a Possible Recruiting ground for the Indian Army', *Journal of the United Service Institution* 24 (1895), 117–24.
Lance, F. 'Recruiting for the Native Army', *Journal of the United Service Institution* 19 (1890), 386–404.

Lindsay, J. 'Chairman's Address', *Journal of the United Service Institution* 1 (1857), 1–7.

MacGregor, Lady. *The Life and Opinions of Major General Sir Charles Metcalfe MacGregor K.C.B, C.S.I., C.I.E. Quartermaster-General in India*, Edinburgh and London, 1888.

Metcalf, T.R. *Ideologies of the Raj*. Cambridge, 1995.

Moreman, T.R. *The Army in India and the Development of Frontier Warfare 1849–1947*. London, 1998.

Napier, G.F.S. 'The Best Method of Recruiting the Indian Armies from sources not hitherto tapped on the assumption that enlistment amongst the recognised martial races of the Indian Empire and its frontiers has been pushed very nearly to its utmost limits', *Journal of the United Service Institution of India* 26 (1897), 199–240.

Omissi, David, *The Sepoy and the Raj: the Indian Army 1860–1940*. London, 1994.

Peers, Douglas M. '"The Habitual Nobility of Being": British Officers and the Social Construction of the Bengal Army in the Early Nineteenth Century', *Modern Asian Studies* 25 (1991), 545–69.

Peers, Douglas M. *Between Mars and Mammon: Colonial Armies and the Garrison State in India 1819–1835*. London, 1995.

Peers, Douglas M. '"Those Noble Exemplars of the True Military Tradition"; Constructions of the Indian Army in the Mid-Victorian Press', *Modern Asian Studies* 31 (1997), 109–42.

Pitcher, H.W. 'Notes on the Military Tribes and Races of the Punjab and North Western Frontier', *Proceedings of the United Service Institution* 3 (1873), 49–56.

Price, H.C.P., 'Notes on the Sikhs as Soldiers for our Army', *Proceedings of the United Service Institution* 2 (1872), 57–70.

Ranken, G.P. 'The Best Method of Recruiting the Indian Armies from sources not hitherto tapped on the assumption that enlistment amongst the recognised martial races of the Indian Empire and its frontiers has been pushed very nearly to its utmost limits', *Journal of the United Service Institute of India* 26 (1897), 261–83.

Reader, W.J. *At Duty's Call: a Study in Obsolete Patriotism*. Manchester, 1988.

Sharma, B.L. 'Looking Back', *Journal of the United Service Institution of India* 100 (1970), 524–46.

Showers, H.L. 'The Meywar Bhil Corps', *Journal of the United Service Institution of India* 20 (1891), 87–95.

Spiers, Edward. *The Late Victorian Army 1868–1902*. Manchester, 1992.

Stocqueler, J.H. 'Address to the Officers of the Indian Army', *The East India United Service Journal* 1 (1833), i–iii.

Strachan, H. *From Waterloo to Balaclava: Tactics, Technology and the British Army 1815–1854*. Cambridge, 1985.

Strachan, H. *The Politics of the British Army*. Oxford, 1997.

Trousdale, William (ed.). *War in Afghanistan, 1879–80. the Personal Diary of Major General Sir Charles Metcalfe MacGregor*. Detroit, 1985.

Tucker, A. 'Military', in J. DonVann and R.T. VanArsdel (eds), *Victorian Periodicals and Victorian Society*. Aldershot, 1994, 62–80.

Tyrrel, Lt.-Col. F.W. 'The Races of the Madras Army', *Proceedings of the United Service Institution* 10 (1881), 11–22.

Welch, M.D. *Science and the British Officer: the Early Days of the Royal United Services Institute for Defence Studies (1829–1869)*. London, 1998.

11

Was there an Oriental Renaissance in Medicine? The Evidence of the Nineteenth-Century Medical Press

Mark Harrison

The first chapter of Raymond Schwab's work *The Oriental Renaissance* is confidently entitled: 'There is an Oriental Renaissance'. He was in no doubt that the translation of Indian and other 'eastern' texts from the eighteenth century wrought a profound change in European attitudes, comparable to the Renaissance of the fifteenth and sixteenth centuries. Only after 1771, claims Schwab, when the French scholar Anquetil-Duperron published his translation of the Persian text, the *Zend Avesta*, 'does the world become truly round' (Schwab 1950, 16). It is undeniable that the discovery of literate non-western cultures broadened the scope of the humanist vision, but does it really merit the title 'Renaissance', with the radical renewal or revival of culture which that term implies? Schwab makes a good case for the impact of orientalist scholarship on the arts – on fiction, philosophy and music – but missing from his account is any discussion of science and medicine, two of the most important aspects of Renaissance humanism in early-modern Europe. Can a case be made for an 'Oriental Renaissance' in these areas too, or were western science and medicine so supremely self-confident that they felt they had little to gain from other systems of knowledge? Using the evidence of medical journalism in and about India, this chapter asks whether it is possible to talk of an 'Oriental Renaissance' in medicine during the nineteenth century. Was Europe's debt to India merely empirical (the acquisition of medicinal drugs and plants) or did contact with other cultures alter fundamentally the concepts and theories of European medical practitioners? Did the interaction between European and Indian practitioners constitute a respectful dialogue (Halbfass 1988; Irschick 1994; Bayly 1996), or did it amount to nothing more than the appropriation of indigenous knowledge for the purposes of command (Cohn 1985; Inden 1990; Arnold 1993)?

The medical periodicals of British India developed as the organs of three types of institution: medical societies, medical colleges and the colonial state. Of great importance in the first half of the nineteenth century were the transactions of the presidency medical and physical societies, the first of which was the *Transactions of the Calcutta Medical and Physical Society*, which appeared in 1825. The *Transactions* were available to anyone who paid a subscription to the Society, including a number of corresponding members located overseas. They were essentially collections of papers read before the societies, with the addition of editorial comment, small news items, and book reviews. To some degree, the transactions provided a forum for professional advancement, although this was more likely to arise as the result of distinguished military or administrative service than because of scientific or medical work.

The establishment of medical colleges teaching western medicine from the mid-1830s led to the creation of a number of journals closely allied to these institutions, the first being the Calcutta-based *India Journal of Medical Science*, founded in 1835 – the same year as the Medical College. The *Madras Quarterly Journal of Medical Science* performed a similar function. However, the transactions of the various medical and physical societies, and journals associated with medical schools, were gradually eclipsed in the second half of the century by the *Indian Medical Gazette*, which was the official organ of the Indian Medical Service. This reflected the greater centralization of medical authority which took place following the transfer of government from the East India Company to the Crown in 1858. While it carried scientific articles, the *Indian Medical Gazette* was quite different from earlier journals in that it was far more concerned with professional matters affecting members of the official medical service (Neelameghan 1963; Crawford 1914).

Towards the end of the nineteenth century, and in the first decade or so of the twentieth, more specialist medical journals began to cater to different sections of the medical profession in India. The *Scientific Memoirs of Medical Offices of the Army of India*, established in 1884, published the research papers of officers in the Indian Medical Service and the Army Medical Department. By this time, a few medical officers were beginning to build careers within the Army medical services largely on the basis of their scientific research and publication; Ronald Ross, discoverer of the mosquito vector of malaria, was one such. However, such individuals were still very much in a minority and distinction in research still counted less than distinction in military service, or simply seniority, when it came to professional advancement.

Medical men working in India outside official circles were able to publish their views on medical matters in a range of other Indian and British medical journals. Public health workers employed by Indian municipalities, for example, contributed to the *Indian Public Health and Municipal Journal*, which appears to have been founded in 1908. In addition to journals based in India, all major medical periodicals in Britain – such as the *Lancet* and the *British Medical Journal* – regularly carried articles on Indian subjects, most of which were written by men who had served or were serving in India. Some periodicals were even founded by men with Indian experience, the best known of which is the *Journal of Tropical Medicine*, co-founded by William J. Simpson (formerly Health Officer of Calcutta) and James Cantlie (formerly a doctor in Hong Kong) in 1898.

Scientific medicine and the assault on orientalism

A number of recent studies have shown that there was considerable interaction between European and Indian medical practitioners during the seventeenth and eighteenth centuries. The exact nature of this interaction, in most cases, can only be guessed at, since sources generally do not reveal details of conversations between European and Indian medical men. What can be stated with certainty, however, is that European practitioners came to rely substantially on Indian knowledge of medical chemicals and plants, since their own medicines seemed unable to treat the different varieties of disease they encountered in India. For the same reason, practitioners of Indian systems of medicine were employed from very early on as subordinate medical personnel by the English East India Company, for which they worked as apothecaries and hospital assistants. Europeans also came to adopt certain Indian customs in the belief that they would help them adapt to life in the tropics. Indian dietary regimes, clothing, and scrupulous personal cleanliness were recommended in numerous eighteenth and early-nineteenth-century medical texts (Harrison 1992, 1996, 1999; Pearson 1995, 1996; Grove 1996; Arnold 1996). This was an accommodation born of necessity but it also reflected the tolerance and openness characteristic of the eighteenth-century Enlightenment. There were also epistemological similarities between western and Indian medical systems: western medicine, like its Indian counterparts, was fundamentally humoral until well into the eighteenth century, and in both systems disease was thought to arise from an imbalance of bodily substances such as water, phlegm or bile (Harrison 1992, 1999; Basham 1976; Burgel 1976).

But to what extent was this 'dialogue' furthered by orientalist scholarship and the discovery and translation of Indian medical texts? Before we even begin to address this question, it is necessary to indicate a countervailing tendency towards a rationalist critique of Indian culture. This began in the late eighteenth century with moves towards the 'anglicisation' of India's judicial and administrative machinery under the governor-generalship of Lord Cornwallis (1786–93), but gathered pace in the early nineteenth century under the force of Evangelical Christianity and the virulently westernizing creed of Utilitarianism (Stokes 1959; Bearce 1961). There was a growing feeling that India was to be governed in accordance with Reason rather than tradition. It is important not to overstate the impact of these doctrines, nor to give the impression that a clear-cut division existed between orientalists on the one hand, and anglicists and utilitarians on the other. Nevertheless, a more assertive and self-confident attitude is clearly evident in the medical press of the early nineteenth century. For example, the preface to the first issue of British-India's first medical journal – the *Transactions of the Medical and Physical Society of Calcutta*, which was first published in 1825 – declared that medical men would have to conduct their *own* investigations into the diseases of India because it was not expected that 'the imperfect science of the *Baids* [*vaidyas*, that is, ayurvedic physicians] and *Hakims* [practitioners of Islamic medicine, that is, *unan-i-tibb*] of India, shall offer any instructive lessons to their better educated brethren of Europe' (*Trans. Medl & Physl Soc. of Calcutta* 1825, iv). The editor of the *Transactions* – which expressed the opinions of Calcutta's most progressive surgeons and physicians – held the increasingly common view that Indian culture had little to offer Europeans: to those of a utilitarian frame of mind, even India's 'sciences' were backward and riddled with 'medieval superstition'. James Mill, for instance, wrote that 'Even medicine and surgery, to the cultivation of which so obvious and powerful an interest invites, had scarcely, beyond the degree of the most uncultivated tribes, attracted the rude understanding of the Hindus' (Mill 1820, vol. 2, 185).

After 1800 most European medical men in India would have agreed that advances in anatomy and physiology had created a gulf between western and Indian medical systems. In particular, the new technique of pathological anatomy, which had emerged from the Paris Hospital at the end of the eighteenth century, had begun to alter fundamentally their perceptions of disease (Ackerknecht 1967; Foucault 1973; Waddington

1973; Jewson 1976; Maulitz 1987). Although most Europeans had long since abandoned a simple (classical) humoral theory of disease, until the early nineteenth century many diseases were still regarded as being due to some 'imbalance' of the bodily fluids. In this sense, western and Indian medical systems had much in common, but pathological anatomists viewed disease as 'localized' in a particular organ or tissues (and as distinct entities), rather than as a general distempers affecting the body as a whole.

This was a fundamental change which, as far as many contemporaries were concerned, drew a line between 'scientific' and 'non-scientific' systems of medicine. Thus, in 1836, the Professor of Medicine at the Calcutta Medical College, Henry Hurry Goodeve, wrote in his 'Sketch on the Progress of European Medicine in the East' that 'Within the last twenty or fifteen years Anglo-Indian medicine has advanced with rapid strides. The immense improvements which have taken place in the medical sciences in Europe have doubtless contributed to this desirable end; for even in these distant regions we feel . . . the influence of scientific discoveries at home' (Goodeve 1837, 152). Confident in the progress made by western medicine, European practitioners came increasingly to hold their indigenous counterparts up to ridicule. R.H. Irvine, writing of the *hakims* and *vaidyas* practising in the western Indian town of Ajmer, wrote that 'Their knowledge appears to be at a very low ebb; their chief reliance upon charms and signs; the materials of their prescriptions often of the most incongruous materials, and laughable even to themselves when they are asked on what principles they prescribe' (Irvine 1838, 191).

These criticisms accompanied moves in the mid-1830s to establish medical education in India on British lines. A Native Medical Institution (NMI) had been in existence since 1822, being established to prepare (Indian and Eurasian) medical staff for subordinate posts in the Presidency medical services. The courses taught at this institution embraced aspects of western and Indian systems and were conducted in vernacular languages. Medical classes were also taught at the Sanskrit College and the Madrassa in Calcutta. The head of the NMI, Mr Tytler, was an avowed 'orientalist' who opposed demands from some members of the Anglo-Indian medical profession that medical courses be conducted in English, on the grounds of the latter's 'intrinsic difficulty' (in other words, its combination of French, Latin and Germanic terms). However, a committee set up to report on the state of 'Native Medical Education' by the reforming governor-general William Bentinck (in office 1828–35) protested that only a few medical books had been translated into Indian languages, meaning that education in the vernacular must necessarily be inferior. It was also critical of the lack of practical education, especially of human dissection, which was anathema to most Hindus.

The committee, therefore, recommended that a new Medical College be established in Calcutta, providing up-to-date theoretical and practical tuition in English (Kumar 1995). In addition, it advised that a number of Indians be provided with scholarships to study medicine in England for five years. These men would be equipped to take up teaching positions at the College on their return (*India J. Medl Sci*. 1835, 98–115). This was very much in line with the universalistic, progressive ethos espoused by the medical profession in India, and was accordingly welcomed by the medical press. The editor of the *India Journal of Medical Science* (an organ closely associated with the medical college) felt that government had satisfactorily addressed the most important issues raised by the committee, but the scheme was not as grand as he and other members of the medical profession would have liked (*India J. Medl Sci*. 1835, 123). The new Medical College opened in June 1835, with only three professors – Mr Bromley, Dr H.H. Goodeve and Dr O'Shaughnessy – to teach every part of the curriculum. The *Journal* also felt that the lack of European students at the College would hold back the progress of the Indians, it being deemed essential that the latter imbibe their 'energetic and aspiring spirit', and that Indian students needed to learn from Europeans how to 'reason intellectually' rather than simply to learn the curriculum by rote (*India J. Medl. Sci*. 1835, 266). Medical periodicals, such as those attached to medical schools and societies, provided one of the few media through which progressive-minded doctors could advance their cause and articulate their conviction that science and medicine should be fundamental elements of any mission to civilize India.

Orientalist empiricism

The triumphal march of western medicine did not, however, blind its practitioners to the uses of indigenous medical knowledge. Expanding on some of the monographic studies of disease in India produced in the eighteenth and early nineteenth centuries, medical periodicals carried numerous articles evaluating indigenous drugs and medicinal plants. George Playfair, an army surgeon and translator of the Islamic pharmacopoeia, the *Taleef Shereef*, recorded encouraging results after using the juice extracted from the Madar plant (*Asclepsias gigantea*) in the treatment of syphilis and remittent fever. The Medical Board of Bengal had even requested some of the medicine for trials at the General Hospital in Calcutta (Playfair 1825). The garrison surgeon of the Nasirabad cantonment in western India had also found a local plant (Anola) useful in the treatment of 'land scurvy', which was common among Indian troops. But the information had been given to sepoys by inhabitants of nearby Ajmer district, and European surgeons had found out about the matter only by chance. With the 'apathetic indifference of the race', recalled Surgeon MacNab, 'those rustics withheld their information when our exigency required it most, and only divulged the secret after our troubles were well nigh over' (MacNab 1837). On other occasions, European practitioners had to resort to 'bribery' to induce Indians to relinquish their medical secrets (Irvine 1838, 201).

The dependence of Europeans on indigenous sources was increasingly resented, particularly because there were pressing financial reasons for obtaining more indigenous drugs. The Medical Boards of the three presidencies were keen to find alternatives to many of the drugs imported at considerable expense from Britain: despite over two centuries of contact with India, the East India Company was still relying predominantly on medicines imported from London. In 1837 the *Quarterly Journal of the Calcutta Medical and Physical Society* reported that the official *materia medica* of the Bombay Presidency consisted of 90 European medicines and 70 procured locally or from other 'Eastern' countries (*Quart. J. Calcutta Medl & Physl Soc.* 1837, 467–8). It is important to note that the qualities of indigenous remedies were no longer assessed simply on the basis of clinical experience; nor was their value generally taken on trust. The Bengal Medical Board, for example, appointed medical officers to conduct systematic chemical and clinical trials before a drug was available for general use (*Quart. J. Calcutta Medl & Physl Soc.* 1838, 155; Bala 1991, 38–57).

Another stimulus to research into Indian medicine was growing competition between European and Asian medical systems. Many European practitioners saw themselves as engaged in a struggle against ignorance and superstition, but in order to compete on an equal footing it was necessary to know as much as possible about traditional practice. Thus, the orientalist scholar Horace Hayman Wilson told the Calcutta Medical and Physical Society in 1825 that he

> had obtained for the information, and probably for the amusement of the Society, the following account of the treatment of the cholera of the Bengali practitioners, from a respectable member of the native community.... The practice he describes is for the greater part the most barbarous empiricism, in which ample advantage is taken of ignorant credulity.

Nevertheless, Wilson stressed 'the propriety of our investigating the means employed by native medicine, in order that we may avail ourselves of such as may be beneficial, and expose the mischief or absurdity of such as may be ridiculous or detrimental' (Wilson 1825, 282–3).

Knowledge of Indian drugs was also considered important in view of the development of medical jurisprudence at the Presidency medical colleges during the 1840s and 1850s. The establishment of these courses reflected the widespread fear of poisoning among Europeans. It was widely believed that Indians possessed an extensive knowledge of toxic plants and minerals, and that murders were commonly committed by poisoning, without being identified as such. It was possible for European doctors to detect the effects of opium or arsenic but, as Professor Blacklock of Madras Medical College put it in 1852,

> we do not know nearly all the poisons which can be obtained by the native population, nor in what instances they are able to baffle enquiry by employing poisons which induce symptoms and appearances similar to those of ordinary disease. The poisoner has far more means at his command in this country of whose effects European medical men are very ignorant. (Blacklock 1852, 31)

But despite the impetus provided by the teaching of medical toxicology in all three presidencies, research into indigenous drugs seems to have become less, rather than more, popular towards the middle of the century. This was a matter of some concern for Dr George Bidie, writing in the *Madras Quarterly Journal of Medical Science* in 1862, who (presumably with the recent war against Russia in mind), drew attention to the dangers of any interruption to medical supplies from Europe.

> Let us not dispose of a medicine because its use is peculiar to India . . . or fling aside a truth because it is mixed up with many crude notions. Great men have led the way, for the illustrious names of Ainslie, Roxburgh and Wright shed honour on the medical service of Madras. (Bidie 1862, 32)

Bidie wanted to revive the pioneering spirit of the late eighteenth and early nineteenth centuries, when European surgeons had travelled all over India to collect specimens of potential use to the Company and of scientific interest (Vicziany 1986; Kumar 1995, 32–72; Grove 1995, 380–473). Roxburgh, for example, went on to establish the Calcutta Botanical Garden, while Whitelaw Ainslie had compiled pharmacopoeia from translations of Persian and Sanskrit texts. Bidie seems to have been part of a broader movement which aimed to revive this tradition of medical botany in Madras. In the early 1860s, the editor of the *Madras Quarterly Journal of Medical Science*, Howard Montgomery, Professor of Botany and *Materia Medica* at Madras Medical College, accepted a number of articles making similar points. One of these was J.J. Wood's 'Gleanings from the Hindoo Formularly' of 1862, which referred to a number of useful remedies listed in this treatise, the *Bit-Laban* (Wood 1862). The same edition also carried a very favourable review of Hugh Cleghorn's *Forests and Gardens of South India*. Cleghorn, who had joined the forest service, was formerly a medical man, whom many saw as following in the same distinguished botanical footsteps as Roxburgh (*Madras Quart. J. of Medl Sci.* 1862, 134–43; Grove 1995, 451–3, 461–2). Recalling earlier anxieties over poisoning, there was also news of several such cases, albeit among Indians rather than Europeans (Moodelly 1862). All this seemed to be aimed at reviving medical botany, which had suffered, in part, from the reluctance of European practitioners to take seriously anything 'Indian'. The same prejudice, according to George Bidie, was having a destructive effect on indigenous medical traditions, which he thought it necessary to revive:

> many of our native subordinates, the sons and relatives of Hakeems, no doubt began life with considerable confidence in, and some form of knowledge of, native remedies, which it is to be feared have been all but lost under the influence of our example. Had we, by the light of Western Science, fostered and modified that hereditary knowledge, what a goodly and useful superstructure might have been erected on such a foundation. (Bidie 1862, 32–3)

Classification and disease theory

The scientific study of India's medicinal plants and minerals might be more accurately termed an 'appropriation' of indigenous knowledge for the purposes of imperial rule, than a dialogue in any meaningful sense. The properties of these substances were seldom accepted on the personal recommendation of Indian practitioners or on scriptural authority alone: scientific testing was thought to be essential. However, some Europeans were more sympathetic to indigenous medical systems, and less than supremely confident in their own. One such surgeon was H.H. Wilson (Kopf 1969, 167–77), who found much that could be admired in the Indian medical treatise, the *Susruta Samhita*. Wilson argued that 'the comparative mildness of the Sanscritic dressings [used in surgery] appears to advantage when contrasted to the cruelty of European surgery even to so late a period as the middle of the seventeenth century' (Wilson 1834, 118). Although more respectful, Wilson still seemed to be implying that little had changed in Indian medicine, whereas European science had progressed rapidly since the Renaissance. But, in other areas of medicine, Wilson was prepared to acknowledge that Indian medicine could make more than an empirical contribution to contemporary practice:

> the Hindu notions, on the subject of leprosy, might form a not unserviceable introduction to the more scientific enquiries, which the better opportunities and greater experience of other members of the Society may enable them to institute. The advanced state of medical knowledge in Europe is a sufficient security, that the errors of these guides . . . , will not lead us astray; whilst from their long experience and accumulated observation, it is possible that some hints may be derived, which may lead us to an improved knowledge and classification, if not to a more successful treatment of the disease. (Wilson 1825, 2–3)

This was a guarded recommendation and one in which western ('scientific') medicine was being defined in relation to the 'errors' of indigenous systems. Nevertheless, it was a view of indigenous medicine which betrays more than the usual empirical interest in therapies and medicinal plants. Wilson was concerned here with what was primarily a *conceptual* problem – that of the classification of disease – and, on the question of leprosy, at least, he thought the nosology of Hindu (ayurvedic) physicians more accurate than that of Europeans. Wilson was critical of the tendency among European physicians to differentiate between the diseases of leprosy and elephantiasis, whereas Hindu practitioners saw them as different manifestations of the same disease. 'This unity of classification', he argued, '. . . appears preferable to that which has been latterly adopted by English writers, who have separated Elephantiasis from lepra, as a wholly distinct complaint' (Wilson 1825, 20). On other matters, however, Indian and European writers were in agreement. Wilson drew attention to the similarity between European and Indian notions of a 'sympathy' between the stomach and the skin and on the causation of leprosy, which Indians and some Europeans attributed to the consumption of rancid food, particularly fish (Wilson 1825, 5–6). This view was still held by some Europeans as late as the 1890s, when a Leprosy

Commission sounded professional opinion on the matter (Government of India 1892, 344). However, it should be stressed that Wilson's preference for the Hindu classification of disease was by no means typical. As the editor of the *Indian Medical Gazette* put it in 1868, 'Their [i.e. Indian medical practitioners'] primary want is that of a scientific nomenclature of disease, theirs being either fanciful, and often utterly unintelligible to the rest of the civilised world' (*Indian Medl Gazette* 1868, 88).

Wilson drew on the writings of elite practitioners from an allegedly 'Golden Age'; like most orientalists, he looked to the past rather than to the present for inspiration. But some Europeans believed that much could be learnt about the nature and causation of diseases from consultation with indigenous peoples. The collection of 'folk' knowledge on health and disease constituted an important part of 'medical topography': an enterprise which dominated Anglo-Indian medicine in the years from 1825 to 1860 (Harrison 1999). Medical topography was principally concerned with the effects of the environment (climate, waters, soils and so forth) on the health of a particular locality, although many topographies also commented on hospitals, medical practice, and even the agricultural or commercial prosperity of an area. All these factors were taken into account when deciding whether a particular locality was 'healthy' or not. For example, after commenting on the high rates of sickness experienced by both sepoys and European troops in the Northern Circars, a range of hills in the Madras Presidency, Assistant-Surgeon Wright of the 8th Regt. Madras Native Infantry observed that 'The original inhabitants of the hills are a diminutive race, with shaggy hair and stunted growth, and bear evidence as to the ungeniality of their natural clime.' It came as no surprise to Wright – given the weakness induced by long residence in the Circars – that the rebellion they had come to put down had been staged by *recent* arrivals of the 'Ooria caste'. These men were equally 'uncivilised' but, coming from the base of the hills and the valleys, were 'brave' and 'well-formed' (Wright 1834, 360). These observations led Wright, like so many of his contemporaries, to the conclusion that each 'race' could prosper only in a climate to which it had become habituated through birth or long residence. However, this opinion was based as much on *indigenous* perceptions of the unhealthiness of the valleys as on European prejudices or medical theory. He recorded:

It is . . . a strange anomaly . . . that the hill inhabitants, when removed to any distance from the spot in which they have been born and acclimated, become subject to attacks of fever – although formerly exempt. *They seem perfectly aware of this* . . . they only levy black mail in the villages, in their immediate vicinity, and seldom venture into the plains. (Wright 1834, 360, emphasis added)

On other occasions, European medical men actually conferred with indigenous peoples in an attempt to discover the principal causes of ill health in their locality (Waller 1842, 105). Some topographers noted that the inhabitants of forests often attributed the incidence of fever – like Europeans – to the rapid decay of vegetation occurring in jungles and on the banks of rivers (Gibson 1838, 40). Such beliefs were similar to those expressed in the ancient medical texts translated by Wilson, and orientalist surgeons such as Playfair and J.F. Royle (Playfair 1832; Royle 1837). It was now known that Indian authorities, such as Charaka and Susruta, attributed some diseases to unseasonal weather or noxious vapours emanating from jungles and swampy low-lying areas (Wise 1867, vol. 2, 27, 32, 37, 80). There were also similarities between Indian texts (contemporary as well as ancient) and classical discourses on climate and human character (Raychaudhuri 1992, 159–60). Thus, indigenous knowledge may have reinforced European ideas about the dangers of particular localities and the peculiarities of racial immunity; ideas which originated in those parts of the Hippocratic corpus concerning *Airs, Waters and Places*. Anglo-Indian practitioners shared, with Hippocrates, the tendency to make general statements about differences between Europeans and 'Asiatics' which they attributed to climate, among other factors, but were also, like Hippocrates, of the opinion that 'Asiatics differ[ed] greatly among themselves' (Hippocrates 1983, 12–16). Yet more often than not popular understandings of disease causation served only to highlight differences between European and indigenous medical knowledge. Edward Waring's 'Medical Notes on the Burmese', published in the *Indian Annals of Medical Science* in 1854, asserted that local medical practice consisted largely of 'charms and incantations' – 'It being a belief commonly entertained by the natives that disease of kinds is the result of the unfriendly influence of some malignant spirit or *Nat*' (Waring 1854, 106).

The 'lunacists'

Indian theories of disease causation were, however, apparent in the doctrines of the so-called 'lunacists': the two or three generations of Anglo-Indian practitioners who thought the moon was a causal factor in fever and some other diseases. The basic premise of the 'lunar theory' of fever was that the moon exerted far more influence over the bodies of human beings in tropical than in temperate zones. The naval surgeon James Lind, for example, had written in 1768 that

> It is a common observation, both at Bengal and Bencoolen, that the moon or tides have a remarkable influence there on intermitting fevers. I have been informed by a gentleman of undoubted veracity, and of great knowledge in medicine, that in fevers at Bengal, he could fortel the precise time when the patient would expire, it being generally about the hour of low water. (Lind 1808, 92–3)

The same opinion was expressed by another well-known 'lunacist', Francis Balfour, in his *Treatise on the Influence of the Moon in Fevers* in 1784 (Balfour 1784, vi). Balfour, a physician at the East India Company's European hospital in Calcutta, believed that certain phases of the moon (the new and full moons) predisposed individuals to attacks of fever; usually of an intermittent variety, but also 'putrid, nervous and rheumatic fevers' (Balfour 1784, 34, 42). The moon's influence upon the body, according to Balfour, was analogous to its influence on the tides, and this could be seen in the way in which his patients' fever seemed to 'ebb and flow' with the lunar cycle (Balfour 1784, 43). Such ideas were popular among Anglo-Indian medical practitioners until well into the nineteenth century (Johnson 1815, 88), despite the fact that they were ridiculed by most of the profession in Europe, where lunar theory was associated with the discredited astrological medicine of the seventeenth century and before (Porter 1995, 376).

That the lunar theory took root in India (among some of its most influential medical practitioners) can be explained by the prevailing view that the tropics were a distinctive disease environment, in which the moon and the sun exerted a more direct and powerful effect on human bodies than in temperate regions (Harrison 1996, 1999). But there may be other reasons for the popularity of lunar theory which were peculiar to India itself, not least the continuing importance of astrology in Indian medical systems. European physicians often consulted *vaidyas* and *hakims*, and it would not be surprising if they had come to share certain of their convictions about planetary influence over disease (Pearson 1995, 1996; Boomgaard 1996). James Lind, for instance, shared the widespread Hindu belief that the solar eclipse could exert a baneful influence, and claimed that some 800 Europeans and 30 000 Indians had perished during the solar eclipse of 15 November 1762 (Lind 1808, 90). The translation of Hindu medical texts from the late eighteenth century was another contributory factor. By the 1840s many Anglo-Indians were able to read for themselves what such author-ities as Susruta had to say about the influence of the moon, and found that his writings corresponded closely with received wisdom about the influence of the moon's 'age' on the course of a disease (Peet 1843, 210).

However, it would be misleading to attribute the longevity of the lunar theory in India simply to the influence of indigenous medical writings and practitioners. The moon was prominent in naval lore, and it is noteworthy that some of the foremost lunacists, such as James Lind, were naval men. Some sailors believed that exposure to the moon's rays caused such conditions as paralysis, vertigo and swelling of the face. As late as 1839 a correspondent to the *Nautical Magazine* claimed that he had seen many newly littered young animals perish in a few hours by the mother's side if exposed to rays of the full moon. He also espoused the popular notion that meat and fish became putrid if exposed to the moon. Such beliefs began to wane during the during the nineteenth century and some experiments with meat were even conducted to refute the doctrine (Peet 1843, 212–13). Nevertheless, there were still medical men who were prepared to attest to the phenomenon (Peet 1843, 214).

The lunar theory of fevers continued to claim the support of Anglo-Indian practitioners until well into the nineteenth century but, by the 1830s, few physicians were prepared to admit anything like the influence claimed by Drs Lind and Balfour. Dr H.H. Goodeve of the Calcutta Med-ical School thought that these men had fair ground for their belief' and he, himself, regarded the moon as 'a very active agent in the periodic changes . . . to which our bodies are liable'. He explained:

> It may not be that the moon itself acts directly upon the human frame . . . but I think few would be prepared to deny the . . . manifest control which the 'lamp of night' exercises upon various phenomena of the air and weather. The moon perhaps 'works at second hand'; but whatever may be its modus operandi, I think we require stronger arguments than have been adduced to overthrow the doctrines of the Lunacists. At the same time, I am not prepared to go to the absurd length to which sol-lunar influences, as he calls it, led Dr. Balfour. (Goodeve 1837, 132)

Goodeve criticized Balfour's treatise as being 'full of the most inconclusive reasoning, supported by a pompous affectation of philosophical prob-lems' (Goodeve 1837, 132). Yet, in the late 1830s there were still many practitioners prepared to believe that the moon had a direct influence, not only upon fevers, but also on chronic diseases. The surgeon James Murray was converted to the lunar doctrine after meeting an army officer subject to frequent, sudden attacks of dizziness and headache. He had also discerned the influence of the moon in cases of epilepsy and of that of a women suffering from 'irritation of the spine' (Murray 1839). As late as 1860, the assistant apothecary J.D. Rozario (probably of Indo-Portuguese descent), claimed that the intermittent fever which had ravaged Bassadore was subject to lunar influence (Rozario 1860).

Orientalist medicine and the colonial metropole

It would not be entirely unfair to say that their willingness to entertain certain Indian medical ideas had led Anglo-Indian practitioners into an intellectual cul-de-sac. This is, perhaps, especially true of the lunacists, whose opinions diverged radically from the mainstream of European medicine, and were of no lasting scientific significance. Yet there was a time, particularly in the years between 1820 and 1860, that Anglo-Indian practitioners made important contributions to the development of medical knowledge and practice in Europe. This contribution was, itself, profoundly shaped by the experience of working in a tropical climate and by consultation with indigenous peoples. Many Europeans who visited India were struck by the relative absence of notions of 'contagion' in Indian medical theory and that India was free from many of the epidemic diseases, such as plague, which had ravaged Europe and the Middle East, despite the absence of quarantine. For free-trade critics of quarantine, such as the radical doctor Charles Maclean, this was conclusive evidence that such diseases were produced by local environmental conditions, rather than by communication from person to person (Pelling 1978, 27–8; Cooter 1982, 96–8). Maclean wrote with approbation of indigenous Indian medical theory and practices, which seemed to confirm his own beliefs (Maclean 1817, vol. 1, 21, vol. 2, 482–4). Nor was he alone: the vast majority of Anglo-Indians were confirmed opponents of contagion in the strict sense of the word, believing that most diseases afflicting the subcontinent were attributable, either directly or indirectly, to the effects of climate. These convictions reflected not only the personal experiences of medical men, who were struck by the difference of India's climate, but also, as we have seen, the opinions of Indian practitioners and of popular understanding of disease.

Although it is impossible to evaluate its importance in relation to other factors, Indian notions of disease causation certainly contributed to the emergence of a distinctive climatic bias in Anglo-Indian medicine, often in conscious opposition to prevailing opinions in Europe. In 1838, the first issue of the *Transactions of the Medical and Physical Society of Bombay*, for example, asserted the centrality of climate to understanding disease in India and stated that Europeans in India were far more at the mercy of 'external' influences than they were at home, where greater attention was paid to the peculiarities of an individual's constitution. Its editor claimed that 'to be slavish imitators of the doctrines and systems of the European schools, is to shew, that we do not estimate our position here, at its true value to science' (*Trans. Medl & Physl Soc. of Bombay* 1838, ix–x). Anglo-Indian practitioners, then, were very conscious that they could make a distinctive contribution to medical science and they began to make their influence felt during the 1830s, in which decade cholera (or 'Asiatic Cholera', as it was then generally known) reached Europe, having spread westwards from India (Arnold 1993, 159–99; Harrison 1994, 99–116). Anglo-Indian practitioners such as James Johnson were critical of the strict contagionist position adopted by the emergency Board of Health in Britain and its imposition of quarantine. They argued that the disease could not be contagious in the strict sense since it seemed to prevail far more in some places than others; its apparent 'preference' for certain localities being due to poor hygiene and unfavourable climatic conditions. This fitted popular perceptions of the epidemic, which seemed to spread unevenly, and contributed to a shift in medical opinion in Britain which began to move away from a strict theory of contagion as an explanation for outbreaks of cholera (Durey 1979, 105–18). It is important not to exaggerate the impact which practitioners with Indian experience had on the debate over cholera in Britain, but the interest taken in their views was celebrated in the Anglo-Indian press. In 1837 the *India Journal of Medical Science* confidently asserted that

> Few men, who have had any experience of fever in tropical climates, believe in contagion. In short, the medical men of India are universally non-contagionists: their belief is grounded on the known fallacy of the doctrine; and they carried their principles and views with respect to cholera into practical effect, and taught a lesson to Europe that is now adopted and will never be forgotten. (*India J. Medl Sci.* ns (1837), 389)

In so far as climate was thought to be a cause of the disease, Anglo-Indian practitioners were in accord with Indian opinion on cholera, first known to Europeans in corrupt forms of the vernacular as 'modechi' or 'mordexi' (Pearson 1996). The Orientalist physician Whitelaw Ainslie wrote that 'It may not be irrelevant . . . to observe that the natives of India themselves also ascribe epidemic disorders to . . . irregularities in the weather, as we learn from the *Guretumnotum*, an astronomical *Sastrum* to be found in the Sheva Pagoda at Tencoushie' (Ainslie 1825, 22). It would be going too far, however, to argue that Anglo-Indian medicine was indebted to Indian medical systems for its distinctive theory of cholera. There was certainly a similarity of outlook but, in cholera, as in other diseases such as fever, Indian writings and practices tended to confirm rather than to determine the opinions of Europeans. It is also important to remember that Ainslie and other orientalists were untypical of the Anglo-Indian medical profession as a whole. As we have seen, many doctors were highly critical of Indian medical knowledge and chose to rely as far as possible on their own observations and experiments. Further, the degree of emphasis which many Anglo-Indian doctors continued to place on climate (as opposed to other factors such as 'contagion' and contaminated drinking water) in the causation of cholera, brought them into disrepute in metropolitan medical circles from the 1860s (*Indian Medl Gazette* 1873, 265). Even in India, the continued insistence of some senior members of the medical profession on the primacy of atmospheric phenomena in outbreaks of cholera was criticized as narrow minded and 'metaphysical', for its want of grounding in 'fact' (*Indian Medl Gazette* 1873, 265).

Conclusion

This study of the medical press in British India shows that India's contribution to western medicine during the nineteenth century was predominantly an empirical one. There can be no doubt that consultation with practitioners of indigenous systems of medicine, and the translation of ancient medical texts, expanded European pharmacopoeia and that this affected therapeutic practices in India, if not in Britain. But the utility and safety of these drugs was seldom taken on trust: indigenous remedies were increasingly subjected to scientific scrutiny so that their active ingredients could be identified. The shift from informal dialogues with indigenous practitioners to scientific trials of Indian drugs from the 1830s, provides further evidence of what Bayly (1996) has seen as a trend in British India towards more systematic and abstract forms of information gathering. This encouraged European doctors to consider merely the active properties of Indian medicines and not the medicine or the medical system of which it was a part. Even then, the extent to which indigenous drugs replaced European ones in the practice of western practitioners is questionable. Anglo-Indian doctors were often frustrated at the disinclination of their colleagues to consider Indian remedies, and the vast majority of medicines continued to be supplied from London.

Conceptually, Indian medical systems made even less of a contribution to western medical practice. Although indigenous and western systems were congruent until the early nineteenth century, pathological anatomy and other developments in western medicine created a gulf that could not be bridged by even the most ardent orientalist. From around 1820, the dominant tendency was for Europeans to emphasize their difference from Indians; to stress the dynamic nature of western science by comparison with the allegedly static or 'degraded' state of oriental learning. This, at any rate, was the message expressed urgently and persistently in the Indian medical press throughout the nineteenth century. The press – which began as the mouthpiece to fledgling colleges and medical societies in the 1820s and 1830s – asserted the centrality of medicine and science to any vision of social improvement. Although the West was for the moment the custodian of learning, science was, as the *Quarterly Journal of the Calcutta Medical and Physical Society* put it, 'of no country' and 'of no rank' (*Quart. J. Calcutta Medl & Physl Soc.* 1837, 156).

Although essentially universalistic in outlook, this reformist agenda was to become increasingly important as a justification and imperative for imperial rule (Adas 1989; Metcalf 1994). By attaching themselves to the van to progress, doctors were also hoping to attract the attention of reform-minded officials in government; some of these officials such as the governor-general William Bentinck, did much to advance their professional agenda. But this is not to say that European practitioners were entirely immune or unsympathetic to the culture in which they found themselves. Orientalist scholars uncovered medical writings which seemed to confirm European ideas concerning the effects of the environment upon health; opinions which, themselves, may have been shaped by consultation with indigenous practitioners. Indian influence is also discernible in writings on the lunar theory of fevers, although the attachment of some Anglo-Indians to the lunar theory served only to alienate them from the majority of practitioners in Europe. We can conclude, then, from the evidence of the Indian medical press, that there is little evidence of an 'Oriental Renaissance' in medicine to compare with that documented in literature, music and the visual arts. This 'Renaissance', if indeed it is appropriate to call it such, was therefore narrower in scope, and far less profound in its implications, than that of the fifteenth and sixteenth centuries.

Works cited

Ackerknecht, Erwin H. *Medicine at the Paris Hospital*. Baltimore, 1967.

Adas, Michael. *Machines as a Measure of Men. Science, Technology, and Ideologies of Western Dominance*. Ithaca and London, 1989.

Ainslie, Whitelaw. *Observations on the Cholera Morbus: a Letter to the Honourable Court of Directors of the East India Company*. London, 1825.

Arnold, David. *Colonizing the Body: State Medicine and Epidemic Disease in Nineteenth-Century India*. Berkeley, 1993.

Arnold, David (ed.). *Warm Climates and Western Medicine*. Amsterdam, 1996.

Bala, Poonam. *Imperialism and Medicine in Bengal: a Socio-Historical Perspective*. New Delhi, 1991.

Balfour, Francis. *Treatise on the Influence of the Moon in Fevers*. Calcutta, 1784.

Basham, A.L. 'The Practice of Medicine in Ancient and Medieval India', in C. Leslie (ed.), *Asian Medical Systems: a Comparative Study*. Berkeley, 1976, 18–43.

Bayly, C.A. *Empire and Information: Intelligence Gathering and Social Communication in India, 1780–1870*. Cambridge, 1996.

Bearce, G.D. *British Attitudes Towards India 1784–1858*. Oxford, 1961.

Bidie, George. 'Indian Substitutes for European Medicines', *Madras Quarterly Journal of Medical Science* 5 (1862), 31–50.

Blacklock, A. 'Medical Jurisprudence', *Madras Quarterly Journal of Medical Science* 1 (1852), 18–32.

Boomgaard, Peter. 'Dutch Medicine in Asia, 1600–1900', in D. Arnold (ed.), *Warm Climates and Western Medicine*. Amsterdam, 1996, 42–64.

British Medical Journal

Burgel, J.C. 'Secular and Religious Features of Medieval Arabic Medicine', in C. Leslie (ed.), *Asian Medical Systems*. Berkeley, 1976, 44–59.

Cohn, Bernard. 'The Command of Language and the Language of Command', in R. Guha (ed.), *Subaltern Studies IV: Writings on South Asian History and Society*. New Delhi, 1985, 276–329.

Cooter, Roger. 'Anticontagionism and History's Medical Record', in P. Wright and A. Treacher (eds), *The Problem of Medical Knowledge*. Edinburgh, 1982, 87–108.

Crawford, D.G. *History of the Indian Medical Service, 1600–1913*, 2 vols, London, 1914.

Durey, Michael. *The Return of the Plague: British Society and the Cholera 1831–2*. Dublin, 1979.

Foucault, Michel. *The Birth of the Clinic*. London, 1973.

Gibson, A. 'A General Sketch of the Province of Guzerat from Deesa to Damaun', *Transactions of the Medical and Physical Society of Bombay* 1 (1838), 1–74.

Goodeve, H.H. 'A Sketch on the Progress of European Medicine in the East', *Quarterly Journal of the Calcutta Medical and Physical Society* 1 (1837), 124–56.

Government of India. *Leprosy in India: Report of the Leprosy Commission in India 1890–91*. Calcutta, 1892.

Grove, Richard. *Green Imperialism: Colonial Expansion, Tropical Island Edens and the Origins of Environmentalism, 1600–1860*. Cambridge, 1995.

Grove, Richard. 'Indigenous Knowledge and the Significance of South West India for Portuguese and Dutch Constructions of Tropical Nature', *Modern Asian Studies* 30 (1996), 121–44.

Halbfass, Wilhelm. *India and Europe: an Essay in Understanding*. Albany, 1988.

Harrison, Mark. 'Tropical Medicine in Nineteenth-Century India', *British Journal for the History of Science* 25 (1992), 299–318.

Harrison, Mark. *Public Health in British India: Anglo-Indian Preventive Medicine 1859–1914*. Cambridge, 1994.

Harrison, Mark. '"The Tender Frame of Man": Disease, Climate, and Racial Difference in India and the West Indies, 1760–1860', *Bulletin of the History of Medicine* 70 (1996), 68–93.

Harrison, Mark. *Climates and Constitutions: Health, Race, Environment and British Imperialism in India*, New Delhi, 1999.

Hippocrates. *Airs, Waters, Places*, in G.E.R. Lloyd (ed.), *Hippocratic Writings*. Harmondsworth, 1983.

Inden, Ronald. *Imagining India*. Oxford, 1990.

India Journal of Medical Science

Indian Annals of Medical Science

Indian Medical Gazette

Irschick, Eugene. *Dialogue and History: Constructing South India, 1795–1895*. Berkeley, 1994.

Irvine, R.H. 'On the Materia Medica of Ajmer; in a Letter to the Secretary of State to the Committee of Inquiry Upon the Vegetable, Animal, and Mineral Productions of Medicinal Qualities, Procurable in India, and the Surrounding Countries', *Quarterly Journal of the Calcutta Medical and Physical Society* 3 (1838), 191–223.

Jewson, N. 'The Disappearance of the Sick Man from Medical Cosmology, 1770–1870', *Sociology* 10 (1976), 225–44.

Johnson, James. *The Influence of Tropical Climates, More Especially of the Climate of India, on European Constitutions*. London, 1815; first edition 1812.

Kopf, David. *Orientalism and the Bengal Renaissance: the Dynamics of Modernization 1773–1835*. Berkeley, 1969.

Kumar, Deepak. *Science and the Raj 1857–1905*. Oxford, 1995.

The Lancet

Lind, James. *An Essay on Diseases Incidental to Europeans in Hot Climates with the Method of Preventing their Consequences*. London, 1808; first published 1768.

Maclean. Charles. *Results of an Investigation Respecting Epidemic and Pestilential Diseases; including Researches in the Levant Concerning the Plague*, 2 vols. London, 1817.

MacNab. 'Some Additional Remarks on Land Scurvy, with Cases to Illustrate the Good Effects of the *Anola*, or fruit of the *Phyllanthus Emblica* in that Disease', *Quarterly Journal of the Calcutta Medical and Physical Society* 3 (1837), 306–10.

Madras Quarterly Journal of Medical Science

Maulitz, Russell C. *Morbid Appearances: the Anatomy of Pathology in the Early Nineteenth Century*. Cambridge, 1987.

Metcalf, Thomas. *Ideologies of the Raj*. Cambridge, 1994.

Mill, James. *The History of British India*, 6 vols. London, 1820.

Moodelly, T.R. 'Cases of Poisoning Witnessed in Nellore', *Madras Quarterly Journal of Medical Science* 5 (1862), 308–21.

Murray, James. 'Cases Illustrative of the Influence of Lunar Agency as an Occasional Cause of Periodical Exacerbations in Various Chronic Diseases', *Transactions of the Medical and Physical Society of Bombay* 2 (1839), 171–80.

Neelameghan, A. *Development of Medical Societies and Medical Periodicals in India, 1780–1914*, Calcutta, 1963.

Pearson, M.N. 'The Thin End of the Wedge: Medical Relativities as a Paradigm of Early Modern Indian–European Relations', *Modern Asian Studies* 29 (1996), 141–70.

Pearson, M.N. 'First Contacts between Indian and European Medical Systems: Goa in the Sixteenth Century', in D. Arnold (ed.), *Warm Climates and Western Medicine*. Amsterdam, 1996, 20–1.

Peet, J. 'An Enquiry into the Evidence which is recorded in relation to the Influence of the Lunar Changes upon certain Forms of Disease', *Transactions of the Medical and Physical Society of Bombay* 6 (1843), 210–30.

Pelling, Margaret. *Cholera, Fever and English Medicine 1825–1865*. Oxford, 1978.

Playfair, George. *The Taleef Shereef, or Indian Materia Medica*. Calcutta, 1832.

Playfair, George. 'On the Madar, and its Medical Uses', *Transactions of the Medical and Physical Society of Calcutta* 1 (1825), 77–102.

Porter, Roy. 'The Eighteenth Century', in L.I. Conrad, M. Neve, V. Nutton and R. Porter (eds), *The Western Medical Tradition*. Cambridge, 1995, 371–476.

Quarterly Journal of the Calcutta Medical and Physical Society

Raychaudhuri, Tapan. 'Europe in India's Xenology: the Nineteenth-Century Record', *Past and Present* 137 (1992), 156–82.

Royle, J.F. *An Essay on the Antiquity of Hindu Medicine*. London, 1837.

Rozario, J.D. 'An Account of Bassadore, and of the Fever Prevalent there', *Transactions of the Medical and Physical Society of Bombay* ns 6 (1860), App. 4, xxiii–xxiv.

Schwab, Raymond. *The Oriental Renaissance: Europe's Rediscovery of India and the East*, trans. G. Patterson-Black and V. Reinking. New York, 1984; first published 1950.

Stokes, Eric. *The English Utilitarians and India*. Oxford, 1959.

Transactions of the Medical and Physical Society of Bombay

Transactions of the Medical and Physical Society of Calcutta

Vicziany, Marika. 'Imperialism, Botany and Statistics in Early Nineteenth-Century India: the Surveys of Francis Buchanon (1762–1829)', *Modern Asian Studies* 20 (1986), 625–60.

Waddington, I. 'The Role of the Hospital in the Development of Modern Medicine: a Sociological Analysis', *Sociology* 7 (1973), 211–24.

Waller, T. 'A Letter on the Fever which Prevailed at Bankote in the S. Concan in 1841', *Transactions of the Medical and Physical Society of Bombay* 5 (1842), 103–5.

Waring, Edward J. 'Medical Notes on the Burmese', *Indian Annals of Medical Science* 1 (1854), 93–109.

Wilson, H.H. 'Kushta, or Leprosy; as known to the Hindoos', *Transactions of the Calcutta Medical and Physical Society* 1 (1825), 1–44.

Wilson, H.H. 'On the Native Practice in Cholera, with Remarks', *Transactions of the Medical and Physical Society of Calcutta* 2 (1826), 282–92.

Wilson, H.H. 'An Account of the Medical and Surgical Sciences of the Hindoos', reprinted from the *Oriental Magazine* (1823), *India Journal of Medical Science* 1 (1834), 115–18.

Wise, Thomas A. *Review of the History of Medicine Among Asiatic Nations*, 2 vols, London, 1867.

Wood, J.J. 'Gleanings from the Hindoo Formularly', *Madras Quarterly Journal of Medical Science* 5 (1862), 127–33.

Wright, Asst-Surg. 'On the Disease locally designated Hill Fever', *India Journal of Medical Science* 10 (1834), 359–62.

12

Purple Prose and the Yellow Press: Imagined Spaces and the Military Expedition to Tirah, 1897*

Glenn R. Wilkinson

In his influential and oft-quoted book, *The Expansion of England*, J.R. Seeley stated that the British in India 'stand out boldly as teachers and civilisers', incurring at the same time vast responsibilities compensated by little or no advantage (Seeley 1909, 291, 353). Whilst a debate about the economic advantages or disadvantages of British Imperialism is beyond the scope of this chapter, it is true that the newspaper reading public gained a great deal from India. They gained primarily an imagined space where they could play out their need to create themselves and their cultural identity. It was essentially an 'imagined' space because few newspaper readers ever got there and their interactions with India and Indians were purely vicarious. It is important, therefore, to examine closely the image that the British public held of India through their primary source of news and information, the daily and weekly newspaper (Koss 1981, 9). In addition, the image presented to and consumed by readers of the popular press is worthy of study in itself in order to ascertain the pervasive nature of impressions of India and their value.

The 'Yellow Press', a common term used to describe the sensationalist and popular organs read by the working and middle classes, was initiated by the onset of the 'New Journalism' in the 1880s and 1890s (Brake 1994, 83). While the origins of the popular press in Britain have been traced back to the ending of the Stamp Tax in 1855 (Lee 1976, 117), the year 1896 marked the high-water mark for the development of the 'New

---

*I should like to thank Caroline Johns, whose editing skills have made this a much better work than it otherwise would have been, and the students in History 3146: Victorian England class at Acadia University, 1996–97.

Journalism' (or, perhaps the low one, depending on one's perspective). In that year, the weekly *Lloyd's Weekly Newspaper* reached the lofty circulation of one million, and the *Daily Mail*, which for many was the epitome of the new mass media for its bright and brash approach, was founded. These two events are significant because they represented the commercial importance of a new type of reader in the lower-middle and middle classes who demanded a new form of newspaper. Circulation and consumption patterns illustrated that these new readers wanted entertaining and improving information presented in a bright and readable manner with bold headlines and sensational stories, rather than the old, tired forms of political intelligence, where newspapers published entire speeches in dense, unbroken columns. The press was no longer seen as a party political tool, but now became a commercial enterprise oriented to mass-reader tastes (Koss 1981, 346–9).

In the following year, 1897, the Northwest Frontier of India was the scene of a number of Pathan revolts that created an enormous amount of interest and anxiety in Britain. Colonel C.E. Callwell, the leading expert on the conduct of 'small wars' or wars in which regular disciplined troops fought untrained local levies, focused on the most important of these risings, which occurred in Tirah. This campaign was 'one of the most dangerous and arduous struggles which British troops have been engaged in since the Indian Mutiny' (Callwell 1906, 289). Callwell points out that a combination of the 'martial instincts' of the Pathans, made up mostly of Afridis and Orakzais, and their use of modern 'arms of range and precision' made this particular expedition most difficult. In addition it was, according to Callwell, the landscape of this part of India which gave the guerrillas a distinct advantage, being a 'land of narrow gorges and steep declivities, of jagged hill-tops and hidden nullahs' (Callwell 1911, vii).

Though Callwell's interest in the Northwest Frontier, and Tirah in particular, concerned the military conduct of 'small wars' and the lessons to be learned from them, the campaign also captured the popular imagination. Many newspapers in Britain and India sent war correspondents to accompany particular military columns in the area, the most famous being Winston Churchill, who accompanied General Sir Bindon Blood into the Malakand, and penned his autobiographical sketch, *The Malakand Field Force* (Edwards 1989, 649). However, it was not the Malakand that received the most attention in the press or made the biggest impression in popular culture. The expedition to Tirah, under Lieutenant-General Sir William Lockhart, included the famous and successful assault of the heights of Dargai by the Gordon Highlanders led by Lieutenant-Colonel

Henry Mathias, a feat that captivated readers and commentators alike. The capture of Dargai was so significant that it was one of only eight panoramic scenes created by Madame Tussaud's waxworks museum between 1885 and 1904 – and the only military scene based in India (MacDonald 1994, 94).

Accompanying the expedition were a number of war correspondents, including Colonel H.D. Hutchinson, who sent letters about the progress of the main column to *The Times*; Captain L.J. Shadwell, special correspondent for *The Pioneer* and the *Daily News*, and Lionel James, Reuters' special correspondent. In addition, Rene Bull wrote dispatches and drew sketches for *Black and White*, an illustrated weekly published in London which focused on Imperial issues (Tiffin 1984, 224), as well as several news agency representatives on the Frontier itself. Given the great expense of supporting a war correspondent in the field (McKenzie 1905, 271), this represents a large investment by the press in war news from the Northwest Frontier. It is also indicative of the belief expressed by the famous *Daily Express* editor Ralph Blumenfeld that wars make newspapers, not the other way around (Blumenfeld 1933, 45).

When examining these images and conceptions of space, it is important to remember that they are *imagined* spaces. They do not necessarily represent 'reality' – their value lay in the fact that readers felt them to be real, and that those who bought newspapers accepted the tropes and metaphors expressed in them every time they handed over their penny or halfpenny. Newspapers, after all, operate in the context of their times and must make immediate connections with their audiences. These are not merely figures of speech or statements of likeness, but ways in which the world can be ordered and made sensible (Edwards 1989, 656–7). Metaphors are the reality through which individuals relate themselves to larger 'categories of identity' (MacDonald 1994, 19), making the study of images and impressions important. Indeed, it is the 'romantic fantasy about brave, noble warriors' which is crucial in understanding vicarious attitudes to India and wars on the Northwest Frontier. Gerard De Groot misses the point when he suggests that the goal of the historian is to uncover *reality*, instead of understanding what people at the time *believed* to be reality (De Groot 1996, 15).

The kinds of spaces evoked by newspaper reports of war on the Frontier are diverse and mutually supporting. They range from portrayals of India's Northwest Frontier as a masculine/martial space, a space of sport, a rugged, uncivilized space inhabited by 'fanatical hillmen', and a hierarchical space, where an order and value of soldiers is emphasized. All of these spaces reflect important cultural attitudes regarding India, held and believed by the readers of the popular press in Britain, and act as ways in which the British defined themselves. Yet perhaps the most basic of images which influence these spaces, and the first to be discussed, is that of newspapers conveying the impression that India was a literary or theatrical background, a mysterious setting where adventures take place.

In his book *The Language of Empire: Myths and Metaphor of Popular Imperialism, 1880–1918*, Robert H. MacDonald suggests that military campaigns in the empire read like romance stories in that they conform to a recognizable pattern of signs and situations and usually have 'happy endings'. These patterns, according to MacDonald (1994, 29–30), are recognizable because they have a familiar vocabulary. Indeed, these patterns become so familiar that they can be arranged into categories of action by individuals and groups, and the consequences of war. Readers could thus respond with ready and appropriate emotions through these standard literary set-pieces. MacDonald (1994, 90–1) recognizes that while these patterns are not necessarily nineteenth-century creations, the Victorians codified these 'emblematic actions' and used them extensively.

These patterns are clearly visible in the news reports found in the pages of the popular press. For example, the *Daily Mail* headline described the attack on Dargai as 'A Stirring Story', while the text went on to state that it was 'one of the most stirring feats of war in Indian Army annals'. The paper outlined the events surrounding 'The Big Battle', including the preparations for the assault, the initial failures by the Gurkhas, the Derbyshire and Dorset Regiments, and the cunning concealment of the Pathans. Finally, the attack of the Gordon Highlanders, who were then 'assigned the same desperate task' (*Daily Mail* 22 October 1897, 5). Colonel Mathias gave a short speech to his troops which, through the news reports, soon became famous and emblematic of the inspirational leadership of British officers. He announced, 'Men of the Gordon Highlanders, the General says that the position must be taken at all costs. The Gordon Highlanders will take it!' (*Daily Mail* 23 October 1897, 5). The paper went on to report that 'instantly the pipers started a swinging, martial skirl, and the highlanders leaped to the attack with Colonel Mathias at their head' (*Daily Mail* 22 October 1897, 5). In 'perfect silence' they 'rushed in the fire zone. Half the men dropped, but the remainder pushed gallantly on . . .' and twenty minutes later, 'the position was won' (*Daily Mail* 21 October 1897, 5). The Highlanders captured the difficult position in grand style and were 'spontaneously cheered' by the other regiments when they bring their wounded, along with those from the Gurkha regiment, down from the heights.

The importance of this episode and its reporting is that it makes for entertaining and stirring reading. For contemporary readers, the serialization of a martial narrative encouraged a demand for more news and for the next issue or instalment of the story, thus emphasizing Blumenfeld's point regarding the commercial importance of war for newspapers, especially when those military events were conducted in exotic locations against worthy adversaries. This serialization was also reflected in the patterns though which narrative and fictional stories were presented in the press throughout the nineteenth century, by those such as Charles Dickens, Wilkie Collins and Arthur Conan Doyle. Exciting and sensational fictional stories were presented in the same serialized manner as news stories because they peaked at regular intervals, they were didactic, and the noble and virtuous either emerged victorious or were later avenged. The interest in these martial stories also came from the feeling that they helped to allay late-Victorian fears of emasculation and racial degeneration, concerns which peaked three years after the expedition to Tirah during the Boer War (1899–1902) (Pick 1989, 5).

India, but in particular the Northwest Frontier, was portrayed as the ideal setting for a stage performance. The landscape was rugged and exotic, but it was also essentially empty, like a stage before the arrival of the actors. *Black and White* portrays the area around Fort Gulistan, the scene of a heroic last-stand, as giving 'a very adequate idea of the desolate and savage loneliness of the whole Samana Range' in southern Tirah (*Black and White* 25 September 1897, 378). Indeed, this impression of an empty stage awaiting the arrival of the actors is reiterated in the drawings and photographs of forts and the landscape in *Black and White* (25 September 1897, 380, 537), the *Penny Illustrated Paper* (25 September 1897, 198), and the photographs of Rene Bull (Bull 1899).

The theatrical aspect of India being portrayed as an imagined space was underscored by the knowledge that Colonel Mathias was himself a fine and respected actor. The *Daily News* reported that he was 'well used to enthusiastic and tumultuous applause . . . [being] a quietly humorous actor of the first rank, as even "the profession" would admit, he has hundreds of times brought down the house in Simla's Gaiety Theatre: one of his greatest successes being in the "Pantomime Rehearsal"' (*Daily News* 25 October 1897, 5). The assault itself was, *The Globe* emphasized, 'no play acting, and assuredly no "Pantomime Rehearsal", in which he took the leading part on Wednesday' (*The Globe* 23 October 1897, 4).

This form of theatre was in a sense didactic, emphasizing certain lessons to be conveyed to readers and for them to recognize in themselves and their society. The actions played out on the 'empty stage' of the Northwest

Frontier of India gave rise to the ways in which it was represented in the newspapers. The most obvious of these was the portrayal of the Frontier as an essentially masculine space where masculinity would be defined and created for readers of the popular press to emulate and support. This was particularly important given the anxieties occasioned by the trial of Oscar Wilde and the debates over fin de siècle decadence caused by such literary productions as *The Savoy* which had first appeared in 1896 (Brake 1994, 148). The antidote lay in warfare, the ultimate gendering activity (Higonnet 1987, 4) and in 1897, the Northwest Frontier was the space in which to exert and to reclaim British masculinity.

Western Indologists claimed that the Hindu nature of India gave the country a feminine, irrational character (Inden 1990, 86). In addition, British India was seen as becoming more feminine through the rise in influence of the memsahib, the notorious Anglo-Indian female figure who was seen to have fostered and accelerated the feminization of a masculine empire, particularly since the Rebellion (Sharpe 1993, 91). But the cynosure of conflict at the end of the nineteenth century in the subcontinent was not with the frail and domesticated Hindus, but with the mighty warriors of Islam, both in Afghanistan and on the Indian hinterland, the Northwest Frontier. The masculinity that the British were afraid of losing could only be tested against the equally masculine Muslims of the north.

War itself was seen as a gender-specific activity where men acted out their roles as distinct from and superior to women, and women were either absent or acted in minor, supporting roles. The *Black and White* Christmas Number for 1897 contained a supplement entitled 'Farewell!', an illustration by R. Hillingford intended as a keepsake to fold out and hang on a wall. The scene is a railway station platform, where a train is being loaded with soldiers, bound for 'the front' via Southampton. The background consists of cheery British troops saying goodbye to their families, while in the centre is a middle-class officer and his wife and children. He is strong, kindly, resolved, while his wife is next to him, gazing admiringly at him, and their children, all girls, are extremely sad though trying to look brave (*Black and White* Christmas Number 1897, Supplement).

This drawing was designed to strike a sympathetic chord with those who had sent their menfolk to the Frontier (or were about to do so in 1898). But it also delineates the separate spheres of men and their women and children. Soldiers occupy the hostile, wild and exotic space of the Northwest Frontier of India (Dawson 1994, 45). The women remain at home in safe, domestic and familiar England, maintaining and extending their responsibilities for the family. In addition, the popular newspapers emphasized and supported the lessons of didactic fiction where women were encouraged to teach men 'moral and spiritual development', to maintain the family while men were away fighting, and for girls to learn 'to accept cheerfully the burden of sacrifice entailed by involvement in Empire' (Rowbotham 1989, 190–1). That the officer and soldiers *are* cheerful meant that the women in their lives had done their job properly and encouraged the men to fulfil their gender role in maintaining the boundaries of Empire.

For men, this departure can be seen as a chance to *escape* the domesticated, stifling world of the feminine and enter into the Frontier – symbol of virility, freedom and adventure. John M. MacKenzie has outlined the nineteenth-century cult of hunting in the British Empire and suggested that it was a means for men to move from constrained and mundane 'civilized' urban space, into 'barbaric' rural space with its concomitant tension and ecstasy (MacKenzie 1988, 42). In this light, it is less surprising to see that the middle-class officer is not *too* distraught at the prospect of the departure.

Yet, women *were* present in the Northwest Frontier, but in ways which emphasized the masculinity of its imagined space. Most of the popular papers related the story of the Fort Gulistan garrison which described the adventures of a number of 'ladies' and children. Fort Gulistan, officially and confusingly also known as Fort Cavagnari, was located approximately 35 miles from Kohat in the Samana Range near Dargai. In August, the newspapers reported that a number of 'English ladies, with several children, still remain at one of the threatened outposts', namely Parachinar, six days' march from Kohat. These 'non-combatants' were the source of some moral indignation, with the *Daily News* stating flatly in a leading article that 'if they are touched, those who touch them, fanatics or otherwise, will have reason to repent it' (*Daily News* 25 August 1897, 4). The spectre of 'fanatical natives' killing or, worse, raping English ladies raised the spectre of the Indian Rebellion (1857–59) and the Christian mission to make Indian sinners 'repent' their misdeeds. This incident also stressed the masculine role of protecting the helpless women and children, and, failing that, seeking their revenge.

The Indian Rebellion was a catalyst that changed and defined the late-nineteenth-century image of India, particularly regarding gender. Jenny Sharpe (1993, 6–8) has noted that the concept and fear of rape of English women by Indian men was a longstanding trope that began when structures of authority began to break down after the Rebellion. These tropes were expressed in the press but also in fiction, particularly in what Sharpe called 'the most popular Mutiny novel of them all', Flora Annie Steel's *On the Face of the Waters: a Tale of the Mutiny*, published in 1896, the year before the Tirah Expedition. Reviewers were to complain that the adventures of Steel's strong heroine, Kate Erlton, imposed the contemporary 'sex problem' on an earlier historical period (Sharpe 1993, 88). Thus, the racial memory of the Rebellion and sexual anxiety of inter-racial rape can be linked to threats to masculinity at home from the increasing presence of women in the public sphere and racial repercussions of growing urbanization.

By 17 August 1897, the women were taken to Fort Gulistan, a martial space where they could demonstrate another of the acceptable roles for women – nursing. Nursing had expanded in the late-nineteenth century and after the Crimean War had become increasingly secular in terms of motivation. Religious conviction was replaced by imperial ardour and a desire for adventure denied to other feminine professions. In 1883, the Royal Red Cross medal was instituted by Royal Warrant for Nursing Sisters and other 'ladies' who displayed merit and special exertions in the field (Summers 1988, 175, 180). In March 1897, the nursing profession was given further publicity with the formation of the Army Nursing Reserve, which would be under the control of the War Office in wartime. Opinion was sharply divided as to the role and arena in which the women were to act, whether women should carry stretchers or be present on the battlefield (Summers 1988, 191–2). The image of the Frontier as a symbol of male virility demanded that this role be a supporting one for women, demonstrated by the almost universal, but brief, attention these women received in the press. Coverage was limited to several lines of type rather than individual stories themselves, reiterating the peripheral role of women on the fringes of empire. Stories such as those of Miss Teresa McGrath and her 'devotion' to a wounded officer, Lieutenant Blain, evoked 'gratitude' from the officers and men defending Fort Gulistan, but little detail in the papers of the lives and background of the women (*News of the World* 19 September 1897, 7).

Though some of the very few women who occupied the masculine space of the Indian frontier were deemed 'heroines' for their acceptable roles as nurses, the main representation of India and the Northwest Frontier is of a space for the display of heroic, masculine martial virtues. Psychologically, the need for heroes is crucial for a society, for they provide important aspects of national identity and cultural meaning, acting as models of acceptable and exemplary behaviour. The nineteenth century made the British military hero a symbol of civilization and order (Dawson 1994, 82–3). Indeed, it was the 'New Journalism' of the late nineteenth century that helped to create and sustain the ideals of the martial hero at the popular level, receiving in return higher circulation figures. At the time of the Rebellion, heroes were high-ranking officers like Havelock, but by the end of the century, British soldiers of all ranks were seen to perform 'deeds of valour of a Homeric quality' (*News of the World* 19 September 1897, 6).

While it can be said that this hero creation occurred in earlier periods (Lieven 1998, 430–1), the speed and ease with which the hero was manufactured and the elevation of the common soldier to warrior-hero was quite unique. An example of this phenomenon is the story of Piper Findlater of the Gordon Highlanders, who won the Victoria Cross for continuing to play 'Cock o' the North' though wounded in both legs during the storming of Dargai. Initial confusion as to the identity of the piper led to the press lauding the exploits of the wrong man, but on the strength of the assertions made by Colonel Hutchinson of *The Times*, Findlater was made the hero (*Lloyd's Weekly Newspaper* 21 November 1897, 5). This confusion and the subsequent attention lavished on Piper Findlater, who later became somewhat of a national sensation, eventually performing 'Cock o' the North' in music halls (Farwell 1985, 323), demonstrated clearly that accuracy in establishing the true identity of heroes was less important than their creation.

The belief that common soldiers could act as models for society through heroic actions was furthered by their presence in advertisements. The Gordon Highlanders in particular generated saleable images associated with courage, determination and toughness which advertisers wanted to exploit in order to sell their products. After Dargai, Highland regiments were featured in several newspaper advertisements, particularly those selling whisky. Pattison's, for example, took out a half-page advertisement in the *Black and White* Christmas Number showing a large number of Highlanders charging with guns firing in hilly terrain (see Figure 12.1). The advertisement associates Pattison's Whisky and the Gordon Highlanders as both being 'Victorious all Along the Line'. It stated that 'the booming of the cannon is nothing to the booming of Pattison's Whisky' suggesting that, like the Highlanders, the whisky was rough but disciplined and steady. Readers were apt to make the connection that if they drank Pattison's brand whisky, they too could demonstrate the heroic qualities of the Gordon Highlanders; consumption of the scotch was the consumption of Scottish martial virtues and heroism (*Black and White* Christmas Number 1897, 25). The similarities between the rugged and wild hills of the Highlands and those of Tirah also added to this sense of connection and offered a romantic escape from the urban squalor of industrial Britain.

263

Figure 12.1 Pattison's Whisky ad, from *Black and White*, Christmas 1897, p. 5.

This connection was ever more in evidence when the news of the assault on Dargai and of Piper Findlater's bravery broke just as Pattison's published a block advertisement with a piper in full Highland dress, 'piping the praises of Pattison's whisky' (*Black and White* 21 October 1897, 4). It can be said that the motif of the Highland piper was an obvious one for a whisky company to select for an advertising image. But the association with that image and its martial meaning demonstrated in India, along with the impeccable timing, reveals a level of deliberate appropriation on the part of the company of a meaningful and positive heroic icon of masculinity.

One of the ways in which these heroics were played out (literally and figuratively) was through the familiar and acceptable tropes of sporting imagery. The hero, as in Henry Newbolt's poem 'Vitaï Lampada' (Dickinson 1981, 38–9), gains the skills and style to die correctly by facing defeat as a schoolboy on the cricket field, a space to be subsumed later into the Imperial battlefield. Sport also can be seen as a substitute for warfare, operating as a guiltless form of bloodshed in the hunt or as football matches (Baden-Powell 1899, 124). For *The Globe*, the soldiers of Lockhart's forces were veteran experts in hill warfare, making them 'up to every move in the game' (*The Globe* 30 October 1897, 4). Sporting events assume evenly matched sides pitting raw skill and determination against equally balanced opponents. However, the warfare on the frontier against Pathan tribesmen created a tension between ideals of fair play and the reality of the mismatched levels of technology available to each side (*News of the World* 10 October 1897, 6).

One way to alleviate this tension was to suggest that the Pathans were much better armed than previous enemies of the British, and that they were a worthy adversary. This is a point stressed by Callwell and one of the main reasons for the study of the Tirah expedition since 'the campaigns of 1897 on the Northwest Frontier of India supply practically the first example of regular troops engaging in operations against savage antagonists armed with modern fire-weapons of precision' (Callwell 1911, 151). It was also implied that the sporting contest in the Northwest Frontier was more fair and equal than other similar encounters. Lionel James, Reuters' special correspondent, wrote in his later account of the expedition that the 'Pathan, while still possessing the natural advantages of country and physical hardihood, is further armed with weapons as precise and deadly as our own' and skilfully trained (James 1898, ix). Recent scholarship indicates that the Afridis, in particular, were armed with a combination of modern Lee-Metford rifles and rather older Martini-Henry and Snider rifles, putting the numbers at perhaps 20 per cent armed with these new breech-loading weapons, mostly of the latter models. While these weapons 'greatly complicated the conduct of hill warfare and made the Tirah campaign strikingly different from all earlier frontier campaigns' (Moreman 1994, 194), they hardly made the 'contest' an equal one. The British had at their disposal searchlights, the most modern rifles, Dum-Dum bullets that expanded to generate horrific wounds (and were banned against 'civilized' enemies), machine-guns and modern mountain artillery (Moreman 1992, 50).

The newspaper reports of fighting in Tirah also recognised these points. *Black and White* utilized a quarter of a page to discuss the importance of Pathan possession of modern arms, stating that the acquisition of a modern high-powered weapon was a status symbol and that the Pathans would risk death to obtain one. The paper suggested that the Pathans stole arms from the British, bought them from unscrupulous European or even British arms manufacturers, or made their own from spare parts or from scratch (*Black and White* 13 November 1897, 602). Yet despite this feeling that the Pathans were well armed, there was a recognition in the press that technological superiority in weaponry was maintained by the British forces. Indeed, this attitude was crucial to maintain the image of the British as morally and intellectually superior because throughout the nineteenth century, technological innovations were linked with advanced civilization and culture. People such as the French sociologist Gustave Le Bon saw India as a whole as inferior in science and technology (Adas 1989, 176), and this perception became stronger as one moved towards the Frontier and away from recognizable edifices of civilization.

These two competing images, the need to see the Pathans as well armed and trained in order to make them a worthy adversary and the belief that British technological and scientific advances deemed them superior to the Pathans, was demonstrated in the press. The *Daily News* told the story of a particular artillery barrage at Shenowari where artillery officers spotted the enemy 4000–5000 yards away and fired their new 12-pounder guns. Up popped one of the Pathans, signalling in good Indian Army form, using familiar signals indicating that the shot went high and to the left. The commander of the guns took the hint from this alleged 'Sepoy deserter' (a further allusion to the Rebellion) and fired again. The paper reported that 'this time, the shell correctly reached its destination and the tribesmen instantly dispersed' (*Daily News* 10 September 1897, 5). While this report might be apocryphal, it emphasized the belief that the British were fighting well-trained soldiers, many being former Indian Army recruits, making the contest more fair and the enemy worthy, but that the Pathans lacked basic intelligence because they directed British artillery onto their own positions. This meant that there was extreme confidence that the British would ultimately win, in spite of the weapons situation, because they were still technologically superior and therefore racially and intellectually superior.

Despite this awareness of uneven distribution of technology, the press cast ridicule on the unwillingness of the Pathans to fight in the open. *Lloyd's Weekly Newspaper* relayed how Major General A.G. Yeatman Briggs recaptured a position near Fort Gulistan by using artillery at a range of 400 yards from a Pathan position. The paper reported that 'here again, the enemy unfortunately shirked a fair fight. As soon as the artillery opened on them they hurriedly retreated' (*Lloyd's Weekly Newspaper* 19 September 1897, 5). *The Globe* felt that it was galling to read about an enemy that would not stand and be annihilated by superior technology in a 'fair fight', preferring instead to utilise guerrilla warfare, a form of fighting seen as 'sneaky' and less 'sporting', and almost impossible to defeat (*The Globe* 13 September 1897, 4).

The point was not lost on some papers however. The socialist paper *Justice*, edited by H.M. Hyndman, recognized in a leading article that the Pathans eventually would be crushed, since 'they have no artillery, no systematic food supply and no well-thought-out scheme of attack or defence' (*Justice* 18 September 1897, 1). The point was not lost on the Pathans themselves either, as many of the newspapers noted. *Lloyd's* reported a 'strange story' circulating Peshawar attributed to Afridi Sowars (cavalry soldiers) suggesting that they would be willing to fight the British in the open if the British advanced without artillery. This, for the Afridi, was a fair and equal fight. If these conditions were met, then the Afridi promised to meet the British 'in open battle, otherwise they will content themselves with guerrilla warfare' (*Lloyd's Weekly Newspaper* 10 October 1897, 6). *Punch* ridiculed this desire for 'equality' by lampooning the Afridi style of dress and, tellingly, of weaponry showing that the Tommies would have to 'dress down' to a considerable degree in order to be equal with them (*Punch* 30 October 1897, 202) (see Figure 12.2).

The *News of the World* looked at this situation slightly differently, complaining that:

> The Afridis are an ingenious if treacherous race. Convinced that the punishment which they so richly merit is now within measurable distance of being inflicted, they have come forward with a proposal for the disarmament of our troops. 'Don't use your weapons of

FROM MR. PUNCH'S SPECIAL ARTIST AT THE FRONT.

"The enemy sent in a message that if the troops would come out and meet them *on equal terms*, they would fight."

TOMMY ATKINS TAKES THEM AT THEIR WORD, AND COMES OUT, ADOPTING THE FASHION OF THE LOCALITY!

Figure 12.2 'From Mr. Punch's Special Artist at the Front', *Punch, or the London Charivari*, 30 October 1897, p. 202.

science,' they say, 'meet us on the plains on even terms, and we shall be satisfied.' As well they might expect a schoolmaster to entertain a similar plea from a disobedient pupil. They treacherously attack our subjects in the first instance, and must face the consequences. (*News of the World* 10 October 1897, 6)

Here, the Afridis are not praised for their tactics which, given the circumstances, were quite effective and made the best use of their resources, but they are condemned for not 'playing' the game sportingly, and for not learning the moral lessons of sporting defeat. By demanding a fair and equal 'playing field', the Pathans threatened to make the contest more difficult and thus make it less likely for a British victory. India, and in particular the Northwest Frontier, could thus be made into a space where triumph was less assured and the sporting heroic virtues of the British less likely to be displayed. When victory did occur, the British triumph appeared to be more deserved and indicative of a superior race. James Belich (1988) noted a similar tendency in New Zealand as the Maoris threatened to defeat the British through the superior defensive structure, the *pa*. The British had to construct justifications for their difficulties to avoid suggestions of their own military inferiority.

Yet despite this, the fact that the Afridis and Orakzais fought stubbornly made India into a space for military training. The British felt they could hone their martial and moral superiority, gained 'on the playing fields of Eton', by engaging with a worthy, though ultimately defeated, adversary. In his book, *Indian Memories: Recollections of Soldiering, Sport, etc.*, Baden-Powell stressed that sport was excellent military training, particularly the Anglo-Indian favoured sports of polo and pig-sticking (Baden-Powell 1915, 30). According to Baden-Powell, it was the Northwest Frontier which was the most important martial space for training. His view of India, similar to that found in popular newspapers, was that 'we as a nation are exceptionally fortunate in having a valuable training ground for our officers in the Northwest Frontier of India, with real live enemies always ready to oblige in giving us practical instruction . . .' (Baden-Powell 1915, 205). The *News of the World* agreed, relating the heroic deeds of British troops, in a war 'forced upon us without the slightest excuse', which has 'become a valuable training ground, not only for our generals, but the entire rank and file in India' (*News of the World* 19 September 1897, 6). The socialist paper, *The Clarion*, recognised this tendency in a slightly different way, suggesting that 'British troops and officers are being afforded plenty of practice in the art of splendid murder' in the Northwest Frontier (*The Clarion* 28 August 1897, 299). While the

News of the World saw the war as thrust upon the British and therefore as a morally untainted training ground, *The Clarion* viewed the war as immoral and thus akin to murder, undermining the British claim of the virtuous high ground. The latter view of *The Clarion* denied the impression of India as a space to display British superiority, either scientific, moral or martial.

Yet most of the newspapers portrayed India as an arena to display and confirm British superiority, albeit within the late-nineteenth-century social context fearful of its loss. Indeed, it was because of this fear, during what has been called the period of *'fin de siècle* Darwinian pessimism' (Harris 1993, 241), that spaces such as the Northwest Frontier were used to demonstrate British martial prowess, masculine virility and 'racial' superiority. This portrayal was accomplished not simply through relaying the exploits of the British themselves, but through discussions of the actions of their own native soldiers and their enemies, the Pathans, both groups described as 'martial races'.

The main advantage these 'martial races' had over the more civilized British, was that they were untainted by the ravages of urbanization, industrialization and decadent luxury, threatening characteristics of the late nineteenth century. It was believed that 'martial races' tended to come from areas that were hilly and cooler in climate, and where martial prowess had been passed on to offspring in a Lamarckian sense (Caplan 1991, 582). Thus the Sikhs, Gurkhas and Pathans were animated, martial and masculine while the Bengalis, for example, were lazy, intellectual and feminine. Recent scholarship has indicated that though contemporary British sources contended strongly that 'martial races' did in fact exist and were useful, the concept is really an invented distinction, reflecting British ideas of masculinity and imperialism (Sinha 1995, 8; Omissi 1991, 1–27).

The Northwest Frontier was portrayed in newspapers as a space where military skills and virtues were demonstrated by these 'martial races', and against which the British could measure themselves and their civilization. The Pathans were praised because they were 'first rate skirmishers' well armed and knew the landscape (*Daily Mail* 27 October 1897, 5), and they displayed 'wonderful audacity' during 'severe fighting' (*Daily Mail* 11 November 1897, 5). The initial fighting demonstrated that 'the enemy fought bravely and with cunning and sought to take our force by surprise ...', the Pathans retreating only after 'a stiff fight' (*The Star* 13 September 1897, 3). Indeed, this was made clear by *The Globe*, which echoed the equally conservative *Morning Post*, when it stated that the 'Afridis and Orakzais are a brave and hardy race, good soldiers worth conquering and winning over' (*The Globe* 22 October 1897, 3). The fighting qualities of the Pathans ensured that the eventual success of the Tirah Expedition acquired additional significance. Defeat of this superb 'martial race' meant that the British were even better, demonstrating their military and logistical superiority, and putting to rest mistaken fears of decadence and sloth.

Yet, while the Pathans were natural fighters, they lacked discipline and control. They were 'fanatics', easily led by their Mullahs who were seen as 'blowing the fanaticism of the rebels into flame' (*The Globe* 13 September 1897, 4). Even the radical press referred to the Pathans as 'fanatics', though the *Daily News* recognized that 'fanaticism is an appreciable disadvantage in a philosophical discussion. But when it comes to fighting, fanatics are at a premium' (*Daily News* 25 August 1897, 4). According to David B. Edwards (1989, 655), those labelled 'fanatic' were denied 'moral status', while those applying the term were afforded an unarguable position of moral superiority, thus making it easier for the latter group to justify their domination of the former. In labelling the Pathans 'fanatics', the British established their own moral superiority and made resistance not only futile but also irrational.

The depiction of the enemy as 'fanatical' had the concomitant image of them as 'superstitious'. At the end of October, many of the papers relayed the story of the Akka Khel Mullah, Said Akbar, who unearthed a long-buried earthen pot which contained a perfectly preserved flag, taken as a good omen of impending victory (*The Globe* 26 October 1897, 4). This augury was portrayed by the papers as mere superstition, and a sign of the backward nature of their adversary, a trait which was seen to be characteristic of India (Tiffin 1984, 232). However, suggestions in the press that General Lockhart was considered in British military circles to be 'one of the favourites of fortune, always bringing luck to the arms of those he commands', evidently did not mean that the British were 'superstitious' in quite the same way (*Lloyd's Weekly Newspaper* 26 September 1897, 12).

While the Pathans were brave and audacious fighters, they lacked the advantages of their neighbours in Northern India, the Sikhs and the Gurkhas. The British native troops were determined, audacious and brave like the Pathans, but they were also disciplined, able to follow orders and well-led. The qualities of the 'martial races' which they shared with the Pathans were channelled though the contact and control of the British. Photographs in Colonel Hutchinson's *The Campaign in Tirah 1897–1898: an Account of the Expedition against the Orakzais and Afridis* make the point by juxtaposing 'before' and 'after' images of two

Gurkhas. The first, '*Gurkhas: The Raw Material*', portrayed the natives in traditional dress, armed with kukri knives, wild-looking and slouching, while the second, '*Gurkhas: The Finished Article*', showed the same men in regimental uniforms, with rifles, alert and at attention (Hutchinson 1898, between 238–9). The positive influence of British training and drill transformed the Gurkhas into a disciplined fighting force, without sacrificing their natural martial talents. The fact that they also wore a recognizable uniform helped in the same way that the Japanese were seen to be 'civilized' in 1904 because they were essentially 'westernised', though they did not lose their martial edge.

The requirement for the leadership of British officers was conveyed in an article in *Black and White* written to praise the regiments involved in the attack on Dargai. The article discussed the role of each unit along with their regimental histories; the Gordon Highlanders were listed first, then the Dorsetshires, the Derbyshires, and finally the Gurkhas, despite the fact that only the Gordons and the Gurkhas were successful in their attack. The article praised the Gurkhas, stating that they were 'fire-eaters from the cradle, all their traditions are warlike, and all their inclinations are towards skirmishes'. Yet, they are 'plucky little hillmen who will go anywhere and do anything when their British officers bid them' (*Black and White* 6 November 1897, 570).

The suggestion that the Gurkhas could go nowhere and do nothing *without* their British officers was reinforced by specific news stories. The papers reported that the leadership of Lieutenant Arthur Tillard, commander of the 3rd Gurkha Guides, was crucial at Dargai. The *Daily News* reported that Lieutenant Tillard:

> was the first man who actually got across [the fire zone], and his men followed his lead manfully. Midway across, in the stormy journey, the Gurkhas appeared to hesitate, whereupon Lieutenant Tillard encouraged them with kindly and stimulating words, while the hail of bullets continued all around him. (*Daily News* 2 November 1897, 5)

In this report, the paper reinforced the image of the Gurkha as a fighter, though with a child-like innocence and rather simple-minded devotion (Caplan 1991, 587). The Gurkhas were seen to need encouragement and kindness like children, rather than the harsh and brutal treatment of regular British troops. Repeated reference to the diminutive stature of the Gurkhas added to this image (*News of the World* 7 November 1897, 7).

A final way in which India was represented in the British popular press, was as a space where ideals of class and caste hierarchies were conveyed and reinforced. India was used to display British superiority, but the images used were complex and subtle. When the actions or deaths of British officers were reported, their full names, ranks, regimental affiliations and, quite often, a lengthy biography were presented at the same time. For example, the headline relating a Pathan attack read, 'Sikhs Massacred', but the Sikhs themselves were not mentioned in detail, while space was given to the biographical sketch which outlined the death of Captain E.Y. Watson, shot in the head by the Pathans (*Daily Mail* 11 November 1897, 5). This unequal distribution of printed space in the press served to reinforce the importance of British officers over native troops in the imagined space of India, and the degree to which readers supported and advanced the idea (see Figure 12.3).

Yet, this differentiation was not merely racial. The officers and men of British regiments were treated in a manner that highlighted and supported their hierarchical class structures, even in lower-class papers. For example, when *The Globe* (19 October 1897, 4) reported 'the sharp fighting', the lists of killed and wounded mentioned officers by rank, name, and regiment, and included brief biographical sketches, while the privates were listed by rank and regiment only. While it might be argued that the paper was conveying its conservative nature, the same thing can hardly be said for the radical *Lloyd's Weekly Newspaper*, which followed suit in reporting a later engagement (*Lloyd's Weekly Newspaper* 14 November 1897, 5).

Black and White went even further in its front-page headline report on the 'Heroes of the Fight at Dargai'. Seven officers were depicted in separate photographs, with Colonel Mathias ('who led the charge') in the centre. Each photograph referred to the officers by their name and rank, and included the decorous prefix 'Late . . .' if the officer had been killed or '. . . wounded', if appropriate, after the officer's name. The following page discussed the photographs, suggesting that they were 'portraits of the most prominent officers who took part in the gallant display of British arms at the Dargai heights', and appended a brief biography of each officer (*Black and White* 30 October 1897, 533–4). Here the newspaper not only adds the extra dimension of individual photographs, but also introduces the idea that some British officers are more prominent than others.

Newspaper representations of India in the late-nineteenth-century popular press reveal more about Britain than they do about India. These ephemeral epistles from the Northwest Frontier and the newspaper envelopes in which they were sent to readers convey popular interests and concerns which are much closer to an *imagined* India than to reality. And yet they remain of the utmost value for what they tell us about the

The native officers of the 16th Bengal Lancers now serving in China

Lt. Baird, I.M.S.   Lt. Rivett-Carnac   Lt. and Adj. Holman Lt. Craik (attached)   Capt. Maxwell   Lt. Sarel (attached)

Capt. Thornton   Lt. Doveton   Col. Alexander   Major Waldron   Capt. Griffiths

The British officers. The 16th Bengal Lancers form portion of the Cavalry Brigade proceeding to China from India. This regiment is composed of Sikhs, Dogras and Jats, three of the best fighting races of India. The officers are in their fighting dress of khaki, which renders them almost indistinguishable from the men at a short distance.

THE 16th BENGAL LANCERS

Figure 12.3 'The 16th Bengal Lancers' from *Black and White Budget*, 22 September 1900, p. 779.

way in which the British saw their world and themselves. The *real* India, just like *real* soldiers, is difficult for historians to grasp, but the India *imagined* by the British and conveyed through the newspapers, virtually their only window to the world, is a concept much easier to ascertain. It was India as an imagined space that was of importance for the British public. It acted as an imagined space where readers could define themselves, partly through what they perceived they were not (fanatical, superstitious, uncivilized), partly through what they believed themselves to be (disciplined, rational, superior), but also through the presentation of values they felt in danger of losing (martial, adventurous, ecstatic). The Frontier was also a gendered space, where masculinity could be displayed and maintained, particularly in the wake of the Oscar Wilde trial. All of these elements were presented to readers through the reporting of warfare on the Northwest Frontier, helping to shape the British themselves. In this way we can ultimately understand that India did indeed compensate for the vast responsibilities incurred by the Imperial power and gave a significant, if subtle, amount of 'advantage'.

Works Cited

Newspapers

Black and White
The Clarion
Daily Mail
Daily News
The Globe
Justice
Lloyd's Weekly Newspaper
Manchester Guardian
News of the World
Penny Illustrated Newspaper
Reynold's Newspaper
Punch
The Star
The Times
Yorkshire Post

Articles

Caplan, Lionel. '"Bravest of the Brave": Representations of "The Gurkha" in British Military Writings', *Modern Asian Studies* 25 (1991), 571–97.
Edwards, David B. 'Mad Mullahs and Englishmen: Discourse in the Colonial Encounter', *Comparative Studies of Society and History* 31 (1989), 649–70.

Hogben, W. Murray. 'British Civil–Military Relations on the North-West Frontier of India', in Adrian Preston and Peter Dennis (eds), *Swords and Covenants*. London, 1979, 124–46.

Lieven, Michael. 'Heroism, Heroics and the Making of Heroes: the Anglo-Zulu War of 1879', *Albion* 30 (1998), 419–38.

Moreman, T.R. 'The Arms Trade and the North-West Frontier Pathan Tribes, 1890–1914', *The Journal of Imperial and Commonwealth History* 22 (1994), 187–216.

Moreman, T.R. 'The British and Indian Armies and North-West Frontier Warfare, 1849–1914', *The Journal of Imperial and Commonwealth History* 20 (1992), 35–64.

Omissi, David. '"Martial Races": Ethnicity and Security in Colonial India, 1859–1939', *War and Society* 9 (1991), 1–27.

Tiffin, Chris. '"Black and White" and the Literature of Empire', *World Literature Written in English* 23 (1984), 224–33.

Books

Adas, Michael. *Machines as the Measure of Men: Science, Technology, and Ideologies of Western Dominance*. Ithaca, 1989.

Baden-Powell, Lieutenant-Colonel R.S.S. *Aids to Scouting for N.-C.Os and Men*. London, 1899.

Baden-Powell, Lieutenant-General Sir Robert. *Indian Memories: Recollections of Soldiering, Sport Etc*. London, 1915.

Belich, James. *The New Zealand Wars and the Interpretation of Racial Conflict*. London, 1988.

Blumenfeld, Ralph. *The Press in My Time*. London, 1933.

Brake, Laurel. *Subjugated Knowledges: Journalism, Gender and Literature in the Nineteenth Century*. New York, 1994.

Bull, Rene. *Black and White War Albums: No. 3: The Tirah Campaign*. London, 1899.

Callwell, C.E. *Small Wars: a Tactical Textbook for Imperial Soldiers*. London, 1906.

Callwell, C.E. *Tirah. 1897*. London, 1911.

De Groot, Gerald J. *Blighty: British Society in the Era of the Great War*. London, 1996.

Dickinson, Patric (ed.). *Selected Poems of Henry Newbolt*. London, 1981.

Fallwell, Byron. *Queen Victoria's Little Wars*. New York, 1972.

Harris, Jose. *Private Lives, Public Spirit: a Social History Of Britain 1870–1914*. Oxford, 1993.

Higonet, Margaret Randolph et al. *Behind the Lines: Gender and the Two World Wars*. New Haven, 1987.

Hutchinson, Colonel H.D. *The Campaign in Tirah 1897–1898*. London, 1898.

Inden, Ronald. *Imagining India*. Oxford, 1990.

James, Lionel. *The Indian Frontier War: Being an Account of the Mohmund and Tirah Expeditions 1897*. London, 1898.

Koss, Stephen. *The Rise and Fall of the Political Press in Britain Vol. I*. London, 1981.

Lee, Alan J. *The Origins of the Popular Press in England 1855–1914*. London, 1976.

MacDonald, Robert H. *The Language of Empire: Myths and Metaphor of Popular Imperialism, 1880–1918*. Manchester, 1994.

MacKenzie, John M. *The Empire of Nature: Hunting, Conservation and British Imperialism*. Manchester, 1988.

McKenzie, Frederick Arthur. *From Tokyo to Tiflis: Uncensored Letters from the War*. London, 1905.

Pick, Daniel. *Faces of Degeneration: a European Disorder, c. 1848–1919.* Cambridge, 1989.

Rowbotham, Judith. *Good Girls Make Good Wives: Guidance for Girls in Victorian Fiction.* Oxford, 1989.

Seeley, J.R. *The Expansion of England.* London, 1883.

Shadwell, Captain L.J. *Lockhart's Advance Through Tirah.* London, 1898.

Sharpe, Jenny. *Allegories of Empire: the Figure of Woman in the Colonial Text.* Minneapolis, 1993.

Sinha, Mrinalini. *Colonial Masculinity: the 'Manly Englishman' and the 'Effeminate Bengali' in the Late Nineteenth Century.* Manchester, 1995.

Slessor, Captain A.K. *The 2nd Battalion Derbyshire Regiment in Tirah.* London, 1900.

Summers, Anne. *Angels and Citizens: British Women as Military Nurses 1854–1914.* London, 1988.

Thomsett, Richard Gillham. *With the Peshawar Column Tirah Expeditionary Force.* London, 1899.

Index

Townsend, E. 116
Transactions of the Calcutta Medical and Physical Society 234, 236
Transactions of the Medical and Physical Society of Bombay 248
Tyrell, Lieutenant-Colonel F.W. 225

Udaipur 171, 176
Union Jack 67
United Service Gazette 212
United Service Institution 213
United Service Institution of India 217–18
United Service Journal 6, 12
United Service Magazine 211
Urdu language 137–8
  relationship to Hindi 138
Urdu periodicals 13, 135–59
  and construction of community 149–53
  and social reform 141–2
  and *adab* tradition 144
  and gnomologia 144
  and British stereotypes 152
  Arab influences on 144–5
  blending science with legend 142
  discussing Indian history 142–3
  frequency and content 136–7
  editors and proprietors 137–8
  government patronage 140, 147
  Greek influences on 144–5
  on moral economy 144
  on technology 142
  prose styles 146–9
'Useful Knowledge Movement' 147
Utilitarianism 236

Victoria, Queen 51, 68, 96
Victoria Cross 68, 75, 78, 80, 262
Visram, Rozina 43

Waring, Edward 244
Washbrook, David 153
Watson, Captain E.Y. 272
Webster, Benjamin 125
Weiner, Martin 109
Westminster Review 8
White, Cynthia A. 54
Wickens, G.M. 145–6
widowhood 33–4, 35, 38
  see also social reform
Wilde, Oscar 174, 259, 274
Wilson, Horace Hayman 239–40, 241–2
Wizard, The 66
women, British
  and imperial mission 52
  charitable activities of 57–8
  reported heroism in 1857 128–9
women, Indian 24, 25
  see also social reform, rape, orientalism
women's periodicals
  and imperialism 51–61
  and Indian women 54
  and religion in India 56–7
Wong, J.R. 4
Wood, Herbert 204

'Yellow Press' 254
Young, Robert 2, 14, 92
Young Women's Christian Association 58
Youngs, Tim 18
Yuval-Davis, Nira 52

Zenana 30–2